D0848861

By Ze'ev Schiff and Ehud Ya'ari:

Intifada: The Palestinian Uprising—Israel's Third Front
Israel's Lebanon War
The Year of the Dove

THE PALESTINIAN UPRISING—
ISRAEL'S THIRD FRONT

INTIFADA

ZE'EV SCHIFF

&

EHUD YA'ARI

EDITED AND TRANSLATED BY INA FRIEDMAN

SIMON AND SCHUSTER
NEW YORK · LONDON · TORONTO
SYDNEY · TOKYO

SIMON AND SCHUSTER
Simon & Schuster Building
Rockefeller Center
1230 Avenue of the Americas
New York, New York 10020

Copyright © 1989 by Domino Press
English Language Translation
copyright © 1990 by Ina Friedman
All rights reserved
including the right of reproduction
in whole or in part in any form.
SIMON AND SCHUSTER *and colophon are*
registered trademarks of Simon & Schuster Inc.
Designed by Edith Fowler
Manufactured in the United States of America

10 9 8 7 6 5 4 3 2 1

Library of Congress Cataloging in Publication Data
Schiff, Ze'ev, 1932–
    Intifada—the Palestinian uprising : Israel's third front /
Ze'ev Schiff & Ehud Ya'ari : edited and translated
by Ina Friedman.
        p. cm.
      1. West Bank—History—Palestinian Uprising, 1987–
2. Gaza Strip—History—Palestinian Uprising, 1987–
I. Ya'ari, Ehud. II. Friedman, Ina. III. Title.
DS110.W47S34 1990   *89–48864*
                                         CIP

ISBN 0–671–67530–3

CONTENTS

FOREWORD

FIVE YEARS AGO we wrote in the Afterword to our last book, *Israel's Lebanon War:*

> . . . The war in Lebanon has in no way tempered the virulence of the Palestinian problem—which is hardly surprising, inasmuch as the roots of that problem do not lie in Lebanon. It was sheer folly to believe that any action there would ameliorate the political conflict between the Israeli and Palestinian nations. If anything, the war has exacerbated the strife between the two peoples. [What lies on the horizon is hazy to us now, but it may well be a civil war between Israelis and Palestinians in the distant future.]
>
> Perhaps the greatest tragedy of the [Lebanon] war, then, is that when it was over and the PLO had been whipped, Israel lacked the wisdom to choose a path to political compromise with the Palestinians, or at least with Jordan.

We were closer to that horizon than we had imagined, and out of the haze burst a war of a wholly new kind for Israel: a popular war fought not by conventional forces armed with standard weapons but by masses of civilians using other violent means. The *intifada* is a war of an unusual style that works in unusual ways, and it contains not only the dimension of two nations in confrontation but a strong element of socioeconomic tension. It is also a war that is still in progress, and we make no pretensions to offer the last word on the subject. But we have come to the conclusion that after two years, this "war within" has reached a crossroads that leads toward negotiations in one direction and away from them in the other. Seeing that a choice must be made, we believe that an examination of where the two sides stand and how they arrived at this juncture is a most timely one.

Each of the partners to the conflict has changed its basic position under the impact of the *intifada*. The PLO has revised its attitude toward a settlement; Jordan has severed its administrative links with the West Bank; the United States has opened an official dialogue with the PLO (which constitutes recognition); and the Israeli government has come around to seeing that it must negotiate a settlement of the Palestinian problem with the Palestinians, not the Arab states, and has therefore put forth a proposal for elections in the occupied territories. The uprising, like the negotiating process, may go on for some time yet, but there is no longer any reason to postpone an interim assessment.

Our aim in writing this book has been to bore through the tangle of emotion, prejudice, and self-interest encompassing our subject and to focus on the heart of the matter. We do not offer a chronological description of developments or enter into every aspect of the controversy that has attended the *intifada* on both sides of the barricades. Our aim is to shed light on the decisive events and isolate key processes, though we have made a point of elaborating on the facts in cases where the situation has been distorted beyond recognition by a plethora of emotional or moralizing accounts or by deliberate misrepresentation.

The point of this book is not to establish guilt, impute blame, or grade the parties on their conduct or performance. Neither is it our aim to fuel the bitter controversy that divides Israel today. Our sole purpose in taking on this venture is to contribute to a better understanding of the tempest that has been raging in our country for two years so that the necessary conclusions can be drawn. Even though we are identified with one side of the conflict, we have been privileged to receive help from the other as well. Many Palestinians have aided us in our research and writing, as have Israelis of all ranks, and the final product reflects this combination of sources on both sides of the fault line. Crucial material was likewise gathered abroad, especially in the United States, though we were also able to glean information from Russian, Swedish, and other European sources with a bearing on the matter.

The ideas presented in the Epilogue are based upon papers we wrote as the Koret Fellow (Schiff) and a Visiting Fellow (Ya'ari) at the Washington Institute for Near East Policy. Our agent, Deborah Harris, once again smoothed the way to publication with her customary graciousness and skill. We have had the good fortune to benefit from the support and insight of Alice Mayhew and the genially tendered aid of David Shipley at Simon and Schuster. To them, and to all the others who have helped us with information, documentation, and counsel, we wish to express our deep appreciation.

ZE'EV SCHIFF
EHUD YA'ARI

Tel Aviv-Jerusalem
October 1989

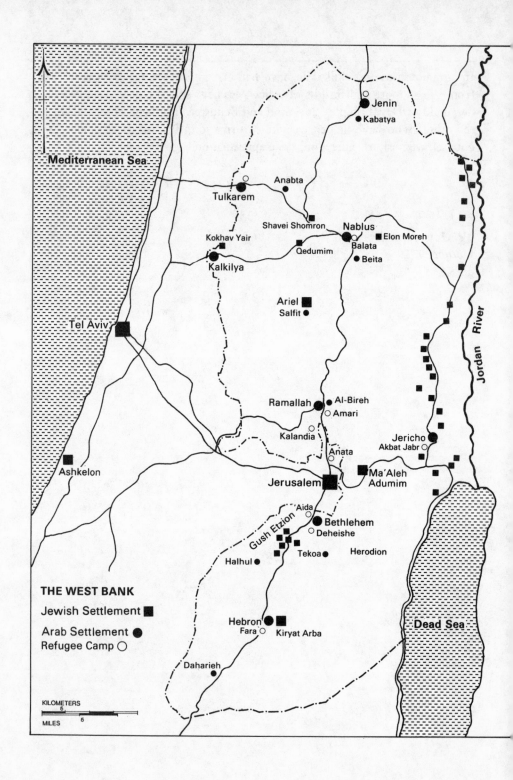

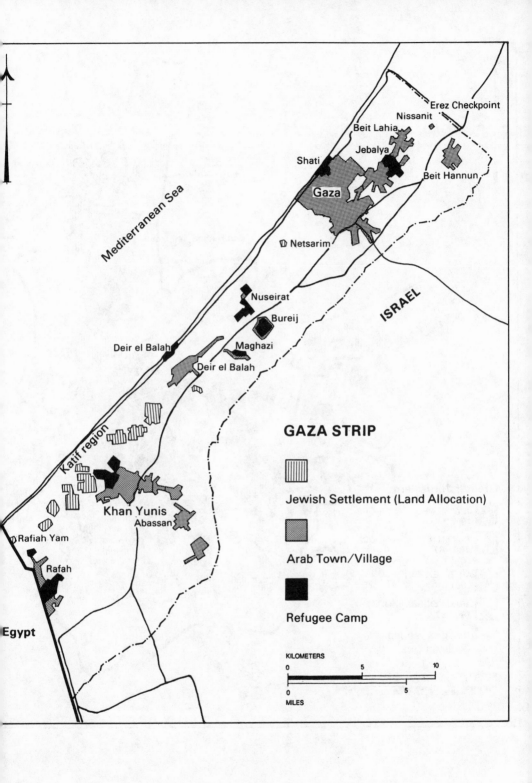

Mediterranean Sea

Erez Checkpoint

Nissanit

Beit Lahia

Jebalya

Shati

Beit Hannun

Gaza

Netsarim

ISRAEL

Nuseirat

Bureij

Deir el Balah

Maghazi

Deir el Balah

Katif region

Khan Yunis

Abassan

Rafiah Yam

Rafah

Egypt

GAZA STRIP

Jewish Settlement (Land Allocation)

Arab Town/Village

Refugee Camp

KILOMETERS

0   5   10

0   5

MILES

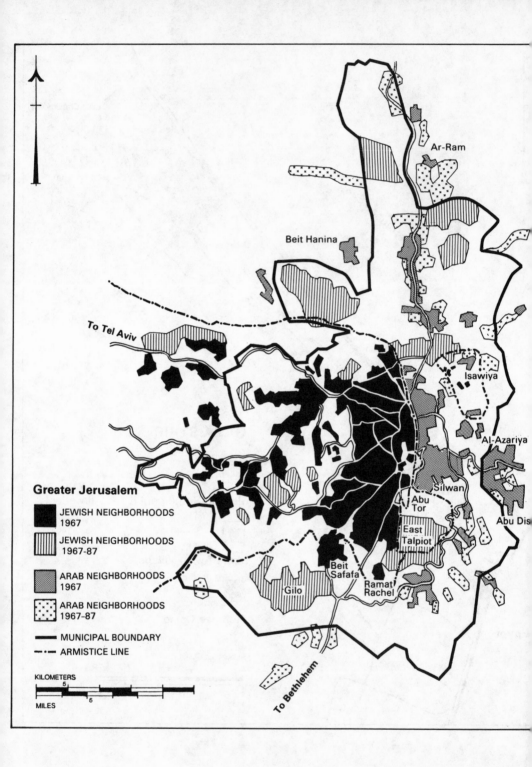

Greater Jerusalem

- ■ JEWISH NEIGHBORHOODS 1967
- ▥ JEWISH NEIGHBORHOODS 1967-87
- ▦ ARAB NEIGHBORHOODS 1967
- ▦ ARAB NEIGHBORHOODS 1967-87
- — MUNICIPAL BOUNDARY
- —·—·— ARMISTICE LINE

KILOMETERS
5

MILES
5

To Tel Aviv

Ar-Ram

Beit Hanina

Isawiya

Al-Azariya

Silwan

Abu Dis

Abu Tor

East Talpiot

Beit Safafa

Gilo

Ramat Rachel

To Bethlehem

ONE | *THE SURPRISE*

THOUGH WINTER had already set in by then, the evening of Tuesday, December 8, 1987, was a warm one in Gaza, and the air was particularly close in Jebalya, the largest refugee camp in the Strip. The heaviness permeating the air that night was a detail that would long be remembered by the Israeli soldiers manning the outpost in the camp, for December 8 was the evening on which the Palestinian uprising broke out. In a sense, it was fitting that the explosion should occur in Jebalya, where some 60,000 people make their home in conditions of appalling poverty, overcrowding, and filth. The violence on December 8 was directed specifically against the army outpost and the soldiers holding it—a company of reservists under the command of a computer programmer and a moshavnik from the Negev. They were the first to experience the surprise that hit the entire Israeli army, indeed all of Israel. But unlike most others, they were to bear the brunt of it—and in more ways than one.

For all intents and purposes, December 8 had been a day like most others in the Gaza Strip. Admittedly, a fatal traffic accident had occurred there in the afternoon, but traffic deaths are so commonplace in Israel and the territories that it often seems the public is totally inured to them. In this case an Israeli truck had hit a car carrying laborers from the Gaza Strip, immediately killing four of the passengers and badly injuring the others. The item was broadcast over the radio as a matter of course—another statistic that was expected to faze almost no one. Then something odd happened: all at once, it seemed, Gaza was abuzz with a wild rumor that was to spark off an unprecedented wave of demonstrations. The crash, this rumor had it, had not been an accident at all but a cold-blooded act of vengeance by a relative of the Israeli stabbed to death in Gaza's main market two days earlier. And by the same token that the crash was no accident, to the residents of both the Gaza Strip and the West Bank the rumor was no rumor but an indisputable fact. By evening a leaflet was already in circulation in Gaza denouncing the killing of the four Palestinians, and the following day the Arabic newspaper *al-Fajr*, published in East Jerusalem, pronounced the death of the four passengers to have been "maliciously perpetrated." Even the mayor of Nablus, Hafez Toukan—an Israeli appointee—took the trouble to protest the "murder" of the four innocent men and declared a day of mourning in his city.

As soon as news of the fatal accident had been broadcast on the radio, the officers of the company in Jebalya sensed that there would be trouble when the funerals took place. But their concern was not shared by all. The head of the army's Southern Command, Maj. Gen. Yitzhak (Itzik) Mordechai, was not even informed of the accident; one of his men evidently decided that since no military personnel were involved, there was no point in "bothering" the general with the news. The men in Jebalya were right to feel uneasy, though. As thousands of mourners returned from the funerals early in the evening, their procession turned into an outright assault on the outpost. Crowds of angry people, young and old, closed in on the barbed-wire fence and began throwing stones into the compound. Shots fired in the air did nothing to deter the rioters, who were shouting curses and chanting the cry "*Jihad! Jihad!*" A patrol was sent out to disperse the demonstrators, but they only regrouped and surrounded the outpost again. Soon rioting had spread throughout the camp, as other army and Border Police patrols became the targets of stones and firebombs. In the past, demonstrations and other disturbances had always broken up at nightfall, when the residents closed themselves up in their homes. This time the rioting began at dusk and continued well past eleven o'clock.

Tired and shaken by the force of the outburst, a few of the reserve company's officers met at the entrance to the Jebalya outpost before turning in for the night. When one of them commented that unless the army sent a conspicuous infusion of reinforcements into the camp there would be trouble the next day as well, the sector commander could hardly contain his impatience. "Nothing's going to happen!" he scoffed at the reservists so easily rattled by the violence. "You don't know these people. They'll go to sleep now and leave for work first thing in the morning, as usual. You'll see."

No additional forces were sent to Gaza. Neither was Jebalya placed under curfew. But few people slept in the camp that night, and by dawn most of its roads and alleyways had been blocked by a combination of heavy rocks, broken furniture, and steel pipes (brought in to repair the chronically insufficient sewage system). One of the army's night patrols saw what was happening but received orders to wait until dawn before dealing with the problem. Meanwhile, the reserve company's fifty-five men closed themselves up in the outpost and waited for the inevitable.

Contrary to the sector commander's confident prediction, the next day boded ill from the very start. Most of Jebalya's residents did not go to work, and by six A.M. the rioting had already flared up again. Students of the Islamic University were milling around the streets of Gaza city, calling on people to come out and demonstrate. In nearby Jebalya thousands of people already filled the streets and countless others stood on their roofs waiting expectantly. A pall of rage hovered over the camp, and there was little reason to doubt that the appearance of troops would trigger an explosion. Nevertheless, out of the compound came two armored personnel carriers preceded by a jeep. Their aim was to break through the roadblocks and make a show of strength, but their mission was doomed from the start. As they moved along the narrow axis dividing the two quarters of the camp, thousands of people stood lining the road and at the windows of their huts and houses, practically touching the vehicles as they passed. At first the soldiers were met by jeers and curses, but soon stones began flying and the men in the APCs realized that if they didn't close the flaps they would be knocked out by the missiles coming from every direction, including the rooftops. A Molotov cocktail hurled out of one of the buildings missed its mark but burst into flames on the street, filling the air with the pungent odor of gasoline. A few daring young Palestinians actually jumped onto the APCs, forcing their drivers to floor the gas pedal and deliberately swerve their vehicles from side to side in an attempt to shake them off.

On one of these zigzags a machine gun and its tripod fell off an APC, and a number of people rushed forward to snatch it. It took a burst of gunfire, while the vehicle was traveling in reverse, to stop them from getting to the weapon, but two of the Palestinians did manage to run off with the ammunition belt. The rioters were not daunted by the shots fired in the air. On the contrary, again and again the soldiers were confronted by frenzied people taunting them in Hebrew and daring them to shoot while they stood rooted to the spot in defiance. Others let out cries of despair—"It's better to die than to go on like this!"—as though the reservists had the power to change their fate or the abominable conditions in the camp. Soon it was evident that the APCs were quite useless in that situation—especially as standing orders forbade the men to fire indiscriminately into a crowd—and the patrol was ordered to return to the outpost.

Another incident developing about 200 meters north of the outpost ultimately led to the death of one of the camp's residents. At 8:30 A.M., Lt. Ofer of the same reserve company and the three men accompanying him in his command car were ordered to disperse the crowd gathered in an open lot before it began advancing on the outpost. Ofer shot off a tear-gas grenade from a distance of a few dozen yards, but rather than scatter, the crowd responded with a hail of stones. One Palestinian teenager with particularly good aim began fleeing as soon as the command car approached him. Seeing him enter one of the houses, Ofer decided—in accordance with his standing orders—to pursue the youth and arrest him.

Two of the soldiers remained standing by the vehicle while the third accompanied Ofer into the house to arrest the youngster. As they left the building, they were met by a barrage of stones from the nearby rooftops. Once again tear gas was shot at the burgeoning crowd, but again it had no effect. The two men escorting the young Palestinian were forced back into the house with him, and within minutes three firebombs had been thrown at the command car waiting outside, two of them scoring hits and setting it ablaze. While two soldiers were busy trying to extinguish the fire and a third was guarding the youngster in the courtyard, the fourth stood by the window of the house firing in the air. Then the youngster's family decided to try and free him; two elderly women assaulted the guard with a pipe and a stick as others dashed into the courtyard to snatch the youth from his captors. Another Palestinian youngster joined the attack and threw a brick at the guard, hitting him in the back. At first the assailants were driven back by more shots fired into the air, but then one of the Palestinians grabbed the rifle by its barrel and tried to wrest it away from the soldier until a burst of gunfire drove him off.

Meanwhile the soldiers standing by the command car were trying to raise the outpost on the vehicle's radio but found that it had been damaged. They also tried to contact Ofer on the walkie-talkie but got no reply. Finally Ofer's voice came over the instrument ordering them to fire at the legs of the approaching mob, since shots in the air seemed to have no effect. The crowd stood about thirty yards from the vehicle and looked as though it was going to rush the soldiers in order to free the youngster. As the throng surged forward, two people were wounded by gunfire and were dragged aside by their comrades; the rest seemed to be worked up into a state of frenzy. Then a third Palestinian was hit, and the forward movement came to a halt. By that point another army patrol had reached the area to help out, and the youngster under arrest was forced into a jeep and driven off. Ofer and his men did not know that one of the people wounded by their fire, seventeen-year-old Hatem a-Sisi, was already dead.

Less than two hours after the incident, Itzik Mordechai, the head of Southern Command, turned up at the Jebalya outpost full of complaints. Why had it been necessary to pursue the boy into his house? Why had the men been so slow in getting out and so quick to open fire? For many a day thereafter, Mordechai remained convinced that this street battle was the reason why the disturbances in Gaza persisted. In his anger, he suspended Lt. Ofer on the spot—before the matter had been investigated and despite the insistence of Ofer's superior that the lieutenant had acted on his orders. The entire company was stunned by the day's events, but it was difficult to tell what shocked them more: the boldness of the people of Jebalya or the behavior of their own commanding officer.

While soldiers were battling refugees in Jebalya, the coordinator of the government's operations in the territories, Shmuel Goren, happened to be a few miles away visiting Brig. Aryeh Ramot, the newly appointed head of the Civil Administration in Gaza. The Civil Administration is one of those sutble devices that has enabled Israel simultaneously to practice occupation and to deny it. As its name implies, it was conceived as a foil to both the letter and the spirit of the Military Government, though still strictly a part of it. The Civil Administration received its own title and identity in 1981, when then-Defense Minister Ariel Sharon assigned to it all the non-security tasks of the Military Government. The result was to forge in the territories a structure of government closely parallel to Israel's own bureaucracy—which is why some observers regard it as a manifestation of "creeping annexation." As coordinator of operations in the territories, Goren was wedged between the head of the Civil Administration and the minister of defense, who is ultimately responsible for the two-track apparatus that has functioned in the territories since Sharon's day. On this visit to Brig. Ramot, an easy-going armor officer with no previous experience in his new role, Goren felt obliged to stress the clear distinction between military and civilian concerns. He advised Ramot to leave anything that even smacked of security affairs to the army and to steer clear of any task that was beyond his mandate or competence. This was a policy to which Goren himself strictly adhered at all times. Yet on hearing the flood of reports coming in from Jebalya, even he couldn't resist going out to see things for himself.

The drive from Ramot's Gaza headquarters to Jebalya takes only minutes, but on that day the officers escorting Goren insisted that he dispense with his staff car and make the trip by jeep. They also chose to approach the camp not by the usual short and well-traveled route but by a roundabout course dictated over the radio from the outpost. At one junction the alley they had taken was blocked by an old refrigerator, forcing them to backtrack in reverse. Finally they were met by two vehicles from the Border Police whose blaring sirens alternated with orders to the crowd, issued over loud speakers, to make way for the convoy to pass. When Goren finally reached the outpost, it looked more like the setting for a chain gang than a military installation: groups of prisoners, hands tied and heads bowed, were crowded together in a corner of the yard opposite a huge pile of the stones that had been thrown into the compound.

When Goren and his escorts left Jebalya that afternoon, again in a convoy of military vehicles, the acrid black smoke of burning tires was billowing into the air on all sides. A short while earlier a report had come through that the riots had spread to the southern end of the Gaza Strip, where a small unit of reservists had run into trouble in the Rafah refugee camp. "The whole city was out on the streets"—or so it seemed to the unit trapped there. "Rafah is no longer in our hands," one of the reservists told the young infantry officer whose unit had been dispatched to rescue him. "It has to be captured all over again!" Another infantryman involved in that operation later commented that he now knew what it must have been like to rescue the men from the surrounded outposts on the Suez Canal at the start of the Yom Kippur War!

Yet for all the drama of that day and everything he had seen and heard, upon reaching Tel Aviv Shmuel Goren phoned the defense min-

ister's military secretary, Brig. Elkana Harnof, and assured him that
the events in Gaza were much the same as the countless disturbances
quelled in the past. There were certain difficulties, to be sure, but he
was confident that Itzik Mordechai would have them under control
in no time. And he wasn't the only one who thought so.

On December 10, the third day of the Palestinian uprising in the
occupied territories and a critical juncture in the development of its
momentum, Israel's minister of defense, Yitzhak Rabin, boarded an El Al
plane and flew off to the United States. Had appropriate action been
taken on that day, it might still have been possible to block the spread
of violence from the Gaza Strip to the West Bank. But the sad fact is
that Rabin and his aides had their sights set so firmly on Washington
that they failed to see what was happening at their feet. The territories
were a powder keg whose short fuse was already burning.

Demonstrations in the Gaza Strip weren't anything new, though
the signs pointing to a difference in their scope and force might have
suggested something about their duration, as well. In any event, the
notion that the defense minister should stay home under these circumstances was never seriously considered, for the possibility that the
Palestinians were bent on revolt did not even occur to the captains of
Israel's defense establishment. Rabin's attention was sharply focused on
the highlight of his Washington agenda: the signing of a memorandum
of understanding on the sale of Israeli-manufactured equipment to the
American government and setting the final price for seventy F-16
fighter planes on which Israel expected to receive a discount. Also
scheduled for the trip was a visit to a number of American military installations and finally an address before a large convention in Florida
on behalf of Israel Bonds. Someone must have been uneasy about the
defense minister's leaving, for on the day before his departure Rabin
held a meeting with his top aides to decide on whether to go through
with the trip. Not a single one of the participants suggested that he
make his apologies to the new secretary of defense, Frank Carlucci, and
postpone the visit. No one even proposed that the trip be pared down
to the bare essentials. The total insouciance in face of the renewed violence in Gaza was striking, almost startling.

None of the three men in the Israeli government who were vet-
erans of the post was chosen as acting minister of defense during
Rabin's absence. Instead, Rabin's stand-in was Prime Minister Yitzhak
Shamir, who was serving in this capacity for the first time. In one sense

Shamir was an ideal caretaker; not known as a mover and shaker in the best of circumstances, he was unlikely to toy with a senior minister's prerogatives—or make tough decisions in his stead. The chief of staff, Lt. Gen. Dan Shomron, who was to report to and advise Shamir, was fairly new to his job (having held it for about eight months) and had never before dealt with widespread disturbances in the territories. Manning the defense minister's office in Tel Aviv was another relative newcomer, Brig. Harnof, who was to brief Rabin daily on all significant developments. On grounds of experience alone, this was not an ideal lineup for crisis management.

From the moment Rabin's plane touched down in New York, the members of his entourage did all they could to assure themselves that the situation in the territories was not serious and that there was no need to cut their visit short. The fact that Defense Secretary Carlucci gave the subject only passing mention was proof positive, in their eyes, that the riots were just another flare-up of the periodic, short-lived unrest so familiar from the past. On December 14 Rabin and Carlucci signed their memorandum of understanding and the defense minister embarked on his visit to an F-16 squadron and two combat-helicopter squadrons—which could easily have been canceled without offending the Americans. Instead, yet another reason was found not to shorten his tour: if Rabin "rushed home," Harnof argued from Tel Aviv, he would only add melodrama to an already overheated situation, blow things further out of proportion, and hand the Palestinians a victory. By that point the television screens in the United States and Europe were filled with grim footage of the clashes in the territories, and it was hard to see how Rabin could have further dramatized the issue even if he had chosen to. Still, such reasoning put everyone's mind at ease, and it wasn't until just before their flight to Florida that Rabin's aides began to consider whether they shouldn't return home after all. Eitan Haber, the minister's media adviser, even asked the director of Israel Bonds, Yehudah Halevy, what the reaction would be if Rabin were to cancel his appearance before the thousands of Holocaust survivors who had come to Miami from all over the United States and Central America. "If it's due to a military problem, we'll find a satisfactory explanation. Such things have happened before," Halevy reassured him. But when Haber asked him to volunteer that information directly to the minister, Halevy begged off gracefully; he was not one to pull another man's chestnuts out of the fire.

The result was that Israel's defense minister was on the other side

of the world during the critical opening phase of the Palestinian uprising, and his absence was sorely felt, especially when it came to making hard-nosed decisions. Perhaps the most important effect was the
failure to pour reinforcements into the West Bank and Gaza immediately. Ironically, however, when Rabin finally did return to Israel on
December 21—some two weeks after the rioting had broken out and
a week after concluding his business with Carlucci—his first move was
a misstep. Met upon landing by Shmuel Goren and Dan Shomron, who
barely had time to brief him, he proceeded to hold an airport press
conference and advertise just how divorced he was from the situation
by informing the world, definitively, that Iran and Syria were behind
the unrest in the territories. Clearly, neither Teheran nor Damascus
had the power to incite anywhere near the level of violence raging in
the West Bank and Gaza. Rabin was looking for a convenient scape-
goat and lashed out wildly at Israel's most fanatic and thus easily
blamed enemies, without a shred of evidence or justification. (Apparently distance was not the only obstacle to understanding, for the acting minister of defense, who had been in Israel all the time, was likewise quick to point a finger at the wrong party. Shamir charged the
Palestine Liberation Organization with fomenting the uprising—and
was equally off the mark.)

Afterward Rabin's apologists claimed, rather lamely, that the minister had been misled in the hasty briefing he received upon landing.
Yet this version of events does not stand up to scrutiny, if only because
all the intelligence experts were by then in agreement that the uprising
had begun as a grass-roots initiative, and neither Goren nor Shomron
had reason to tell Rabin otherwise. Shamir could also have spared himself the embarrassment of misleading the public, for at least one intelligence report written during that period stated explicitly that the PLO
had not fomented the riots in the territories; it had merely jumped on
the bandwagon once they were in progress. In any event, the prime
minister might not have played down the gravity of the situation, dismissing the riots as a fleeting episode, had he gone out into the field
and talked with the men who were facing the Palestinians day in and
day out. They, at least, sensed from the start that something had
changed—radically.

The reservists in Jebalya were acquainted with the Gaza Strip
from their stint in the same outpost in June–July 1985, but they soon
realized that there was no comparison between the two periods. What

they found especially astonishing was the audacity of the demonstrators who, undeterred by gunfire, attacked the APCs and tried to grab weapons right out of the soldiers' hands. Even before the first riots broke out, the men had sensed a change in the atmosphere. But they had come to that conclusion on their own, and it raised many angry questions. Why hadn't they been briefed about the shift in mood? Why hadn't they been told that the area was on the brink of an explosion? Their initial briefing by officers from the sector command had been brief and sloppy. No one mentioned that just a few weeks earlier the group calling itself the Islamic Jihad had drawn masses of people out into the streets for unprecedented demonstrations or that a decision to deport its leader, Sheikh Abd al-Aziz Odeh, had prompted an assault by some 2,000 people on the Jebalya outpost. No one set down guidelines on how the reservists were to conduct themselves when confronting civilians in threatening situations. And despite the recent spate of violence in the camp, no one issued special equipment for dealing with such incidents. The entire company had to share a total of four canister tubes for launching tear-gas grenades from rifles. Its vehicles had no spare tires, and when the demonstrations began one of the company's sergeants actually had to steal windshield protectors from the regional garage!

The company's preparatory exercises were further proof that none of the responsible officers or intelligence men from the local command had any inkling that the reservists might be faced with mass demonstrations. There had been no training in crowd dispersal or riot control. Other than a single demonstration of shooting tear-gas grenades and rubber bullets, no exercises had been held in either of these methods. After the first assault on the outpost, the men of the company were understandably disgruntled about their poor preparation, and their officers demanded answers to a number of troubling questions. They were not actually ignored; a few senior officers, including the brigade and divisional commanders and the chief of staff of Southern Command, paid visits to Jebalya. But when the reservists asked if they would be outfitted with special equipment for dispersing demonstrations—clubs, helmets, shields, and the like—the response was always the same: a patronizing grin and the promise that "everything will be fine!" What disturbed the company most, however, was that whenever its commanders asked for clear instructions on how to act in the face of civil disturbances, the reply was consistently evasive. "You have to judge by the situation" was usually the only guideline that senior officers were willing to supply.

Needless to say, after Lt. Ofer's dismissal, the frustration over what the men of his company saw as a lack of direction and support from their superiors turned to outrage. On the last day of their tour, still smarting from the short shrift they felt they had all received, fifty-nine of the company's officers and enlisted men signed a petition to the chief of staff protesting the "lack of guidance, backing, and appropriate equipment given to soldiers of the Israel Defense Forces holding the territories" and making an appeal for Ofer's reinstatement. "In our opinion," the men wrote, "Lt. Ofer acted according to orders, for hours, and in highly difficult circumstances. He displayed valor, daring, leadership, and fixity of purpose, all while exercising maximum judgment, and in our view he deserves to be decorated for his actions."

At the urging of their battalion commander, the men waited a month to send off the petition in the hope that Ofer's dismissal would be reversed, they would all be summoned to a discussion about their experience, and the appropriate conclusions would be drawn from it. When none of this came to pass, they sent their appeal to the chief of staff. But the result was a chain reaction of anger that proved catastrophic for the company's command. Miffed by their independent action, their battalion commander immediately sent off a letter of his own calling the petition "insolent" and asking Shomron to ignore it. The chief of staff complied, leaving the whole matter to the discretion of the battalion and brigade commanders, who took out their pique by dismissing two more of the company's officers—its commander and his deputy—for having signed the petition along with their men. In protest, two veteran sergeants asked to be relieved of their duties, leaving the company's command a shambles. Thus rather than highlight grave oversights and problems of communication between the various levels of command, the effect of the soldiers' appeal was to destroy the backbone of their company. It was not the IDF's finest hour.

If Itzik Mordechai was quick to anger over the handling of the violence in Jebalya, he was also quick to grasp that it was not a passing vagary and that Israel was facing a whole new phenomenon. His primary concern was that the force at his disposal, which sufficed to hold the Gaza Strip during periods of calm, would be swamped by the mobs of demonstrators and that his men would be provoked into shooting indiscriminately. Before Rabin's departure, therefore, he asked for additional troops, but the request was denied, almost reflexively. The use of reinforcements had become a rather sore point in the IDF, because they usually came at the expense of the army's training schedule. Consequently the chief of staff and his deputy had issued strict orders against pulling units out of their training programs to handle problems of current security, and since neither man imagined that the rioting would snowball into an uprising, they were disinclined to honor Mordechai's request. Shomron's refusal remained in force even after he had visited the Gaza Strip on December 15, for he held to the belief that the riots were just a gust of turbulence that would soon blow over. Most members of the General Staff tended to agree; neither Mordechai's persistent uneasiness nor the fact that the Shin Bet (General Security Services) was recommending the dispatch of reinforcements and a roundup of agitators did anything to change that. It would take quite a while before most of the generals understood that profound changes had occurred within Palestinian society—changes they had neglected to notice—and that like it or not, they had an uprising on their hands.

For his part, the acting defense minister was unaware of Itzik Mordechai's request, for he never made an appearance at General Staff meetings to hear the thinking on the subject. Instead he relied exclusively on reports from the chief of staff, with whom he held regular phone conversations. Shamir was treated to a description of the rioting in one meeting with Shomron, but most of that conversation centered on the possibility of placing limitations on the media (to which the chief of staff was firmly opposed). Some of the other ministers had urged Shamir to summon Rabin home, but he was unresponsive to the idea; in fact, although he spoke with Rabin a number of times, he never so much as broached the subject. Similarly, the idea of sending reinforcements into the territories was mentioned in Shamir's office, but he did not raise the matter at the next cabinet meeting, for he was convinced that the present disturbances, like all the previous outbursts instigated by the PLO, would quickly burn themselves out. Little did he suspect that Yasser Arafat and his associates had been no less surprised by the timing, and particularly by the vehemence, of the riots.

On Friday, December 18, Dan Shomron was again scheduled to visit the Gaza Strip, but before leaving his office he took a call from Ezer Weizman, a former minister of defense and now Labor minister-without-portfolio in the National Unity Government. "What's going on there?" Weizman asked with characteristic bluster. "Have you lost control of things?" Weizman had just spoken with the Egyptian ambassador, Mohammed Basyuni, who had expressed deep concern over the high number of casualties in Gaza. Indeed, it was impossible to

deny that the toll had risen from day to day. Shomron quietly reassured him that the IDF had matters in hand, but apparently the call
had its effect. In any case, that was the last time that either Central or
Southern Command, which were dealing with the violence in the occupied territories, suffered from a shortage of troops.

Speculation on whether the dispatch of reinforcements at the start
of the uprising would have changed the course of events soon developed into a full-blown controversy. Some military men have insisted
that a swift, massive, and energetic reaction to the violence would
have nipped the uprising in the bud. Even had it come at the cost of
many casualties, they argued, such an action would still have saved the
hundreds of lives lost during the subsequent months of rebellion. From
a purely tactical standpoint they may be right, especially as the uprising was a spontaneous action. The longer it was allowed to continue,
with the IDF seemingly irresolute, the more it picked up momentum.
In East Jerusalem, for example, the Israeli police were equally surprised
by the eruption of rioting and attacks on a number of Jewish neighborhoods. But they quickly massed thousands of men from all over the
country, and their forceful response restored relative calm. On the
other hand, those who argue that the uprising could have been quashed
by a greater show of force ignore the reasons behind it: the buildup of
national, economic, and social grievances that would have led to an
explosion in any case. A larger military force might have cut the initial
wave short, but it would not have changed the circumstances that
brought it about. All things considered, a sustained rebellion was only
a matter of time.

For those willing to see them, there had been countless signs that
serious trouble was afoot in the territories, and certainly the uprising
did not break out abruptly after a period of calm. In the course of
1987, and especially during the latter half of the year, various symptoms made themselves so manifest that either all of Israel had gone
blind or those who did make out the drift of events simply chose to
ignore it. The boldness of the demonstrators in the territories had
reached the point where they were attempting to attack Israeli soldiers,
including high-ranking officers, and snatch their weapons away. In
August an Israeli officer was shot and killed at midday on the main
street of Gaza before the eyes of dozens of people—none of whom
made an effort to help him or even called for an ambulance. Firing
into the air to disperse demonstrations had become a fruitless exercise;

the demonstrators merely jeered at the troops, as though intent on drawing them into a confrontation. More than once in the course of November, Israeli employees of the Civil Administration abandoned their cars in panic on the streets of Gaza, later to find only their charred remains. Many of the actions that were to characterize the uprising—throwing stones and firebombs at Israeli vehicles and during demonstrations, distributing leaflets on how to operate against Israel, holding commercial and school strikes, and showing the Palestinian flag—had actually been current during the months before its outbreak. A perusal of the operations log kept by the Civil Administration in Gaza showed a steep rise in most kinds of civil disturbances over the previous year: 133 percent in the number of demonstrations and riots, 178 percent in the burning of tires (487 incidents up from 172), 140 percent in the throwing of stones, and 68 percent in the blocking of roads.

The more these incidents multiplied, the more difficult it was for the IDF to bring them to a halt, and the more Israel appeared weak in Palestinian eyes. With the army's deterrent image badly battered, the Palestinians had less to fear from Israel's clout, and their boldness began to escalate. After the murder of the IDF officer in Gaza, the employees of the Civil Administration were ordered to commute to their jobs in groups, so that many of them traveled in convoys—and even then they shunned the main road through Gaza, preferring a circuitous route that bypasses most of the Strip. There was nothing secret about this new arrangement; it functioned day in and day out in full view of the Gazans, who made a habit of standing outside the administration's headquarters to watch the stream of Israeli vehicles pass through the gates. Moreover, most of the Civil Administration's staff, including its complement of army officers, made a point of leaving Gaza before dark. Some Israelis actually preferred, whenever possible, to use cars with Gazan license plates. In time even the military was given orders to skirt the obstacles laid on the roads and avoid clashing with rioters. None of this was lost on the Palestinians, of course. A survey conducted by the Civil Administration showed that the local population took these precautions to be a sign of cowardice and concluded that "the rioters have placed the Israeli administration under siege." As the investigating officer would ultimately phrase it: "The erosion in our image did not occur overnight; it was a process of retreat, concession, and hesitation, a collection of small victories over the administration, with each little triumph having reverberations ten times greater than the actual significance of the victory itself."

Yet despite this protracted buildup of confidence, when the periodic incidents turned into a bona fide uprising that spread to the West Bank as well, Israel was surprised—and not just on the tactical level, as certain government and military figures would now have us believe. Until the uprising the Israelis knew that they must be prepared to fight on two fronts: a regular war against standing armies and both an open and secret war against terrorism. By their rebellion, however, the Palestinians opened a third front of mass, unarmed, civilian violence—a new kind of warfare for which Israel had no effective response. Since the standard tools of military might are not designed to handle defiance of this sort, the IDF was wholly unprepared for the uprising in terms of its deployment, its combat doctrine, and even its store of the most basic equipment. The result was that overnight Israel was exposed in all its weakness, which was perhaps the real import of the surprise. The shock of being caught off guard was further aggravated by Israeli's failure in addressing world public opinion; it was simply incapable of making a case for its position while its army was shooting down unarmed women and children.

Much of the surprise was about the way in which the Palestinians conducted themselves. The Military Government had been dealing with sporadic outbreaks of rioting for years, but they had usually been the work of students and other young people guided by the Palestinian organizations. This time the outburst was spontaneous and encompassed the entire population: young and old, male and female, town and country, religious and secular. But above all it was the sheer number of people that catapulted the riots into a full-blown uprising. The revolt spread like wildfire to cities, villages, and refugee camps. None was prepared to oppose it; indeed, the sense of solidarity during the first months of the uprising had never been stronger in Palestinian society, long known for its divisiveness. Israel was no less astonished by the readiness of the Palestinians to bear the weight of casualties and suffering, from over 500 dead and 8,500 wounded in the first two years of the insurgency to long commercial strikes, weeks without working or bringing in pay, and oppressive curfews and blockades. Equally unexpected was their self-restraint. Despite their animosity and rage, the Palestinians did not resort to arms—giving them a distinct advantage in the contest for sympathetic public opinion. There was a modest collection of arms within the territories, and even these few weapons could have wreaked havoc among unsuspecting Israelis, especially civilians. But the Palestinians appreciated almost instinctively that restraint was in their own self-interest; resort to arms would only justify the IDF's sweeping use of its far superior fire power and cause the Palestinians punishing losses.

Though the uprising claimed few Israeli casualties, in many respects Israel's unpreparedness for it was even less excusable than the surprise it sustained in October 1973 at the start of the Yom Kippur War. For in 1973 Israel failed to see what its neighbors were concocting over the border, but in 1987 it was oblivious to what was cooking in its very own back yard. In 1973 its Military Intelligence and political leadership misread the implications of a single Arab military move, but in 1987 Israel's political leadership and entire intelligence community failed to discern a process already well advanced among a population under its own tight control. Worse yet, the country's politicians, along with most of their constituents, flaunted their blindness by behaving as though the Palestinians would forever remain resigned to whatever Israel did in the territories. Turmoil was raging right under their windows, but they chose to ignore whatever was incongruent with their prejudices and dreams. One member of the General Staff compared the situation to placing an empty kettle on the fire and being startled when the top blows off.

Damage is not always measured in terms of casualties, and one certainly cannot compare the toll in a clash between regular armies with the losses incurred when troops face unarmed civilians. But in calculating the cost of the uprising, Israel must take into account such intangibles as the harm done to its political standing, the setback in its struggle for supportive public opinion, and the diminishment of its moral stature, especially in the eyes of its friends and of Diaspora Jewry. Viewed in these terms, Israel has suffered far more damage as a result of the Palestinian uprising than it did from the Yom Kippur War. Yet the reaction to this latest setback has been radically different. In 1973, once the fighting had ended, the blunder that made Israel so vulnerable at the start of the war prompted such a public outcry that the government was forced to appoint a commission of inquiry into the matter. But the fact that Israel was surprised by the Palestinian uprising has passed almost without comment in Israel's usually tumultuous political arena. How did such a situation come about, and why have the Israelis accepted it so tamely?

That the gathering storm went unnoticed probably traced to the fact that no single person or agency regarded itself as fully responsible for the territories, so that from an administrative standpoint the subject was allowed to fall between all the possible stools. Neither did any one officer or official believe himself responsible for assessing what was likely to happen there or for gauging the perils that Israel would face by continuing to control a million and a half Palestinians who did not want to be subject to its rule. Various bodies within the defense establishment each focused its attention on a specific aspect of the broad subject of "the territories," yet neither the prime minister nor the minister of defense—who should have been aware of the gaps—called for a change in the structure of the system. The same held for the Ministerial Committee for Security Affairs, which had a number of former defense ministers among its members.

When Dan Shomron was about to move into the chief of staff's office, he was approached by one of the officers who was well acquainted with the situation in the territories and told: "You will be remembered as the 'chief-of-staff of the territories.' " Shomron scoffed at the idea. He was looking forward to revolutionizing the IDF and preparing it to function on the "battlefield of the future." As for security problems in the territories, he hoped and assumed they would be no worse than in the past and therefore did not place them anywhere near the top of his agenda. The results were evident throughout the IDF.

Military Intelligence is responsible for assessing Israel's state of national security, in the broadest sense. Yet strictly speaking its mandate does not extend to any threat from within—and so far had the distinction between Israel and the territories been eroded that the West Bank and Gaza already qualified as "within." Hence the risks to Israel as a consequence of its control over the territories—including an outright revolt—were never addressed in the situation reports that Military Intelligence submitted to the prime minister, the defense minister, and the cabinet. Nevertheless, it cannot evade responsibility for the surprise merely because the subject under scrutiny was classified as an internal threat. As the body dealing with the problem of Palestinian terrorism and monitoring Palestinian political affairs, the IDF's Intelligence Branch was aware that for all intents and purposes the Palestinians' long military struggle against Israel had come to naught. It also knew that the futility of this endeavor was among the primary reasons for the frustration eating away at the Palestinians in the territories, yet it made no effort to determine how they would be likely to react to the unqualified failure of this policy: by a revolt, civil disobedience, or perhaps a variation on one or both of these courses. For this reason alone, Intelligence Branch should have been charting and reporting the general trends in Palestinian society.

Toward the end of 1986 Military Intelligence did, in fact, forecast that serious disturbances could be expected in the territories in the coming year. But beyond making the prediction, it did not press the matter at all by raising it for deliberation by the government. After the uprising had begun, when this forecast was shown to the head of Intelligence Branch, Maj. Gen. Amnon Shahak, as evidence that his men had not been derelict in their duty, his response was emphatic. "This means nothing," he countered, "because we didn't nag anyone, we didn't delve into it, and when we were called to appear at a cabinet meeting, we didn't insist on a thorough discussion of the issue."

Yet the blame does not lie with Military Intelligence alone. The files of General Staff Branch do not contain a single comprehensive assessment of the situation in the territories. Its approach to this subject had always been confined to purely tactical considerations, specifically how many men would be needed to hold the territories. This narrow view of the problem was undoubtedly the reason for the IDF's slow response to the uprising, its lack of proper equipment, and the failure to prepare its troops for such a contingency. Instead of drawing up a regular situation assessment, the army fell back on the standard operative assumption that the violence in the territories would not exceed the dimensions known in the past. Members of the high command noted the growing restiveness in the territories but held to the belief that the status quo would continue for years to come. In 1986 the then-deputy chief of staff, Maj. Gen. Amir Drori, did propose a change that might have made a considerable difference a year later. Drori pushed for the creation of a regular battalion for the West Bank, making it possible to respond promptly with a larger standing force whenever the situation required. But because of internal squabbling over which of the regional commands would "donate" this force, the proposal was eventually shelved.

On another level, Col. Yigal Carmon of the National Defense College, which often serves as a framework for clarifying ideas, challenged the view that maintaining a larger force in the territories was the proper approach to the problem. In a paper entitled *Coping with Security Problems in the Territories: A Re-evaluation*, he explored the implications of the fact that it had taken twenty-eight companies to restore order on the West Bank after the riots in August–September 1985. Carmon argued that the very need to send in so large a contingent "exposes a fundamental difficulty, not an incidental one." He also concluded that "the true dimensions of the security problem in the territories are beyond the capabilities of the Shin Bet and the IDF," so that placing the task on their shoulders "is doing them an injustice."

Essentially Carmon held that Israel was focusing solely on the symptoms of the Palestinian condition, such as terrorism, rather than on the political factors behind them. As a former adviser on Arab affairs to the Civil Administration in the West Bank, he was able to testify that this narrow approach had created ideal conditions for the PLO to make inroads among the local population. Hence the best solution to the violence was to launch an all-out war against the political arm of the PLO. He called for stronger measures against expressions of identification with the organization. He also wanted to restrain the Arabic press in East Jerusalem and particularly to block the flow of PLO funds into the territories. Yet even this paper did not go much beyond trifling with symptoms in suggesting that a crackdown on the PLO's nonmilitary organs would restore calm to the territories. Like so many others, Carmon completely ignored the economic and social problems plaguing the territories and the national aspirations of their inhabitants, which even Israel had recognized in the Camp David accords as "the legitimate rights" of the Palestinian people. In any event, his report sat gathering dust on the shelves of the college's library and had no impact on either national policy or even the public debate on the territories.

Similar papers were prepared by more junior officers. In the Nablus District, for example, one of the experts drew up recommendations stating that due to the IDF's tenuous hold over the territories, it should concentrate strictly on securing the axes of transport. He also decried all the vain notions of creating Palestinian institutions that would prop up Israel's rule, adding a footnote quoting the elderly Palestinian leader Hikmat al-Masri—among the more moderate and cautious political figures in the territories—as saying that "even the asses are rejecting the occupation by now!"

Of Israel's other security arms, the Shin Bet, or General Security Services, certainly cannot evade responsibility for the surprise that rocked Israel in December 1987. For in contrast to Military Intelligence and other branches of the IDF, it was specifically created to deal with the internal threat to Israel. The service's mandate is clear: to thwart acts of sabotage, terrorism, and espionage and prevent both sedition and political subversion. Nevertheless, when the defense minister attempted to extend these duties to providing advance warning of disturbances, the head of the Shin Bet, Avraham Shalom, balked. This happened during Moshe Arens's term as defense minister (February 1983–September 1984), when the incident of riots and other civil disturbances in the territories rose sharply and the coordinator of operations in the territories, Rehavia Vardi, called attention to the fact that not a single one of the intelligence bodies was responsible for alerting the army to prepare for them. Arens proposed that the task be assigned to the Shin Bet, but Shalom complained that he already had enough on his hands and lacked sufficient means to handle this aspect of security as well. Despite this demur Arens persuaded Prime Minister Shamir to back his suggestion, and the Shin Bet was ordered to supply advance warning of riots and other civil disturbances in the territories.

There still remained much room for misunderstanding. Shalom assumed that since the Civil Administration's advisers on Arab affairs and the coordinator of operations in the territories maintained direct contact with the residents of the areas, they would monitor and report on noteworthy trends in Palestinian society, including the possibility of widespread civil disobedience or violence. Thus the Shin Bet geared its monitory efforts primarily to tactical needs, providing such details as the time, place, and organizers of demonstrations. Precisely who was responsible for analyzing the public mood in the territories remained unclear, and certainly it could not be said that the Shin Bet was particularly attuned to the Palestinians' feelings. Of course its agents were keenly aware—perhaps more than anyone else in the Israeli administration—of the despair and frustration so prevalent among the Palestinians and of the cavalier treatment they received at the hands of the army, their Israeli employers, and "the system" in general. Yet even this "intelligence" was not reflected in any of their assessments, and they definitely did not sound an unequivocal warning that rebellion was in the air. Perhaps the best evidence of its failure in this realm was that the Shin Bet noted the mounting strength of the radical Islamic Jihad and its influence on the population in Gaza well before the uprising, yet it too was surprised by the force and scope of the explosion in December 1987.

It would appear that the service had foundered on two accounts. By focusing so sharply on tactical matters, it ended up with a case of tunnel vision, losing sight of the forest for the trees. At the same time, its penchant for maximum, even exaggerated, secrecy—considering that the safety of agents was not at stake in these circumstances—led it to keep too much of its knowledge to itself. There were other forces at work too. As a result of the "No. 300 Bus Affair," in which two terrorists were killed after their capture and senior members of the service suborned witnesses to cover up their involvement in the incident, the Shin Bet had suffered a severe internal crisis. It came, moreover, on the heels of the war in Lebanon, which had forced the service to divide its resources between the occupied territories and the southern part of Lebanon, severely taxing its agents. Not surprisingly, then, matters that had always been accorded lower priority, such as political subversion, became even less consequential now. Finally, the scandal that had tainted the Shin Bet's image and exposed it to strident public criticism diminished its prestige in the eyes of its own principals. This would appear to be the only explanation of why the cabinet did not follow its early recommendation to send reinforcements into the territories and make widespread arrests—one of the very few cases in which the Shin Bet's advice on such a vital issue was not accepted with alacrity.

But the buck did not stop there, either. The coordinator of operations in the territories, who was directly subordinate to the defense minister, was unquestionably the man with the greatest sway when it came to the conduct of the occupation. When the uprising broke out, Shmuel Goren had occupied this post for four years under two successive ministers: Moshe Arens of the Likud, who had proposed him for the job, and Labor's Yitzhak Rabin. A seasoned intelligence man, he had come to the position from the Mossad without having been tainted by its record in the war in Lebanon, and Arens undoubtedly believed that his intelligence background would stand him in good stead.

Goren's views carried considerable weight with both the ministers he served, and he soon won a reputation as a "string puller" whose influence extended into the prime minister's bureau as well. There was no aspect of governing the territories that he did not touch upon, to one degree or another. For example, he was in charge of liaising directly with the Americans on matters that fell into his province, and he used this channel to maintain indirect contact with the Jordanians, conveying his messages to them quickly. Goren also presided over all domestic political contacts with the territories and was known to guard this prerogative jealously. He would not tolerate meetings between prominent figures from the territories and Israeli officials—including ministers—that had not been cleared with him in advance, and more than one such meeting was canceled due to the pressure

Goren placed directly on the defense minister's or prime minister's bureau. His presumption reached a peak when he intervened to prevent the late Rashad a-Shawa, the former mayor of Gaza and one of the most distinguished personalities in the territories, from meeting with Israel's president, Chaim Herzog. When Herzog discovered what had happened, he bitterly protested the affront to the presidency. But Goren had a way of shrugging off such protests, pleading that the policy set down for his office was to fight the PLO by every means possible, and he was merely doing his duty to the utmost.

By the very nature of his position, the coordinator of operations in the territories had many antenna out in the field. Ever since Ariel Sharon had ordered that a clear distinction be drawn between the activities of the army and those of the Civil Administration, the latter had assumed full responsibility for contacts with the Palestinian population and was subordinate in this sphere to the coordinator of operations in the territories. The military commanders in the West Bank and Gaza dealt solely with security affairs (which were broadened to include contacts with the Jewish settlers). This arrangement gave Goren something of a monopoly on direct access to and information about the local Palestinians—a point, incidentally, that was confirmed by the army through complaints that its own knowledge of what was going on in Palestinian quarters came mainly through the filter of the Civil Administration and the security services. Goren's prime sources were his advisers on Arab affairs, who were presumably in close touch with the Palestinian population and prepared daily and weekly reports on their activities. These summaries were supplemented by research on specific subjects, some of which was done by outside experts. But even the best of these papers usually evinced a pronounced reluctance to draw any definitive conclusions, and hardly ever did they contain a penetrating political analysis of the facts they revealed. The best example of this kind of pussyfooting was a research paper on the future of the Gaza Strip published shortly before the outbreak of the uprising. Though it was brimming with data pointing to increasingly intolerable conditions for the inhabitants of the Strip by the year 2000 (and perhaps for precisely this reason was kept a classified document), Goren refused to append any forthright conclusions about what its findings implied for Israel's policy toward Gaza.

The Civil Administration's portrayal of the situation for consumption outside the political and defense establishment was considerably more disingenuous. In its information booklets, which were little better than propaganda leaflets, it managed to avoid mention of the real, grim facts of life in the territories, and the picture it did convey was a highly skewed one. On the twentieth anniversary of the Six-Day War, to cite but one example, the coordinator of operations in the territories published a full-color booklet on the accomplishments of the Civil Administration. The photograph on the cover showed a field of golden wheat, and inside, printed on expensive glossy paper, were pictures of playgrounds and health-care centers for the Palestinians—as though their lot under the occupation was all sweetness and light.

Considering this propensity to touch up reality in pastel colors, is it possible that the coordinator of operations in the territories and the Civil Administration deceived themselves as well? More than any other official, Goren was in a position to keep his finger on the pulse of Palestinian life in the territories. The Shin Bet was undoubtedly better informed about subversive activities, but the Civil Administration was supposed and presumed to be in touch with the mood among broad sectors of the population. Nevertheless, Goren's people have argued that it was not their job to warn the army of an approaching outburst of violence. Formally speaking they were right; that responsibility lay with the Shin Bet. On the other hand, if, as Goren has claimed, he could not have foreseen the impending explosion, he must have been oblivious to the enormous buildup of negative energy in the territories—meaning that he was ignorant of the most critical development of all! The fact is that Goren's reports on the eve of the uprising related to wholly marginal matters. On December 5, for example, a mere four days before the outbreak of the rioting, one of them stated that rumors of Israeli preparations for a military attack on Syria were "at the focus of public interest in the territories."

The longer the violence went on, the more the brunt of public criticism was directed specifically at Goren. During a consultation of Labor Party ministers, Rabin was urged to see to his dismissal but rejected the demand. Goren also came under sharp attack when the Knesset Foreign Affairs and Defense Committee met to discuss the uprising. The deputies spoke as though he alone was accountable for Israel's delinquency in facing the Palestinian issue, yet this very committee had suffered from a similar lapse of foresight. For the better part of a year, one of its subcommittees had carefully studied Israel's security doctrine, calling dozens of experts to testify and solemnly debating the issues. But at the end of its deliberations, when the subcommittee published a report containing a detailed chapter on the hazards Israel faced, not a single word was said about the prospect of rebellion by the Palestinians in the territories. Even when the deputies discussed the specter of disruptions in the mobilization of the reserves, no one raised the possibility that the flow of units to the front might be impeded by popular resistance in the West Bank. The subcommittee simply ignored the Palestinians' potential to mount a major challenge, thus overlooking possible pitfalls in the IDF's deployment.

In the final analysis, however, nowhere was the total disregard of the Palestinian issue more conspicuous than in the government of the National Unity coalition, which made a habit of avoiding sensitive issues. In army circles this special brand of squeamishness had become the object of outright ridicule. Attempts to maneuver or cajole the cabinet into discussing the changes taking place in Soviet policy, for example, were all but fruitless. A senior intelligence official who requested that an urgent security matter be raised for discussion in the cabinet was told by one of the prime minister's aides, "What's the rush? After all, our situation has never been better!" And in a similar vein, despite admonitions from various security experts, the government continued to avoid reviewing its policy toward Israel's own Arab citizens. Even after the uprising had broken out, two whole weeks passed before the cabinet was convened to discuss the persistent and unprecedented violence—and then only after Ezer Weizman had complained vigorously that the ministers were not being kept abreast of affairs.

At various times Labor ministers appointed ad hoc groups of experts to advise them on the territories. Shimon Peres had a team that included the Arabist Emanuel Sivan. Gad Ya'akobi, the minister of economy and planning, put together a group that included, in addition to Sivan, the former military commander of the West Bank, Benyamin Ben-Eliezer, and ex-intelligence chief Shlomo Gazit. At a meeting held early in 1986, the consensus among these men was that the creation of a clear policy on the territories was long overdue. Ben-Eliezer even warned that a rebellion was in the offing if the political and economic problems in the territories continued to go untended. Yet these frameworks, if not perfunctory, were highly limited in their influence both because their findings were not circulated through the standard channels and because no minister ever made a crusade out of the information gleaned from his experts.

And a crusade was what it would have taken to make the country sit up and listen. For the sad truth is that when it came to the occupied territories and their Palestinian inhabitants, there seemed to be a collective mental block in Israel that the national leadership, most of the experts, and even a large portion of the press was unable to overcome. The Jewish public tended to repress the Palestinian issue entirely, relating to the territories as though they were a distant land. In a sense the Israelis discovered the territories twice: at the end of the Six-Day War, when attention was riveted on their historical landscape with all its biblical landmarks, and again some twenty years later, in December 1987, when the Palestinian population made it impossible for them to cling to the blinders that had made the million and a half Arabs under Israeli military rule so conveniently invisible. In the interim, however, a new conception had taken hold: that the Palestinians were not a factor in the Middle East equation. Above all, this conclusion was reached because the Palestinians simply did not exist in the political consciousness of most Israelis. Yet it was supposedly justified by the reasoning that since they had no aspirations other than the destruction of the State of Israel, the Palestinians had disqualified themselves as partners to negotiations on the settlement of the Middle East conflict. Both the major parties in Israel, Labor and the Likud, were at most prepared to accord the Palestinians oblique recognition by discussing their problem with others—the Jordanians, the Egyptians, or the Americans—but never with the Palestinians themselves. Curiously enough, the Arabs had once taken a similar tack by obliterating the word Israel from all their books and maps, insisting that there was no such place and that any negotiations on the Middle East dispute would have to be conducted through the United States. Israel's adoption of a parallel policy toward the Palestinians had a similarly damping effect on the peace process.

The block of the two major parties was evident in every step they took. As far as the Israeli Right was and is concerned, the territories might as well be a virgin wilderness, as the Arabs inhabiting them are regarded as little more than tree trunks. The conclusions that beg to be drawn from the demographic patterns of the two peoples living in the Greater Land of Israel are irrelevant to right-wingers; otherwise they would concede that if the territories are incorporated into Israel, the Jews will soon become a minority in their own state! Those members of the Right who do apprehend the dangers inherent in their plan to annex the territories have begun to espouse a so-called transfer of their Arab inhabitants. But despite all efforts to befog the issue and even portray it as a humanitarian gesture, since it is unimaginable that the Palestinians would leave their homes of their own accord, the real import of their proposed "transfer" is expulsion.

The mindset of the Labor Party is a more complex affair, but certainly the party is no less to blame for the deterioration of the situation. Throughout the history of the Israeli-Palestinian conflict, Labor has exhibited an amazing talent not only for missing political boats but for continuing to wait for them long after they had left port. The mental block of this sector of the political spectrum was best exemplified by Golda Meir's pronouncement that there is no such thing as a Palestinian people. Moshe Dayan, meanwhile, systematically undermined the one blueprint for territorial compromise, known as the Allon Plan,* while suppressing the emergence of a native Palestinian leadership willing and able to deal with anything beyond municipal affairs. Many of the home-bred Palestinian leaders with the potential to become negotiating partners—the local leadership that Israel claims to be searching for today—were deported to Jordan during the years when the Labor Alignment was in power. Labor is to blame for the procrastination of the 1970s and shares full responsibility for the prevailing belief that the Palestinians in the territories would forever resign themselves to the occupation. Certain hawks in the party have even argued that the occupation is irreversible. By acquiescing in the status quo of occupation for over two decades, the leaders of the party effectively endorsed the belief that Israel, a nation of three-and-a-half million people, could go on repressing another nation of some two million souls indefinitely and with complete impunity.

In retrospect, a few of Israel's leaders have tried to absolve themselves of all blame for the straits in which Israel now finds itself; to claim, like the bodies in charge of governing the territories, that their authority extended only to a narrow sector of the problem. Defense Minister Rabin, for one, has contended that his mandate was confined to maintaining security in the territories and that the responsibility for all other issues, such as the political ramifications of the occupation, lay elsewhere. Yet such claims are tantamount to pleading that a minister is accountable only for implementing national policy, not for setting it. In Israel's form of parliamentary government, ministers bear collective responsibility for the government's failure to chart and pursue a sane and defensible policy for the state. At the very least, by failing to see that no agency was responsible for the investigation and assessment of

---

* The proposal whereby the Jordan Valley, Judean Desert, and other areas deemed necessary for establishing a defensible border were to be held by Israel, but the Arab-populated mountain ridge running down the center of the West Bank would be ceded to Jordan as part of an envisioned Jordanian-Palestinian state.

the overall situation in the territories, the ministers of Israel's government—and perhaps Rabin most of all—are responsible for once again leaving their country vulnerable to harm.

Thus the greatest responsibility for the surprise lies with Israel's political echelon, the men who stood at the helm of state when the uprising broke out. Most of them suffered from clouded vision when it came to relations between the Arabs and the Jews—and particularly between the Israelis and the Palestinians. Some were at best wise after the fact, but all of them consistently failed to see what lay ahead. They allowed themselves to feed off information that warped their judgment, and they had great difficulty raising their thinking above the level of exhausted political slogans. Thus anyone interested in knowing what was *really* going on in the occupied territories could not rely on information processed through the Israeli establishment. For Israelis, at least, this is one of the most significant and sobering lessons to be learned from the Palestinian uprising.

For whatever consolation it might be to Israel, no less startled by the outbreak of the uprising was the once and future regent of the West Bank (or so, at least, some Israeli, Palestinian, and Jordanian diehards chose to continue believing): King Hussein of Jordan. For years, but especially in the months prior to the uprising, the Jordanians had conducted themselves in the territories with the aplomb of aristocrats. They were confident—even as the revolution was approaching—that despite the Israeli occupation and the great gains made by the independent Palestinian organizations at the grass-roots level, it was Amman that really controlled much of what went on in the West Bank and to a lesser degree in the Gaza Strip as well. The Jordanians pursued their affairs in the territories with Israel's knowledge and consent (and under especially cordial conditions when Labor ministers were in charge of foreign affairs and defense). They also enjoyed the blessings of the United States, which was pumping considerable sums into Jordan's development program for the West Bank. Yet King Hussein also believed that his status in the territories was assured by the strength of his followers there, many of whom received their salaries from Jordan's state coffers. Hussein and the PLO had been having a rocky, on-again off-again affair ever since the 1974 Rabat summit had officially recognized the PLO as the sole legitimate representative of the Palestinian people. They seemed to have been in an off period since the Amman summit conference in November 1987, at which the Palestinian cause had been totally eclipsed by the Gulf war, and Hussein had been giving the PLO the cold shoulder. When Arafat proposed renewing his dialogue with Jordan, for example, Hussein did not even give him the courtesy of a reply, and the king summarily rejected the idea of re-establishing a joint political committee. Moreover, in a letter sent to the United Nations on the occasion of its conference on Palestinian rights, Hussein played up Jordan's special role in advancing the Palestinian cause and pointedly made no reference whatever to the PLO.

The Israeli Foreign Ministry was impressed by Jordan's record in the occupied territories, if only for its seeming resilience. On the very day the uprising broke out, the ministry's Center for Political Research published a special report on the upsurge in Jordanian activity following the Amman summit. It noted that "the swift, efficient, and open organization of the pro-Jordanian camp in the territories has proven that when it closes ranks, it is able to hold its own against the PLO's supporters and even gain the upper hand. Jordan will now try to extend its influence and increase the [Palestinians'] dependence on Amman."

Both Shimon Peres and Yitzhak Rabin were more than willing to aid in that effort. Once again they touted Labor's conception of the "Jordanian option"—whereby Israel and Jordan would solve the Palestinian problem between them—as the cure to all ills. They also behaved as though this approach were official policy, when in fact neither the Israeli nor the Jordanian government had ever endorsed it and it was anathema to the Likud. A week before the riots broke out, Rabin invited seven members of the Jordanian Parliament living in the West Bank to the headquarters of the Civil Administration for a chat on Jordan's development plans for the territories. And it must be said that the Jordanians contributed to keeping the illusion of the "option" alive. Even after the uprising was in progress, their officials continued to visit the territories and perform their duties with an air of business as usual.

Shortly before the rioting began, a rumor made the rounds that the United States was going to hold a secret meeting in Aqaba between State Department officials and senior diplomats from the American embassies in Amman and Tel Aviv to discuss ways of aiding the Jordanian Five-Year Development Plan for the territories. Washington felt sufficiently confident about Hussein's standing, particularly in the West Bank, to cover parts of this program with funds from the Pentagon's research and development budget, and the Aqaba meeting was to discuss the allocation of the $23 million scheduled to be transferred to Jordan by the spring of 1988.

To prepare themselves for this important meeting, on December 7 the directors of the Health Departments throughout the West Bank were summoned to meet with the Jordanian minister of health in Amman. On the agenda was the construction of medical centers in various cities and towns and of a new hospital in East Jerusalem, for which Israel had promised to give its approval. At the same time, Jordan sent a number of its own people to the West Bank and Gaza Strip, so that when the riots began there were three Jordanian officials in the territories: Dr. Sa'adallah Sa'adallah, who headed the Planning Department of the Jordanian Ministry of Occupied Lands; Rateb Amr, the director of its Department of West Bank Municipalities and Town Councils; and Hashem a-Shawa, who was in charge of the development program in Gaza but had not visited the area for at least a year and was now scheduled to spend about a week there. Shawa informed the Israeli officials who met with him that Jordan was pleased with the rate of progress on the projects in the Strip—unlike the situation in the West Bank—and was quite satisfied with the way in which the 150,000 dinars allocated to Gaza were being spent. The Jordanians had many plans for the Gaza Strip, he told them brightly. But even as those words were being spoken, the uprising was already overtaking both a-Shawa and his government, and all their ambitious plans remained tucked away in drawers in Amman. Hussein and his button-down bureaucrats were as removed from the realities of life in the territories as the overweening Israelis, and they too were to pay a heavy price for their presumption where the Palestinians were concerned.

"Uprising" does not begin to do justice to the Arabic word *intifada*, which soon became the rubric for the explosion in the occupied territories. Its literal meaning is the shivering that grips a person suffering from fever, or the persistent shaking of a dog infested with fleas; but in political terms it has always been associated with relatively limited or brief upheavals, such as the Kurdish revolt, the 1983 split within the Fatah, and even the 1977 riots in Cairo. The "copyright" on its use in the Israeli-Palestinian context belongs to Yasser Arafat, who failed to see in the early reports reaching his desk anything out of the ordinary about the eruption of riots in the territories. Since he regarded the events in Gaza as just another spasm of violence that would pass within days, it did not occur to him to offer a more appropriate name for the phenomenon—or, in fact, to treat the situation any differently than he had similar instances in the past. (Shortly before his death in April 1988, Arafat's deputy, Halil al-Wazir—better known as Abu Jihad—

coined another term for the events in the territories: "*haba*," meaning storm or tempest. But by that point "*intifada*" had already stuck.) So it was that the "sole legitimate representative" of the Palestinians living under occupation displayed much the same blindness as the occupiers.

In historical perspective, Arafat's mistake in underrating the riots may have been even graver than the Israelis', for it attested to an astounding degree of estrangement between the self-styled popular leader and the people he presumed to have led. That Arafat and his colleagues were way off in assessing the mood that had spawned the riots was not anything new. For years they had misgauged the magnitude of distress in the territories, and just as they had never plumbed the depth of despair that had settled over the Palestinian masses, neither could they appreciate the great swell of energy that now surged up to the surface. If Arafat and the others had even dreamed that the territories contained so vast a reservoir of "revolutionary potential," as they put it, they would have wasted no time in placing the struggle for the "interior" (the population under Israeli control) at the top of their scale of priorities. But they were insensitive to that potential before December 1987 and thus forfeited their strongest card in favor of a supreme effort in a different and—as history had already proved—utterly pointless direction: rebuilding the PLO's military infrastructure in Lebanon.

Four or five days passed before Arafat sensed that something radically different was going on in the territories. He saw a unique opportunity to make political capital—if he acted quickly. But not everyone in the PLO was quite so perspicacious. When Arafat had recovered enough from his apathy to call for an emergency meeting of the Security Council, his representatives at the United Nations were about to board flights that would carry them to Cuba for the Christmas recess. More than ten days after the outbreak of the rioting, many of the PLO people outside the territories were still convinced that the violence was just a passing squall, and they did not consider canceling their personal plans. Until the end of December, the PLO headquarters in Tunis refused to concede that such widespread demonstrations were possible without direction from seasoned activists. Yet when the staff of the PLO's Occupied Lands Department and the various committees of its Western Sector* began manning the phones to find out what was really happening in the field, most of their contacts reported that they had not organized and were not involved in the demonstrations. In fact,

* The clandestine apparatus that directs terrorist operations against Israel.

they were equally astonished by the degree of daring exhibited by the rioters, especially in the refugee camps. Some of them also reported that rather than carry the Palestinian flag, the demonstrators were waving little green banners (green being the traditional color of Islam), that there were no posters of Arafat in the streets, and that the crowds were not shouting the PLO's classic slogans. If not all the news was bad, it was only because the local observers were as removed from reality as their patrons abroad. "This is a dress rehearsal" was how a few of Arafat's more prominent supporters in Gaza put it, assuring their callers that the rioting was an outpouring of rage directed only sporadically by the Muslim fundamentalists and that the Israeli army would have it subdued in a matter of days.

The focal figure in this network of contacts was Abu Jihad, who, as the coordinator of the Fatah's activities in the territories, had most of the major lines of communication under his control. His sole aim during the first weeks of demonstrations was to urge the Fatah's followers in the West Bank and Gaza to join the violence and further its momentum. Working out of the PLO offices in Athens, Cyprus, and Cairo, either by phone or by using messengers who crossed over the bridges from Jordan, Abu Jihad's people began pressing the trade unions, youth committees, and individuals identified with nationalist circles to fuel the riots by getting their supporters out on the streets. In days of frenetic activity, they made hundreds of calls, sent their ideas by facsimile, even broadcast instructions over the PLO Radio from Baghdad, reminding their people to make sure that the demonstrators were carrying portraits of "Brother Commander Abu Ammar" (Arafat) and that graffiti commending the PLO was scrawled on as many buildings as possible.

In essence, this torrent of communications was a desperate attempt to jump on the bandwagon that was already careening forward, but it also attested to the confusion and chagrin that pervaded the PLO's offices abroad. Abu Jihad's staff often contacted figures who were totally cut off from events or passed on the names and phone numbers of people who had never been known to participate in demonstrations. Close to ten days passed before circles identified with the PLO printed up their first handbill in Gaza; two weeks elapsed before the organization's supporters geared up to distribute the first of their leaflets in Nablus—and that at a time when the fundamentalist factions had already circulated quite a few leaflets that met with a hearty response. Three days after the outbreak of the rioting, George Habash's Popular

Front for the Liberation of Palestine disseminated a leaflet marking the twentieth anniversary of its establishment, but it made no reference to anything remotely resembling the *intifada*.

Back in Tunis, the idea of calling a general strike likewise evolved slowly, as did the realization that the situation required consensus and a common effort by the organizations represented in the PLO.* Rather than order his "troops" in the territories into action during December, Arafat accommodated himself to the dictates from below. The first move to unite the PLO's factions in the territories into a Unified National Command came from the ranks of the local activists. Meanwhile, plans for holding a strike and systematically escalating the riots were being laid by the fundamentalist groups, at least some of which were engaged in a bitter struggle with Arafat's loyalists. The consequences of confusion and delay were not lost on the leaders of the PLO, who took note of the eager popular response to the leaflets of the Islamic Jihad and the Islamic Resistance Movement in Gaza, as opposed to the lukewarm reception to their own call to strike and demonstrate on the anniversary of the founding of the Fatah, January 1, 1988.

For all this concern, however, a month after the outbreak of the *intifada*, Abu Jihad was still working on outdated assumptions and had difficulty taking the measure of the sudden quake. On January 7 he reported his impressions to the PLO Central Council in Baghdad, sheepishly admitting that only recently had he begun to consider ways of harnessing and developing the *intifada*. At that stage he was already pondering the idea of escalating it into a show of "all-out civil disobedience," but he could not overcome his old habit of evaluating events according to how much material damage had been caused to Israel, rather than highlighting the signal fact that people from all classes of society had joined in the demonstrations. Hence he droned on and on at that closed meeting, counting off by make and year each of the Israeli vehicles damaged in the territories and detailing every fire set in branches of Israeli banks, police stations, and telephone exchanges. It would take still longer for him to grasp that wrack and ruin was not the true measure of what he himself had described as "a fateful juncture."

A "popular revolution" was nowhere to be found on the PLO's agenda because the realistic prospect of one ran counter to the expe-

* Fatah, the Popular Front for the Liberation of Palestine, the Democratic Front for the Liberation of Palestine, the Palestine Communist Party, and a number of smaller groups.

rience accumulated over the years. During the latter half of 1967, Arafat had headed a highly ambitious operation to spark off an armed rebellion within the territories captured by Israel in the Six-Day War. Living in the vicinity of Ramallah under the alias of Dr. Fawzi al-Husseini, for over two months he personally directed a large network of saboteurs who were hastily trained in Syria, under the supervision of Abu Jihad, and infiltrated back into the Israeli-controlled West Bank via Jordan. Fairly soon, however, the entire network came to grief, not least because few of the Palestinians were prepared to offer it cover and aid. Its members were gradually driven out of the cities and villages into caves and the open countryside, where they were hauled in by the hundreds. Arafat fled his own hideout in the middle of the night just steps ahead of his Israeli pursuers, and the experience firmly set him against the strategy of making the occupied territories the base of anti-Israeli activity. He was sure that the Israelis would promptly derail any effort to organize a serious underground, while the notion of a mass unarmed struggle was never even considered because it contradicted the tenet summed up in Arafat's oft-quoted motto: "The solution will come through the barrel of a gun." Thus having made the principle of the "armed struggle" the *sine qua non* of all the PLO's activities, veteran leaders such as Arafat and Abu Jihad were practically incapable of grasping that arms were not necessarily their most effective weapon. Ever since 1967 they had operated on the assumption that the inhabitants of the territories, loath to endanger themselves in a serious confrontation with the Israeli authorities, were unlikely to spearhead the Palestinian national struggle. It took time for them to absorb the enormity of their mistake.

Initially, therefore, Arafat's most pressing aim was to prevent the erosion of the PLO's standing in the territories—specifically in favor of an indigenous Palestinian leadership that might agree to have truck with Israel and neutralize the "outsiders" completely. The praise he and his associates lavished on the inhabitants of the territories was meant to appease and encourage them, but it also reflected their surprise at what they saw in the film clips being shown on television. By the time of the Baghdad meeting, Abu Jihad had no choice but to pronounce that the "interior" had become the real, decisive arena of struggle, and he immediately instituted a complex maneuver to help the organization adjust to the new situation. But it was not until well into January 1988 that the PLO recovered its balance and ability to lead.

□

The *intifada* was an assertion of defiance that bubbled up from below, a statement by the legions of Palestinian youth who felt bereft of a future; the high school and university students doomed to choose between indignity and exile; the tens of thousands of laborers who made their living in Israel but were expected to remain invisible; the veterans of Israeli prisons who were more convinced than ever of the justice of their cause but saw their people sinking deeper and deeper into hopelessness. In short, it was the work of the Palestinian masses, and that is why it surprised everyone: the complacent Israeli authorities, the over-confident Jordanians, the self-satisfied PLO leadership, and even local Palestinians regarded as influential figures in the territories. A popular revolt with all the hallmarks of a genuine revolution, it erupted suddenly and created a new strategy for the Palestinian struggle that confounded both the PLO establishment, scrambling wildly to keep up with events from afar, and the native leadership whose constituents were suddenly spinning out of control. Above all, however, it delivered a sharp reminder to the Israelis that they simply could not go on blithely ignoring the twenty-year-old Palestinian problem festering right in the middle of their collective lap.

TWO

THE LONG AND WINDING FUSE

AT PRECISELY SIX O'CLOCK on the morning of May 18, 1987, the duty officer of the Gaza Central Prison began his routine head count of the close to 700 prisoners crowded into the cells of the huge fortified police station that serves as the IDF's headquarters in Gaza. Upon reaching Cell No. 1 in the Security Wing, which houses the members of terrorist organizations, he immediately noticed that something was awry: six of the twenty-five prisoners were missing, and a further check of the cell showed that the bars over the window had been sawed through with files. After warning their cell mates against trying to join in, so as to keep the noise at a minimum, the escapees had jumped from the cell window down to the inner courtyard, cut through the barbed wire covering it, and climbed over the wall right onto the main street of Gaza, which at that early-morning hour was already humming with people on their way to work in Israel.

This was the first successful escape from the country's most heavily guarded prison—after years of failed attempts by Arab security prisoners—and in the shock and confusion that followed precious minutes were lost before forces were dispatched in pursuit. But once set in motion, the search was a sweeping one. Navy ships stopped the fishing boats already out on the water and forbade the others to leave shore; troops and Border Police began combing the area's citrus groves; and the Shin Bet pumped all its sources in an effort to discover where the fugitives were headed. One of the six escapees was actually caught a few days later, but he wouldn't breathe a word about the intentions of the others. And in the absence of indications to the contrary, it was assumed that the fugitives would sit tight in their hideouts or slip over the border into Egypt. In fact they had escaped specifically to perpetrate a series of explosive actions that would crescendo into a resounding blast before the year was out.

The six escapees were the vibrant hard core of the youngest terrorist organization in the Palestinian arena: the Islamic Jihad. Calloused killers who acted in the name of their ideals, for the past year they had been operating as a band of assassins spreading mayhem on the streets of Gaza. All of them were young (under the age of twenty-three) and lacking in military training; all had undergone the difficult experience of arrest and interrogation and had not broken. Most Gazans had regarded them as a group of reckless fanatics touched by an excess of ambition and childish bravura. But then came their daring escape—the very stuff of heroic legend—and overnight the Jihad became an object of pride and identification, kindling the imagination of tens of thousands of Palestinian youngsters and charging the enthusiasm of whole sectors of the population that had little in common with its simplistic world view. Driven by the zeal of "born-again Muslims," the six fugitives had set a personal example by their courage, resourcefulness, and ability to strike at Israel and survive. They were the match held to the long and winding fuse leading to the *intifada*.

The most notorious of the six desperados was twenty-one-year-old Imad Siftawi, who had been tried and convicted of murdering three Israeli civilians in Gaza in the autumn of 1986: two Jewish taxi drivers from the town of Ashkelon and an Israeli Arab from the village of Abu Ghosh, just west of Jerusalem. In each case the murder was committed in cold blood, with calculated brutality, in broad daylight and in full view of dozens of people. But even before turning to terrorism, Imad had been fairly well known among the youth of the area as the son of Asa'ad Siftawi, one of the leading Fatah figures in the Gaza Strip.

A burly man with a thick moustache and a musical pattern to his speech, the elder Siftawi had spent five years in prison for his part in organizing terrorist squads at the end of the 1960s. Ever since his release in 1974, however, he had eschewed all terrorist activity for he was convinced there was little to be gained from a local armed struggle—to say nothing of the fact that the Shin Bet would nip in the bud any attempt to organize one. In any case, Siftawi assumed that he was under surveillance and could not afford to make any imprudent moves. He did, however, open his home as a regular meeting place for the supporters of the nationalist camp in Gaza. The activists in the Shabiba—

the Fatah's youth movement—looked up to him as a staunch and judicious ally who helped spread their propaganda in the United Nations Relief and Works Agency (UNRWA) school under his direction.

Though admired by the Shabiba, Asa'ad had difficulty winning the heart of his own radical son, who believed that the Fatah's policy of holding anti-Israeli demonstrations was a sign of squeamishness and that there was no substitute for violent action. The debate between father and son went on for a number of years, much like the political arguments in countless other families. In this case, though, the two men were divided not only by the generation gap but by Imad's rejection of his father's modern outlook. The young Siftawi favored a retreat into the bosom of Islam. Like thousands of other Gazans over the past decade, he had turned his back on what he disdained as hollow patriotism and set out to seek redemption in his Muslim heritage. Asa'ad Siftawi was steadfast in his loyalty to the PLO; his son regarded that fidelity as an alibi for indolence.

As a student at the Islamic University in Gaza, Imad had been deeply involved in the titanic struggle waged between the tightly knit, activist religious faction and the less intense but far more popular nationalist camp. The Israelis had tacitly encouraged the rise of the religious front in the Gaza Strip and welcomed the rivalry between the two camps as a handicap to the PLO—that is, until the friction threatened to get entirely out of hand. Although, on the face of it, the contest was for public support and positions of power, it often deteriorated to the level of raw vendetta, costing at least one life (a lecturer at the Islamic University) and leaving a trail of injured, including victims of stabbings and acid attacks. In May 1986 a member of the Siftawi family itself was shot by a supporter of the Popular Front for the Liberation of Palestine during a heated quarrel. The subject of discord: smoking in a taxi cab during the fast of Ramadan.

In a roundabout way, one of these attacks changed history. For when Asa'ad Siftawi was worked over by a goon from the Islamic Congress—the front organization of the religious faction—Imad decided to sever his ties with the group. Apart from resenting the affront to his father's honor, he had reached the conclusion that the Congress was more interested in settling scores with the PLO than in working against the occupation. He had also decided that he could no longer acquiesce in its binge of internecine brawls. So together with a handful of close friends, he joined the clandestine movement that had recently split off from the Congress: the Islamic Jihad.

The Jihad's aim was not only to sound a call to arms against Israel immediately—a measure that the leaders of the Congress had scrupulously avoided—but to forge a new doctrine that would make the fight against Israel the condition of an Islamic revival and the return to religious values. While the Congress and other groups more disposed toward the PLO believed in educating the public by means of mass propaganda, the Jihad stood for personal, one-on-one indoctrination. And rather than infiltrate existing institutions or work through charitable societies, like the other factions, it chose to build a network of subterranean bunkers and let its actions speak louder than words. In the course of 1987 the Islamic Jihad would do to the PLO exactly what Arafat had done to the Arab states twenty years earlier. Just as the Fatah had pushed President Nasser into a clash with Israel in 1967, the fighters of the Jihad would now force the PLO into a mass confrontation with Israel's troops in the territories. Essentially they invoked Arafat's old "theory of entanglement"—the idea that the weak and the few could manipulate their betters in strength and numbers—and it worked like a charm.

According to estimates commonly accepted at the time, on the eve of the uprising the Islamic Jihad numbered no more than 300 activists, some of them organized in cells of only five to seven members. Unlike the supporters of other Muslim organizations and societies, the Jihad's people went out of their way to remain anonymous, even nondescript. They were ordered not to grow beards—contrary to what some traditionalists hold to be an explicit command from the Prophet Mohammed—and to forgo the *jalabiya*, the long cotton or linen robe worn by Muslims who adhere to traditional ways. For the most part they drew their ideas from the sermons preached in five mosques: three in Gaza, one in Rafah, and above all the Sheikh Izz-al-Din al-Qassam Mosque in the village of Beit Lahiya near Gaza (Qassam having been a pious Muslim who led a collection of terrorist gangs in northern Palestine and preached a *jihad* against the British and the Jews until being killed in a clash with British troops in 1935).

Credited with importing the militant approach into Gaza are two graduates of Zakazik University in the Nile Delta, known as a hothouse of Muslim fundamentalism. The first to return from Egypt was the physician Fathi Shkaki, and in 1981 he was joined by Abd al-Aziz Odeh, a lecturer in Muslim law who received a position at the Islamic University and preached in the Qassam Mosque. They were followed by students deported from Egypt after President Sadat had been assassinated by another fundamentalist group. Shkaki became the Jihad's political leader and was arrested by the Israelis in the spring of 1986 for smuggling arms and inciting violence. Making the best of the situation, he turned his trial into a show of defiance, lecturing the court on his doctrine and drawing crowds of Gazans to its sessions until he was ultimately convicted on both charges. As a result of the publicity, moreover, his pamphlet *Khomeini: The Islamic Solution and the Alternative* was in great demand among the youth of the area. Odeh, meanwhile, steered clear of any prosecutable offense, after having spent eleven months in prison for incitement. From time to time, though, he did see to the publication of thin pamphlets known as "Islamic Notebooks" and occasionally even of a small, illegal journal entitled *al-Bayan* ("The Proof").

Shkaki and Odeh's disciples went under a variety of names—the Islamic Vanguard, the Revolutionary Islamic Current, the Independents Movement—and subscribed to ideas that most of the local youth still shied away from. Chief among their principles were admiration for Khomeini's Islamic Revolution (in contrast to the majority view of Iran as a Persian threat to the Arabs); the belief that only dramatic steps, not gradual reform, could raise the Islamic nation out of the nadir to which it had declined; the tenet that death in the service of Islam (*shahadeh*) was the loftiest of values; and a preference for mobilizing the masses in a struggle "for the sake of Allah" over an effort to save the individual's soul. This mix of ideas, spiced with abstruse scholarly arguments and quotations from the Koran, was absorbed only slowly—and even then more by the intelligentsia in the Gaza Strip than by pious common folk. Its attraction for the young firebrands like Imad Siftawi was the call to immediate action. Reduced to its simplest, the doctrine of the Islamic Jihad holds that the redemption of Islam requires first of all a war for the liberation of Palestine, since the power of the faithful cannot be revived as long as Israel exists as the spearhead of Western culture in the heart of the Muslim world. This principle was of course the interface between the Jihad and the PLO. Notwithstanding the gap between the religious fervor of the first and the secular nationalism of the latter, both movements were dedicated to advancing the struggle against Israel; and it was on this point of compatibility that the Jihad and the Fatah were to build an alliance.

Though initially indulgent of the fundamentalists, the Israeli authorities grew increasingly uneasy about the specter of terrorism fed by religious zeal. When the Shin Bet noted the unique determination of this new breed, all the other security organs concurred that it would be "very difficult" to clamp down on them. So they adopted a two-pronged strategy of curbing the most visible activists while trying to disrupt the contacts between the religious faction and the Fatah—especially after the Civil Administration in Gaza warned that a link was forming between the local fundamentalist zealots and the PLO.

What had indeed emerged was a loose connection, rife with suspicion and jealousy, between the Islamic Jihad and the Fatah's Organization 1977 Committee (an operational body under the command of the Western Sector) that both sides perceived as a temporary expedient. To Abu Jihad, the head of the Western Sector and a man eager to pump fresh blood into his worn military staff, the movement of young fundamentalists seemed an excellent recruiting ground. He also made it a policy to try to place under his aegis any new faction that arose outside the PLO, as a way of forestalling competition. Despite all the scorn it had heaped upon the Palestinian establishment, the Islamic Jihad was a natural target of just such a maneuver.

To form the link between the two organizations, Abu Jihad wisely chose two of his aides who had shown a marked leaning toward the "new-wave piety" so characteristic of the Jihad. One was Bassem Sultan, better known simply as Hamdi, an operations officer who had planned (among other actions) the May 1980 attack against Israeli settlers outside Hadassah House in Hebron, which took six lives. A tall Hebronite in his mid-thirties, he had twice served out sentences in Israeli prisons before starting a meteoric career as the commander of terrorist networks. During the revolution in Iran, Hamdi placed a photograph of the Ayatollah Khomeini on his desk, began chanting his prayers at the appointed times each day, and took up an ascetic lifestyle. The same was true of Ghazi al-Husseini, another veteran of Israeli prisons who went on to become an operations officer of Black September and may have had a hand in its attack on the Israeli athletes at the Munich Olympics. Ghazi grew a beard and began putting out an elaborately printed journal in which he extolled the PLO in the Jihad's fiery style and depicted the war against Israel as a religious injunction rather than a national duty. (Incidentally, Ariel Sharon twice demanded that Israel take punitive action against their commands in Amman, but the majority in the cabinet apparently suspected that he was merely looking for a way to sabotage the contacts then being sustained with King Hussein. The Jordanians were asked to keep an eye on the two men and stop them from causing any real damage, but they did so with only partial success.)

The main liaison between these two men and the clandestine cells of the Jihad was Sheikh Asa'ad Bayoud a-Tamimi, who had been deported from Hebron for incitement in 1980 and whose short book, *The Disappearance of Israel: A Koranic Imperative*, became the rage among the young fundamentalists in the territories (though few copies had evaded the net of the Israeli censor). After his deportation Tamimi became Teheran's chief Palestinian protégé, twice visiting Iran and receiving the royal treatment. Khomeini's associates tried to lure him into declaring himself leader of a movement to supplant the PLO, but Tamimi would agree only to the far more modest role of a spiritual mentor who would keep an eye on the connection with the Fatah so that the Jihad would not be dominated by it. For the youngsters of the Islamic Jihad, he was a patron with much to offer. Well connected with the fundamentalist Muslim Brotherhood in Egypt, its functionaries in Jordan, the religious factions in Lebanon, and of course the ruling circles in Iran, he could bring the budding underground two precious commodities: sources of funding and channels of communication. No less important, his constellation of contacts protected him from being crushed by the bear hug that Abu Jihad would surely extend at the first opportunity. Through Tamimi, then, the clandestine cells of the Jihad acquired a dimension of political depth and a champion outside the country who urged them to act.

The odd alliance between those who adored Khomeini as sage and redeemer and those who abhorred him as an enemy of their cause bore fruit in a series of bloody attacks in the territories. The Fatah supplied the planning and the weapons, the Jihad the manpower. The most spectacular of these actions was a grenade attack on the cadets of the IDF's Givati Brigade during their swearing-in ceremony at the Western Wall in October 1986, in which the father of one of the soldiers was killed and a dozen others were wounded. The bond between the members of the Jihad in the West Bank and Gaza solidified during their common sojourn in Israeli prisons (for most of the perpetrators of the attacks were quickly apprehended). By the time the first of these prisoners were released in the mass exchange engineered by Ahmed Jebril in May 1985, the ground had been laid for a clandestine network that stretched across the length and breadth of the territories. At the end of 1987 smaller networks of the Islamic Jihad were operating underground in half the refugee camps on the West Bank, a handful of villages in the Nablus-Jenin-Tulkarem triangle, and every village, town, and camp in the Gaza Strip. Until the escape of Siftawi and his comrades, the Jihad had put its strength to the test only once—in the elections for the student council of the Islamic University—and took a considerable beating: barely 4 percent of the student body supported the movement's list. Its great leap forward really began when Siftawi and the others holed up in a building within sight of the IDF's Gaza headquarters and, despite the relentless search for them, resumed their campaign of "armed propaganda": a new spate of terrorist attacks. The hunted transformed themselves back into hunters, and in the last months of 1987 their small organization sprang back from defeat to become the vanguard of rebellion with the resounding battle cry of *"Jihad Now!"*

The ground in the territories was at any rate burning by then. In a sense, the *intifada* actually began over a year before its declared inauguration; the actions of the Jihad merely boosted the shock waves that had continued sporadically throughout 1987. But the powers that be in Israel refused to look the changing reality squarely in the eye. Various and often pat explanations were given for the jagged rise in the number of violent incidents. Rather than try to bring the larger picture into focus or seek out the common denominator of the frequent flareups, there was a distinct preference for scrutinizing each case under a magnifying glass and offering answers on an individual basis alone. Thus the uprising was allowed to advance through the year on a steady uphill course, flexing its muscles and gathering strength for the moment when it would manifest itself in a mass, sustained outburst.

There is little point now in spelling out each and every stage of its climb. Suffice it to say that there was enough evidence of a trend to merit serious deliberation by the Israeli defense community. But there was also a catch: statistical data had long been accepted as the most accurate gauge of the security situation, and on the face of it the frequency of such familiar phenomena as demonstrations on memorial days, stones thrown at Israeli vehicles, processions and riots by university students, and terrorist attacks seemed no greater than in previous years. The same was true of the number of arrests on grounds of security offenses. Yet hidden behind the graphs and tables, and overlooked by the soothing professional assessments, were two trends of decisive significance. The first was a sharp rise in the number of assaults and "disturbances" by youngsters unaffiliated with any of the Palestinian organizations (up to 60 percent of all the incidents). The other was a concomitant rise in the instances of "direct action" by Israelis living in the territories—wild retaliatory gestures ranging from a rampage to shatter the windshields of Arab vehicles in the streets of Kalkilya (with Daniella Weiss, the secretary of Gush Emunim, calling the signals) to a nocturnal shooting spree in the Deheishe refugee camp by residents of Kiryat Arba (many of them members of Meir Kahane's Kach movement).

After each of these incidents, more and more Palestinians were beset by the feeling that Israel was having a very hard time coping with the violence and that anarchy lay just a step or two away. To aggravate the mood even further, the settlers' abusive behavior toward Israel's own troops, including officers of the highest rank, was infecting their Arab neighbors with a similar sense of contempt. Yet there was ambivalence about the army's role in the territories, and most Palestinians were the first to admit that the difficulty in restraining the hotheads on both sides was essentially to their detriment. They worried that with feelings running so high, if the IDF appeared to falter there was a good chance that Arab-bashing would become the preferred option for any Jew who felt threatened, frustrated, or just plain mad. That certainly seemed to be the direction in which things were going when a mob of Jewish ruffians from Jerusalem's Shmuel Hanavi quarter ran amok in East Jerusalem after one of their friends had been stabbed to death in the Old City. Many observers have commented on the symmetry of extremism in the Israeli-Palestinian conflict, yet in this case both sides were reacting less to one another than to disappointment in their own instruments of power. Settlers took the law into their hands on the grounds that the army was not doing enough to protect them; Arabs acted on the assumption that the PLO was either indifferent or ineffectual, and if it was deliverance they sought, they would have to achieve it on their own.

The most radical conclusions bred by this climate were reached by the Shabiba in the Balata refugee camp, which effectively declared the area closed to the IDF. Hugging the eastern outskirts of Nablus, Balata contains some 14,000 people living in circumstances of acute congestion—meaning some 40 houses packed onto each of its 65 acres. About half of the camp's breadwinners worked in Israel, many others being employed by the wealthier residents of Nablus. As a rule, however, Balata functioned as a closed unit: most purchases were made from shops inside the camp; all primary and junior-high-school education was imparted within its bounds; and it even boasted free clinics and two mosques, which hosted a growing number of worshipers as the return to religion made headway among the young.

The Shabiba movement (officially called the Youth Council for Social Activity) was established in Balata in 1982 after the local youth club had been disbanded and its clubhouse sealed up by the army for functioning as a Fatah recruitment center. The irony was that the Shabiba flourished even more than its predecessor and soon developed into an effective instrument for serving and controlling the population as a whole, just as it had in dozens of other places. It also established its dominance with enviable dispatch. After the camp's Israeli-appointed *mukhtar* (headman) had been wounded in an ambush and gladly relinquished the post, the UNRWA people working in Balata readily bowed to the authority of the Shabiba's leaders—a mixture of students from the two colleges in Nablus, released security prisoners, and ordinary thugs. Members of the movement's rank and file patrolled the camp's alleyways at night, usually masked and sometimes armed with iron chains to leave no doubt about their sway. They forced whole families to leave Balata in shame because their sons were suspected of collaborating with the Shin Bet. But "squealers" and "finks" were not the only ones to feel their sting; an assortment of drug dealers, pimps, and the proprietors of pool halls were also treated to a taste of their wrath. The Shabiba stood firm in its mission to preserve public and national morals and soon won unchallenged control over most aspects of life in the camp.

Its most visible enterprise in Balata was volunteer work in the area of maintenance: paving streets, upgrading the sewage system, hauling away garbage, and renovating the mosque. But above all, the camp's young people were drawn to the movement-sponsored sports activities, such as ping-pong and volley-ball tournaments, field races, and the perennial favorite: soccer. In fact the soccer field was a veritable mecca of recruitment, with new members going on to activities of political and educational value—be they evenings of folklore and nationalist poetry or laying wreaths in the cemetery and sending candy to the families of security prisoners. Beside cultivating support for the Fatah, the Shabiba tried to ease the social distress in Balata by working to lower the sum of the *mahr* (bridal price) demanded of young men, for example, and "urging" wealthy physicians from Nablus to treat patients for free.

In this way the Shabiba became the address for almost every matter concerning the youth of Balata, who generally felt deprived and forgotten. Little wonder that expressions of loyalty to the movement gradually took on the form of violent actions, from tracking down collaborators to preventing laborers from going to work on strike days and ultimately enforcing the decision to keep Israeli soldiers and policemen out of the camp. Stones flew day and night in Balata, even when IDF lookouts were posted on rooftops for weeks at a stretch, and Molotov cocktails became such a nagging problem that IDF patrols simply preferred to avoid the camp as much as they possibly could.

In effect, then, Balata had declared a revolt even before December 1987, setting itself off bounds to the Israeli administration and closing ranks around an unarmed militia of youngsters from the Shabiba. The longer the Civil Administration wavered over the response to this challenge, the less inclined the IDF was to flaunt its presence in Balata, and the greater the gains made by self-rule. What's more, the threat that these gains would become an example to others was ignored by the army's senior command. Everybody knew that "straightening up Balata" would require a major operation, perhaps even a grim toll of casualties—and no one wanted to deal with a prospect like that. So the subject was shunted aside, postponed from one meeting to the next. Finally, after considerable delay, the IDF entered the camp in battalion strength about a month before the outbreak of the *intifada*. Its plan was to mount house-to-house searches and make mass arrests in an effort to break the hold of the Shabiba. The "invasion of Balata" was a showdown, the ultimate test of the "liberation model" established in the camp—and it climaxed in a stunning Israeli defeat.

After sealing off the camp, the army sent in motorized patrols to circulate through its alleys and assemble hundreds of men in the school yard for identification and interrogation. The members of the Shabiba had definitely been caught by surprise, not only by the timing of the action but by the size of the force, which was far larger than any fielded in the past. At first the residents seemed stunned. But in the course of sifting out the suspects, a buzz of ferment began to spread through the collection of detainees. One by one, those whose names appeared on the wanted list were picked out of the crowd, handcuffed, blindfolded, and ushered over to a corner of the yard. At one point the women who were huddled around the edges of the area started shrieking wildly and pressing forward in an angry mass. As if picking up their cue, the detainees immediately began to jeer at the soldiers, tearing open their shirts and thrusting their bare chests out against the barrels of the Israeli rifles. Soon calls to resist actively could be heard from the vicinity of the mosque, and the curses shouted at the troops were punctuated by the thud of stones hurled from a distance. At the height of the commotion, the head of Central Command, Maj. Gen. Amram Mitzna, was summoned back to Balata, for his officers rightly feared that they might have to open fire to keep the crowd at bay. Determined to avoid a blood bath, Mitzna promptly brought the operation to a halt. It was a wicked game of brinkmanship they played in Balata, and the IDF backed down first.

The army had managed to arrest about half of the few dozen activists of the Shabiba, the Democratic Front, and the Islamic Youth on its wanted list. Still, the people of Balata had every reason to be heartened by the fact that they had forced the Israelis to yield under pressure. For the first time since 1967, Israel's security forces were prevented from carrying out their mission in the territories, and word of the victory soon spread far and wide. On December 7, just a day before the outbreak of rioting in Gaza, the Shabiba leaders who had escaped arrest published a special victory handbill. "We have set an example through the length and the breadth of the land," they exulted. "We call upon you to stand together . . . Every household can contribute gas, boiling water, and stones; the craven soldiers can be hit from every rooftop." Cautioning the residents to display "prudence in every move" and prevent "the administration's flunkies" from pushing the camp into "situations that are best avoided," the authors of the flier added that "we alone, not the enemy, are responsible for determining when and where the clashes will take place." As the crowning touch to their achievement, they ordered the Palestinian policemen living in Balata never to wear their uniforms within the camp, not as a rebuke to the men themselves but as testament to the fact that the police force is "the government's instrument of oppression." Today we know that this was a portent of things to come.

There were other "liberation models," of course, but their electrifying effect seemed to have been tempered by a new-found realism. For an entire generation, notebooks with bright orange covers—primers on the ins and outs of clandestine activity—had changed hands among the youth of the territories and been devoured at covert meetings of the Shabiba's cells. It goes without saying that all the copies uncovered by the Israelis were confiscated and their readers promptly punished for possession of seditious material. Nevertheless, the territories were absolutely awash with this "struggle literature." *Pamphlet Number 1*, a detailed guide on how to run a demonstration, included pointers such as hoisting the slogan-painted banners at the start of a march, so that the crowd could master the rhythmic chants, and dividing up tasks between carrying placards, leading the chants over bullhorns, extending first aid, and removing anyone known to be working for the Israelis. It also recommended choosing the route of a march carefully, so that the participants could disperse quickly and safely if the army appeared.

Another pamphlet cautioned against excessive enthusiasm on the part of the march leaders; it did, however, commend the torching of any shops that remained open during the procession—though only if the organizers had utterly despaired of persuading their owners to cooperate. Molotov cocktails, the same pamphlet advised, usually caused only slight damage; to achieve the desired effect, therefore, a number of them would have to be thrown in succession (after the perpetrator had secured a reliable route of escape). There were yet other reservations about firebombs: even under the best of conditions, it was easy to miss the mark; targets often did not catch fire; and in too many cases it was the attackers, not the soldiers, who were injured by these crude devices. The authors also reasoned that since the IDF opened fire on anyone spotted with a Molotov cocktail, and sometimes even demolished the houses of those who were caught, they might as well use genuine weapons. At any rate, the chapter concluded, the firebomb had become increasingly popular among the youth in the territories only in the absence of a real armed struggle.

The most interesting thing about these underground publications was their frank treatment of the countless failed military operations against Israel. Even as the PLO-in-exile refused to take a serious look at its record on this score, inside the territories the downfall of the armed infiltrators was subjected to close scrutiny. Considerable space was devoted to analyzing their tactical errors in choosing targets, creating camouflage in the field, and calculating the necessary amount of explosives. Equally disquieting was the breakdown of trust among their members, and examples were even given of complex operations that had come to grief because of romantic triangles. But the main lesson of these booklets, discussed in detail and at great length, was of an entirely different sort. For years Israel had been planting agents by the hundreds within the Palestinian organizations. Some had managed to rise to sensitive command positions; others were included in the units sent over the border to sow havoc in Israel. Thus more than once, the notebooks observed, a squad member had deliberately misled his comrades and then, under cover of darkness or at a bend in the road, made off to warn the enemy. In fact, as one booklet conceded, "Many a squad has fallen victim to the treachery of one of its members." These revelations were the PLO's open admission that its military arm was riddled with collaborators and that even its intelligence services were powerless to halt the systematic penetration of their ranks.

The underground literature also dealt almost obsessively with the subject of how to behave under interrogation, incidentally exposing another of the PLO's most irksome weaknesses: the speed with which its activists broke under pressure, divulged secrets, informed on comrades, and agreed to work for the Shin Bet, enabling it to refresh its sources of information. *The Philosophy of Confrontation: Behind Bars* was undoubtedly one of the more popular books among youngsters who had to decide whether to graduate from attending demonstrations to assembling bombs. In the space of 250 pages, its author tried to sum up the accumulated experience with Israeli interrogators, enumerating their favored tricks of the trade and suggesting ways to avoid their traps. Yet rather than feel reassured by the thorough advice, many of the youngsters who gobbled up descriptions of these battles of wits between cunning Israeli officers and their callow Palestinian foes were actually discouraged from testing their own strength in this plainly lopsided contest.

Indeed, the overall effect of this candid approach was something of a paradox, for the young people in the territories learned just how dangerous it was to be involved in armed actions, how fragile was the PLO's protective shell of secrecy, and how vastly superior the Israelis were at the cat-and-mouse game of counterintelligence. The authors of these pamphlets had intended to teach their readers to respect and observe the rules of conspiracy; instead they fostered a tendency to avoid it altogether. The fact is that during the 1980s the supporters of the Shabiba and other pro-PLO groups grew increasingly reluctant to cross the line between affiliation with a public framework and membership in an underground cell. After all, everyone knew—and the various pamphlets virtually confirmed—that Israel had a whole legion of informers spread throughout the Palestinian population. And considering the degree to which they had penetrated even the PLO, they were sure to be apprised of any attempt to establish new cells in the territories. Thus in the months prior to the uprising, there was a marked growth in the membership of the quasi-legal Shabiba but a decline in faith that its patrons could be trusted to protect the identity of those who answered the call and joined the "armed struggle." In short, while the PLO retained its magic as a symbol, an address, an object of identification and loyalty, it had lost much of its organizational appeal. New recruits came in all the time, but they opted for "soft" activities—like the programs of the Shabiba and the student councils—while the hard core of armed fighters was steadily ground down. The dynamics of this trend would later explain much about the special temper of the *intifada*.

Along with this reevaluation of the PLO's accomplishments on the military plane, toward the middle of the 1980s young people in the territories began to take a fresh look at *summud* ("steadfastness"), the main slogan that the PLO directed at them—and here a genuine revolution took off at a dizzying pace. In *summud* Arafat conveyed an unmistakable message: the residents of the territories were to cling to their land with all their might, foster their national identity, strengthen their ties with the PLO, and wait for the job of ending the occupation to be done by their brothers on the outside. A strategy demanding fortitude alone, it was meant to spare the people of the territories the assumption of tasks that were beyond their competence. Ultimately, of course, in assigning the territories a distinctly passive role, this reading of *summud* implied that all the "big decisions" were to be made by the PLO in exile. Demonstrations, for example, were regarded not chiefly as a means of placing pressure on Israel but as an opportunity to scout out new recruits for the PLO's operations abroad, just as the Shabiba had initially been designed to groom activists for terrorist operations and was never judged by its effectiveness in other spheres, as was so amply demonstrated in Balata, for one.

Opposing the minimalist version of *summud*, with greater boldness as time went on, were a number of instructors who had received their degrees from American and West European universities and were gaining influence in colleges on the West Bank. In June 1987, when a seminar on the occupation was sponsored by the East Jerusalem daily *al-Fajr*—considered all but an official organ of the Fatah—one of these instructors turned it into a platform for the first public expression of sharp disagreement with the PLO's dictates from abroad. In the presence of the Who's Who of Fatah loyalists in the West Bank, Dr. Hisham Awartani, a lecturer in economics at a-Najah University in Nablus, took strong issue with the line being followed by the movement's leadership. It goes without saying that his style was academic and the barrage of criticism issuing from his lips was not delivered on a flat trajectory. Nevertheless, it hit the mark square on.

Awartani, a thin and rather austere-looking man, had no political ambitions and was barely recognized outside of his university. Yet without even knowing it, perhaps, he became a spokesman for countless others chafing under the occupation when he lectured, in English, on the "new mood among the Palestinians" and noted that "for the first time in our turbulent economic history, we must confine our glance within the borders of the homeland." Awartani criticized the PLO's priorities in parceling out funds within the territories. He argued that instead of encouraging independent economic initiative and productive activity, Arafat was rewarding parasites and whole sectors of the population that contributed naught to the Palestinian economy. The result, he strongly implied, was that the PLO was funding the creation of a new class of idle university graduates, and instead of creating work for the people abandoning agriculture in favor of jobs in Israel, it was squandering a fortune on superfluous services run by unqualified people. In short, he decried the "corruption" and "tragedy" that the Palestinians abroad were bringing down upon their brothers at home.

The few dozen guests applauded politely at the end of the lecture, but its repercussions were far greater than one would have expected of an academic paper. From then on, grumbling about the PLO's self-centered interpretation of *summud* began to grow louder and more widespread. What began as a theoretical and presumably naive critique of the PLO's assistance program soon inspired a deeper look into other areas of endeavor. The young journalist Daoud Koutab stirred up a quickly suppressed scandal when he began poking around a subject that had always been shrouded by a conspiracy of silence: embezzlement and waste by the agents who distributed the assistance funds. Dr. Sufian al-Khatib, a noted cardiologist and member of the Popular Front, ridiculed "that clown" Arafat from every possible platform, and at Bir Zeit University Sari Nusseibeh and Azmi Beshara had their students re-examine the PLO's basic doctrine in light of Hegel, Marcuse, and Frantz Fanon. Suddenly the PLO seemed to have lost its total immunity to probing questions, and *summud* changed from the watchword of quiet perseverance into a call for the residents of the territories to think—and perhaps act—for themselves.

Before long, students were carrying this intellectual leaven back to their native cities and towns. The new gospel was never articulated in explicit terms, but the gist of it was clear: the PLO was showing signs of wear and tear, and the effects of the 1982 debacle in Lebanon were all too obvious. Most of its troops had been dispersed among camps in the remote reaches of Iraq, Sudan, Yemen, and Algeria and could no longer be expected to fulfill the hopes once placed on them. Neither did Arafat's diplomatic efforts augur a breakthrough of any kind in the foreseeable future. What the PLO appeared to need was a transfusion from the territories, not only of more sophisticated means of pursuing the struggle but of fresh, unconventional ideas. Against this background Sari Nusseibeh publicly toyed with the notion that the local Palestinians should demand Israeli citizenship, thus creating a challenge that Israel would be loath to face. Hanna Siniora took this thinking a step further in proposing that the Arabs of East Jerusalem officially run a slate in the municipal elections, with the aim of becoming the deciding factor in the formation of a coalition. From his Center for the Study of Non-Violence, Mubarak Awad spread his Gandhian ideas of passive resistance, and in the Arab Thought Forum Ibrahim Dakak weighed proposals for encouraging a "cottage economy." From working off imported theories, the intellectuals in the territories began originating a few of their own. Ideas of this sort outraged some people, who denounced them as ludicrous intellectual exercises. But essentially they embraced the compelling and—as events would prove—appealing conclusion that the Palestinians in the territories must accomplish for and by themselves what their leaders abroad were unable to do: not just abide the occupation but give it a swift kick where it would hurt the most.

Curiously enough, the PLO's inattentiveness to these rumblings was matched only, perhaps, by the indifference of the Israelis themselves. For just as Arafat and his colleagues, like politicians from time immemorial, were less than eager to take a hard look at their own failings, neither were they willing to respond to the signs of impatience coming out of the territories. Naif Hawatmeh, head of the Democratic Front, did not believe conditions were ripe for defeating the occupation and asked little more of the Palestinians than to "avoid repeating the mistakes of 1948," by which he meant averting their expulsion from the territories. Dr. George Habash of the Popular Front spoke of the need to resume military actions in the territories, but his expert on such operations was thinking in terms of small, mobile squads that would at most try to harass the IDF in Hebron and the Gaza Strip. Even Haled al-Hassan, a veteran leader of the Fatah and former "foreign minister" of the PLO who never shrank from taking exception to his colleagues' views, would recommend nothing beyond trusting to the "forces of self-destruction" whose tracks he imagined he could see all over Israel. Thus even the *enfant terrible* of the PLO, unable to conceive of a bold new strategy, clung instead to the naive hope that Israel would obligingly do to itself what the PLO could not.

It was mostly in the junior ranks of the organization that grave doubts were being expressed about this sclerotic approach. Yazid Halaf, well known for his articles in Palestinian journals, attacked the habit of acting for action's sake "without knowing what we're likely to stir up and what aim is being served." "We sit in our offices or lie around our bases," he added, "not even bothering to dig a trench although we know the Israeli air force will return to hunt us down. What's the point in sending squads [over the Lebanese border] into Kiryat Shmonah when the response will be the obliteration of half a Palestinian refugee camp?" Sabri Jiryas, editor of the journal *Shuoun Falastiniya* ("Palestinian Affairs"), believed that the answer lay in an armed rebellion in the territories, "even if it is only with the simplest of revolvers." He called for the renewal of armed resistance "in a way that will accord [us] at least teeth to bite and nails to scratch with"—by which he meant 100 to 200 volunteers who would act to destroy the Israelis' sense of security in the territories.

To the best of our knowledge, the only person in the PLO abroad to appreciate the potential of a mass popular rebellion was a little-known, low-ranking activist by the name of Ahmed Shahin. About two months before the outbreak of the *intifada,* Shahin published a polemical piece that elicited only a mild response in the PLO and did not win much attention in Israel either, though it was translated into Hebrew. Entitling the piece "A Dynamic Program That Won't Mark Time," he forecast that after twenty-two years of hegemony by the Palestinians in exile, the political initiative, as well as the actual direction of affairs, would soon pass on to the residents of the territories themselves. Contrary to the opinion of his comrades, Shahin held that conditions in the West Bank and Gaza Strip were promising for a struggle in the form of demonstrations and civil disobedience, so that the leaders of the PLO would have to begin sharing power not only with activists who had been deported from the territories but with those still living there. He urged Arafat to overcome his old fear about the emergence of an "alternative leadership" and to develop the PLO's "forces on the inside." The local inhabitants themselves were encouraged to "challenge Israel to a duel," for unlike Arafat they did not need a *laissez passer* from one of the Arab states to make contact with the enemy. Neither were they obliged to resort to arms, for they could choose from a variety of other means of resistance. The task ahead was to turn the Palestinian problem into a major headache for Israel. "Every occupation has its price," Shahin wrote, and "the Israeli authorities will not end theirs as long as it costs them less than what they gain."

□

On the streets, meanwhile, there were countless "telltale signs," in the argot of Israeli Intelligence, that even without exposure to seminars and journals, the residents of the territories were coming to much the same conclusion. On August 8 the fugitives from Gaza Prison shot and killed Captain Ron Tal of the Military Police in cold blood right in the middle of downtown Gaza, leaving the Israeli defense establishment rather shaken. Defense Minister Rabin himself rushed to the site of the murder and, standing over the fresh blood stains, gave his permission to impose a curfew on all of the Gaza Strip—contrary to the advice of ranking members of the Civil Administration. Shmuel Goren, who had not been consulted on this decision, subsequently objected that the large contingent of troops required to enforce the curfew would only exacerbate the tension. Worse yet, the period of effective "house arrest" and searches in the cities and camps would turn all the inhabitants of the Strip into partners in the struggle, while only proving to them that there were clear limits to the army's power.

Two weeks later the spotlight shifted to Jerusalem, where the first attempt to carry off a suicide attack following the model set in south Lebanon was thwarted by the Shin Bet. A young Bethlehemite named Attaf Alian had intended to blow herself up in a car packed with explosives in the heart of the capital. Hussein Zahiri, the engineer from the West Bank town of Tulkarem who had prepared her for the operation, was not a religious man but had planned the operation for the Islamic Jihad, thus enhancing its prestige even further.

In a single week in September, three Israelis suffered stab wounds in the West Bank and a reservist was stabbed to death while waiting at a bus stop in Israel proper. (The police later established that his assailant was a young man from the West Bank village of Yamoun who had previously murdered a pregnant Arab prostitute because he mistook her for a Jew.) Another incident typical of this run of events was the stabbing of a Jew—during an argument over the painting and renovation of his house—by a young member of the Toun family of East Jerusalem. The suspect was arrested a few days later but escaped detention during a meeting with his lawyer. On his flight northward he went on to stab an unsuspecting Israeli soldier and take his M-16 rifle before ultimately escaping to Egypt. At some point the weapon was deposited for safe keeping with the imam of one of the mosques in Nazareth and later made its way back to the West Bank village of Sur Baher, where the fugitive's brother became the chief organizer of the riots during the early days of the *intifada*. This particular chain of events is just one of dozens of examples of the tie between random attacks by lone Palestinians in the course of 1987 and the collective explosion at the end of the year.

In the summer and autumn a variety of developments in and around Jerusalem encouraged the city's Palestinian population to take a considerably more confident stance in their dealings with the authorities. Tires were repeatedly set afire in the village of Silwan without eliciting any real response. Buses running along the main road to the Jewish neighborhood of Neve Ya'akov, on the northern outskirts of the city, were stoned almost daily, with the police seemingly helpless to do anything about it. Israeli vehicles traveling to the suburban settlement of Ma'ale Adumim suffered the same fate, albeit less frequently, while the railway track running through the Arab village of Beit Safafa (which now falls within the municipal boundaries of Jerusalem) was repeatedly blocked by piles of stones.

When wealthy residents of the Arab neighborhood of Beit Hanina met to discuss an alarming rise in the number of robberies and attempts to extort protection money from merchants, one young man proposed that they establish a kind of private Civil Guard, rather than ask the police to beef up its presence in the area. His idea was to recruit the most violent of the extortionists for guard duty, on salary, and thus kill two birds with one stone: restore peace to the neighborhood, without calling in the Israelis, and send the local burglars to practice their skills in Jewish areas. At the other end of the social scale, in the Anata refugee camp and the neighborhood of A-Tor on the Mount of Olives, bands of young people organized to put a stop to the flourishing drug trade. Jewish addicts frequented these areas because they could purchase a better grade of heroin for less than half the price of inferior smack on their own side of town. Although the *mukhtars* of these areas complained about the incessant frays related to drug trafficking, the police—by the testimony of its own officers—were "slow to respond." As the authorities discovered after the fact, there were also a number of significant incidents that had not been reported at all; for example, the *sulkha* (reconciliation) reached among the Jewish and Arab residents of the Armon Hanatziv quarter after a number of assaults and brawls, and the vandalism perpetrated against the property of Kibbutz Ramat Rachel, ending with a half-hearted apology by the *mukhtar* of the adjoining Arab village.

Throughout the territories and East Jerusalem, an atmosphere of unrest pervaded the educational institutions during the entire school year. Most of the hundred or so activists arrested in the demonstrations of December 1986, which had erupted in response to the fatal shooting of two university students during a major riot, were released by the end of the year and returned to their classrooms more determined than ever to lead their schoolmates onto the streets. The universities were closed intermittently throughout 1987, either on orders of the Civil Administration or due to paralyzing disputes between the student councils and the school administrations. More often than not, however, it was the high school juniors and seniors who took pride of place in the growing number of street incidents, for they knew that they had little to lose and less to look forward to. Even if they went on to college, they had only a slim chance of ever being employed in their chosen professions and would probably end up working at unskilled jobs in the Israeli economy, just like their friends who had chosen to forgo a higher education. To get the demonstrations going, these young agitators would usually make a beeline to the nearest girls' school and try to lure or incite its students into leading their procession; it was well known that the presence of girls stirred young men to minor feats of prowess—or at least made it very difficult for them to sit these actions out on the sidelines.

Time and again Palestinian principals and teachers warned the Israelis of the turbulent mood among their charges, but for the most part their warnings fell on deaf ears. In any case, the Civil Administration tended to pull back from supervising or even closely monitoring affairs within the schools under its jurisdiction. This withdrawal reached its height in the Gaza Strip when the Civil Administration directed its Israeli educational-affairs officer and the supervisors under his command to refrain from entering the schools, for the sake of their own safety. They were routinely supplied with field reports, of course, but these documents dealt solely with pedagogical matters and never touched upon the sensitive and highly relevant subject of political activity in the schools. Thus wholly by default, groups like the Shabiba were able to enforce their will not only on the students in Gaza but on their teachers and principals as well.

The new mood of aggression was carried right into the offices of the Civil Administration, where Palestinians applying for licenses—or whatever else required their being in the good graces of the Israelis—felt game enough to snap at officials, flout instructions, or simply refuse to take no for an answer. Israeli field workers, they noted, no longer visited places in the Strip once considered their stamping grounds, unless they were accompanied by an armed escort. When one district commander warned that as a result of this decline in performance Israel stood to lose control over the area, his superiors assured him that the civilians working for the administration were just looking for a pretext to demand a raise in salary. But the Palestinians saw this state of affairs for what it really was: a sign not only that, on the civilian level at least, Israel was backing off but that its retreat from involvement in every aspect and level of Palestinian life was an expression of fright. And of course the Israelis really had lost their ability to operate freely in the hot spots of the Gaza Strip.

Even with the Shin Bet committing all its energies to the Strip, it took until the first week of October to track down the band of fugitives from Gaza Prison. In the interim, they continued to strike at the Israelis in the area, after twice throwing grenades at the Military Government's headquarters in Gaza, laying an ambush for a Shin Bet vehicle, and wounding its passengers. They also assassinated two Arabs suspected of collaborating with Israel. Emerging from their hideout once a week—a frequency without precedent in the history of local terrorism—they consistently managed to hit their mark and get away again. But their run of success ended on October 1, when the Shin Bet finally collected enough leads to trap them.

First, a three-member Jihad squad led by one of the fugitives, Sabah a-Souri, tried to drive through an IDF roadblock and was killed by the soldiers' gunfire. (To make up for the setback, the Jihad spread the inflammatory rumor that Souri had been captured alive and was shot by the soldiers despite having raised his hands in surrender.) Then, on the evening of October 6, an ambush closed in on the rest of the fugitives, who were on their way to carry out another attack. Shin Bet agents reinforced by troops from the Special Unit to Combat Terrorism were waiting in Gaza's Seja'iya quarter for the arrival of two Peugeot 504s—one red, the other white—that would be carrying members of the Islamic Jihad. The white car bore only its driver, who was supposed to serve as a scout and ensure his comrades' successful escape. The red car carried three men: two of the fugitives and another member of the Jihad, all of them armed with Kalashnikov rifles as well as explosives, revolvers, and a hand grenade. When they caught sight of the Israeli force, the drivers of both cars began to careen wildly through the streets of Seja'iya, drawing curious residents out onto their balconies to see what the gunning of motors and squealing of tires was about. At one point the driver of the white car abandoned his vehicle and ran for his life but was quickly cut down by a sharpshooter. His comrades in the second vehicle opened fire on their pursuers, fatally wounding twenty-seven-year-old Victor Arjwan of the Shin Bet before being killed by the spray of bullets directed at the car. Searching their hideout afterward, investigators found a Polaroid snapshot of all four men, armed and grinning, that had been taken just before their last foray into the night. Imad Siftawi was the only one to slip out of the net that had closed in around him. By the next day it was known throughout Gaza that he had reached Egyptian soil safe and sound.

If anyone thought that the backbone of the Islamic Jihad had been broken by these actions, within days it was clear that quite the opposite was true: the battle in the streets of Seja'iya had enhanced the aura of heroism surrounding its activists. Not only had they evaded the ubiquitous security forces for months, it now came out that they had been hiding right under the army's nose and had nonetheless managed to strike at the IDF and the Civil Administration until falling as free men, weapons in hand. The gun battle fought on October 6 was transformed into a legend of valor, replete with the motifs that speak to the hearts of young men: pride and courage, the spirit of self-sacrifice, and a martyr's death on the altar of the nation's freedom. It spread throughout the Strip and reverberated in the public prayers for the souls of the fallen, the sermons following them, and the handbills commemorating the memory of the victims.

Most of these handbills, which were printed in thousands of copies, opened with the well-known Koranic verse: "Do not regard those who have died for the sanctification of the holy name as deceased, for they live on and will receive their reward from Allah." The flier passed out in Rafah went on to remind its readers that "the bitter repression of our people continues day after day [bringing] death, torture, exile, internment, and deprivation. But with Allah's help all the Jews' methods will fail, and success will be the prize of the heroes who have given their lives for [their belief in] one or the other: freedom or death." These assurances were followed by the claim, designed to fire up its readers, that the women soldiers in the Askhelon Prison make every Arab woman visiting a member of her family strip down to her underwear and submit to a body search. They then photograph "our mothers and sisters to blackmail them into working for Israeli Intelligence, threatening that otherwise the pictures will be published or even used to fabricate [photos of them in more compromising] positions."

(Strangely enough, considering its indignation over the affront to feminine modesty, this particular handbill ends with the heartening reminder that whoever falls in the service of the cause is awaited in Paradise by seventy-two beautiful women!) Portraits of the men who had died in the Seja'iya shoot-out were distributed freely on every street corner, and another handbill circulated throughout the Strip called for a general strike on October 10. "Do not betray heroes by forgetting them," it chided. "Do not return to work or your usual routine. Let us paint the skies of Palestine with the blood of heroes and turn the fallen into ghosts that will pursue the Jews everywhere and for all time!"

Demolishing the houses of four members of the Islamic Jihad— at Yitzhak Mordechai's insistence and contrary to Shmuel Goren's advice—only boosted the resentment into unrest. And although the funerals of the "martyrs" were held after dark, with only a small group of mourners allowed to attend, in the atmosphere created by the strike it was impossible to prevent riots from developing the next day. October 10 was the first time a general strike had been called by the Islamic Jihad, rather than the PLO, and both sides were astounded by the huge response. Israeli units stationed at flash points and particularly sensitive junctions arrested dozens of people, but the demonstrations went on nonetheless. Thousands of people crowded around the mosques and the courtyard of the Islamic University to hear rousing speeches by well-known religious figures. Soon the streets of Gaza were cluttered with burning tires and overturned garbage bins. Israeli vehicles were stoned on the roads, and in the city of Gaza dozens of bearded young men tried to mount a kind of human-wave assault on the police station—an event without precedent in the entire history of the occupation. Before the day was over some twenty people had been injured by Israeli gunfire, but the Islamic Jihad had scored an incontestable victory: what had begun as a hunt for five dangerous men climaxed as a head-on clash with the entire population of Gaza.

The Islamic motif, it must be said, was not confined to Gaza alone. In Jerusalem 2,000 Muslims blocked the Moghrabi Gate, the main entrance to the Haram a-Sherif or Temple Mount (site of the al-Aqsa Mosque and the Dome of the Rock), after members of the Jewish group known as the Faithful of the Temple Mount announced their intention to hold prayers outside al-Aqsa on the Jewish holiday of Sukkot (the Festival of Tabernacles). The angry crowd was dispersed by a large force of policemen, who were attacked by a hail of stones and bottles before resorting to the use of clubs and tear gas. Afterward, the members of the Jewish group were permitted to hold their prayers on the Temple Mount, prompting the Supreme Muslim Council to publish a sharp protest. At about the same time, a brawl broke out between Jewish and Muslim worshipers in the Cave of the Patriarchs in Hebron.

By the end of October, the driving power of the religious impulse was plain for all to see. It had been demonstrated in Jerusalem as well as Gaza that a sizable portion of the population was willing to pit itself against the police, the army, and other security forces in violent confrontations. The fireball was teetering at the edge of the slope, yet even at this late date senior Israeli officers and officials failed to see that a fresh approach was needed. Yitzhak Mordechai of Southern Command held a meeting to warn notables from the Gaza Strip against allowing the rioting to continue—as though they actually had any control over events—while the head of Central Command, Maj. Gen. Amram Mitzna, spoke of introducing a new sharpshooter rifle that would make it easier to zero in on the leaders of the disturbances.

The events of the last weeks before the start of the uprising read like a classic countdown to ignition. On October 28 a student was killed in a clash with troops at Bethlehem University and the school was closed for three months by order of the Military Government. On November 10 a schoolgirl from the Gazan town of Dir al-Balah was shot to death by a Jewish settler after his car had been stoned, and his release on bail stirred a new wave of resentment. On the following day, two other schoolgirls were injured in Gaza by fire from an Israeli car that had been stoned. Coincidentally or otherwise, on the same day the Islamic University was closed by the Israeli authorities.

November 10 also brought the announcement that the government had decided to deport Sheikh Abd al-Aziz Odeh, the leading figure in the Islamic Jihad—a move that bespoke a profound misreading of the public mood and led to a resumption of rioting. Soon all of Gaza was coated with handbills signed by the Muslim Brotherhood. Denouncing the planned deportation, they charged that "throughout history the Jews have remained crooks, charlatans, and schemers who trample our honor and kill women, children, and old people" and described Odeh's deportation as "another nail in the coffin of their demise." Photographs of his children were published in all the papers, and a rash of petitions decrying the decision circulated throughout the Strip. The protests reached proportions that astounded the IDF. Over 1,000 people took to the streets in Jebalya, for example, and the behavior of the crowds was far more threatening than before. In the past the demonstrators had always kept their distance from the outpost in that camp, at most shouting slogans at the soldiers within earshot; now they tried to scale the fence surrounding the compound!

On November 21 there was another general strike in the Gaza Strip, again called by the Islamic Jihad and again accompanied by barrages of stones and bottles together with roadblocks of burning tires. "The light of fire and revolt" was how a new Jihad handbill described these episodes in instructing its readers that "we are standing on the threshold of a new era, a time to attack the forces of evil! Today they are frightened and find no rest from the monster of their own making." The Jihad's activists painted the town green with quotes from the sermons that Odeh had preached in the al-Qassam Mosque and most of all with the counsel: "All who embrace the Koran to their hearts know neither submission nor despair."

A few days earlier, an announcement had been made about the impending deportation of Dr. Mubarak Awad, a Jerusalem-born champion of nonviolent resistance who had studied in the United States, become an American citizen, and returned to his native city on a tourist visa that was now expired. Thus together with the uproar over Odeh, protest actions were being held in Jerusalem on behalf of Awad.

Yet probably the most potent, and from the Palestinian standpoint stirring, event of that period occurred on the night of November 25, when a terrorist from Ahmed Jebril's Popular Front for the Liberation of Palestine–General Command flew a hang glider over the Lebanese border, landed alongside an army camp, penetrated the facility, and killed six men before being shot dead. This spectacular attack on a military installation thrilled the Palestinian masses and prompted a swell of admiration for the daring of a lone fighter (in this case a Syrian) who infiltrated the headquarters of a combat brigade and terrorized the Israeli soldiers within—as all were able to learn from the lurid reports on the flight of the camp's sentry featured in the Israeli press. It now appeared that the members of the Islamic Jihad were not the only ones capable of bold action.

There followed a number of incidents and reactions in staccato rhythm. On November 29, as every year on the anniversary of the 1947 U.N. vote to partition Palestine, demonstrations centered on the schools—some of which were closed by the decision of their own administrations. Two days later an Israeli salesman was murdered in the heart of Gaza and the entire area was placed under curfew, with hundreds of people being hauled in for interrogation. Two days after that Radwan Abu Ayyash, chairman of the Journalists' Association in the West Bank and a leading Fatah activist, was arrested and placed in administrative detention for six months. Feelings were also running high over a number of issues of strong symbolic import. Israel's takeover of most of the franchise of the East Jerusalem Electric Company had long been a particularly sensitive matter, and the prospect that many of the company's employees would be laid off now made it all the more infuriating. Deep drilling at Herodion, southeast of Bethlehem, raised fears that Israel would deplete the West Bank's water reserves—another very sore point for the Palestinians. Most provocative of all, however, was the announcement by Industry and Trade Minister Ariel Sharon that he had purchased an apartment in the Muslim Quarter of the Old City. This move was no mere striving for upward mobility or a prudent investment in real estate, the Muslim Quarter being among the more rundown areas of the city. It was a political statement that was rightly interpreted by the Palestinians as another sign of the Likud's intention to squeeze them out. That these menacing signs were taken far more seriously by the Arabs than they were meant by the Israelis is less relevant than the fact that even in these last moments before the explosion, the authorities were oblivious to the turbulence swelling under the lid of the occupation.

So it was that the raw materials of anger and frustration built up to a critical mass. The litany of Palestinian fears and grievances that had festered for an entire generation went on and on. The difference at the end of 1987 was a new sense of self-confidence nourished by the latest round of riots, the single-handed attack on the army camp, the derring-do of the Islamic Jihad, and the clout of the youngsters of Balata—all made even more pronounced by the signs of confusion and capitulation on the part of the IDF. Together with the latest moves suggesting Israel's intent to strip the Palestinians of the last of their assets and resources, these events seemed to confirm the belief that having reached a nadir, the residents of the territories had no other choice but to take their fate into their own hands. They had new models of heroism; they had begun to conquer their fear of the army; and most important they had very few illusions about the future awaiting them if they did not cast off the chains of their own anxiety and act. If they continued to hope that a solution would come from without, soon it would be too late. And the mass demonstrations of October and November had proven at least one thing: those who took to the streets enjoyed the support of countless others who were convinced of the Koranic dictum that the Jihad had turned into a battle cry: "Allah helps only those who help themselves!"

THREE | *THE ENRAGED PROLETARIAT*

LET THERE BE NO DOUBT about it: though it developed into a statement of major political import, the *intifada* began not as a national uprising to throw off the yoke of foreign domination but as rebellion of the poor, an awesome outburst by the forsaken and forgotten at the bottom of the social heap. Wave after wave of the deprived and despised seething at the base of the Palestinian pot blew the top off and let their fury spew into the streets. Crowds of refugees bonded by a solidarity of despair whipped themselves into raptures of release for their pent-up rage, tearing up paving stones, overturning garbage bins, and showering traffic with volleys of stones. Leaderless and without a defined aim, thousands joined together in a rite of chaos. Unfazed even by rifle fire, the men in the mobs tore open their shirts, thrust out their chests, and continued to press forward amid a din of war cries and wails of mourning. From the stench-filled alleys came a roar of protest that echoed throughout the land as the oppressed and indigent rose up to end the long indifference to their plight. What Israel had so long refused to see was splashed across the horizon. All that had been suppressed, quashed, shelved, ignored, papered over, pushed aside, and swept under the carpet for two decades now forced its way out into the open, tearing through the veil of hypocrisy and self-deceit that what Israel had practiced for over twenty-one years was a "benevolent occupation."

Israelis and Palestinians have both tried to paint a very different picture of those first days of December 1987, each for their own reasons. Yet the testimony of the rioters themselves leads almost inexorably to the conclusion that the rebellion was kindled by the depressing conditions in which Israel kept the inhabitants of the territories, not the visions planted in their hearts by the PLO; that it was initially powered by the hardship of getting through each day, not the hope for a brighter political future; that its impulse was to smash the system that scorned the Palestinians as individuals and violated their dignity as people, not just to salvage their honor as a nation by raising the banner of independence. It was with a sense of nothing more to lose that thousands of refugees grabbed at hoes, axes, sticks, stones, and whatever else came to hand to march out and proclaim that they would no longer stand for being treated like the dregs of humanity. Indeed, the early hallmarks of the revolt were reminiscent of riots in the slums and inner cities of other countries, and given the same ghastly conditions the people of any other nation—Filipinos, Poles, or Jews—would probably have responded in much the same way.

The leaders of the PLO, still struggling to digest the rebellion's spontaneous genesis, naturally tried to minimize the social motive behind the unrest, for fear that it would overshadow the political one. Even so respected a thinker as Feisal Hourani, a leading Democratic Front activist, expressed the fear that the PLO would suffer in the eyes of history unless it demolished the view that the riots were caused by the buildup of pressure on the impoverished classes, rather than by the efforts to cultivate a Palestinian national consciousness. For their part, Israelis up through the highest echelons have displayed an equally resolute refusal to acknowledge the misery of large sections of the Palestinian population, lest it be taken as evidence of their own short-sightedness and neglect. Thus leading figures across the political spectrum have clung to the argument that incitement from without and subversion from within were the real reasons why whole neighborhoods of seemingly crazed people poured out into the streets to hurl themselves at Israel's soldiers in spasms of violence. But that was just not so, and Yasser Arafat can no more change what happened by peddling a self-serving version of history than Yitzhak Shamir or Yitzhak Rabin can. What fueled the early stages of the *intifada* was the fathomless frustration of people trapped by a system that threatened to perpetuate their lowliness and force their children into an equally hopeless future. Seen through the lens of persecution, the traffic accident of December 8 struck many Palestinians as clear proof that not only their dignity but their very survival was at stake; that beyond being denied the right to a decent existence, their lives counted for so little that the Israelis could declare open season on them with complete impunity.

Thus even without the added dimension of national friction and the PLO's efforts to lay the foundations of independence, it was probably inevitable that the Palestinian poor would one day try to cast off the crushing burden of their own inconsequence. The climate in Israel not only denied that the Palestinians were entitled to political rights, it pointedly ignored the disgraceful conditions in which so many of them lived. Indifference and disdain made the lot of second- and third-generation refugees particularly bitter. Not a finger or voice was raised to help them. Israel behaved—perhaps unwittingly but certainly consistently—as though it was intent upon legitimizing norms of discrimination and abuse, kneading the people who had come under its rule into a spineless mass devoid of any will of its own. In this sense Israel had only itself to blame for the bitterness and defiance cast up against it. The more it whet the refugees' sense of desperation, the further it stretched the thin membrane of their self-restraint, and the consequences were predictable. After decades of a reign of negligence, it would awaken from its long slumber on a cushion of apathy to the terrifying roar of a landslide.

The true face of the *intifada* at this opening stage could be seen in the detention centers that absorbed the rioters arrested in the refugee camps of Gaza. These detainees represented a good sample of the people leading the demonstrations, yet contrary to expectations most of them had no previous record of arrest, nor were they known to be active in any of the Palestinian movements. Though absolutely green, none of them was quick to break under interrogation, and all stood on their right to meet with a lawyer immediately. Indeed, from December 9 onward the Israelis met a wealth of new faces that merged into the profile of a demonstrator unknown until then. To solve this and other puzzling aspects of the violence, such as the reason for the force of the outburst, an Arabic-speaking officer was asked to make a quick survey of these early detainees. After personally interviewing about a dozen of them, collecting impressions from the professional interrogators at a detention facility, and piecing together findings from the testimony of over 100 prisoners, he formulated some sobering conclusions that were not very pleasant reading for the handful of people to whom he addressed his report.

One of the survey's startling findings was that hardly any of the detainees were familiar with the clauses of the Palestinian National Covenant or knew of its existence. They were unable to repeat the most common slogans used in the PLO's routine propaganda, and even the central concept of the Palestinian struggle—the right to self-determination—was completely alien to them. None of them listened to the evening broadcasts of the PLO Radio from Baghdad (which are barely audible above the heavy static in the Gaza Strip). They could not say what resolutions had been adopted a few weeks earlier at the Amman summit and were unaware, and unconcerned, that the Palestinian issue had been left off the agenda of the Reagan-Gorbachev summit in Washington. In fact, these phalanxes of rock-throwing youth appeared to be completely ignorant of political affairs—almost, it seemed, to the point of deliberately ignoring them. They did not regard themselves as the foot soldiers of the Palestinian national struggle; they were just simple people steeped in the routine of their daily lives who happily did without reading a newspaper. Throughout Gaza the detention centers were filled with sullen young men who saw themselves as victims of governments and politicians of all persuasions, including their own. They were not devoted followers of Yasser Arafat or anyone else, and it was not from this class of instinctive rebels that the PLO drew its support.

Yet the detainees were not a collection of ruffians or people from the fringes of Palestinian society. Subsequent surveys taken in these facilities showed that for the most part the participants in the riots were simple laborers, men who worked from dawn to dusk and were in many cases the sole supporters of large families. In the past, high school and college students had been the most animated element in Palestinian demonstrations; now the center of gravity had shifted to people over the age of twenty who lacked a high school diploma and were employed in unskilled jobs—the classic "dirty work" that Israelis so disdained. Most of them had never been involved in demonstrations before and by exposing themselves to arrest had jeopardized the welfare of their dependents. One of these prisoners, the father of an infant, was asked whether he wasn't concerned that the baby would starve in his absence. "Allah will look after her," he replied with a shrug of resignation.

Another point common to these early detainees was that they worked in Israel and were usually able to communicate in Hebrew. When asked to explain their reasons for joining in the riots, all of them cited much the same motive: the feeling that they had suffered a grave personal injustice at the hands of their Jewish employers or colleagues. Each prisoner had his own story to tell, but the gist of their experiences was similar: at one time or another they had been subjected to verbal and even physical abuse, cheated out of their wages, set to work under inhuman conditions, and exposed to the sweep of the dragnet that followed every act of terrorism. All complained of the insult and humiliation repeatedly suffered at army roadblocks and checkpoints: the nasty tone in which they were addressed, the body searches accompanied by shoves and shouts, the derision they were forced to endure in front of family and friends.

The Erez Checkpoint, which is the main gate from the Gaza Strip into Israel, took top billing in these testimonies. The detainees told of being delayed for three hours or more, without explanation, upon returning exhausted from a week's work in Israel. They described the long lines of cars waiting to undergo security checks, the arbitrary confiscation of identity cards, the passengers pulled off buses without cause. One prisoner even told of a convoy of decorated vehicles—obviously a wedding party—being halted at the checkpoint and the groom being ordered to dismantle the seats and wheels of his car as his bride and her family looked on in mortification. Many spoke emotionally of the countless times they had been ordered to stand up against a wall with their hands in the air and legs spread apart to be frisked. Some also complained of cash being confiscated during security checks; others described instances of unabashed sadism, such as being forced to imitate barking, bleating, or other animal sounds before being allowed to drive on. Thus the checkpoint, which the Israelis considered a minimal security measure, was a regular ordeal for the residents of the Gaza Strip—just as the roundup of all Arabs in the vicinity of a bombing or other terrorist action seemed vital to the Israelis but sorely aggravated the Palestinians' sense of vulnerability. These workers may have felt particularly defenseless in Israel—exposed to the whim of anyone in uniform—but they had little reason to feel safer in their own homes in Gaza. Soldiers might (and did) break in on them in the course of a search, surprising couples in their beds and shaming fathers in front of their children.

The response of the interrogators to this recital of woe was also instructive. Even though these harassments had been going on for years, they were surprised to learn how deep suspicion and hostility ran among the rioters—to the point where most of these detainees (the exceptions being the better educated) fully believed that the December 8 traffic accident had been a deliberate act of vengeance. If anyone thought that a vicious lie of this sort could not possibly be credited, it soon emerged that in the grim mood permeating the Strip, its inhabitants believed the Israelis capable of almost anything. Laborers who were sent to sleep in stables and cellars—often locked in from the outside, lest they go out for a breath of fresh air and be discovered*—had no problem suspecting Israelis of malicious intent. Youngsters who spent hours by the roadside waiting for prospective employers to drive up and check their muscles, and the look in their eyes, before offering them the chance to earn a day's wages had equal reason to regard Israel as a cruel place where they had no hope of ever winning a drop of sympathy, to say nothing of respect. Again and again these prisoners voiced the same bitter grievance: "We're treated like animals."

In the last analysis, the surveys done among the detainees proved beyond a doubt that rather than tear down divisions, the close contact between Israelis and Palestinians had created a wall of hatred. The longer the acquaintance with Israelis lasted and the more intimate it became, the stronger the Palestinians' feelings of alienation, animosity, and envy. Naturally there were also instances in which strong, stable friendships had grown up between the detainees and their Jewish employees or acquaintances, but the Palestinians tended to regard such ties as exceptional cases that in no way mitigated their rancor toward Israel. Those who knew Hebrew and were able to understand the insulting comments made within earshot—or, indeed, right to their faces—were burning with resentment. Every night tens of thousands of laborers who had left their homes before dawn to eke out a living in Israel returned with an ever greater burden of repressed anger against the country that mocked their right to equality and ravaged their dignity. They were discriminated against in wages, barred from joining Israeli unions, and forbidden to form workers' committees of their own, while huge sums were deducted from their pay for benefits (such as social security and pensions) they would never receive.

That wasn't the whole story, of course. The opportunity to work in Israel gave the population of the territories the means to fund a considerable improvement in their standard of living, whose signs were everywhere. The number of telephone subscribers multiplied sixfold, the number of tractors ninefold, and the number of private cars tenfold. Compared to the pre-1967 era, there was a steep rise in the purchase of electrical appliances, in the standard of health, and even in the popularity of leisure activities; many Gazans, for example, frequented the nightclubs of Ashkelon. Yet the natural tendency was to look around and ahead, never back. While recognizing the improvement in their

* Residents of the West Bank and Gaza Strip are forbidden by law to remain overnight in Israel without special permission.

welfare, the laborers from Gaza were equally aware of the yawning gap between them and the average Israeli. They also knew that over the same period the Palestinian refugees in Jordan, at least, had enjoyed a rate of economic growth that was even more impressive. Israel may have felt noble for enabling them to come as far as they had, but the Palestinians in Gaza were more conscious of the empty half of their glass—like the fact that the overcrowding in the Gaza Strip had grown steadily worse. Indeed, this situation was hard to ignore with over 40 percent of the Gazan population living three or more to a room (compared with only 1 percent among the Jews of Israel). Relatively more Gazans maintained cars than Israeli Arabs, but the chances of solving their housing problems were far less promising, since building starts in the Strip were on the decrease and had been for quite a while. In real terms, then, it was possible to buy television sets, refrigerators, and washing machines, but the prospects of relieving the human crush in Gaza diminished with each passing year and the desire to approximate the standards encountered in Israel came up against a solid wall of neglect.

From the perspective of the refugees, who comprised more than half the population of the Gaza Strip and were the majority of the Palestinian laborers employed in Israel, the contrast between the quality of life on the two sides of the Green Line was downright painful. Not surprisingly, then, the data collected during the initial phase of the riots showed that the number of refugees interned in the detention centers was double that of the indigenous residents from nearby cities and towns. They arrived with a highly developed sense of deprivation and, as earlier surveys done by the Civil Administration had shown, were strongly motivated to improve their lot—not least because of the higher quality of the schooling they had received in the UNRWA institutions. Nevertheless, wherever they went, these refugees bore a stigma of inferiority. Hardly any of them owned land or other major assets. They had few opportunities to earn a livelihood except as salaried workers— and then usually on a temporary basis. A study completed at the beginning of 1987 cited among the trends characterizing the refugee population the ability to adjust quickly to technological changes and the striving for achievement and self-fulfillment, alongside a decrease in the demand for higher education (which no longer seemed to offer its beneficiaries a suitable return on their investment). It was therefore with good reason that the Israeli social scientists who did this study marked the refugees as "the prime agents of change" in the years to come, meaning the group most likely to take the initiative in altering the direction of its life.

The slow process of rehabilitating the refugees, which had begun in 1973 and essentially consisted of constructing apartment buildings and extending financial aid to people building on their own, came to an almost total halt in the 1980s. By the end of 1987 a mere 8,600 families had been resettled in new housing. It was clear that at that rate the camps would never be dismantled, for it would take at least fifty years to improve the condition of the other 33,000 families while natural increase proceeded at more than double the pace of construction. Even if a greater investment were made in housing, it would inevitably be of low quality, and the planners themselves warned that cheaply constructed three- and four-story buildings would soon deteriorate into slums. A truly effective solution—or so one official believed—would cost close to a billion dollars, and Israel saw no way of raising anywhere near that sum. Thus although the government deliberated the issue from time to time, its discussions always ended much as they had begun. The fact is that Israel regarded the rehabilitation program as little more than window dressing, but it could have been a boon to both sides. When the riots broke out, the residents of the new neighborhoods, who had benefitted from government aid and were relatively well off, stood apart from their former neighbors in the camps and were slow to join the protests—telling evidence of the lost opportunity to check the urge to violence with a more generous and humane policy.

By the same token, the Arab-run municipalities in the Gaza Strip usually related to the nearby camps with a chill bordering on hostility. When the Civil Administration tried to make the Gaza Municipality extend its services to the surrounding refugee camps, it responded by cutting off their water supply. The permanent residents of the Strip used any excuse to show that they regarded the refugees as outsiders whose presence in the area was unnatural and unwanted. This attitude was also to affect the course of the riots when the refugees exploited the chaos to give their neighbors back as good as they got.

One survey taken in the detention centers showed that 185 out of the 231 people in the sample fell into the fifteen to twenty-four age group. These young people had not only been raised on the heritage of want that marks the life of any refugee but had also imbibed their parents' tradition of mourning towns and villages lost within Israel proper. While traveling to and from their jobs, they passed by places their parents had once called home. Often they found themselves building villas for Jews, picking produce in their fields, or washing pots in their eateries on land they regarded as their own patrimony. In Israel they felt like invisible men, while in Gaza they were treated like human blight. On one side of the Green Line they encountered the ugliest aspects of Jewish society—voracious materialism, latent (if not blatant) racism, an intolerant system of norms and laws—while on the other they came up against a barrier of Arab contempt. These men who could not scrape together the *mahr* demanded of every Arab groom watched their Israeli peers disport in bars with lascivious young women (at least by the standards of their puritanical society) and saw their Gazan peers move into homes built for them upon their marriage. One class of Palestinians mixed with another and together they brushed up against Israelis every single day, but the gaps between them remained unbridged. On the contrary, the closeness bred distance, the contact alienation.

A few months before the outbreak of the *intifada*, the coordinator of operations in the territories was presented with a classified study entitled *The Gaza District up to the Year 2000*. A thick tome brimming with charts and figures, it proved to be one of the grimmest documents ever submitted to the Israeli defense establishment on developments predicted for Gaza in the coming decade. The report was written by an independent team of civilians—including a city planner, an economist, and a sociologist—on information drawn mostly from the files of the Civil Administration and other government agencies. Neither its authors nor the officers who appended an introduction framed any definitive conclusions or made any distinct recommendations to the government. Still, whoever reads this report cannot miss the overall implication that the Gaza Strip is a cancer that, unless subjected to radical treatment, will steadily drain the vigor of the State of Israel. Even if only some of the report's predictions are borne out, there is every reason to believe that Israel will soon be on its knees begging all and sundry to do it the mercy of taking Gaga off its hands.

These conclusions were left to the reader and not spelled out in unequivocal language because the parties who had commissioned the report forbade its authors, in no uncertain terms, to enter into matters of direct political import. Thus the chapter dealing with sociological questions deliberately avoids the issue of the mutual dependence between Israel and the Gaza Strip, including its political and economic ramifications. Neither was anything said, even obliquely, about the bearing of the forecasts on Israel's national security, despite the obvious expectation that control of the Gaza Strip would become increasingly difficult and require a larger allocation of forces. In fact the report did not explicitly warn its readers of anything, lest plain talk evoke the wrath of the ministers it was presumably designed to serve—though its authors prudently chose to ascribe their reticence to the "sensitive political nature" of the material.

In the end, they needn't have taken such care to appease the politicians by calibrating their dose of realism, for despite its obvious importance this study was quickly shelved together with all the other disagreeable documents about the bleak future of the territories. It was distributed among twenty officials, but curiously enough the prime minister was not one of them. The only person in the Foreign Ministry to receive a copy was one of the minister's junior advisers, and not a single member of the Ministerial Committee for Security Affairs got to glance at it, though it was circulated within the IDF, the Defense Ministry, and the Intelligence community. Little wonder, then, that no serious discussion was ever devoted to its findings or the conclusions they implied.

The report's most alarming prediction was that the Gaza Strip would break every known record of population density before the twentieth century was out. Concentrated on a narrow strip of sandy soil 28 miles long and between 3.5 and 8 miles wide are 634,000 Palestinians.* Since only 360,000 people inhabited the area when Israel captured it in 1967, the population had grown by over 75 percent during the first two decades of occupation. In the five-year period of 1981–1986 alone, the Palestinian population of the Strip rose from 507,000 to 634,000—and these figures continue to swell, with the average annual growth rate at 4.3 percent. It is true that natural increase has declined somewhat, though not due to any significant change in infant mortality or in the mortality rate in general. The report estimates that life expectancy in the Strip will increase from sixty-three to sixty-nine years of age, and the trend of continued growth is also evinced by the proportion of children and teenagers in the Gazan population: in 1988, 59.1 percent of the total population of the Gaza Strip was under the age of nineteen and 76.9 percent was under the age of twenty-nine. The upshot of all these statistics is that within twelve years or so, the Arab population of the Gaza Strip will have grown by over 50 percent! A

* According to the figures of Israel's Central Bureau of Statistics for the end of 1986.

conservative estimate puts the number of Palestinians living in Gaza by the year 2000 at 957,000; the pessimists forecast a total of 1,053,000.

This picture is virtually one of a human time bomb ticking away at Israel's ear, a weapon with the potential to wreak far more damage than the strictly conventional sort. For unless some dramatic development takes place soon, it is Israel that will have to govern, employ, and create a minimal infrastructure for these swarms of people—and it can barely cope with the wretched mass of humanity in Gaza as it is. Thus Yasser Arafat is quite justified in boasting that the Palestinians have a nonconventional weapon of their own: the "biological bomb" represented by the womb of the Palestinian woman. Although the fertility rate of the women of Gaza continues to decline by 0.5 percent every five years, in 1987 it stood at an average of 7.2 children per woman and in 2000 it will still be an average of 5.7.

As the population density continues to mount, so will the physical pressure and emotional friction until life in the Gaza Strip becomes utterly intolerable. The worst problem threatens to be the availability of water—and not just for agricultural purposes, for it is the consumption of drinking water that stands to rise appreciably with the growth of the population. The greater the demand on local wells, the more sea water will penetrate the water table, making its yield ever saltier until it is no longer potable. The study also notes that since the Gaza Strip has no facilities for purifying sewage, "the quality of the water will steadily decline as a consequence of pollution as well. Even now the water in certain areas of the Gaza Strip is unfit for drinking. About 3 million cubic meters of impotable water are currently pumped in the Gaza Strip, and by the year 2000 the figure will rise to about 7 million cubic meters," leaving Israel with little choice but to supply the Strip from its own overburdened sources.

In addition to the water crisis, the little land available to the Gazan population today—whether for housing or for agriculture, roads, or public facilities such as schools and hospitals—will shrink even further before the end of the century. And with land so scarce, the population density in Gaza is expected to grow to unbearable proportions. Some 5,000 new families join the population every year, but less than 40 percent of them currently receive their own housing unit, so that by the turn of the century 84,000 families will have augmented the population but under the best of circumstances only 27,000 new units will have been built to accommodate them. Even were it to be revived at its original pace, Israel's project to rehabilitate the refugees would be an exercise in futility, because overcrowding would promptly reduce every spanking new neighborhood to a slum. The sense of suffocation will penetrate every sphere. Experts warn, for example, that with earnings going toward the purchase of vehicles to get people to and from their jobs in Israel, Gaza's main roads will be completely jammed during the "rush hours" unless huge investments are made in paving new ones. The amount of cultivated agricultural land is expected to decline by 15 percent in the coming decade alone. Aggravating the situation even more is the fact that rather than place state lands at the disposal of the Palestinians, Israel is holding these reserves for the few Jewish settlers in the area—a total of some 2,500 people, including 150 yeshivah students. These settlers comprise only 0.4 percent of the Strip's total population, but they have already been awarded some 28 percent of the state lands and are clamoring for more!

Considering this collection of relentlessly negative trends, with the chances of economic development being nil, as the Palestinian proletariat grows in size and discontent the persistence of violence is all but assured. Outbursts are likely to follow one upon the next, with rising frequency, because the prime condition for revolt has already become a standard feature of Palestinian life: the inhabitants of the Gaza Strip have absolutely nothing to lose.

Trapped at the bottom of the economic and social pecking order, the refugees were naturally the most rebellious class in the territories, and it was therefore from the camps that the gospel of revolt came forth. But their experience regarding Israel and Israelis was in no way exceptional; other population groups also suffered the kind of treatment that disposed them to join in the uprising. The largest category was unquestionably the Palestinians who worked within the Green Line—a total of some 100,000 people, only half of whom are refugees but all of whom seem to have suffered a similar trauma. They were joined by the Palestinian farmers who had been forced to abandon their fields because of the discriminatory regulations that Israel imposed to protect its own agriculture and the price ceilings and quotas set by Jordan on the exports over the bridges. As the Palestinian farmer was gradually being squeezed out of the market, his credit was reduced, his yield per acre shrank, and the size of his cultivated area followed suit. The result was that like the refugee camps, many villages became reserves of cheap labor for Israel's industries and services.

This stagnation—actually retreat—in the agricultural sector was accompanied by a standstill in the development of Palestinian industry that can be traced to the same two sources, namely, Israel's determination to protect its own industries and ensure a competition-free market in the territories, and Jordan's dam on the flow of manufactured goods from the Palestinian economy. As a result, throughout the twenty-two years of occupation only a few entrepreneurs developed medium-sized and relatively primitive plants, leaving the prospects of local employment at an absolute minimum. For the same reason, unemployment has spread like a plague among the graduates of the seven universities established in the West Bank (with Israel's permission) since 1967. In the 1970s the territories "exported" skilled workers to other Arab states, but the crisis in the Gulf oil economies has diminished their chances of finding work abroad, while opportunities have steadily closed to them in Jordan as well. Thus a total of some 15,000 Palestinian college graduates were estimated to have been unemployed at the outbreak of the *intifada*. And since only one out of eight Palestinian graduates finds work in his profession, most of those who were employed had settled for jobs as unskilled laborers, mainly in the construction industry. Even the Palestinian merchant was cramped by a system that stymied almost every attempt to foster growth and modernization.

In stunting the development of the Palestinian economy by harnessing it to Israel's priorities and needs, the occupation made any improvement in the Palestinian standard of living conditional upon some direct link to the economy inside the Green Line. Worse yet, the Palestinians found themselves completely at the mercy of the Civil Administration in every sphere of economic life. Each request for a permit, grant, or dispensation entailed an exhausting wrestle with a crabbed bureaucracy of mostly indifferent but sometimes hostile clerks and officials—a veritable juggernaut of 400 Jewish mandarins managing thousands of Arab minions bereft of all authority. Complex tax and customs laws, restrictive marketing arrangements, and a slew of bewildering decrees and regulations were the weapons used to hold the territories hostage to the Israeli economy. By the 1980s, moreover, the Palestinians derived no compensating advantage from this situation— such as the appreciable rise in the standard of living that had mollified them during the first years of the occupation—so that their honeymoon with Israel came to a bitter end. As far as they could see, the "symbiosis" between Israelis and Palestinians was more accurately described as the relationship between a horse and its rider.

By the end of 1987, the pressure in this steam boiler had reached the point where both the rural population and urban middle class were straining for release when the refugee-camp dwellers finally blew the gasket. By its own devices, Israel had given all the strata of Palestinian society—with the exception of a small group of middlemen and labor contractors—good reason for wanting to smash the status quo. They all felt choked by a bureaucratic octopus. They all felt subjugated to alien interests. And to make it even worse, they all felt the terrible crush of being piled up together at an absolute dead end.

The odd part about this aspect of the occupation is that while in matters of security there is logic to a system of close supervision and perhaps even a strong hand, there was no defensible reason for the economic clamp that Israel placed on the territories. It was the product of sheer despotism, selfishness, and greed; of the flight from fair competition and an addiction to easy profits made by exploiting workers in a depressed market. Yet it must be said that Israel did not aim for this situation from the outset. It was born less of malice than of sheer thoughtlessness: the Israelis extended to the territories the same bureaucratic system that had long plagued their own lives because they knew no other way. The difference is that whereas this system irritates Israelis by making them scurry from pillar to post for every stamp of approval, wasting years of their collective time, when applied to the Palestinians it became nothing short of tyranny. The Israeli has ways of dealing with the highhandedness of the state; he can appeal to the national ombudsman or the High Court of Justice, if necessary. Not so the Palestinian: without union backing a simple laborer is reluctant to complain when employers abuse him or hold back his wages; a businessman has difficulty exposing deceit and corruption; a peasant has no way of getting fair prices for his produce; and a college graduate cannot insist on being hired for a job commensurate with his education and skills. The result was that in more ways than one, painful as it is to admit, a "slave market" of sorts came into being in the territories.

Daniel Doron, the director of the Center for Social and Economic Progress, was quite forthright in describing this situation:

> When the government makes life miserable for Jewish workers and businessmen, the Jews console themselves with excuses . . . that such economic tyranny is necessary for reasons of security, for the sake of social justice, and for Jewish national independence. But such justifications are cold comfort to the Arabs. Few Arabs, moreover, come under the

aegis of the strong public sector in Israel . . . most of them are nonorganized labor or small businessmen. Neither do they have recourse to the array of defensive measures that the Jews have developed vis-à-vis the government, such as pulling strings or joining one of the pressure groups that are able to obtain exemptions or perks. In the Israeli economy, where most of the resources are divided on the basis of political clout, the Arabs have no way of getting ahead—except by specifically political means.

Because of this basic inability to protect themselves, over the years the tens of thousands of Palestinians who made their livelihood in Israel and the hundreds of thousands who have suffered economic oppression in the territories developed into Israel's enraged proletariat, a class that saw no way out of its abominable state except by a political revolt. In short, Israel's economic system was the real driving force behind the radicalization of the Palestinian public. It was the piston of the *intifada*.

As the suffocation and anger mounted in the territories, three events that occurred toward the end of 1987 raised the tension even higher. On November 8, when a three-day Arab summit conference opened in Amman, King Hussein spared no effort to douse the PLO with insult and scorn. He failed to meet Yasser Arafat at the airport and demonstrably snubbed him during the rest of the conclave. Worse yet, though held a mere twenty-five miles from the West Bank, the summit in his capital pushed the Palestinian question onto the sidelines and devoted itself solely to the Iran-Iraq War. At the same time, Hussein's loyalists in the territories used the opportunity to organize an unprecedented show of strength. The editors of *a-Nahar* ("The Day"), published in East Jerusalem, collected thousands of signatures on a petition espousing the "unification of both banks [of the Jordan]." The signatories' names filled eight whole pages of the pro-Jordanian daily and were broadcast nonstop on Jordanian television. Caught off guard, the PLO's supporters quickly mustered for a fierce counterattack, backed by evidence that some of the signatures had been obtained by fraud. Nevertheless, the flap proved to Hussein's advantage, for it created the impression that his supporters had gathered enough strength to take on their PLO rivals. Fear that the so-called Jordanian lobby in the territories would now try for a comeback was compounded by the shame of seeing Arafat and all that he stood for so rudely neglected at the summit. It looked as though the rest of the Arab world, bored with the enduring plight of the Palestinians, was quite prepared to abandon them to the care (and caprice) of King Hussein, while Israel was only too happy to open doors for the Jordanians in return for help in maintaining its control over the territories. The prospect of Jordan regaining its status and power in the territories was actually quite dubious, but each time this bogey was conjured up it never failed to inflame emotions, doing far more harm than good. Soon after the Amman meeting, the Palestinians suffered yet another demeaning blow when they discovered that their cause had also been left off the agenda of the Reagan-Gobachev summit in Washington.

Early in December work was completed on Ariel Sharon's apartment in the Muslim Quarter of Jerusalem's Old City, and the minister announced plans to hold a housewarming. Since Sharon lived on an expansive private farm in the northern Negev and was eligible for hotel accommodations at the government's expense whenever he had to stay overnight in the capital, his purchase of property in the Muslim Quarter (with funds provided by wealthy Jews who support one of the yeshivahs in the Old City) was clearly a political act—and a highly provocative one at that. A certain *modus vivendi* obtained in the Old City. For centuries it had been customary for the followers of the various faiths to live in separate quarters, and preserving the distinctness of these sections had always been important to Jerusalem's successive rulers. In 1948, after capturing the Jewish Quarter and taking its surviving inhabitants prisoner, the Jordanians turned its houses over to Arabs. But nineteen years later, when the Old City fell to the IDF in the Six-Day War, Israel was determined to restore the *status quo ante*. As work began on renovating the Jewish Quarter, all the families that had taken up residence there since May 1948 were evicted. In fact, no Arabs were allowed to live in the quarter as a matter of principle. When one of the residents appealed his eviction on the grounds that it was an expression of racial discrimination, the High Court of Justice ruled against him, invoking the long-standing division of the Old City along ethnic lines.

Sharon brazenly violated this arrangement and didn't stop there, for he and his associates promised that other Jews would follow in his wake. From the Palestinian perspective, the flow of Jewish residents into the crowded Muslim Quarter could mean only one thing: Arabs would have to be removed to make room for them. Thus Sharon's much-vaunted entry into the Muslim Quarter was taken by many Palestinians as it was undoubtedly meant to be: a sign that their days in the area were numbered.

It was with good reason that this threat was perceived to be far more serious than the fantasy of a single Israeli minister. Sharon's housewarming turned into a public occasion demonstrating widespread support for his initiative. The *intifada* was still regarded as just another flareup of rioting when hundreds of guests arrived at Sharon's new home to join him in lighting the first candle of the festival of Hanukkah. The leading celebrant was none other than Prime Minister Yitzhak Shamir. He was accompanied by a throng of other ministers and notables—and not only members of the Likud Party—who came to celebrate Sharon's "breakthrough" into the Muslim Quarter. Even though the Labor ministers and Mayor Teddy Kollek were not present that night, the ceremony had an official air about it. Hundreds of policemen were assigned to protect the house and its guests. Sharon's Arab neighbors were placed under tight scrutiny (which felt to them more like harassment). And the fact is that dozens of Border Policemen and Shin Bet security people have been guarding the building in three shifts ever since—naturally, at the taxpayer's expense. Sharon proclaimed that his presence in the Muslim Quarter would bring security to the Old City, but no such thing has transpired. And then there is the delicate matter of public probity: for all the brouhaha, at the end of the housewarming Sharon and his wife did not remain in their new home, preferring to retire to a hotel on the Jewish side of town; and despite the drain on manpower to secure it, they have yet to make this apartment their permanent address.

The Israeli press generally took a dim view of this "one-man settlement" done in the pre-state style of "creating facts on the ground," but many Palestinians continued to believe that Sharon's move was part of a sinister plot to force them out. The word "transfer" had been in the air for quite a while, and everyone knew that it was a euphemism for the mass expulsion of the Arab inhabitants of the territories. At first only fanatics like Meir Kahane of the racist Kach movement had indulged in such talk, but in the mid-1980s the notion spread to other, more "respectable" circles of Israeli society, including the ruling Likud Party. In July 1987 so senior an official as Deputy Minister of Defense Michael Dekel, known to be a Shamir stalwart, called for the dispatch of Palestinians into Jordan, arguing that "transfer is the only way to solve the Palestinian problem." And he wasn't the only one to pick up the refrain. The more that relations between Israel and the Palestinians deteriorated, the more right wingers realized that far from being the solution to the conflict, the annexation of the territories would only exacerbate it. Thus the idea of transporting the Palestinians to their "homeland in Jordan" began to acquire a following on the Israeli Right. Hearing such ideas bandied about so openly in Israel, and remembering what had befallen their people in 1948, many Palestinians were filled with dread. In light of this new "fad," moreover, a number of recent events looked increasingly like a diabolical scheme to dispose of them.

The most conspicuous of these events was Israel's encroachment on the franchise of the Arab electric corporation, which was seen as a bid to destroy one part of the Palestinian infrastructure that had been created with great effort and care. The East Jerusalem Electric Company was the largest Arab enterprise in the West Bank. Though poorly managed (from a strictly commercial standpoint) and burdened by debt, it was nonetheless an object of pride for the Palestinians, who regarded the company as a cornerstone of their independence. The problem from Israel's vantage was that its facilities had failed to grow with the times, and residents of the Jewish neighborhoods built over the Green Line complained bitterly of the company's inadequate service, so the government decided to connect them directly to Israel's national grid. On the night of December 6, 1987, when officials of the Israel Electric Corporation entered the company's offices with a police escort to cut the supply of electricity to these neighborhoods, the move was read as another attempt to infringe on Palestinian prerogatives. The following day the pro-PLO organ *a-Sh'ab* ("The People") described this curtailment of the company's franchise as "part of the policy of destroying the Palestinian national institutions." Some of the company's employees were convinced that Israel and Jordan had joined in league to "destroy the company's national character," though the pro-Jordanian *a-Nahar* warned darkly that expropriating part of the franchise would severely affect the relations between Jews and Arabs and the company's chairman was summoned urgently to Amman to report on the action.

In the eyes of many Palestinians, the move against the electric company was consonant with what they saw as Israel's attempts to gain control of the water sources on the West Bank. South of Jerusalem, in the area of Herodion, a quiet battle had been going on for months over a new source of water and the right to exploit it. Because of their justified concern that excessive pumping from wells in the West Bank would damage the water table in Israel proper (which is directly linked to aquifers east of the Green Line), the Israelis have controlled the water sources in the territories with an iron hand. Palestinians are forbidden to sink wells without permission, drilling permits have been awarded only for drinking water, and even then the Israeli authorities have not been particularly generous. In 1986 the state comptroller devoted a special chapter of his annual retport to the subject of water in the territories and noted, for example, that when Tulkarem began suffering from a shortage of water for domestic use, the Civil Administration turned down the mayor's request to sink an additional well.

On the other hand, the Jewish settlers in the territories have enjoyed two to three times the water quota of their Palestinian neighbors—and then often pumped even more than they were allowed. After resigning as head of the Civil Administration in the West Bank, Brig. Gen. Ephraim Sneh observed that the amount of water pumped for an Israeli resident of the West Bank is twelve times as much as the amount pumped for a Palestinian. One reason for this huge disparity is that the quotas are not entirely under the control of the Civil Administration. In 1982 then-Defense Minister Ariel Sharon ordered that the management of the water system in the West Bank be turned over to Mekorot, the Israeli water company, which was granted a forty-nine-year lease on its waterworks. It soon became obvious that Mekorot was developing the water sources primarily for the Jewish settlements. In one case, on its own cognizance Mekorot went so far as to expropriate land from an Arab to drill a well for a nearby Jewish settlement. Not only did the company fail to receive the necessary approval from the Civil Administration, it never compensated the Palestinian for his land! Sneh has claimed that 92 percent of the water supplied by Mekorot was consumed by Jewish settlements, while the state comptroller established that Mekorot supplied the Jewish settlements in the West Bank with quantities of water far surpassing the limits set by the Water Commission (which governs Israel's national water policy). In 1986 the Jewish settlements exceeded their water quotas by 36.4 percent.

With these details hovering in the background, it is hardly surprising that the proposal to use a new drilling method near Herodion was received by the Palestinians with great suspicion. The aim of the project was to increase the flow of water to Jerusalem, including the city's Arab neighborhoods. The new technique, which called for sinking a deep shaft and inserting large pumps, promised to ensure twice the drawing power from the large aquifer in the area of Bethlehem— a reservoir that had not yet been exploited at all. Some hydrologists contended that while this system would indeed enhance the water output, it would also endanger all the other wells in the area, most of which serve Arab communities. The controversy went beyond hydrological issues, however. Jordan expressed strong opposition to the project as being prejudicial to Palestinian interests. Even the State Department became involved when its legal experts argued that although Israel, as an occupying power, had the right to exploit water sources for the benefit of the local inhabitants, it was not entitled to transfer the water to its own territory—and Jerusalem, for this purpose, was considered sovereign Israeli soil.

The Palestinians viewed the matter far more simply. To them the project was sheer theft, a scheme to wrest control of one of their natural resources (perhaps the sole reserve of water left in the West Bank) as part of a broader plan to reduce the Palestinians to a state of national indigence and then drive them out. The Civil Administration duly promised the mayors of the surrounding cities that they would be represented before Mekorot. Shmuel Goren further made the drilling conditional upon a commitment to give the needs of the Palestinian inhabitants first priority and, should existing wells in any way be damaged by the new method, to compensate the population with water from another source. It was also established that the price of water for the Palestinians would be fixed by Mekorot in collaboration with the Civil Administration and that any disagreement on this matter would be decided by the minister of defense. When word of this compromise reached the Jewish settlers, they sent a cable to Rabin calling it a "racist" arrangement that would work to their detriment. But none of these conditions calmed Palestinian fears. Bethlehem's Mayor Elias Freij, regarded as a moderate man in both his politics and his demeanor, bitterly denounced the Herodion plan, for he knew that linking Jerusalem to such a rich source of water would only militate against a future Israeli withdrawal. "In our region water is more important than oil," Freij pronounced. "Those who try to obtain my agreement to the plan do not understand that anyone who supports it will be considered an unpardonable traitor."

To his surprise Freij received support for this position from an unexpected source: the head of the West Bank's Civil Administration, Brig. Ephraim Sneh. A few months into the dispute, however, Sneh resigned from his post after holding it for over two years. Rabin urged him to stay on, though it was known that Sneh intended to enter politics as a member of the Labor Party. Yet what hastened his departure was less personal ambition than bitter arguments with his immediate superior in the government hierarchy, Shmuel Goren. The Herodion water project was one subject of disagreement between them, though not necessarily the most provocative; they also clashed over such questions as whether to permit the reunification of families, which Palestinian leaders to meet with, and whom to appoint as mayors. As might be expected, the settlers regarded Sneh as an obstacle and wanted him out quickly. For the Palestinians, however, his leaving was a genuine setback. They regarded Sneh as an address for their grievances and took his departure in October 1987 as the loss of the one person in the Israeli administration who showed them any understanding.

Thus chained to their poverty and gradually despoiled of their land, the Palestinians of the "enraged proletariat" felt trapped in a system that seemed designed to grind them down to the dust of humanity so that at an opportune moment Israel could blow them over the border in a single puff. In the eyes of this new class of self-perceived peons, Israel had lost the last of its inhibitions. Gone were all the moral and political constraints they could once have looked to as bulwarks against exploitation, dispossession, and expulsion. The outcries of Israelis against these trends were erratic and weak. Far too many Jews had convinced themselves that Kahane and his ilk were a noisy but marginal phenomenon, while to the Palestinians they were merely the most vulgar symptom of the terrible plot about to engulf them. The inhabitants of the West Bank and Gaza were fraught with fear of Israel's appetite for what was left of the Palestinian resources in the territories; filled with dismay at the prospect of a renewed Jordanian stewardship; and sore with insult over the indifference shown them by the Arab world and the Great Powers.

But most of all they were bristling with fury over the crude discrimination practiced against them and the crass arrogance that demeaned them further with every passing day. They seethed over Israel's presumptuousness, which had led it, in the words of a leaflet put out by one of the fundamentalist groups in Gaza, to "assault both the land and the people": the land in a series of expropriation actions and the building of settlements "by force and coercion, skulduggery and seduction"; the people by "inhuman behavior" toward defenseless individuals, the arrest and abuse of thousands, the collection of ruinous taxes, even the barring of kin from attending their relatives' funerals. "That is the nature of the bullying coward, the vengeful weakling who wanted to believe that our people had sunk to the depths of despondency and would yet fall at its feet to beg for mercy." And so, the leaflet concluded, "the outburst was inevitable" as an eruption of pure rage.

It was by dint of that rage that by the end of the first week of December 1987, many of the million and a half Palestinians in the West Bank and Gaza Strip were ready to claw their way out of the pit of humiliation and despair that had become their lives—and to do so on their own. In the beginning, at least, that was the crux of the *intifada*.

FOUR | *FIRST FRUITS*

THE FIRE THAT BEGAN in Jebalya was carried on the wind to Khan Yunis, then to al-Bourej, Nuseirat, and Ma'azi—the nearby "central camps"—and on to Rafah in the south. With the entire Strip ablaze, the flames spread to Balata, then down to the Kalandia camp by Ramallah, infecting most of the West Bank as well. In Gaza the hard core of the Islamic Jihad, who had first inspired the people to defiance, dispensed with their deep cover to assume the direction of a number of large demonstrations. They incited the public over loudspeakers, feverishly churned out handbills, coated the camps with slogans, and turned the crowds at the martyrs' funerals against the small army patrols, so that time and again the Israelis were surrounded and subject to threat. Soon the professional preachers joined in the effort, according the turmoil a religious motive and prescribing assaults upon the soldiers as a divine imperative. In this way the *intifada* zigzagged its way forward from town to town and funeral to funeral, from one prayer for the fallen to the next, with the blessing of the imans and ulemas.

As the hell of Gaza turned into pandemonium, the frenzy was not directed against the Israelis alone. From al-Bourej, Nuseirat, and Ma'azi, thousands descended on the fields of the area's landed residents, trampling and looting their crops. Jebalya rang with cries of "First the Jews, then Rimal!" (Rimal being one of the more affluent neighborhoods of Gaza), and graffiti in the commercial district threatened all who failed to join in the riots. Hundreds of youngsters from the Shati camp on the Gaza coast overran the nearby Shifa Hospital, flooding the wards where the injured lay and meeting the troops (who had been summoned by the staff) with a hail of stones and firebombs from the roof and courtyard. Thousands of refugees marched on the cities to draw their residents into showdowns with the army. Only in Dir al-Balah did the refugees meet with difficulties when they tried to bring the uprising from the camp to the town, for the army was able to halt their procession en route. Nevertheless, they managed to make their point, and when the military moved to penalize the refugee camp, the townsfolk begged to be included in the punishment so as to avert their neighbors' vengeance.

To fuel the fear of Gaza's indigenous population, word got out that the refugees intended to swoop down on the groceries and other city shops if they began to suffer shortages. The traditional leadership—old-guard types widely referred to as "notables"—actually begged the Civil Administration to restrain the refugees and block their access to the towns, for the specter of looting terrified the commercial classes. They were also vulnerable to the weapon of boycott, and here a double standard was at work. The refugees stopped patronizing the urban shops in response to strike calls from the Islamic Jihad, but during the strikes the stores within the camps remained open. In effect, the poor were trying to bully their more established neighbors into honoring the code of the *intifada* while readily ignoring it themselves. Typical of this phenomenon was the example of a young man from Nuseirat who was caught setting fire to a small truck that carried laborers to jobs in Israel. Asked where he was headed, the "rebel" replied matter-of-factly, "To work. I have a job in a plastics plant outside Tel Aviv."

The opening wave of riots and demonstrations lasted for twelve consecutive days in which whole sections of Gaza, the largest of the Palestinian cities, were blocked by stone barricades or burning tires with crowds of youngsters defending them. The entire city reeked of scorched rubber as black smoke billowed upward for hours at a stretch. IDF patrols were systematically stoned; gangs of teenagers sprang out of the citrus orchards to attack traffic; and hundreds of people gathered around the mosques practically inviting the army to disperse them by force. At the same time, the *intifada* maintained the tenor of a social revolt against the local establishment. In the climate of smashing conventional frameworks and abandoning all restraint, lowly fruit pickers lorded it over plantation owners and charwomen scolded the gentry. Men employed in Israel turned viciously on their "benefactors"—the Arab contractors who hired and paid them—and pummeled the drivers who ferried them to and fro. School children forced their teachers to join in demonstrations, and women defied their husbands by abandoning their kitchens for combat roles in the streets. On the face of it, at least, the social glue that held Palestinian society together had melted in the fire meant for the Israelis; the old class structure had been washed away in the flood of fury aimed at the occupation. Those whose opinions had never been heeded before suddenly emerged as trend setters, for the "hoi polloi" became the dominant force in society. The impact of this facet of the uprising cannot be underestimated, for beyond reversing social roles it played havoc with the internal balance of forces. Yesterday's leaders swam madly along with the current for fear of being swamped by it. The old "nationalist camp," scions of well-to-do families and themselves successful professionals, faded into irrelevance. At the end of the first week of the riots, some of them tried to organize a sit-down strike in the Gaza headquarters of the Palestinian Red Crescent only to discover that there was no longer any interest in their meek and decorous protests.

The baton had passed on to others: firebrands who knew how to inflame crowds and send them off to seek violent contact with the troops; masters of mania who stoked the public's urge to shriek and smash. No longer were demonstrations limited to specific population groups, such as students. On the contrary, the stunning effect of the protest derived from the participation of all ages and classes. In the worst of the incidents, even grandmothers came out in numbers. Merchants who had often watched students' protest marches with scowls of irritation now closed their shops and joined the people in the streets. Laborers who had always been prompt to report for work now forgot their jobs and stayed put behind the barricades. The fashion of masking one's face with a *kaffiyeh* color coded along political lines—red for leftists, green for fundamentalists, and black for Fatah—was instantly *de rigueur*. Slingshots for launching anything from stones to marbles became all the rage, and buildings were covered with a panoply of slogans to inform, encourage, and intimidate.

If graffiti was the free press of the *intifada*, the handbills were its bible and signal corps combined. "He who is immersed in water does not fear getting wet" observed one leaflet distributed at the end of the first week of riots. Echoing what dozens of preachers were telling their flocks and Shabiba leaders had impressed on their charges, its message was clear: all the dead and injured would not halt the escalation of the uprising. "Though cascades of blood stream forth every day, our people are in a better position to show patience and perseverance than [the Israelis] are." "The whole world now realizes that a people that seeks death cannot die!"

During these first days of the uprising, it was unquestionably the circulars of the religious organizations that carried the day. The Islamic Resistance Movement, a militant outgrowth of the fundamentalist trend, portrayed the revolt not just as the rejection of the political status quo but as a mass movement of return to the precepts of Islam. Thus it was not the State of Israel that was the enemy but "the Jews, brothers of the apes, the murderers of prophets," so that "each drop of blood should be turned into a firebomb or explosive to tear Jewish bowels apart." Not that the fundamentalist groups ignored the political aspect of the uprising. "This is not a movement to chase after peaceful solutions or to sanction autonomy and an international conference," one of their leaflets declared. "It is a movement against all that, a movement for liberation and an end to the occupation." The final battle had begun for all of Palestine, and coexistence with the Jews was unthinkable, even as a temporary expedient. Yet just as the uprising spelled the end of Arafat's approach—or so the fundamentalists would have their followers believe—it also embraced a dimension of spiritual reawakening and moral purification. A handbill distributed in Rafah, for example, described the IDF as "tired and terrified," the Arab rulers as "somnolent," but the people in the territories as "returning to their roots." It spoke of a process that would lead to the eradication of prostitution and drug abuse, a new commitment to self-sacrifice, a revival of self-respect and self-confidence. It forecast changes in the fabric of social relations and a return to the old values of solidarity, mutual aid, and caring for the needy. The *intifada*, this leaflet promised, would purify the Muslim soul and prepare it for making Palestine the springboard of a renaissance throughout the Muslim world.

The handbills of the Islamic Jihad were even more emphatic and dwelled on Israel's confusion. "All evidence points to the fact that our people's path is rising toward the sun," one flier proclaimed, "while they are on the skids into the dustbin of history." Describing the uprising as a wind from Allah "that has already filled the Israeli soldiers with dread" and caused them to "flee from women and children" as "their bullets were stopped by stones," another leaflet promised: "Today they are crying, 'Save us from this hell!' Today they know that they are losing and will not be able to remain here. Today they are losing and know that *we* have nothing to lose." A leaflet distributed in

Jebalya as early as the fourth day of the *intifada* had already concluded that "Today they realize the future belongs to us and that they have reached the end of the adventurous era of the Zionist dream."

The handbills of all the fundamentalist groups called for the liberation of Palestine "down to the last grain of sand." They exhorted their readers to make a show of daring in the fateful duel of "the faithful against the infidels." They spoke of death as a coveted aim. But most important, perhaps, they consistently denied the PLO any part in this glorious revolution and reinforced the impression that help would not come from any other Arab source, so that the inhabitants of the territories must place their faith in their own self-sacrifice. As a leaflet circulated by the Islamic Resistance Movement explained:

> The Jews expected the generation that has grown up since 1967 to be a wretched and humiliated one, a drugged generation, a generation of informers schooled in defeat. What has happened instead is an awakening of the Muslim people . . . Events have reached the point where the news agencies speak of [the streets] as battlefields. Every day the soil soaks up the blood of the pure. This is part of the price of glory and salvation. This is the *mahr* of the dark-eyed girls [who await the fallen] in Paradise.

As a rule, these leaflets were mimeographed or photocopied and were passed out during prayers by six- and seven-year-olds or piled at the entrance to the mosques so that each worshiper could take a copy. Other methods of distribution included tossing bundles of leaflets onto the streets from moving cars during the pre-dawn hours or sending young men out at night to slide them under doors and plaster them on telephone poles. Certainly it paid to make the effort, for the effect of these handbills was electrifying. In writing to relatives abroad, for example, various Gazans adopted their style in describing their own feelings about the stormy demonstrations. "These are days of truth that should have arrived long ago," one such letter stated:

> We have begun to understand how the Algerians could have sacrificed a million and a half people, how Iran is capable of sacrificing thousands of men. The start of this uprising is a familiar one and its end is predictable, but it is the road in between that counts! It is winter here now, yet the earth is watered not only by rain but by the blood of the fallen, whose scent is like the intoxicating fragrance of perfume.

□

The one island of calm in the midst of all the uproar was Jerusalem. Yet it was precisely the quiet in Israel's capital that inspired a move to transform the Palestinian violence from yet another flash in the pan into a sustained popular uprising.

Two brothers, one an electrician and the other a construction worker, were among the first to appreciate the great potential of the turmoil that had overtaken Gaza. They followed the spread of the riots to Nablus and Ramallah but assumed that the initial enthusiasm would dissipate once the army began responding in earnest. What this nascent uprising needed, they believed, was an immediate achievement, some dazzling triumph to charge its momentum and clearly set it apart from all the previous, short-lived waves of protest. Only one arena was fitting for such an action—Jerusalem—and the two brothers planned to send a jolt of violence through the streets of the holy city. Instead of squandering their resources on a costly effort to set scattered camps afire, they wanted to mount a single vigorous, well-aimed action that would echo around the world and boost the *intifada* onto an entirely new plane.

Thirty-three-year-old Mohammed Labadi and his twenty-eight-year-old brother, Majid, were known in limited circles—and to the Shin Bet, of course—as activists in Naif Hawatmeh's Democratic Front for the Liberation of Palestine. To all appearances, nothing distinguished them from thousands of other young men who belonged to one of the outlawed Palestinian organizations and had done time in Israeli prisons. Neither of the Labadi brothers had made much of an impression on any Israeli interrogator; nor did they enjoy a special reputation among the young people in the territories. In fact there was a distinct air of humility about them: both led quiet, modest lives and were not above doing hard physical labor, when necessary, to support their families. Certainly no one thought them capable of mounting a large-scale operation.

Mohammed's wife, Amal Labadi, had lived with relatives in the United States for a while but ultimately preferred to return to her homeland. The mother of two pre-schoolers, she still found time for political work on the Democratic Women's Committees, the feminist arm of Hawatmeh's organization. Majid was married to a young woman from one of the Gaza camps whom he had met while studying at Bir Zeit. The whole family, including parents and sisters, comprised a close-knit, active political unit that aided and nurtured its members.

All the Labadis were models of ideological rectitude and dedication to the nationalist cause. Unlike many others, however, they were also prepared to take personal risks and had nothing but contempt for the "radical chic" gestures of the PLO's more noted spokesmen in Jerusalem.

Once a day Mohammed Labadi reported to the desk sergeant in the Ramallah police station. A few rehearsed sentences, a question or two, a small check on the report sheet, and the short, dark, mustachioed man had fulfilled his obligation: by the terms of the restriction-of-movement order issued against him, Labadi was forbidden to leave the bounds of Ramallah and had to prove, every twenty-four hours, that he was indeed in the city. He was meticulous in observing that order for fear that any deviation would land him back in administrative detention. Since being recruited into the Democratic Front twelve years earlier, he had been detained for interrogation four times—the longest period being a year and a quarter—always for agitation or sedition.

Prison had in no way decreased his appetite for action or his faith in the merits of the struggle, though he did refine his methods to conform with the assumption that he was under surveillance. During his various stints behind bars, Labadi had proved himself a charismatic leader who was able to impress his comrades with the need for strict discipline and who served as their spokesmen vis-à-vis the prison administration. These interludes had contributed to his political development as well as his leadership skills. In the argot of his fellow security prisoners, Labadi had graduated from the "higher academy" with honors, having both proven his stamina and broadened his education. He was rewarded for these gains by a promotion in status and extension of authority in the front's shadowy hierarchy.

For appearances' sake Labadi held the title of deputy chairman of the Workers' Association—a collection of trade unions identified with the Democratic Front—and in this capacity openly engaged in recruitment, wage struggles, and the allocation of welfare supports. Majid worked closely with him, and among their achievements was the founding of a cooperative of print workers in Shuafat (some of whom would play an important role in the second stage of the *intifada*). The covert side of their activities was running a network of cells in the Jerusalem-Ramallah region, as well as maintaining contact with front members in the Gaza Strip through their brother-in-law Jamal Zakut. Mohammed Labadi took a *nom de guerre* to conceal his identity from even some his own comrades, and it was as Abu Samer ("Father of the Black

Man") that he began playing a pioneering role at the start of the uprising.

As a disciple of Naif Hawatmeh's school of Marxism, Labadi genuinely believed in the power of the few (necessarily strong-minded
people) to fire up the many, and his own vanguard was meant to draw
the masses in its wake. It was undoubtedly for this reason that the
spontaneous start and erratic course of the riots left him feeling uneasy.
While most Palestinians still perceived the violence as something of a
tornado—certainly rampant but just passing through—Labadi was fum-
ing because the Fatah people, who are the majority of the organized
Palestinians, were making no effort to control it. He was also aware of
the fundamentalists' role in fueling the Gaza riots and feared that if the
PLO did not put in a convincing appearance, and soon, the Jihad would
run away with the show. He may even have known that the front's
leaders abroad, similarly concerned about the effects of the chaos, were
appalled that Arafat seemed to be so taken with it. Indeed, one of them
tore into the chairman's "Bonapartism" for relying on some "mystical
tie" with the masses in the territories instead of building a solid and
reliable apparatus there.

Had Israel moved to round up known political activists at the start
of the riots, the Labadi brothers would undoubtedly have been on the
list. But that was a road not taken, leaving Mohammed and Majid,
along with many of the people who would soon join them, free to get
on with their plans. What caught their eye was the seeming complacency of the authorities in Jerusalem and the fact that the eastern,
Arab, half of the city had remained almost eerily quiet while the rest
of the territories were in full revolt. The staid residents of East Jerusalem's wealthier quarters were hardly types to take to the streets, and
the plain fact is that Israel held the area plus a belt of nineteen surrounding villages—containing a total of 120,000 Palestinians—with a
force of just 150 policemen. (All army units had been removed from
the city upon its unification in June 1967.) Even after the onset of riots,
no steps were taken to reinforce this contingent or place it on alert,
as though the Palestinians in the capital were above the susceptibilities
of their brothers everywhere else. This was a telling oversight, and the
Labadis marked it well.

Since Jerusalem was still virgin territory, Mohammed Labadi decided to go for two aims with one effort: to set the city alight, thus
bringing the violence to Israel's doorstep; and to do so by a deliberate,
controlled, and concerted effort of PLO activists. His scheme was to

bring in volunteers from Gaza and Hebron as the agents for importing the riots to Jerusalem. Emissaries were dispatched to mobilize these youngsters, who were put up in the homes of comrades or acquaintances, in a church, and even on the premises of one of the city's Arab hospitals. Altogether a team of about forty young people was raised for the mission. They were briefed on precisely where and how to act so that as many places as possible would explode at the same time. The preparations were completed in total secrecy, without so much as a hint leaking out to the police or the Shin Bet. Spreading out through the city's Arab neighborhoods, the Gazans and Hebronites, along with a handful of local activists, introduced themselves under nicknames or aliases. Saturday, December 19, was set and kept as D-Day even after special measures had been taken to secure the Old City for a visit by Italy's President Francesco Cossiga. Thus it was by intent and instigation, not infectious anger, that the tumult spread from remote, isolated Gaza onto the streets of Israel's capital.

The riots broke out seemingly abruptly but definitely simultaneously in a number of places at precisely 9:20 A.M. As barricades of burning tires appeared in the commercial district of East Jerusalem, mobs of demonstrators sprouted out of nowhere and rampaged through the streets, trashing branches of Israeli banks, burning municipality vehicles, and destroying Israeli-owned restaurants. Students scrambled out of their classrooms to stone traffic on the Mount of Olives and by Abu Dis, Shuafat, Jebel Mukaber, Azariah, and Sur Baher, while hundreds of others converged on predetermined spots to hold violent demonstrations. It didn't occur to the Israelis that the riots had been organized in advance—and by outsiders, at that—until clashes resumed in the surrounding villages two days later. One clue suggesting outside agitation was the fact that the demonstrators often threw stones at such Arab institutions as the Muqased Hospital on the Mount of Olives, youth clubs, and the Coca-Cola warehouse in Anata, where no fewer than 150 Palestinians were employed (the Gazans directing the violence were less than discriminating in their choice of targets). Eleven of these outsiders were arrested within a week, but before being caught they had managed to involve no fewer than 5,000 Jerusalemites in the riots, thus more than achieving their aim. For all intents and purposes, the city had been cut in two with the Green Line restored in the form of mounds of earth and garbage, overturned trash bins, and piles of stones. The 300 extra policemen rushed to the capital were not enough to handle the burgeoning number of hot spots, for as soon as units were rushed to one place, violence broke out in another. The coup set in motion by the Labadi brothers had acquired a momentum of its own.

When the inhabitants of eight villages surrounding Jerusalem blocked their access roads with earth or stone barricades and proclaimed themselves "liberated territory," initially the police followed the army's example of responding with a "counter-blockade," created with the help of bulldozers. The assumption was that, tiring of their isolation, the villagers themselves would soon clear away the obstructions in order to drive to work and enable supplies to reach their stores. As matters turned out, the barriers remained in place. Rather than travel by car, the villagers simply walked to the main road and took public transport, while behind their barricades the flags they had painted on giant sheets fluttered proudly from rooftops and electricity poles. The *mukhtars* of these settlements, who remained in close contact with the authorities, warned the police that by keeping the population out of the reach of the Civil Administration, the "double-blockade" system promoted the young radicals by default. But the police reasoned otherwise. "Let the Arabs stew in their own juice" was their motto in trusting to attrition to do its work. They did not even try to enter Sur Baher, for example, leaving the village to its own devices for a full month and a half.

During this phase a Hebrew University student by the name of Mahmoud a-Toun (whose brother had earlier fled to Egypt after killing a civilian and wounding a soldier with a knife) effectively took over Sur Baher and its sister villages, and his story is typical of the way the riots developed. Identifying himself as Abu al-Izz ("The Father of Glory"), Toun entered the villages only at night, his face covered by a *kaffiyeh*. (During the day, the villagers believed, he hid out in one of the derelict buildings of a Bedouin encampment near the Jewish settlement of Tekoa.) In a series of talks he persuaded the four rival factions in Sur Baher—the Democratic and Popular fronts, the Fatah, and the Fatah breakaway faction led by Abu Moussa—to form an alliance. In this way he gathered around him a hard core of some seventy young men who were able to impose their will on Sur Baher and nearby Jebel Mukaber by a mixture of threats and blandishments. Once they realized that the police had no intention of breaking into the villages, Toun and his people devised a more daring strategy. Rather than just barricade themselves in, they decided to slip past the blockades and carry out raids on nearby Jewish neighborhoods. On the evening of January 17, they called upon the inhabitants of Sur Baher and Jebel

Mukaber to gather for a raid on the adjacent neighborhood of Armon Hanatziv, and in no time a mob of some 7,000 Palestinians armed with hoes and axes began marching on the Jewish houses. Arriving posthaste, the police cut the wires of the mosque's loudspeaker system—which was broadcasting the call to action—set up barricades in their path, and warned the inflamed villagers not to come any further. The marchers ultimately agreed to turn over their "weapons," as the pale and shaken *mukhtars* of the two villages scolded the police with cries of "Where have you been up until now?"

Thereafter the police were less sanguine about leaving the villages on their own. Toun remained on the loose, personally setting fire to an Israeli bakery truck and burning tires by a monument to the fighters of Israel's Sixteenth Brigade. He also continued to hold sway in Sur Baher, for although the police had a photograph of the mysterious leader, his face was masked by a *kaffiyeh*, so that it took some time for them to ascertain his true identity. Twice he managed to slip away from them via a tunnel near the village café. But after a series of patient stakeouts, he was finally caught on February 10 and revealed under interrogation that he had been recruited two years earlier by Abu Moussa's faction of the Fatah during prayers in the al-Aqsa Mosque.

Five days earlier "Operation Forethought" had been launched to regain control of the Arab neighborhoods of Jerusalem with the aid of over 1,000 policemen brought in from all over the country. Some impatient Jerusalemites believed it was more of an afterthought and that the action was mounted only because Prime Minister Shamir had expressed great concern over developments in the capital. But Jerusalem was sensitive ground, and the operation was not begun until a special committee had been formed to coordinate between the police, the Shin Bet, the ministries of Defense and Justice, and the Jerusalem Municipality. On February 15, two months into the *intifada*, a contingent from the police's special anti-terrorism unit took up position on the Haram a-Sherif (or Temple Mount) to prevent the outbreak of demonstrations at the close of the Friday prayers in al-Aqsa. Despite (or perhaps because of) its presence, what ensued was a pitched battle between police and demonstrators, replete with tear gas, clubbings, and an absolutely unprecedented incident in which one of the policemen was caught by the rioters and beaten to within an inch of his life. To a degree, both sides were sobered by the experience. The Israelis realized that the sight of such mayhem against the backdrop of the mosques— transmitted by satellite around the world—did them far more harm than good. In the Arab camp, such prominent figures as Anwar al-Khatib (governor of the Jerusalem District during the period of Jordanian rule) warned the imams in charge of the mosques that by allowing riots to develop in the compound they were virtually inviting the Israelis to desecrate the Muslim holy places. Thereafter the police changed their tactics, stationing men at a safe distance from the mosques so that even if the worshipers emerged from their prayers in full cry, the demonstrations would have a chance to exhaust themselves before precipitating a clash.

At the same time the police took another tack to convey to the Arabs of Jerusalem that unless the violence stopped, life would become increasingly unpleasant for them. This strategy was a subtle but systematic campaign of harassment that took the form of stopping and searching vehicles, conducting body searches, and collecting no fewer than 4,000 identity cards to sift out agitators. Cars were also stopped to check the condition of windshield wipers and seat belts or see to it that the driver and passengers had paid their taxes. Equally potent was a new rule forbidding Muslims from outside the city to pray on the Haram a-Sherif, and everyone entering a mosque had his identity card checked for this purpose. Neighborhoods noted for recurrent violence, such as A-Tor, were placed under curfew—over the bitter objections of Mayor Teddy Kollek—and the police set up checkpoints within the villages themselves. They also took stock of all the garages in the Wadi Joz section so that rioters intent on burning tires would have to steal them off Arab vehicles. (On days of dearth, they resorted to puny bicycle tires!) All told, in the three months from December through February, about 1,000 people were arrested in the Jerusalem area, with charges of agitation and violence pressed against 700 of them.

As the tactic of quelling resistance by administrative harassment gradually proved itself, the strict orders forbidding the police to open fire were reinforced. Commanders warned that if any man did use his weapon, he had better be prepared to prove that his life had been in real and present danger, and "not to his superior officer but to a judge." Even the use of .22-caliber bullets (designed to wound but not kill) was absolutely ruled out. Thus the contest in Jerusalem followed lines very different from the one in the territories. For months not a single person was killed in the capital despite severe rioting and even assaults on Jewish neighborhoods that sometimes caused extensive damage. After the initial outburst on December 19, the strong police presence in the city prevented the renewal of widespread demonstrations and halted the process of whole villages sealing themselves off behind barricades. Still, as Jews disappeared from the shops and markets of the Old City and East Jerusalem, it was clear that the unity of the city had been reduced to a mere geographical fact and that the quiet was an artificial one. The front-line cadres had been removed from the streets by successive waves of arrests, but the air of rebellion remained.

As word of the special Jerusalem action spread, thousands of activists like Mahmoud a-Toun made their presence felt in the territories, jumping at the opportunity to keep the cauldron boiling. The Labadi brothers had achieved their triumph and, as they had hoped, their success in the capital fed the fires burning elsewhere. A ranking expert in the Israeli defense establishment later summed up this stage in a carefully worded memorandum stating that "the [riots] broke out *spontaneously* but were subsequently organized by *many* local elements having little coordination between them but aided by incitement from the PLO. The initiative has come from the [territories]." The fact is that during the first month of the uprising—which Palestinian observers like Sari Nusseibeh agree was a unique period—the violence reached undreamed of proportions: 26 Palestinians were killed by Israeli gunfire and some 320 were injured (two-thirds of them between the ages of seventeen and twenty-nine), while 56 soldiers and 30 Israeli civilians were injured by stones and bottles. In a single month the army's operations logs registered no fewer than 1,412 separate incidents of demonstrations, stonings, tire burnings, blocking roads, and raising barricades. At least 109 firebombs had been thrown in various places, in addition to twelve instances of arson, three grenade attacks, and the discovery of six improvised explosive devices. Over and above the hundreds of rioters and others detained for participation in disturbances, by January 9, 1988, some 270 Palestinians had been arrested for sedition or maintaining ties with terrorist organizations.

These figures are the dry facts of what had become an heroic epic for the Palestinians and would long be remembered by the Israelis as a difficult time of weakness bordering on impotence. It is no exaggeration to say that in the course of a month the Military Government had been reduced to a mockery and Israel had lost complete control over the Palestinian population. But even as the weeks passed and the IDF gradually regained its hold over villages, towns, and the axes of transport, the situation never returned to what it had been before December 8. The instruments of occupation had been damaged beyond repair and in any case could not be mended by force. Old habits of resignation gave way to a spirit of rebellion; the long tradition of capitulation to Israel was supplanted, almost magically, by a mood of defiance. There were signs all around that the populace had learned to appreciate its abilities and the weakness of its enemy. Thousands of people made it a habit to carry fresh onions or small bottles of perfume as an antidote to the effects of tear gas. Fleet young men brandishing slingshots became national heroes, and overnight a dozen hymns of praise were composed to the "warriors armed only with stones." Detention became a status symbol, bruises a badge of courage, and public appeals for pardons—which were once common—had become a thing of the past. The wounded were spirited out of hospitals, lest they fall into enemy hands. Corpses were whisked off the streets before they could be claimed by the Israelis for postmortems. More than once, the dead were carried out of morgues to trills of triumph in processions of song. Even members of the refined middle class, who had always held their children back from joining the struggle in the streets, now felt obliged to support the demonstrations, contribute to the "emergency funds," and profess their loyalty to the new "revolutionary order."

Faced with this display of dauntlessly aggressive behavior, the IDF was helpless to respond. It was as though all the traditional roles had been switched. An army that prided itself on taking the initiative, dictating the moves, and besting the enemy through flexibility and speed was reduced to reacting to such petty provocations as bottles, stones, and the taunts of children. Having lost control of the territories, it was beginning to lose its own composure—a reversal that brought a sharp rise in Palestinian confidence. After the refugee camps, urban neighborhoods and countless villages were transformed into hostile areas that could be entered only by a substantial military force. Large contingents were tied down on observation duties, street patrols, and even round-the-clock defense of sections of roads, once the army realized that after being opened by mobile patrols, axes were soon blocked again by stones, a new kind of "land mine" (scattered nails or broken glass), or puddles of oil that sent jeeps careening into a skid. Even when the roads were open, traveling them became so hazardous that military vehicles had iron grates welded over their windows as protection against stones. Keeping even a modicum of order in the territories required a conspicuously high profile, yet even with a beefed-up force, each day the army had to establish its hold anew. Many villages forced Israeli units to "conquer" them repeatedly, with great effort, in the space of short periods. The terms of skirmishes were dictated by teenagers, sometimes even by children, while troops weighed down by battle gear scurried from one trouble spot to the next. Hardly a day went by without violent confrontations or a week without Palestinian fatalities. The army, in the words of one member of the General Staff, was sprawled on a bed of hot coals, any one of which might burst into flames at unpredictable intervals. After twenty-one years of an implicit *modus vivendi*, in a matter of days the West Bank and Gaza Strip had become the scene of an all-out fray between a native population and an occupying power.

By the end of the first month of the uprising, it was impossible to deny that Israel's policy in the territories was utterly bankrupt. The system that had enabled the occupation to continue for over two decades simply collapsed in the face of the violence and, much to the consternation of the Israelis, none of the old rules applied any more. The basic lines of that system, fashioned back in June 1976, had not been updated since. At that time, following a brief flare-up of rioting, Yitzhak Rabin's government discussed and approved a program formulated by Defense Minister Shimon Peres and Minister of Police Shlomo Hillel. Set out in a document of over thirty clauses, it prescribed a formula for holding the territories over an extended period that generally echoed the philosophy of "benevolent occupation." The program's aim was to minimize intervention in the lives of the Palestinians and allow them to pursue their lives unmolested as long as they obeyed the law and did not defy the occupation. To keep those conditions absolutely clear and reduce the chances of disturbances, the government established "a clear-cut policy of reward and punishment," promising benefits to those who cooperated with the administration and sanctions against those who did not. Patient talks with local leaders were used to achieve a "tacit understanding" on the "rules of the game." In the event that rioting did break out, the military was to "isolate the hot spots" quickly and use the Border Police as the principal force for restoring order, with the army proper being used "for reinforcement only." Direct contact between the security forces and the rioters was to be avoided as much as possible, so that in most cases the preferred tactic was to clear the streets by proclaiming a curfew.

Clause Fifteen of this document stressed that since "respect for human life is the highest value," troops were allowed to open fire only in self-defense in life-threatening situations. The section on "operative means" permitted the adoption of such drastic measures as sealing off the whole or parts of a city, imposing a curfew ("whether as an operative measure or a punitive one"), and resorting to arrests, fines, back-to-work orders, house arrest, banishment from an area, and even deportation from the country in what were characterized as "special cases." Neither did it rule out sealing or demolishing houses, closing schools and firing teachers, postponing exams, withholding salaries, suspending budgets, and delaying projects as legitimate means of maintaining order by making disorders unprofitable.

In the ensuing years this policy worked to limit demonstrations to the student population or to places that could easily be isolated from their surroundings. But with the advent of the *intifada,* the "tacit understanding" no longer held—not least because the leadership of the community had passed to the kids in the street. Nonintervention was replaced by the conspicuous presence of troops. The Border Police were overwhelmed by the multitude of incidents and the magnitude of events. Rather than calm the atmosphere, the permissible means of deterrence seemed to rile it, and the troops repeatedly found that they had to resort to their weapons. Thus from maintaining quiet by means of a big carrot and a little stick (in the form of a barely visible force), Israel switched, for lack of choice, to a massive use of the most flagrant and brutal tools of occupation. In place of the low-profile Civil Administration, the Military Government returned with unprecedented clout. Instead of preserving order by administrative means, the army pulled one company after another out of maneuvers and sent them into the territories. From a marginal task handled by a small, lean apparatus, the occupation became Israel's national obsession, while for the Palestinians it grew into an obtrusive threat and omnipresent challenge, a contest between the might of an army and the plight of a people. Every hour of every day, civilians faced down soldiers somewhere in the territories in a relentless test of strength that left no room for compromise. Every deterrent and punitive measure was tried; all the army's resourcefulness was evoked to improve its performance. But the *intifada* did not yield and would not subside.

It was clear almost from the start that the IDF was quite unprepared for a contest of this sort, for its wealth of hard-earned experience had come from a very different kind of warfare. The five wars in its history, the commando raids, and other actions had made it one of the world's most experienced armies. But this rich operational background and the wealth of tips and pointers passed down from one generation to the next had been gained from confrontations with armed opponents, from terrorist squads to regular armies. What the IDF now had on its hands was a mass civil uprising: not a war fought with tanks, planes, and artillery or a border skirmish with armed men but a challenge posed without weapons, a contest against bottles, stones, and firebombs. And strange as it sounds in retrospect, the prospect of such an uprising was not included among the possibilities that the army was to take into account. There had been several waves of civil disturbances over the twenty-one years of Israeli rule in the territories, but never had they encompassed such great numbers of people in so many places at once. And never had they been so sustained or so closely covered by the media. For the first time in its history, the IDF encountered a threat that it was quite at a loss to handle—and in an area that it had considered almost a footnote to its operational designs.

In the past, each time it was suggested that the IDF create special units to deal with civil unrest in the territories, the proposal was turned down by the senior command for fear that they would deteriorate into "a professional occupation force," as former Chief of Staff Moshe Levi once put it. In Levi's eyes, at least, there was something so odious about a force built expressly to quash civil resistance that he preferred to have all the army's combat units do occasional duty in the territories, handling problems as they arose. (In a similar vein, a small unit of dogs was trained for use against rioters but was kept out of action for obvious reasons.) However, the army did consider various ideas for equipping the troops with more effective means of riot control. For years the General Staff shopped around for vehicles equipped with water jets for dispersing violent demonstrations, but although a model was finally chosen, it was never purchased. Other options ranged from devices for shooting electric arrows and coating the streets with slippery dust to nets for trapping demonstrators and an array of concoctions (from sneeze bombs to soporofic sprays) that would put rioters out of commission. Nothing came of all the talk, however. And when the need actually arose to deal with widespread disturbances, the army lacked even the most elementary riot gear: shields, helmets, and clubs. At the start of the uprising, it had only a meager store of rubber bullets. Tear gas was in short supply, and the local manufacturer fell so far behind demand that large quantities had to be bought up abroad and sent to Israel by special airlift.

During the opening weeks of the uprising, the General Staff was in a state of utter disarray. At first it refrained from sending reinforcements into the field. Then it dispatched them but failed to provide directives on how to act in the face of crowds of inflamed demonstrators. The plain fact is that the men of the Israel Defense Forces had no idea of how to disperse demonstrations professionally. They had neither been trained for the task nor were psychologically prepared to handle it. They did not know how to enter a house for the purpose of making arrests. Though equipped with tear gas, they had never been drilled in its effective use and had to learn from bitter experience that it was all too likely to waft back in their direction and affect the troops more than the rioters. No less frustrating to the soldiers was the Tom-and-Jerry quality of the provocations. They might scatter a group of stone-throwing youngsters from one alleyway only to meet them again in the next one, or clear the barricades off a road just to find that it had been closed again behind them. The IDF's hesitation and confusion during the first, critical days of the uprising were not lost on the demonstrators, who drew encouragement to step up their pressure. As their daring mounted and the disturbances spread, there were days when the insurgents' control of large chunks of territory was beyond question.

From the soldiers' standpoint, the greatest problem was handling the demonstrations made up of thousands of people. Such instances were particularly menacing in the Gaza Strip, where it often seemed as though a sea of people—young and old, women and children—were out on the streets, and the small foot patrols might turn a corner and suddenly find huge crowds bearing down on them. If they tried to close in on the demonstrators, they faced the risk of having their weapons snatched away or even of being trampled by an angry mob. Isolated vehicles were equally helpless against throngs of this sort. In fact, none of the standard tactics seemed to work in such situations, and the Palestinians had a way of finding an answer for everything. When the field commanders switched from the more vulnerable foot patrols to motorized actions using jeeps and command cars, for example, the Palestinians sprinkled the roads with nails or broken glass to puncture the tires.

The composition of the crowds was another problem, since the number of women was particularly high and young children mixed in freely among the demonstrators. The streets of the refugee camps had always teemed with children, and even mass violence did not seem to change that fact of camp life. But the role of women had changed to a critical one, not only because they could be as aggressive as the men but because their very presence in a confrontational setting seemed to be an inciting factor. Given these circumstances, gunfire would have claimed dozens of random victims, many of them inevitably being women and children. But though loath or forbidden to use live ammunition, the soldiers found that they lacked the alternative of rubber bullets; and when the latter were supplied, they proved ineffective at a range of over 15 yards. In the days when most of the demonstrators had been high school or college students, it was enough for a lone soldier to come forward, open his fly, and begin tugging down his pants to send the mortified girls in the crowd scattering in a panic. But such ruses had no effect at all in the camps. Aware that the soldiers were forbidden to shoot, the demonstrators sneered at their impotence.

For years the army's policy on demonstrations had been to single out and arrest their leaders or, if that proved impossible, to wound them—and them alone. Standing orders were to do whatever necessary to avoid injury to innocent bystanders or harm to the public at large. Senior commanders were forever drumming it into their men that every Palestinian killed during a disturbance was a net gain for the PLO and net loss for Israel. But now, with demonstrators flooding the streets, it was impossible to single out the leaders of the disturbances. And even if they could be identified, there was no way of hitting them without risking injury to others. Neither was it possible to pick off the people hurling firebombs once they had melted into a crowd. That the old orders proved irrelevant only added to the confusion, and since the troops were forbidden to fire indiscriminately, they had no choice but to back down in confrontations with crowds.

The old standby in critical situations—placing an area under curfew—was an equally unsatisfactory solution. Though long considered an effective measure during times of unrest, from December onward it proved to be an expensive approach that invited further tests of strength. In the past the Palestinians had always obeyed orders to remain closed up in their homes, enabling the army to enforce curfews with a minimum of manpower. With the onset of the *intifada*, however, breaking the curfew became a national sport. In one particularly unsettling incident, upon meeting massive resistance from the residents of al-Bourej in the Gaza Strip, the infantry company assigned to impose a curfew had to withdraw from the camp and regroup before virtually mounting an assault to disperse a wild mob with clubs and gunfire. It was a harrowing experience for soldiers and a frightening lesson for the camp's inhabitants.

The longer the uprising endured, the clearer it became to both sides that they had embarked upon a stage in the Israeli-Arab conflict in which Israel was unable to apply its military strength. The IDF's main weapons systems—be they planes, tanks, rockets, or artillery—were totally irrelevant to the challenge, and the common soldier was given to understand that he was not entitled to resort to deadly force. Thus without even seeking it, the Palestinians had found a way to neutralize Israel's enormous military advantage. In one of the greater ironies of Middle Eastern history, by the most primitive of means the Palestinians achieved what all the Arab armies over the course of two generations had repeatedly failed to do: strip the IDF of its ability to maneuver quickly and prevent it from manifesting its might. Many weeks were to pass before the army adjusted to these new circumstances and equipped its men with more appropriate means of action, but by then the uprising had acquired enough momentum to keep going anyway.

Due to the impression that the absence of weapons in Palestinian hands added to the IDF's difficulties, all local terrorist actions were brought to a halt. Eventually Arafat would try to take credit for this practice, and he strictly forbade his associates to make any quotable statements encouraging the rioters to take up arms. Yet the restraint was really an instinctive reaction on the part of the people who had wrought the "rock revolution." In point of fact, until Arafat's change of heart, the PLO abroad bombarded its squads in the field with orders to put their guns and explosives to use. But the men on the spot preferred the new style of confrontation and simply ignored these directives (with the exception of a few who attempted to plant booby-trapped cars but were stopped in time by the security services).

The resolve to eschew an "armed struggle" with the Israelis sometimes led to strange situations. When a soldier dropped his rifle during a disturbance in Nablus, one demonstrator went bounding after him to return it, while his comrades stopped their shower of stones and gave out whistles of encouragement instead. The thirst for weapons was satisfied by carving rifles out of wood or assembling revolvers out of pistons, pipes, and a bit of ingenuity. The PLO Radio gave detailed instructions on how to prepare Molotov cocktails, whip up "hand grenades" on a sugar base, and mix noxious brews from materials easily obtained in pharmacies and barber shops. But bona fide weapons were never to be found in the hands of the insurgents; even collaborators were instructed to turn in their army-issue revolvers before being accepted back into the fold.

On January 1, 1988, a second radio station joined the effort. Calling itself al-Quds (Jerusalem), it transmitted from Dara'a in southern Syria and was picked up loud and clear throughout the occupied territories. The station was run by Ahmed Jebril's Popular Front for the Liberation of Palestine–General Command, but its broadcasters were careful not to stress their political affiliation or allude to the faction's bitter quarrel with the PLO,* so that within days they had attracted an audience of hundreds of thousands of listeners. With the aid of the Arab press services in East Jerusalem, a steady flow of reports from the territories was relayed to the station via liaisons in Western Europe. In addition to being a source of hard news and filling the airwaves with anthems and marching songs inspired by the *intifada*, al-Quds broadcast instructions on strikes, threats against collaborators, and praise for the camps, towns, and neighborhoods that excelled in their defiance. Nevertheless, months were to pass before Israel took steps to jam these broadcasts—and was pleased to discover that despite early fears, the Syrians kept Jebril from jamming Israel's Arabic-language broadcasts in return. It was not until the summer of 1988 that al-Quds was able to begin shortwave transmissions and again reach its audience of eager listeners in the territories.

The inauguration of these broadcasts had another less manifest but ultimately important effect. Jebril's control of the airwaves, coupled with the religious slant of the demonstrations in Gaza, left Yasser Arafat feeling increasingly uneasy. From afar, at least, it sometimes seemed that the PLO was losing its position of unquestioned supremacy among the Palestinian organizations. "Voices dripping with venom are going on about the orphaned uprising that has no father and the barren leadership that has no sons" read one communication distributed on Arafat's behalf. "This is a bogus claim," it continued, "and we will not be wiped out by a stroke of the pen or by falsifications written in cheap ink." Thus while still struggling to gain control of the *intifada*, Arafat was already dabbling in an equally important task (from his standpoint, at least): rewriting history as it was being made. Through a group of associates and outside sympathizers, including the Egyptian Communist theoretician Lutfi al-Huli, Arafat saw to it that his own version of the rebellion's genesis was bruited about. The aim of this campaign was to convince the world that the idea of the uprising had originated in Arafat's office, that he had personally given the order for it to begin, and that it had been engineered exclusively by his loyalists.

In the account put together to salvage his honor, Arafat had issued

---

* Jebril broke with the PLO at the end of the war in Lebanon in protest of Arafat's "defeatist" political line and dictatorial demeanor within the organization.

the call for rebellion on October 17 in a broadcast to the territories that spoke of an uprising "in every village and city, in every refugee camp and prison" and stressed the need to increase the use of stones, knives, and firebombs. While this broadcast definitely took place, it was no more than a routine affair—just another one of the speeches that Arafat made on any number of occasions to express his bond with the Palestinians in the territories. Yet by the second month of the uprising, it was conveniently being cited as the chairman's personal signal to his followers to rise up and defeat the occupation by a stroke of mass defiance, rather than the "armed struggle" he had been prescribing for two decades. "D-day," this rendition continues, was originally scheduled for November 9, the second day of the emergency Arab summit held in Amman (when a flurry of demonstrations had indeed taken place, not on Arafat's orders but in response to reports that the summit was being devoted exclusively to the Gulf war). Fortunately, the chairman was quick to grasp his error in timing and called the demonstrations to a halt, lest they be misconstrued as a bid to disrupt the summit's proceedings or embarrass its participants. Consequently, this specious version concludes, the Fatah people in the territories decided to postpone the uprising to December 8—which is of course the date on which it began. It must be said that this tendentious reconstruction of events was never seriously challenged. Not that Arafat's partner-rivals in the PLO let his grab for glory pass without comment. The Democratic Front observed, with characteristic acerbity, that this portrait of Arafat as a man with the power to get tens of thousands of people onto the streets with a single speech was patently absurd.

Indeed, it sometimes seemed during the opening weeks of the violence that the PLO's main contribution to the uprising was hyperbole. Its spokesmen acclaimed the *intifada* as a "qualitative leap" and waxed rapturous about the "change in the strategic balance." Presumably inspiring slogans like "Blood will defeat the sword" and "Our strength lies in our weakness" were coined by the dozen, and at one point the PLO's security chief, Salah Halaf (Abu Iyyad), challenged Israel to a "duel at high noon." But behind the exultant rhetoric lay fears, expressed by the PLO leadership as early as the end of January, that the pace of the rebellion was slowing down. In most cases the initiative remained a local one and lacked organizational backing. The Fatah generally urged its followers to provoke the Israelis but issued no clear instructions on targets or priorities (merely suggesting the more the better). The Communists would not commit their clandestine network to a coordinated effort, and the two "fronts" were quick to commend rebellion but could not get their strongholds (like the Deheishe refugee camp outside Bethlehem) to respond. The Muslim Brotherhood on the West Bank steered clear of organized involvement in the riots, while the students at Bir Zeit were the greatest disappointment of all: after barricading themselves on campus, flying the Palestinian flag, and holding a series of stirring assemblies, when they realized that the army had no intention of forcing its way into the university, they packed up and went home. Ironically, it was the youngsters at this hotbed of Palestinian nationalism who seemed to have the greatest difficulty finding their sense of direction. Thus the picture from December through the end of January was anything but definitive. Taking it all in, Mahmoud Abbas (Abu Mazen), who holds the "Israeli portfolio" in the PLO's top echelon, felt confident in forecasting that "the uprising will continue for two or three months and then break out again in a year or two."

He couldn't have been more wrong, yet most of the Israeli experts would have tended to agree. On December 23 Shmuel Goren, the coordinator of operations in the territories, reported that the riots were "dying down" as a result of the talks between the Civil Administration and leading figures in the territories, the winter weather, and the exhaustion of the population. By the last day of the month, fantasy had crept into a classified situation report stating that "life has gradually returned to normal." This equanimity on the part of the Israeli authorities was presumably based on evidence that the wave of violence had already crested. Indeed, at the end of the second week of the uprising there was a misleading calm in the Gaza Strip, and demonstrations were not renewed there until after the deportation of Sheikh Odeh and four other Jihad activists on January 30. This move was one of Israel's worst tactical errors during the early phase of the *intifada*, for it again brought feelings to a head and prompted a second general strike that was observed by all Palestinians, without exception. Even so, the situation was not unequivocal. At the end of January the schools were opened again, and attendance in the Gaza Strip reached over 70 percent. In various places on the West Bank, parents organized voluntary guard duty to prevent their children from holding demonstrations. The winter recess in the West Bank was moved up a week, and a few of the universities and other institutions of higher learning were closed by their own administrations (with the rest being shut by order of the area commander). What violence there was continued to center on the refugee camps, as youngsters from Kalandia and Amari blocked the main road near Ramallah and demonstrations by school children spread to other districts.

The relative lull late in January was essentially part of a gradual shift in gears that transformed the *intifada* from an infectious outburst into an ongoing and truly mass uprising. It was about then that the *kaffiyeh*-masked youngsters began to shift the focus of confrontation from the alleys of the refugee camps to the main streets of the cities. Their quickly accomplished aim was to paralyze commercial life and push the business community—traditionally the most moderate sector of Palestinian society—to the forefront of the uprising. Young people from the casbah of Nablus and the slums of other cities joined forces with kids from the camps to drag the middle class off the fence so that their struggle could be waged on the backs of the people with the most to lose. It was not a particularly difficult task. In a private conversation, one well-heeled merchant explained to the military governor of Bethlehem that he and his fellow-tradesmen feared the *shabab* ("kids") far more than anything Israel could mete out. Boys silently signaling merchants of their power—by lighting a match in front of their shops, for one—soon gave rise to a telling new Arabic proverb: *"Walad bisaker balad"* ("A child can close down a city").

The IDF knew of the merchants' dilemma. But rather than walk away from this challenge (as it eventually would), the army chose to make it yet another test of strength, insisting that shops remain open during certain hours or for the duration of a general strike. The result was a spate of assaults by both Palestinian ruffians and Israeli soldiers on shops and their hapless owners. Too late was it conceded that Israel had played right into the youngsters' hands by agreeing to their rules of rebellion by proxy. They forced the timorous tradesmen onto the front line of the *intifada*, then the army came along and punished these shopkeepers for defiance! It was not as if this paradox went unnoticed. Senior officers complained of the wanton damage being caused by the conscripts sent out to break the strikes and warned that such actions would only aggravate the hostility in the territories. But such warnings went unheeded, and the merchants knew that if they were doomed to suffer anyway, it was better to sustain damage from Israeli youngsters than from their own.

There were yet other, more positive aspects to this transition. In time the psychologist Dr. Yusef Abu Samarah of Bir Zeit University would provide an eloquent, though in our view exaggerated, description of the new social phenomena that emerged from the whirlwind of events at the close of 1987. He accorded great significance to the spread of behavior that had earlier been demonstrated on only a modest scale: voluntarism and a willingness to help others; mutual solidarity between neighbors of different classes; and a willingness to make concessions and sacrifices. Others believed that a whole new scale of values—the ethic of a fighting people—was quickly evolving in the territories. They wanted to see the *intifada* as the cure for all the ills of a society that was finally discarding its shell of neglect, apathy, and exploitation and being cleansed by a return to simplicity and a devotion to national duty.

Mohammed Nasser, one of the most original thinkers in the West Bank, is another intellectual who perceived the *intifada* as both a social and political upheaval. He wrote in a small book (which was denounced and banned by the PLO) that at the start of the uprising it was as if an alarm clock had gone off in the soul of every Palestinian in the territories, urging him to arise and act without waiting for calls or exhortations. A disciple of the Popular Front for the Liberation of Palestine (turned leader of the Israeli-backed Village Leagues), Nasser saw the *intifada* as a revolution against both the Israeli occupation and the Palestinian "aristocracy"—those prosperous and well-connected families who had not only managed to protect their assets under Jordanian and Israeli rule but had effectively taken over the leadership of the so-called nationalist circles because they blended so well with the Fatah's local spokesmen. He warned that the uprising would ultimately fail unless it stripped this class of its privileges and denied its members their traditional position as leaders and spokesmen. Nasser read what was happening in the streets as the birth of a new class of leaders who understood that a thorough overhaul of Palestinian society was a vital condition of the *intifada*'s success. The fact is that trends in these directions did indeed take shape early in the uprising, but not with anything near the salience described by sympathetic observers like Nasser and Abu Samarah.

It was not until the summer of 1988 that the first Israeli assessment of the rebellion's effect on Palestinian life was composed in the Defense Ministry. Written by Colonel Shalom Harari, one of the Civil Administration's leading experts on Arab affairs, it attempted to analyze the social and psychological changes that had occurred as a result of what Harari termed the rising power of the "violent man in the street." Harari conceded that the behavior patterns of the population in the territories had taken a new direction, though he doubted whether this change could be characterized as a genuine "social revolution." He also noted the "revolutionary mood" that was overturning long-standing conventions and introducing new ones in their place but advised that it was essentially based on rumors and illusions that had no basis in reality.

The most conspicuous examples of the change engendered by the riots were the advertisements published by landlords announcing voluntary reductions in their rents, or cases such as the wealthy merchant from Ramallah who traded in his Mercedes for a battered jalopy to express his identification with the youngsters who now ruled the streets. But more subtle symptoms of upheaval had a greater impact on society at large. Many middle- and upper-class Palestinians were possessed by anxiety and complained of insomnia brought on by fear of Palestinian toughs and Israeli soldiers alike. Wealth and the protection of one of the stronger clans had not merely lost their potency as guarantees of security, they turned the rich into easy targets of blackmail and intimidation. On the family and village level, life often seemed to be spinning out of control. Boys of twelve and thirteen or even younger publicly defied their parents, and the heads of clans were appalled by the insolence of people who would never have dared to offend them before. Teenagers turned viciously on their fathers even in the more conservative villages, and in one incident a group of girls stoned their own parents for trying to stop them from demonstrating. The old rules were changing for their mothers, too, as the image of the Palestinian woman underwent considerable revision. While few women had joined demonstrations in the past, and then only quiet protest actions, masses of them now sought violent contact with the soldiers without fear of compromising their "feminine modesty." The fact is that about one-fifth of the wounded during the first three months of the *intifada* were women and girls.

No less important, Harari noted, was the way in which the Palestinian population felt about itself. Not only was it glorying in its accomplishments, to the point of euphoria, it was moved by a sense of moral superiority over Israel precisely because of its underdog status. The weak are strong was the gist of this philosophy. They display munificence toward their armed oppressors by refusing to stoop to terrorism. They have achieved internal unity (in contrast to the obstreperous divisiveness that marks Israeli life). They have overcome their fear (while sowing panic in Israeli hearts). They have learned to live modestly, accept hardship, and help the needy (unlike the materialistic soldiers facing them). And of course they share a profound conviction that the *intifada* represents just and logical demands (compared with the bitter debate in Israel over the response to it). Though vulnerable to criticism on the grounds of excessive idealism, this self-portrait had a critical impact on events, for the belief that the *intifada* was reshaping the Palestinian national ethos was a mainstay of its endurance.

The blow that the Labadi brothers delivered in Jerusalem was the *intifada*'s first high point after the initial Israeli setback in Gaza. Two days later came another surprise stroke—and again in an area beyond the jurisdiction of the Military Government: the Arab community of Israel. Israel's Arab citizens were meant to serve as the "lungs" of the *intifada*, as the tacticians of George Habash's Popular Front so graphically put it. They were not asked to lend a hand in the uprising or to serve as the "brains" behind it; their task was to pump it with oxygen. This aim was achieved early on by a mass protest action that was all the more impressive because it was the first time that the Arabs of Israel had made common cause with their brethren in the territories to end the occupation and permit the establishment of a Palestinian state.

During the first days of the *intifada* the leaders of the Israeli-Arab community held their peace, not least because, like so many other Israelis, they were cast into confusion and dismay by viewing the clips from the territories shown on the nightly television news. On December 17, just over a week after the outbreak of rioting, the National Committee of Chairmen of Arab Local Councils convened in the Galilean town of Shefaram for a session that had been scheduled well in advance and was to discuss a number of standard issues. As soon as the meeting opened, however, representatives of the Democratic Front for Peace (formerly the New Communist List and still popularly referred to by the Hebrew acronym for that name, Rakah) took the floor to propose a new agenda centering on one issue alone: the demonstration of solidarity with the Arabs of the occupied territories. The rest of the participants in the forum seemed stunned. They had not been prepared for such a move, and a few of them were instantly on their feet opposing it on the grounds that any kind of protest action would be construed by the Jewish public as joining in the uprising. But the Rakah people, who make up half of the committee, insisted that the full plenum be convened to vote on the question the following day.

This plenum is an impressive body representing the entire leadership of the Israeli-Arab community. Most of its members are elected officials, and in addition to the chairmen of the Arab local councils it includes Knesset members from all the parties (with the exception of the Druze deputies). Also represented are members of the watch committees responsible for monitoring developments in spheres of special concern to the Arabs (such as land expropriation and education). High-placed officials, such as supervisors in the Ministry of Education and members of the Histadrut (National Labor Federation) Executive, sit side by side with representatives of the radical Sons of the Village movement, which effectively denies Israel's right to exist. In attendance at this particular meeting was Abdullah Nimer Darwish of Kafer Kassem, one of the more influential sheikhs heading the Islamic Movement, which calls for a return to religious values and practices. Until that day Nimer had refused to sit in the same room with the Communists, but in light of the grave circumstances he put aside his differences with Rakah and came to the meeting to influence its decisions.

In the charged atmosphere that filled the hall, only one decision could have come out of that meeting—and well the Rakah people knew it. Whoever was opposed to a solidarity strike simply made it his business to stay away that day, and not a single participant even raised an alternate proposal. Hence the unanimous vote to hold a general strike and rallies in support of the inhabitants of the territories was pretty much a foregone conclusion. One could even say that the members of the forum had borrowed a leaf from the book of their Jewish compatriots. Just as Jews could not remain indifferent to the discrimination against their brethren in the Soviet Union, they argued, so the Arabs of Israel were entitled to express their protest over the treatment of their brothers in the territories. A manifesto published by the Sons of the Village movement went so far as to declare that the Palestinians on both sides of the Green Line are "a single body." Still, some caution did prevail; in an effort to signal the Jewish public that their aim was not to join in the uprising, the members of the plenum called their strike, scheduled for December 21, "Peace Day."

It was more than a common concern for the inhabitants of the territories that fashioned the vote at that meeting, however. The other, albeit covert, element behind the decision taken at Shefaram was the PLO. In what was perhaps one of the sharper ironies of the day, though the PLO had been surprised by the initiative taken in the territories, it had long been trying to move Israel's Arabs to action and control its sympathizers from afar. In scores of phone calls from abroad, senior PLO officials now urged these "fellow-travelers" to take a stand—if not quite to throw in their lot with the Palestinians over the Green

Line, at least to aid the cause by holding demonstrations to rally world public opinion. Inevitably, however, the action taken by Israel's Arabs also focused the rest of the country's attention on two trends that had long been known to Israel's security services, namely, the PLO's growing appreciation of the potential of the Israeli-Arab community (especially in terms of advancing the Palestinian cause) and the strengthening of ties between Israel's Arab citizens and the organization at war with their country.

The strike on "Peace Day" was a considerable achievement for the national leadership of the Israeli-Arab community and astonished the country's Jews—though it must be said that their surprise was again a result of self-delusion. To the degree that they thought about it at all, most Jewish Israelis assumed that regardless of what happened in the territories, the Arab citizens of Israel would not intervene; that they would always lie low, button their lips, and above all strictly observe the law. The sad fact is that most Jewish Israelis rarely if ever considered the complex position of their Arab countrymen or, indeed, related to the entire Palestinian question as any more than a tangential footnote to their lives. From time to time a terrorist attack claiming innocent victims might turn their apathy into fleeting pain or outrage. But in almost every case such attacks were perpetrated by Arabs coming from outside the country; Jewish Israelis were not expecting to meet Arab violence from within.

And then, at the very heart of Israel, main arteries were being blocked, stones were thrown in Jaffa, and public transport was attacked in Lod, exposing Jewish children to injury as a result of Arab anger. The violence was not restricted to the mixed cities of Jaffa and Lod, which have an Arab minority living in dire poverty. In Nazareth, the Arab capital of the Galilee, a lone Rakah activist decided to ease the reins of restraint far more than his party superiors had approved, and spurred by his exhortations a crowd of demonstrators attacked the police station with stones. (Afterward, when the other partners to the strike accused Rakah of violating the decision to shun violence, the party's leaders claimed that the assault had been the work of "marginal elements.") Even more unsettling were the events in Wadi Ara, where demonstrators from the Arab city of Um al-Fahm blocked the main road connecting the coastal plain with the Jezreel Valley. The mayor of Um al-Fahm is a Rakah man, but the radical Sons of the Village movement enjoys a particularly large following there, as do a number of militant religious elements. The closing of the road was anything but a peaceful maneuver. In what appeared like a human-wave assault to the small unit of police sent to Um al-Fahm with strict orders not to fire on demonstrators, young men streamed down the slopes lining the road and began hurling Molotov cocktails and volleys of stones. The reinforcements summoned to cope with the violence failed to arrive because at precisely that time an urgent call for help had come from Nazareth, where the police station was under siege. The result was that a main axis of transport in the very center of Israel was rendered impassable for close to two hours.

If the previous weeks of violence in the territories had left any Israelis untouched, the outbursts on "Peace Day" finally shocked them out of their complacency, for suddenly the turmoil had crossed the invisible line that continued to exist in the Israeli imagination and had infiltrated the country's heartland. Clearly no one could flee from the Palestinian problem now; far from being confined to the territories, it had surfaced in all its virulence within walking distance of downtown Tel Aviv. The initial response to this rude awakening by the country's ruling circles was predictably bellicose. The head of the Likud faction in the Knesset, Chaim Kaufmann, impetuously suggested that the military government that had been in force over the Israeli-Arab community from 1948 to 1966 promptly be reinstated. Prime Minister Shamir and his followers cited the violence as proof of their oft-repeated claims against the Palestinians. "This is not a struggle for a Palestinian state in the territories," they harangued. "It's an all-out struggle against the State of Israel. [The Palestinians] have their eyes on Tel Aviv and Haifa as well. They want everything!"

On closer examination it turned out—and not for the first time— that reactions of this sort missed the point. What "Peace Day" revealed was not the innate hostility of its participants but the extraordinary power of its organizers. This was the second time that leaders of the Israeli-Arab community had demonstrated an ability to rally their constituents to action on a nationwide scale. (The first was the strike on "Equality Day," June 24, 1987, when the issue had been government discrimination against the Arab community in the allocation of funds for education, development, and other spheres that come under the jurisdiction of the local and municipal councils.) "Peace Day" was observed by the overwhelming majority of Israel's Arabs (only among the Druze and Bedouin communities was the response notably poor). Some 80 percent of the Arab employees stayed away from their jobs, and as a rule the few who did show up in Jewish factories and businesses had taken the precaution of spending the previous night outside their villages, so that they would not have to run the gauntlet of friends and neighbors on their way to work.

Beyond demonstrating that the Arabs of Israel have cultivated a talented and outspoken leadership, the success of "Peace Day" accorded these leaders a sense of power and confidence they had not enjoyed before. The fact that various quarters of the Jewish public had expressed understanding for the motives of the rioters in the territories gave their Arab countrymen the hope that there was also a degree of understanding for their own protest action. Equally important, the Jewish public was made aware of the interplay between the events in the territories and the new mood among Israel's Arabs. The Arabs of Israel had clearly chosen to demonstrate their identification with the *intifada,* though most of them were careful to maintain the distinction between identification and actual participation.

Even in its opening days, then, the Palestinian uprising was able to boast a number of impressive achievements. The rebellion that had spread from Gaza to the West Bank reached new heights in Jerusalem; the Arabs of Israel had demonstrated support for their Palestinian brothers; and the Arab world, at least, was awash with rhetoric extolling the heroism of the generation raised in the shadow of the occupation. On December 22 the United Nations Security Council passed a resolution denouncing Israel for its response to the violence (with the United States pointedly refraining from the exercise of its veto). Reports from Western capitals spoke of growing sympathy for the "Palestinian David" in its struggle with the "Israeli Goliath"—and all this had happened in the space of a few weeks! The PLO knew that aggravating the chaos and bloodshed would strengthen its demand to have an international force, or at least United Nations Observers, sent to the territories. Most Palestinians therefore had ample reason to keep the rebellion going while trying to create more effective channels of organization. After weeks of running wild, the "fighting public" in the territories was thirsty for firm leadership—and there was no dearth of candidates to supply it.

FIVE

BETWEEN ROCKS AND A HARD PLACE

ON THE OPPOSITE SIDE of the barricades, the situation had a rather different slant to it. There seemed to be no lack of people with ready advice on how to handle the uprising, and not one of them had a good word to say for the army—though not for the reasons one might tend to expect. The minority view in the Israeli cabinet* was expressed by Ezer Weizman at the first meeting held after Rabin's return from America, which was also its first serious discussion of the *intifada*. Typically, Weizman minced no words in stating his position.

"Get out of Jebalya and let them burn each other up!" he barked at the chief of staff when he had completed his situation report. Shomron, a man of very different temperament, returned Weizman's glower with a blank stare and icy silence, leaving the defense minister to speak for the army. Rabin was quick to oblige.

"What are you talking about?" he snapped. "They'll burn Jebalya, and then the fire will spread everywhere!"

This prickly exchange between the two Labor ministers was but a mild expression of the political controversy surrounding the IDF. Actually it was quite by chance that the criticism came from Weizman that day. As the uprising dragged on, more often than not the com-

---

* Because of its unwieldy size, with twenty-four ministers, the Israeli government was further subdivided into two bodies: the ten-member cabinet, which operated as a Ministerial Committee for Security Affairs; and the informal "committee of prime ministers," including only Shamir, Rabin, and Peres.

manders of the army heard the most bitter criticism—and of a diametrically opposite nature—from the Likud ministers. Thus for the second time in five years, the Israeli army found itself being sent into action despite a deep division in Israeli society over the way it was being employed and the aims it was to achieve. The first controversy of this kind, sparked by the war in Lebanon and stoked by broad public protests, centered on the government's misuse of the IDF to realize farfetched political goals. This time, however, though opposition to the government's policy was again in evidence, the strongest criticism was directed against the army proper. And it came not from the public but from a number of ministers, primarily of the Likud Party, who hammered away at the message that the army was either too squeamish or too inept to suppress the uprising quickly and, either way, was simply not doing its job. History is filled with examples of armies that failed to prevail in war because the governments they served imposed crippling constraints on them. During the *intifada*, however, the stereotypes of ruddy, reckless generals and pale, prudent pols were suddenly reversed, and it was the politicians who scored the army for being "too soft." The upshot was that even the toughest field commanders came out looking more temperate and restrained than some of the self-styled statesmen seated round the cabinet table.

The most aggressive in his complaints against the IDF's handling of the rebellion was Yitzhak Moda'i of the Likud's Liberal Party.* Well known for his quick wit and sharp tongue, Moda'i, an ex-finance minister, was not particularly noted for his military acumen—beyond the battlefields of Liberal Party politics. Nevertheless, he was quick to take the IDF to task. "If the army is incapable of quashing the uprising," he snarled during one of the meetings devoted to the *intifada*, "its commanders should come right out and say so"—the implication of course being that they should step aside and give someone else a chance to do the job. The chief of staff was not insensitive to such innuendo, but neither was he about to run the army on the basis of vague, albeit stinging, comments. "The army is acting according to the government's instructions" was all he would say in tossing the ball back to the ministers. But his message to them was equally clear: if they did not agree with his handling of the affair, the cabinet would have to issue, and assume direct responsibility for, specific directives on how it wanted the army to proceed. And although he never used the word resignation,

* Formally speaking, until recently the Likud was not a political party in itself but a block of two right-wing parties, Herut and the Liberals.

Shomron's statements strongly intimated that if the majority of the ministers were dissatisfied with his performance or issued orders by which he could not abide, he would not hesitate to relinquish his post.

That, however, was not the way the ministers chose to play the game. Instead, what was never said explicitly in cabinet meetings came out in cynically calculated leaks and snide insinuations about "leftist generals" who were disinclined to suppress the uprising because it vindicated their political philosophy. One paper published the unattributed swipe that when the General Staff wants something badly enough—as it did the IDF's withdrawal from Lebanon or the cancellation of the project to build the Lavie fighter plane—it hasn't the least compunction about demanding it of the government in no uncertain terms. But in the course of the *intifada*, no demands were made for greater leeway in attacking the problem; no commander could be heard clamoring for the right to exercise an "iron fist" against the insurgents. The obvious conclusion, the paper reasoned, was that the high command preferred to use "kid gloves" in dealing with the Palestinians.

Dan Shomron never lost his composure during these skirmishes with the ministers, though clearly he was peeved by the barrage of reprobation. Yet the brunt of the criticism was aimed not at the chief of staff himself but directly at Maj. Gen. Amram Mitzna, the head of Central Command. A bearded, soft-spoken kibbutznik, Mitzna was clearly too open-minded for right-wing tastes. His outspoken criticism of the settlers who had rampaged through the Deheishe refugee camp a few months before the uprising, or who otherwise used the guns given them for self-defense to punish and intimidate Palestinians, had raised many a scowl in the Likud and the parties further to the right. Mitzna's opponents also had a powerful ally in Ariel Sharon, who had forgotten neither the general's criticism of him as minister of defense during the Lebanon war nor his request for a leave of absence in protest over Sharon's refusal to resign after the Sabra and Shatila massacre. Indeed, when Mitzna was promoted to major general and posted as head of Central Command, in whose jurisdiction most of the Palestinian population and Jewish settlements are concentrated, Sharon made sure that the chief of staff was apprised of his fury over the appointment. But Shomron did not even flinch. In fact he backed Mitzna so staunchly that the messenger who brought word of Sharon's displeasure could well have come away with the impression that the chief of staff would take any censure of Mitzna to be a personal attack upon himself.

It is not difficult to see why Mitzna's approach set noses out of joint on the Israeli Right. At the height of the riots he reminded his officers that in subduing the uprising Israel could not afford to alienate the Palestinian population completely or prejudice future negotiations toward a political settlement. The right-wingers wanted less finesse and more clout from their generals. At one meeting Sharon dressed Mitzna down for the mild punitive measures being employed against the Palestinians, while other Likud ministers decried the army's leniency in applying collective punishments. Another member of the Likud's Liberal wing, Justice Minister Avraham Sharir, offered his considered opinion that if destroying the homes of people suspected of sabotage and murder did not have a sufficiently daunting effect, whole blocks of buildings should be demolished—whereupon Yitzhak Moda'i chimed in, "The IDF has been given an assignment and should carry it out!"

"It seems to me," said Mitzna when given leave to reply, "that some of the ministers fail to grasp the implications of what has been said here. Israel is a country ruled by law, and the IDF must operate within the confines of that law."

Hearing the remark as an attempt to preach to the ministers, Sharon started as though he had been bitten by a snake. Shamir let it be known that he was likewise offended by the comment, leaving Mitzna with little choice but to apologize.

Still, the moral and legal considerations involved in setting the army against civilians continued to preoccupy the men responsible for its actions in the field. They were aired not only by Mitzna and at closed meetings but by other generals and on public occasions—indeed, sometimes in the most unlikely of places. Speaking before hundreds of Jewish settlers in Kiryat Arba outside Hebron, for example, the head of Southern Command, Yitzhak Mordechai, dwelled on the high moral standards that the IDF had always tried to inculcate in its men. Kiryat Arba had long been known as a hotbed of anti-Arab militancy, and Mordechai—an officer known for his no-nonsense approach to his duties—was far from what the settlers mocked as a "bleeding heart." Yet on that occasion, in the presence of the prime minister, he too chose to stress that anyone who believed that the army would discard an entire system of values or tailor it to the demands of the "war" that Israel was fighting in the territories was laboring under a grave delusion. Not that this difference of opinion was settled on Mordechai's say-so. When Yitzhak Moda'i—one of the few ministers who bothered to visit the Israeli forces in the territories—came to Mordechai's own bailiwick, the Gaza Strip, he took the trouble to declare that if the

Likud won the forthcoming elections, the uprising would be put down within less than three weeks. He did not accept Mordechai's assessment that if the IDF fired indiscriminately into crowds, for example, it would imperil not only innocent civilians but a whole way of life and that the Israeli public would not stand for such behavior.

Moda'i and Mordechai were not the only two men in the cabinet-army face-off to contradict each other. Other members of the General Staff made statements that clashed head-on with the official line presented by the prime minister himself. "I don't see anyone representing the residents of the territories other than the PLO," Maj. Gen. Amnon Shahak, the head of Intelligence Branch, publicly observed. And contrary to Shamir's assurances that the uprising would burn itself out quickly, Gen. Mitzna warned that it could go on for years! He also stressed, as did the chief of staff, that the army could deal with only the symptoms of the *intifada*, not with its causes. Its task was to ensure that law, order, and a satisfactory level of security were maintained, but that was not to be confused with addressing the reason for the civil disorders.

This was the crux of the dispute between the generals and the ministers from the Likud: Dan Shomron, Amram Mitzna, and other members of the General Staff repeatedly stated that the solution to the *intifada* could not be a military one. The uprising, they explained, was a political problem and would have to be attacked by political means. Not that they argued against the use of force to contain the violence; obviously Israel could not abide by a situation of anarchy. But they wanted no illusions that military repression would dissolve the reasons behind the uprising, and they insisted that since those reasons were primarily political, only a political solution would assuage them. It was as though the IDF command were saying to the Israeli government, "It is not our place to intervene in political affairs, and we would not presume to tell you what the best course is for Israel. All we are saying is that while the IDF can subdue the violence to a certain degree, at some point the government of Israel will have to deal with the problem through political measures."

There was hardly anything outlandish or even original about this approach. Rabin himself had said as much in declaring that Israel would not be able to solve the Palestinian problem by force (though he warned that neither would it allow its actions to be dictated by Palestinian violence). But a large sector of the Likud, and certainly of the parties to the right of it, would not hear of such reasoning from Rabin or the generals. Sharon, for one, insisted that the solution to the *intifada* lay purely in military action—implying that raw repression would do the trick—and he was enraged that the generals suggested otherwise.

Another object of contention was similarly a matter of principle and had to do with the constraints upon the IDF in dealing with the violence. Again and again the generals explained that moral considerations aside, the army operated within the framework of the law. Thus a soldier could not be ordered to use his weapon contrary to its provisions, for if he did so and was brought to trial, he would not be entitled to claim in his defense that he had acted under orders from his commander—or a general, or the chief of staff, or even the minister of defense. When it comes to actions that are patently illegal, Israeli soldiers bear personal responsibility for their deeds. Ministers, on the other hand, are covered by parliamentary immunity, so that it was easy for them to suggest that soldiers should wantonly shoot Arabs; they ran no risk of prosecution for advising others to commit criminal acts. In one exchange on this subject, the chief of staff went so far as to say that if the IDF acted in contravention of the law, it would cease to be an army and deteriorate into a rabble—to which Ariel Sharon retorted that in that case the law would just have to be changed!

As time passed, though deterrent measures grew steadily harsher, the dispute between the General Staff and some of the Likud ministers remained in force because it derived from clashing world views, not merely differences over the correct operational approach. Those who denied that the uprising had resulted from the pressures and exigencies of the occupation insisted that it could be suppressed by force. They were confident that once put down it would never rear its head again, and they necessarily regarded the solution as solely a military matter. Following their logic, if the uprising had continued for months, the only explanation was that Israel had failed to exercise its power properly. Hence there was something wrong with the army's orders, their implementation, or the people issuing them. As far as most of the Likud ministers were concerned, the problem lay not in their perception of the situation but in the way the army and the security services were handling it.

Given these profound and persistent differences, the prime minister and his cabinet faced the ticklish question of whether to forbid the generals to express their opinions. Should they gag the man who headed Israel's intelligence effort and was responsible for assessing the state of the country's security? Or require field commanders to keep their observations to themselves? In the summer of 1988 tension between the cabinet and the high command became so aggravated that, on his own responsibility, Rabin came to a General Staff meeting and asked the generals to be more circumspect in expressing their views in public. A few Likud ministers did their best to dispel the impression that a credibility gap existed between their colleagues and the General Staff, but the problem could not be concealed. After the incident in which a teenage girl from one of the Jewish settlements was killed in the village of Beita while on a hike in the northern West Bank, some of the Likud ministers refused to accept the conclusions reached by the army and the Shin Bet, namely, that the girl had been killed by bullets discharged from the gun of the Israeli escort and that the people of Beita had not shot at the hikers at all. Just before the cabinet was to discuss the findings, a number of these ministers convened a separate session with some of the youngsters who had been on that hike and proceeded to interrogate them in a crude effort to discredit the investigation done by the country's security organs!

Late in the spring of 1988, the Likud ministers decided it was in the best interests of all concerned to shift their criticism of the General Staff onto the defense minister. They began portraying Rabin as the real culprit for failing to make the army act more forcefully. At one point Sharon even demanded that the prime minister exercise his prerogative and fire Rabin (a most unlikely prospect, considering the composition of Israel's National Unity Government). Moreover, what Sharon was saying in speeches and over the airwaves many other Likudniks were saying in private, abroad as well as at home: if they had been in charge of the Defense Ministry, the *intifada* would have been over long ago.

The fact is that Rabin really was the man to reckon with on the handling of the uprising, for the army's campaign was actually being directed not by the General Staff but by a special body called the Territories Forum. The General Staff executed policy, but it was this forum, a nonmilitary group headed by the defense minister, that was formulating policy. Rabin invited to the forum's weekly meetings all the bodies operating in the territories, regardless of whether they were in the Defense Ministry's jurisdiction. The forum was composed of the chief of staff and his area commanders, the coordinator of operations in the territories, the prime minister's military adjutant, a senior representative of the Shin Bet, a representative of the police, the army spokesman, and the defense minister's mdia adviser. None of these participants had the least doubt that the man who was making the decisions and directing this war, for better or for worse, was Rabin himself. He delved into the smallest details and followed up decisions to see that they were carried out satisfactorily. Because of his temperament, Dan Shomron accepted the role of a staff officer, rather than fight for his prerogatives as commander of the forces fighting the *intifada*. The result was that—more than any of Israel's earlier wars, and certainly no less than the 1982 invasion of Lebanon—the campaign against the *intifada* was run by Israel's defense minister. Its achievements and failures were primarily his, and Rabin essentially admitted as much in declaring that any complaints about the subject should be addressed to him.

Still, the generals sensed that this shift of the criticism onto Rabin was merely tactical. As long as complaints against the army came from the settlers—who howled that they were not receiving the protection they deserved—and from liberals or the Left—who charged that Israel's soldiers were using excessive force—the high command was prepared to live with them. But it was understandably touchy about the criticism coming from politicians, on either side of the aisle, for ever since the start of the uprising it seemed that the political echelon had conveniently absolved itself of all responsibility for the situation and dumped it on the army instead. Paradoxical though it seems, considering the standard in most other democracies, in Israel one was more likely to find people of genuine liberal leanings in the senior ranks of the army than in the parallel level of government. The sanest bady in the country—in terms of contending with the *intifada*, at least—was the IDF General Staff!

In the middle of January, when it was already obvious that the violence was not just another round of sporadic rioting, the IDF changed its deployment in the territories. Two divisional commands divided the West Bank between them and a third was established in the Gaza Strip, whereupon the territories filled with thousands of soldiers. As in wartime, new commands were created and outside units were attached to them for the purpose of carrying out their new tasks. One of these commands, which received responsibility for the northern West Bank (Samaria), was that of a standing armored division whose men left their tanks, APCs, and field guns to patrol the streets with tear gas and clubs. The units attached to this command as reinforcements came from every corner of the IDF: tank crews, paratroopers, artillerymen, engineers—conscripts and reservists alike. They were also joined by draftees who had barely completed basic training and were still wet behind the ears. Boys fresh out of boot camp, trained for elite combat units like the Paratroops and the Golani Brigade, found that their first assignment was to chase after stone-throwing children. Even the young men in flight school—the cream of their generation—rotated into the territories, and when a large detention camp was set up at Ketziot in the Negev, the Air Force took on the unsavory task of guarding it. As pressure on the IDF mounted, even volunteers came forth to help shoulder the burden: veteran reserve officers from the kibbutzim and moshavim asked to be called up and serve in the territories alongside the young conscripts during this "difficult hour" for the Israel Defense Forces. The number of men swelled to the point where it proved necessary to open up the emergency stores and draw on equipment usually reserved for wartime.

But the real import of the change ran in other directions. Suddenly thousands of young Israelis discovered the occupied territories, their inhabitants, and above all the refugee camps—which had always been beyond the pale to the average Israeli—and for many this encounter was a great shock. It was as if they had suddenly stumbled upon a dark, dirty secret about the occupation, a side of it they had never been forced to consider before. Neither was this a freak encounter or one they would be spared again in the future. Over the previous twenty years, a few companies of Border Police and a few hundred soldiers had done all the "dirty work" of an occupying force. From time to time a reserve unit was assigned to duty in the territories, and the army relied on the fact that if the Military Government needed further help, reinforcements could always be sent from one of the training bases in the area. But now, with the *intifada* in full swing, the occupation could no longer be maintained by a skeleton force.

The irony was that all the reinforcements pumped into the territories did not seem to suffice. By early January the trouble spots were as common in the cities of Nablus, Jenin, Hebron, Kalkilya, and Tulkarem as in the refugee camps across the West Bank. More and more villages built barricades on their access roads and proclaimed themselves "liberated territory." The uprising posed a major threat to traffic, and wherever they turned it appeared to the troops that their presence was no longer a deterrent. Since all the points of rebellion could not be dealt with simultaneously, the army turned first to the cities, leaving the "liberated" villages for later.

Other than the persistent violence, the most prominent expression of rebellion in the cities was the all-out commercial strike, and the army seemed unsure about how to handle it. Given the choice of forcing the merchants to open their shops and serve the public (for which the Israeli administration was, after all, responsible) or leaving the Palestinians to stew in their own juice, the army seemed to change its policy from day to day. First it tried to compel the shopkeepers to open their stores; then it decided to weld the shutters closed on the striking shops so that their owners would not be able to open them when they chose to. The effect of this battle of wills with the Palestinian tradesmen—many of whom were striking under duress—was to draw still more people into the circle of enmity. Four months after the outbreak of the strike, a decision was made to ignore it, since the Palestinians suffered from it the most. Yet the situation was not quite so simple; for by living with the strike, Israel had effectively reconciled itself to the main symbol of defiance and the disruption of normal life.

It took less time for the IDF to appreciate that because of varying conditions, the uprising could not be handled identically in the West Bank and the Gaza Strip. While Gaza can easily be isolated from the Palestinian heartland, the West Bank *is* that heartland. Moreover, the fact that East Jerusalem is an integral part of the West Bank had a profound effect on the rebellion there. Jerusalem means the holy places and access to foreign consulates, news outlets, international agencies, and the headquarters of Palestinian organizations, while Gaza is remote from these centers of activity; not even the Israeli media have local correspondents there. The Strip can also be isolated—cordoned off, if necessary—because there are no more than four or five ways of entering it, whereas travelers have access to the West Bank on some 250 different roads (a point raised by the army when the government considered barring the press from the territories). The settlers and other Israelis traveling to the Katif area in the southern part of the Strip can easily bypass the teeming center of Gaza, the refugee camps, and the other cities, but those headed for the many settlements in the West Bank have no choice but to drive through Arab cities or past villages and simmering refugee camps. The number of Israelis traveling in the two areas is likewise very different: only 2,500 Israelis live in the Katif area, but some 70,000 people populate the Israeli towns and settlements on the West Bank, and most of them travel the roads regularly because they earn their living within the Green Line. Even differences in topography come into play, Gaza being a flat plain and the West Bank a mountainous area cut by many wadis.

The choice of an operational plan was influenced by economic differences, as well. The Gaza Strip was all but completely dependent on Israel in this sense, whereas the West Bank had its own agricultural and industrial resources and greater reserves for holding out under Israeli pressure. On the other hand, the Gaza Strip was harder to handle from the standpoint of the population density and the fact that its indigent populace had little to lose. In addition, the fanatic Muslim element was far more active in the Gaza Strip than in the West Bank.

There were also differences dictated by political frontiers. Because the uprising extended beyond the territories ruled by the Military Government, the task of suppressing it was not handled exclusively by the army and the Ministry of Defense. The army was not responsible for events in East Jerusalem, for example, although it was there that the uprising's political and media activities were centered. The result was a series of blatant contradictions attesting to poor coordination in Israel's struggle against the uprising. In the territories the army often shot at people raising or flying Palestinian flags and forced elderly Arabs to erase slogans from walls, while in East Jerusalem the Democratic Front was allowed to hold an impressive show of strength by having its members march, in uniform, at the funeral of a comrade who had died of an illness while serving a long prison term. The procession was even joined by two Arab members of the Knesset!

Considering the sum of these factors and lacking experience in quelling a mass civilian uprising, the IDF had to find its way by trial and considerable error, with a chorus of critics at its back. The most strident and persistent of them was Ariel Sharon, who harped on the claim that he held the key to the problem—indeed, that he had already solved it once and could readily do so again. He was referring to the outbreak of terrorism that had rocked the Gaza Strip at the start of the 1970s. But the equation he drew between that period and the *intifada* was transparently fallacious, for the struggle then had been against a few hundred armed men, with the civilian population of Gaza staying well clear of the strife. In the early 1970s most Gazans were too interested in exploiting the opportunity to earn their living inside the Green Line to jeopardize it in any way. Hence there was little doubt that as soon as the troublemakers were captured, the wave of violence that had convulsed Gaza would pass.

And that is precisely what happened. As head of Southern Command, Ariel Sharon had his forces relentlessly stalk the terrorists—many of whom were hiding in bunkers—and their number dwindled from week to week. Often Sharon found that he was having a harder time with his own superiors than with the people of Gaza, because the chief of staff and minister of defense tended to be wary of his zeal and were reluctant to approve the actions he proposed. The issue then was whether to extend the pressure of punitive measures to the population at large, so as to keep new people from joining the terrorist groups. Sharon was not concerned about causing casualties as long as he was able to instill a healthy fear of the army in the residents of Gaza, but his superiors refused to endorse this approach. In retrospect they were right in believing that harsh deterrent measures were not necessary, for as soon as most of the terrorists were caught, the Gaza Strip quieted down for a long while. Once it had, moreover, Defense Minister Moshe Dayan decided to transfer responsibility for the Strip from Southern to Central Command—a highly artificial arrangement that was obviously enacted to wrest the area from Sharon's control. Thus in flaunting his experience with terrorism in Gaza, Sharon was distorting the issue considerably, as the *intifada* bore little relation to the situation almost two decades earlier. Not a collection of desperate terrorists but the entire population, from children to the elderly, was engaged in the struggle now, and their weapons were stones, not guns.

Almost as soon as the *intifada* broke out, the army began to debate the use of punitive measures as a way of quelling the unrest without causing physical injury. No other army has ever made this formula work, for the critical balance of its components is so delicate that it inevitably shatters. Nevertheless, as the riots spread the IDF was pressured to punish the rebellious population without mercy, and suggestions on how to do so were aired freely by ministers, the Knesset Foreign Affairs and Defense Committee, even retired military men. Like the French in Algeria, many Israelis believed that the "iron fist" was a sure panacea. Every lull in the rioting was instantly hailed as a return to quiet and stability. When the violence inevitably resumed, the setback was received with bafflement and demands for ever more vigorous measures. Like other regimes and ruling classes that had encountered similar defiance, the Israelis took the uprising personally. They saw it as an act of impudence, an affront to the prestige of the state and often to their own personal honor. The government and media tried to portray it as a spate of "civil disorders," rather than a mass popular revolt, and as an isolated event, rather than the climax of a long, all-embracing process. At first the insurgents were depicted as rabble-rousers disturbing the peace of their fellow-Palestinians, whose only desire was to continue living amicably under Israeli domination. As the rebellion mounted they were described as an unruly mob that understands only the language of force. If these refrains sound familiar it is because, with eyes wide open, Israel was repeating the mistakes made by the British in India, the French in Algeria, and the Americans in Vietnam.

As more and more voices demanded stringent action, the military establishment found itself in a difficult quandary. "People are constantly pressuring us to come down hard on [the Palestinians]," Dan Shomron related. "But I'm also thinking about the future, about the question of who we will have to live with here, and I'm trying not to burn our bridges." Indeed, the army's senior command exercised considerable restraint in allowing the use of collective punishment and in framing the directives for opening fire on civilians. The army could have obtained Rabin's permission for almost any punitive measure it desired. In fact the defense minister had given the chief of staff and regional commanders carte blanche to administer almost anything classified as a punishment: widespread arrests, the demolition of houses, even preventing the Arab population of cities or whole regions from reaching their jobs in Israel.

Thus the choice of a strategy for quashing the uprising was dependent upon the army more than any other body—and the army remained cautious. It was not eager to allow its men to fire at people throwing Molotov cocktails, for example, for fear that casual bystanders would also be harmed. The senior command also reasoned, and explained to Rabin, that among the thousands of soldiers injected into the territories were men who were likely to pull the trigger without thinking twice, either because they were frightened or because their political philosophy commended it. Hence a broad license to shoot could lead the army into precisely the situation it was trying to avoid. Rabin accepted this argument and left the decision on drawing up guidelines to the chief of staff and the area commanders—that is, until firebombs became a common occurrence. Once it transpired that the insurgents were intent upon using them along the main arteries, especially to precipitate clashes with the settlers, Rabin issued unequivocal orders to shoot anyone hurling a Molotov cocktail, regardless of the circumstances. He also insisted that prompt and harsh punitive measures be taken against suspects, including the demolition or sealing of their houses. And it must be said that this policy of swift retribution resulted almost immediately in a sharp decline in the use of firebombs.

Of course the army's caution and self-restraint did not hold under all circumstances, especially as its commanders were under pressure from below as well as above. The rank-and-file was demanding permission to shoot in response to any provocation—often in the hope that their weapons would compensate for the injury to their pride—and a good many of their direct commanders, from junior to middle-level officers, supported this approach. But the chief of staff, his deputy, Ehud Barak, and the commanders of the two areas affected by the uprising, Yitzhak Mordechai and Amram Mitzna, were torn between two fears. Though concerned that a ban on using weapons would result in a collapse of discipline and damage to moral, they were equally worried that too broad a license to shoot would cause the IDF, which had always prided itself on being a moral and humane army, to sink to the level of ruthlessness for the sake of expedience.

What could not be avoided was the extensive use of collective punishment, and the longer the uprising continued, the more the IDF found itself resorting to tactics that ranged from cutting off phones and electricity to placing extended curfews on villages, towns, and whole cities, which made it impossible for tens of thousands of people to go to work. The uprooting of trees and occasionally whole orchards that had served as cover for people throwing firebombs left ugly scars on the countryside. Demolishing the homes of those involved in sabotage actions or caught with Molotov cocktails (a policy inherited from the British, who had practiced it liberally during their mandate over Palestine) could likewise be classified as collective punishment, since all the members of a family suffered by it. Until the *intifada* the decision to exercise these options had required the approval of the defense minister, but as the rebellion spread their authorization was left to the area commanders. A similar process affected the uprooting of trees, which could be ordered only by an area commander at the start of the uprising but was subsequently left to the discretion of a divisional one. A divisional commander was also entitled to impose a curfew for up to a week, along with widespread arrests, in any city in the territories.

Next to deportation, the demolition of houses was considered the harshest punishment applied in the territories, and it often elicited emotional reactions from Israeli no less than Palestinian witnesses. Soldiers and their officers, all the way up to the senior command, were the first to admit that turning whole families out of their homes and destroying a building while its residents stood by keening and wailing was the worst assignment they had to carry out. "I console myself with the thought that this punishment may lessen the violence," remarked a senior officer who was in charge of dozens of demolition and sealing actions, "but deep in my heart I know that what we're doing will prompt others to react against us violently in revenge." Once considered an extraordinary measure used only against terrorists who had confessed to grave acts of sabotage, the demolition of houses became a common means of administrative punishment during the *intifada*. It was even employed in East Jerusalem, where the Israeli authorities had been careful to avoid resort to administrative punishment since 1967.

Gen. Mitzna, who was convinced of the deterrent effect of these demolition actions, was able to cite cases in which fugitives had been turned in by members of their own families in return for assurances that their homes would be spared. In other instances villages sent word to the authorities that they would do their best to maintain order if this particular sanction was not used against them. Yet despite its effectiveness, Mitzna did not recommend extending the use of demolition or turning it into regular procedure—as the settlers and their supporters were demanding—for to retain its impact it would have to be a highly selective means of punishment. Indeed, when the demolition of houses became more widespread, the tone of the reaction to it changed. As the deafening crack of the explosion and rumble of collapsing masonry faded, shouts of "*Allahu akbar!*"—"Allah is great," the traditional battle cry of the Arab *jihad*—could be heard resounding through whole neighborhoods and villages as an ominous sign of defiance.

Questions also began to be raised about the wisdom of punishment by deportation. Despite the controversy over the legality of this course,* deportation orders were issued against fifty-eight people in the first two years of the uprising. Of the range of administrative punishments, deportation was presumed by almost all the Israeli security experts to be the most dreaded. Thus as the *intifada* spread, so did the pressure from the settlers and other elements on the Right, including ministers, to deport hundreds of agitators and members of the popular committees (the community-level leadership) in one fell swoop. Their assumption was that the shock caused by such a wholesale expulsion would have a deeply sobering effect upon the recalcitrant Palestinians. A compromise was reached in the decision to prepare deportation orders against

---

* Article 49 of the Fourth Geneva Convention (1949), to which Israel is a signatory, prohibits "individual or mass forcible transfers, as well as deportation of protected persons from occupied territory . . . regardless of their motive." However, Israel's High Court of Justice has ruled that it cannot issue a judgment based on this protocol because it has not entered the canon of Israeli law via legislation by the Knesset.

twenty-five heads of popular committees. Some concerned citizens, including Israel's president, Chaim Herzog, suggested that deportation be made a provisory punishment and that the orders be rescinded if the candidates renounced their actions and mended their ways.

Not until the *intifada* had entered its fifteenth month was the deportation policy reconsidered, and then Rabin confessed that it might not be a particularly efficacious one. In the past the subject had always been approached solely from the security standpoint, with the sole consideration being the impact of a particular deportation on the events of the day. How these deportations would affect the state of the Palestinian leadership in the territories was never seriously examined. Nor did anyone stop to consider whether Israel was not, in fact, repeating the mistake it had made at the end of the 1960s, when it deported hundreds of Palestinian leaders (including many pro-Jordanians) who are regarded by today's standards as moderate and pragmatic. It was hard to miss the paradox of Israel's quickness to deport anyone who showed signs of genuine leadership while complaining that there were no Palestinians of stature in the territories to talk to about negotiating a settlement. The Palestinians who were prepared to denounce terrorism (like the leaders of the much-derided and now defunct Village Leagues) were scorned by Israel as not representing the mainstream, while those who did give authentic expression to the Palestinian mood were promptly booted out. Many of the security experts who recommended the deportations were aware of this internal contradiction, as well as the ambivalent effect of the policy. But rather than lock horns with the cabinet— divided as it was into two camps that perceived the Israeli-Palestinian conflict in radically different ways—they contented themselves with weighing the issue according to its narrowest and most immediate implications.

The collective punishments were unquestionably painful to the Palestinian population, but they did not quell the uprising. On the contrary, they may well have stiffened the resistance of the Palestinians, and certainly they contributed to a deepening of their enmity. There were places where the IDF tried to break the spirit of the inhabitants and conspicuously failed to do so. The two examples that immediately come to mind are the large village of Kabatya in the northern West Bank and the al-Bourej refugee camp in the Gaza Strip. Kabatya was chosen for such treatment because it had been the scene of the lynching of a collaborator, who had undoubtedly sealed his fate by killing a four-year-old child while shooting at the mob that descended on his home to get him. After surrounding the house for hours, during which the victim's desperate calls for help went unanswered, the people of Kabatya finally broke into it, stabbed and beat the man to death, and strung his corpse up from an electricity pole as a gruesome warning to others of his kind. Repelled by such behavior, the senior command decided to punish the entire village in the belief that only a vigorous response would prevent similar attacks from occurring elsewhere. Kabatya was literally placed under siege. Dozens of people were arrested and all work was halted in its marble quarries and fields. Even the electricity was cut off, and food was allowed into the village by special permission only. These conditions continued for weeks. Yet although Kabatya's *mukhtars* assured the army that all their constituents were peace-loving people, other suspected collaborators woke up each day to find coffins standing under their windows. And a few days after the siege was lifted, Palestinian flags could again be seen flying from electricity poles, as though the villagers were telling their erstwhile jailers: "You haven't broken us after all!"

The army decided to make an example of the al-Bourej refugee camp due to the resignation of its local council, which was read as an act of defiance. The message it wanted to convey to the people of al-Bourej was that if they did not abandon their course of civil disobedience and resume the management of their own affairs, the army would be forced to run the camp and they would find themselves considerably inconvenienced. Here, too, a concentration of no less than 18,000 residents was placed under siege, with the electricity cut off and restrictions placed on the entry of food and supplies. Only residents with permission (in the form of a green card specially issued for the operation) were allowed out to their jobs in Israel. As part of the punishment, all debts to the tax authorities were collected with inordinate vigor, so that even the bearers of green cards could not leave the camp without first proving that they were in good standing with the tax collector. High school students stopped at demonstrations were barred from taking their matriculation exams. Enormous pressure was applied in every field and every quarter. But despite it all, the population would not give ground. One group or another held a protest demonstration almost every evening, and young people made a habit of sleeping in the orchards near the camp to avoid the threat of arrest. Other regimes might have taken far more drastic steps, but due to its social and political makeup Israel could go only so far in applying collective punishments—and that was not far enough to break the people of al-Bourej.

□

As collective punishments proved to be of limited value, the search for more effective measures continued. A few weeks into the uprising Israel's soldiers were equipped with clubs and given permission to beat their adversaries. Oddly enough, considering the firestorm of criticism it brought down on Israel—even by Jews who had long supported the state and some no-less-questionable policies of its successive governments—this new approach was instituted quite casually, almost incidentally. In analyzing their problems in handling demonstrations, many field officers noted that the frustrating game in which armed soldiers chased after the youngsters who had just provoked them was probably the most degrading situation of all for the Israelis. Instead of waiting for the Palestinians to taunt and attack, they believed the Israelis should be seeking contact with the demonstrators. Such an approach would also keep the soldiers from opening fire unnecessarily, because it was the distance between the troops and the stone throwers that encouraged shooting whenever a missile hit its mark.

This was the thinking behind the introduction of the club as a tool of riot control. Before distributing these new weapons to thousands of its soldiers, the IDF had been typically thorough in investigating which item would suit its needs. It checked and double-checked various options until it had found the best bludgeon money could buy: light, easy to handle, and not likely to break even when administering the heaviest of blows. (Ironically, the firms that manufactured these clubs employed mostly Arab workers from the Gaza Strip, so that it was Palestinians who produced the truncheons used to beat their brothers.) Yet thorough as it was in choosing these weapons, the army proved to be less responsible in issuing guidelines for their use. The official order accompanying the clubs, which had Rabin's publicly stated backing, was to apply force—meaning to beat rioters. As a rule of thumb that might have sufficed. But as a considered directive to the men at the "front," it was simply too vague and allowed for too much freedom, so that predictably, perhaps, its immediate effect was to let a rather mean genie out of the bottle. "We did not appreciate the full implications of the order," Amram Mitzna confessed in retrospect, and in one case in which soldiers were tried for the results of a beating—namely, the death of a Palestinian from Gaza—Shomron himself was called to testify about the intent of the order, because so many interpretations had emerged in the field.

But the blunder went beyond the creation of confusion, for in large measure the new policy achieved exactly the opposite of what it was supposed to. The high command saw the choice before the troops as shoot and kill or to beat and injure, and given the circumstances the latter was definitely to be preferred. Excessive reliance on rifles would only leave a swath of blood dividing the two peoples and spark the desire for revenge. Many junior officers explained the new policy to their men in this way. But obviously they failed to make their point, for in the end the blows were bestowed with a force bordering on fury and on a scope that suggested an army out of control. Rather than being hailed as a symbol of sanity, or at least the lesser of two evils, and rather than being used with discretion to subdue rioters resisting arrest, the club reverted to being an emblem of barbarity and was employed with abandon by men who had simply let the uprising get their goat.

There was of course no comparison between the number of deaths resulting from beatings and bullet wounds. Still, the extent of the injuries caused by the new policy was harrowing. Considering that whole corps of soldiers were engaged in battering away at defenseless civilians, it is hardly surprising that thousands of Palestinians—many of them innocent of any wrongdoing—were badly injured, some to the point of being handicapped. There were countless instances in which young Arabs were dragged behind walls or deserted buildings and systematically beaten all but senseless. The clubs descended on limbs, joints, and ribs until they could be heard to crack—especially as Rabin let slip a "break their bones" remark in a television interview that many soldiers took as a recommendation, if not exactly an order. Thus rather than curb the violence and hatred, the use of clubs served to fuel them. And it is unimaginable that the Palestinian desire to retaliate for the lives lost to bullets was in any way mitigated by the beatings. One intelligence officer well versed in life in the territories has noted in this context that just as many Palestinians turned to sabotage and terrorism in revenge for having been humiliated by Israelis, "the hundreds, perhaps thousands of the people left in casts by Israeli soldiers will translate into thousands of others who wish to avenge them: fathers who have seen their sons battered and children who watched in terror as their fathers were clubbed."

No sooner had the order gone out than word of excesses, unjustified beatings, even sheer sadism echoed back from the field. Junior officers were often seen to join their men in clubbing people without cause. Since the decision on when to administer a beating, to whom, and for what reason was left to the discretion of the individual, before long reports flowed in of soldiers thrashing people in their own homes just for the hell of it. Proof that whole families fell victim to the truncheons was readily observed in the hospitals, where women, children, and the elderly were brought for treatment. Detainees were beaten after being taken into custody, as a punishment in itself, and some hapless souls were beaten twice in succession. The operations log of one of the brigades assigned to Gaza contains a report by the Shin Bet about three badly bruised Arab youngsters who were encountered on the main road in the Katif area. The three had been beaten by soldiers for returning from work after a curfew had gone into effect in Jebalya. Following the assault they were driven southward to the Katif area, and the Shin Bet people came upon them as they were attempting to walk home. The Israelis drove them back to Jebalya, but it subsequently came out that upon entering the camp they were again stopped by soldiers—once more for violating the curfew—and were treated to a second beating, after which all three required hospitalization.

Strangely enough, despite the immediate outcry in Israel and abroad, weeks passed before attempts were made to clarify the circumstances in which clubs were to be used—and even then the guidelines were drawn up by individual units rather than the high command. The senior officers of one division issued the following directive: "1. Force may be used against violent persons while the violence is being committed. After a rioter is caught, he is not to be beaten." Yet even here, a subsequent clause contradicted the first: "2. Anyone violating a curfew who attempts to flee should be beaten and returned to his home," meaning that a beating was permissible regardless of whether or not violence was committed and irrespective of the reason for the violation (conceivably the "culprit" had gone out to call a doctor for a member of his family). This same order went on to state emphatically that "Local police are not to be beaten!"—a warning suggesting that some of them already had been. The explanatory section of the order further stated that "force is to be exercised only against isolated targets," meaning individuals, not entire groups (probably a reference to families). "No warrant exists for causing damage to property, except when a rioter has fled and is hiding in his house—and then only after urging him to open the door and surrender himself." Yet even these directives were less than stringent, and since they were issued to tired and frustrated soldiers in often ambiguous situations, hitches were bound to follow.

Another few months were to pass before this same division revised the directives to its men. Beatings were still permitted, but now the orders addressed themselves to details such as where the strokes should fall ("Force is not be used against sensitive parts of the body [lest it] endanger life"). This latest gloss also stated that beatings were not to be administered as punishment and couched this prohibition in the strongest of terms: "Force may be used against violence and those resisting arrest while the violence is being committed, up to the point of capture. [But] the exercise of force against anyone who has been stopped, is under arrest, or is already in custody and is not behaving violently is absolutely forbidden." The division's commanders had become so sensitive about the treatment of the Palestinians that the revised orders even warned: "Local inhabitants are not to be humiliated."

But still there was a flood of excesses—far more than the army was at first willing to admit. During the initial phase of the *intifada*, the willful disregard or disobedience of orders reached alarming proportions. Officers tended to avoid the subject of the beatings in talks with their men because they themselves were confused about the issue, and some had reason to recall Amram Mitzna's comment that "there's a little devil in every one of us." But as proof piled up that what were dismissed as "exceptions" had become routine, if not exactly the rule, and that people were being beaten in their homes, in detention camps, and as a means of unprovoked abuse, the senior command finally moved to put a stop to the phenomenon. Rabin, Shomron, and members of the General Staff embarked on tours to talk with the men in the field—and were met with a frankness they might rather have been spared.

"What did you imagine would happen?" one of the soldiers asked when the defense minister and chief of staff visited his unit in Nablus (after a number of its men had been arrested for clubbing a stone-thrower already under arrest). "The rubber bullets and tear gas are ineffective. You gave us the clubs. What did you think we'd do with them?"

"Of course detainees were beaten," another admitted. "What do you expect of a tired soldier who has been cursed and stoned and has caught the kid who hit him? Anyone would take out his anger and beat him black and blue."

When the soldiers complained of a lack of support from their superiors, they were assured that no one who obeyed orders would have cause to feel forsaken; the army would stand behind him. But still the improprieties continued, while pressure mounted to allow soldiers to shoot down their assailants, regardless of age, sex, or circumstance. Hearing this demand while on a visit to a kibbutz in the Jordan Valley,

Amram Mitzna retorted sharply, "Are you suggesting that we shoot women and children for throwing stones? Yes, sometimes even a stone can kill, but that's no reason to go around shooting the people who throw them. This is Israel, not Syria!"

For all their chagrin over the results of the new strategy, it must be said that the army's commanders were astonished by the strident reaction to it from the very outset, both in Israel and abroad. Rabin, too, confessed to being puzzled by the response, for he honestly believed that the policy would be received not only with understanding but as evidence that the IDF's only motive was to save lives by replacing bullets with bludgeons. Instead he found that he had merely traded one can of worms for another. In an age in which thousands of people succumb to "smart bombs" dropped from advanced aircraft or to missile-borne war heads and poison gas, it is somehow possible to take acts of mass but anonymous killing in one's stride because they are effected from afar, by the touch of a button, and the suffering of the victims is left to the imagination. But when a man is beaten in range of a TV camera and his face, distorted in pain, looms large on the screen, the public's response tends to be far more vehement. This is all the more true when a country's defense minister takes personal responsibility for the order to beat civilians, making it easy to infer that the wanton violence is a policy dictated from above.

Outraged complaints reached Israel from all sides, and in a twist that left some officials bewildered, the reaction to the beatings was stronger than to the shooting of demonstrators, demolition of houses, or deportations. The office of Israel's president had difficulty coping with the swell of letters on this issue. Missives poured in from Jewish intellectuals, rabbis, and community leaders, to say nothing of organizations that had for decades unfailingly championed Israel's cause. ". . . The inexperience of the Israeli army in riot control and other police functions, and the frustrations of Israeli soldiers as they confront young Palestinians hurling stones and petrol bombs . . . may explain but they cannot excuse . . . the use of excessive force against civilians" read a statement by the AFL-CIO Executive Council. More often than not, however, the protests were less starchily phrased but bespoke deep vexation. "What's happened to you over there?" was the exasperated cry heard over and over again.

What had happened, sad as it is to say, is that the troops were brutalizing the Palestinian population because the *intifada* had brutalized the IDF. For years the Isareli army had managed to avoid having to deal with the occupation on any serious scale. Then the uprising came along and weighed the troops down with a multitude of distasteful tasks. All efforts failed to prevent the Israeli soldier from becoming hardened toward the people facing him across the barricades. Before anyone could stop it, the use of force against tens of thousadns of civilians had dragged the younger generation of Israelis down to the level of brute violence. There could hardly have been better proof of the claim that the administration of the territories was a corrupting influence on Israeli life and that the vision of a "benevolent occupation" was but an exercise in self-delusion. As if to make the point incontrovertible, the most embarrassing (and hitherto unthinkable) things happened. On a standard visit to one of the army camps, high school students in the Gadna* were let into a detention room, in contravention of orders, and proceeded to beat the detainees. A woman soldier serving in another camp was tried for clubbing blindfolded prisoners being held there, and drivers who had brought senior officers to a detention camp for consultations or inspection tours passed the time by battering prisoners. The office of the military prosecutor dealt with these cases, but not every incident was brought to its attention. Worse yet, on a number of occasions it was subjected to immense pressure to let such offenders off without a trial.

In time, however, the struggle to maintain the IDF's moral stature was joined by the army's judicial system. The military courts simply did not allow soldiers to get away with excesses. Typical of their approach was the shock expressed by the court that tried the case of four soldiers from the Givati Brigade charged with causing the death of Hani a-Shami, a resident of Jebalya, as a result of a merciless beating. As the judges noted in their verdict:

> We were appalled to hear some of the witnesses express hatred and contempt for the lives of members of the population ruled by the military forces. We shuddered when we heard that soldiers stood by and watched the degrading scene of detainees—handcuffed, helpless people—being beaten inside a military camp while they themselves remained indifferent to the sight and deaf to the screams of the victims. An attitude of "anything goes" was applied to these people merely because they were suspected of participating in demonstrations and belonged to a hostile population. . . . How could we have reached the point where combat soldiers from a select

* Paramilitary training required of all high school students in Israel.

unit, who we believe have received a good education, could have been so delinquent in their behavior? How could they have cast off all the values that their parents and educators instilled in them and have undergone a psychological metamorphosis?

Induration was the process that most of the soldiers and a few officers in the territories experienced during these months. "At first I was shaken by every Arab death, especially if a child had been killed," one senior officer related of his own experience. "I thought about the victim, I thought about his family, and it was as if every loss pained me as well. But the more time passed and the more people died, the more I noticed that I wasn't reacting anymore, that I just didn't care. I took in the announcements about the deaths—of women, of children—with complete equanimity. I had become calloused, just like everyone else. We all underwent a change to one degree or another during our duty in the territories."

Almost from the start of the uprising, the psychologists attached to the field units advised their commanders to keep an eye on those men with a tendency to overreact—be they officers or enlisted men—so that they could be kept from stooping to savagery. As professionals they appreciated that the operations in the territories were a different kind of warfare entailing great emotional wear and tear on the troops, and they feared that duty of this sort would corrode the soldiers' self-image. To avert a collapse of morale, they also recommended increasing the troops' social activities and seeing to it that every new unit sent into the field receive detailed briefings and thorough explanations of the conclusions reached by its predecessors.

At this early stage there were still few reserve units deployed in the territories, and the army was wary about fielding them. The natural expectation was that the part-time soldiers would bring along the political views they subscribed to as civilians and that sharp differences of opinion might rend the army from within. There was also concern that a considerable number of reservists might refuse to serve in the territories, on moral or political grounds. While arguments about national and army policy raged among the conscripts, as well, they did not shatter morale or threaten the solidarity of units that had a strong esprit de corps. However, the young soldiers were particularly vulnerable to the effects of frustration. Surveys taken among the eighteen- to twenty-one-year-olds doing their three-year obligatory service found that most of the soldiers believed that the beatings had a daunting influence on Palestinian violence but, except for a handful of sadists, they were not keen on administering them. Some even expressed anger at the country's political leaders for allowing the situation to reach the point where soldiers had to engage in such activity. The prevailing view among the units in the territories during the first months of the uprising was that they had a job to do; few enjoyed it, but it had to be done like any other. Even those who felt that they were obliged to club their adversaries often expressed pity for the Palestinians. Yet the combination of anger over the need to wield a truncheon and sympathy for the victims of their blows did not lead to a wave of conscientious objection or rank insubordination; the overwhelming majority of the men simply did as they were told. To paraphrase the popular characterization of Israeli soldiers ("They shoot and they cry"), they beat and they bitched; they battered away at civilians, with or without cause, and felt enormously resentful about it. In a very real sense, this experience marked off a generation of young Israelis; their elder comrades-in-arms had never known anything like it.

It should not be surprising, then, that many soldiers felt the need to talk about their feelings, share their experiences, and warn their countrymen about what their actions implied. This impulse had likewise come out in previous wars, but the public and political community had been more willing to listen then. *The Seventh Day*, a collection of talks with soldiers published after the Six-Day War, became a national bestseller, and no one questioned the sincerity of the feelings recorded there. But when it came to the *intifada*, the Israeli soldier could find no outlet for his bitterness. The country's political leaders were at best ambivalent about the problem, and appeals to the public met with a torrent of cynicism, scorn, and snide accusations that the "bleeding hearts" were "Arab lovers" or better yet that highly serviceable catchall, "stooges of the PLO." Considering the highly partisan and passionate nature of Israel's political culture, the only figure many soldiers felt they could turn to was the country's apolitical president, Chaim Herzog. He was generally receptive to their requests to meet with him. The one group he pointedly refused to see were men from Yesh Gvul ("There's a Limit!"), the protest movement that urges Israelis to refuse to serve in the territories, lest a meeting be construed as according their program legitimacy.

The outspoken comments of one delegation of fifteen soldiers who had just completed reserve duty in the West Bank reflected what countless others were feeling. One by one they told the president that the demands made upon them by the interminable occupation and the revolt against it were brutalizing them—and, by extension, all of Israeli society—in their dealings with the Palestinians. The process was an elementary one: to preserve the army's deterrent capacity—a euphemism for the ability to cow the Palestinians into submission—the soldiers had to treat civilians roughly, if not downright savagely. Their success in this role, they feared, came at the cost of their own humanity. Too easily could they lose sight of the fact that their assignment was fundamentally the repression of human beings, decent people just like themselves. The creed that had always been the mainstay of the IDF's self-image—that morality and respect for human life cannot be suspended even in wartime—was steadily being eroded by the demands of occupation. It led the men to reflect that oppression inevitably exacts a high price of its practitioners. Some of them observed that doing reserve duty along the borders was radically different from serving in the territories, where "the problem is not a military one, though the politicians don't appreciate that." They all spoke of being caught in a no-win situation and decried the lack of any serious efforts to reach a political settlement. But the most striking sentiment of all was their fear of sinking into a state of moral torpor. "It pains us to see what's happening to the army," one man agonized aloud. "We can testify that despite the calls for restraint, the 'exceptions' are becoming the rule." "What we need now," another remarked, "is authoritative leaders to remind us, day and night, that the people we are dealing with out there are human beings made out of exactly the same stuff as we are."

Not long after this audience with the president, another group from the same brigade asked to meet with President Herzog and presented a different point of view. Most of these men lived in one of the Jewish towns or settlements in the territories, which undoubtedly influenced their feelings and outlook. In any case, they told the president that the army's moral strength had not been diminished by its actions in the territories; if anything, it had been tempered by the difficult tests the troops had had to face. They also denied reports of frustration or weariness among the soldiers, though they did express concern about the ability of some of their comrades to bear up under the new conditions of "combat." Yet one of the men in even this group observed that "the soldiers should feel uncomfortable when they operate against a civilian population, because if this keeps up there's a risk of desensitization and moral collapse."

□

The *intifada* profoundly affected the IDF in other ways, too, and the longer it persisted, the deeper the changes went and the more damaging they became. On the training level, the uprising changed the IDF's annual work program beyond recognition, forcing the General Staff Branch to shorten various courses and cut back on exercises. The problem was especially acute for the reserve units, whose training had suffered even before the uprising due to cuts in the defense budget. Close to 200,000 Israelis served in the territories in the two years following the outbreak of the *intifada*. Many reserve units did not see their artillery or armor for quite a while. The IDF was proud of the fact that it had absorbed sophisticated equipment into its reserves, but in many cases the soldiers in these units had yet to train on it.

Instead, this army that throughout its history had pondered, planned for, and generally grappled with purely military issues now abruptly entered the province of police duties on a grand scale. Before long, the army began to acquire a distinct resemblance to the Border Police—except that the latter performed its function far more effectively. Added to this burden were tasks that are disdained by any advanced army and unquestionably despised by the armies of the democracies. Suddenly the IDF found itself in charge of large prisons and huge detention camps filled not with prisoners-of-war but with the civilians for whose welfare Israel is responsible. That they held as many people as all the country's prisons combined was not surprising, since the figures on internment were startling. During the first year of the uprising, 29,000 Palestinians were arrested, with charges being pressed against 8,000 of them. The army also held some 5,000 people for a six-month term of administrative detention (without benefit of trial), and upon completing it some of the detainees—like Feisal al-Husseini, the doyen of the local PLO leadership—were promptly sent back for another. Minors arrested for participating in disturbances were held in Farah, a special prison near Nablus run by the army, for the police and Shin Bet drew the line at expending their energies on interrogating children!

The cost of this approach was a heavy one, and not just because the IDF was taken to task for violations of the Palestinians' human rights. It took considerable manpower to run this system, which came at the expense of other pressing needs. Instead of holding training exercises, whole companies of reservists were assigned to guard the thousands of people being held in makeshift detention camps in unspeakable conditions. This debasement of duties inevitably tarnished the IDF's image in the eyes of its own men, leaving a number of disquieting questions about the future. Would young officers agree to sign on in the regular army for another year or two when they realized that a good portion of their service would be spent putting down the rebellion in the territories? And if not, how was the army to maintain its officer corps? How would the reservists react upon discovering that, far from having their annual service quota cut, they would probably be spending sixty rather than thirty to thirty-five days on reserve duty—and in the territories, no less! And in the broader sense, how would this extra, open-ended disruption of everyday life affect the country's economy, universities, and the whole hallowed institution of a citizens' army?

Another troubling change had to do with the soldiers' attitude toward the media and democratic values in general. It began with complaints about the way they were being portrayed on television and in the press. Many soldiers felt they were being shown in a distorted light because the camera captures only the dramatic moments of a confrontation—the "action"—while the background to the shot is either not documented or ends up on the cutting-room floor. Their resentment over this built-in bias of broadcast news only increased when TV cameras caught soldiers committing excesses for which they were subsequently tried. It was also aggravated by the often obtrusive presence of photographers and cameramen. The *intifada* drew to Israel hundreds of foreign journalists who followed the violence up close, standing literally a step or two behind the soldiers. More than once camera crews hampered the conduct of routine operations, and the men in the field were convinced that the very presence of journalists inspired hostile activity, since the scene was often calm until TV cameras appeared.

Notwithstanding the special apparatus and trained staff of the Army Spokesman's Office, the Palestinians proved far more adept at exploiting the presence of the media to their advantage. Though organized in only the most rudimentary fashion, they geared up to serve the foreign journalists in a variety of ways: as escorts, drivers, and translators; by setting up meetings and interviews; and by relaying reports from the field with enviable speed. Alongside the Palestinian press, various information services with direct lines to the uprising's Unified National Command operated without interference in East Jerusalem. Both sides appreciated that in the special struggle between them, the press was a weapon in its own right; that in a war for hearts and minds, radio, television, and the printed press are the equivalent of artillery. The information services were therefore a highly important component of the Palestinian arsenal. Yet out of concern for its image as a democratic state, Israel allowed these "big guns" to operate behind the lines. From this standpoint, the *intifada* was an uprising deluxe.

As time went on and nerves became frayed, Israel's soldiers reacted to the media with growing intolerance. They disparaged the axiom that a free press is integral to the fabric of democratic life and demanded that journalists be barred from the territories—or at least that the cameras not be allowed to dog them as they went about their work. Some soldiers went so far as to charge that the Israeli press was doing deliberate harm to state security, while complaints against the foreign press were considerably more heated and included accusations that journalists were extending aid and comfort to the insurgents. Tension sometimes reached the point where it turned ugly: more than once cameramen were assaulted by soldiers for defying their orders or just getting in their way.

This animosity toward the media and the values it represents gave the high command cause for concern, and soon the Education Corps went into high gear, arranging lectures and running symposia on the role of the press in a democracy. Divisional commanders issued orders clearly stating that "the area is open to the media, and members of the press are not to be prevented from moving or operating freely. Limited areas can be closed to the media for sensitive periods, but in no case is violence to be used against the media staff; nor are they to be treated rudely." A special pamphlet on the uprising prepared by the IDF's chief educational officer devoted an entire chapter to this subject, pointedly reminding its readers that:

> The media are a part of the twentieth century, like the computer and the jet plane. . . . In contrast to your other assignments in the army, you have various attendants in [this] war: Israeli civilians, the local inhabitants [Palestinians], and hundreds of journalists, photographers, and television crews are following you and viewing all your actions in the field. This is a fact of life when you operate in big cities and [other] populated areas. The presence of photographers has a direct effect upon the Arab inhabitants, who are interested in exploiting the . . . event to set their cause before the world

and present themselves as poor souls confronted by armed and violent soldiers. The photographers and correspondents do everything possible to get better shots and relay more dramatic pictures, for above and beyond their obligation to report [the news] they are engaged in competition among themselves. It could conceivably be claimed that treating the media properly would interfere with your mission, but such thinking misses the point. We must exploit the media to our own advantage, using them to show that Israeli soldiers conduct themselves with determination and restraint.

Such explanations may have checked the soldiers' harsh behavior toward the press, but they did little to change the basically hostile feelings.

In addition to its effect on the IDF proper, the uprising also changed the slant of the work undertaken by the Shin Bet. In the past, top priority had always gone to uncovering and foiling sabotage operations. Like every body of its kind, the Shin Bet had invested great effort in penetrating its adversaries' networks—in this case the Palestinian organizations themselves. It had displayed the patience to succeed at deep, long-term infiltrations, and these efforts bore fruit in its uncommon success at frustrating the PLO's armed struggle. During the *intifada*, however, it was forced to concentrate on identifying activists and quickly thwarting more popular actions, like processions and demonstrations—the gist of this change being the difference between a security service and a secret police. The *intifada* also forced the Shin Bet to spread its own network ever further and thinner, recruiting more agents and running them under conditions far more complex than in the past. Finally, it subjected the organization to an unprecedented burden by adding to its responsibilities the evaluation of the general condition and mood of the Palestinians in the territories. Of course the uprising had also forced the army to take on new assignments. But unlike the IDF, whose system of reserves enabled it to rotate its men, the Shin Bet could draw only upon its own full-time professionals, forcing it to perform these additional tasks without expanding its staff. Given these circumstances, it was hard to believe that in the long run the Shin Bet could escape the enervating effects of the *intifada* and emerge from it unscathed.

While the IDF was hard put to manifest its talents in the territories, outside the country this was emphatically not the case and, according to Palestinian claims, it struck at the PLO on two separate occasions. The first action forced the PLO to scuttle its plan for launching the so-called Ship of Return; the other deprived the organization of its leading military figure, Abu Jihad, plunging it into temporary disarray.

Striking back at the Palestinian leaders responsible for terrorist operations had been a point of principle for the Israeli security services ever since the PLO achieved recognition as a political body in 1974. Regardless of their status elsewhere, in Israel the PLO's leaders continued to be regarded purely as terrorists. They were even defined as such by a law passed in the Knesset in 1986, making them fugitives from the long arm of the Israeli law. Some of these leaders, like Zuheir Muhsein, head of the Syrian-backed a-Saika, paid for their deeds with their lives. Others, like George Habash, evaded capture when the best laid plans went ruefully awry. In the case of Habash, a plane he was scheduled to take but failed to board at the last minute was intercepted and forced to land by the Israeli Air Force, causing the government considerable embarrassment.

Strangely enough, it was Menachem Begin who took pains to ensure that the PLO's leaders would come to no harm at the hands of his compatriots. He considered them as no better than a pack of murderers. But his own deep animosity toward these men was matched by a determination to steer clear of anything that smacked of political assassination. It is doubtful whether this policy derived from a fear that any assault on Arafat or his colleagues would set off a round of mutual bloodletting at the leadership level. Like all of Israel's prime ministers, Begin knew that his counterpart in the PLO would suffer no qualms about having him shot down in cold blood were the opportunity to present itself. But that did not weaken his resolve. Although his prohibition was suspended during the siege of Beirut, when Israel tried unsuccessfully to eliminate the Palestinian leadership—Arafat above all—once the fighting ended and the PLO was evacuated from the city, Begin reverted to his earlier principle. He may have referred to the PLO chairman as a "two-legged animal" and often compared him to Hitler. But it is to Begin that Arafat owes his life, for the prime minister categorically rejected a plan to have him cut down by a sharpshooter as he boarded the ship that was to evacuate him from Beirut.

If the taboo on harming Arafat could be understood on grounds of his notoriety, the same could not be said for his deputy (and close friend since youth), Halil al-Wazir, better known as Abu Jihad.

As the equivalent of the PLO's defense minister and chief of staff combined, Abu Jihad had long been in the Israelis' sights (metaphorically speaking). He often personally briefed the men sent out on missions to assault Israeli civilians and was known to have done so in the case of the March 1978 slaughter of the passengers hijacked in a bus on Israel's coastal road. Nevertheless, Begin refused to approve plans to liquidate even people on this level. Ironically, then, had he been prime minister at the time of the *intifada*—and not suspended his policy, as he did during the Lebanon war—events might have unfolded differently.

As the uprising wore on and the PLO increasingly influenced its direction, it was obvious that the one man with the talent and pragmatism to manage the rebellion from afar was Abu Jihad. Thus it was perhaps only natural to assume that eliminating him would cause the *intifada* a crippling setback, or at least deal a stunning blow to Palestinian morale. As Abu Jihad sat waiting for news about an operation he had ordered, a squad of gunmen broke into his Tunis villa. Raising his gaze from the communication he was preparing to his people in the territories, he instantly grasped that the men standing before him were Israelis and that for him the game was up. According to the account given by Abu Jihad's widow, before he could even reach for the revolver in his desk drawer, he was killed by a spray of bullets. One of the assassins busied himself filming a video of the room while his comrades gathered up all the documents they could lay their hands on. Wazir's wife and children watched mutely as the men fled the villa; then they put through calls to the family's two elder sons (who were studying at American universities by permission of the United States government) to relay the bitter news.

Abu Jihad's death was indeed a grave blow to the PLO but far from a master stroke in terms of the *intifada*. It is true that without him the uprising lost some of its backing from abroad, and occasionally its local leaders bemoaned his absence. But they nevertheless maintained their contact with the PLO (albeit less efficiently) and continued to run affairs on their own. In a broader perspective, it is doubtful whether the assassination secured Israel any formidable advantage, especially as it did nothing to bring discussions between Israel and the Palestinians any closer. It was a classic anti-terrorist action that probably set the PLO's military arm back considerably. It was also the kind of operation at which Israel excelled, and may therefore have been a temporary boost to the IDF's morale. But on the strategic plane, the elimination of Abu Jihad was almost incidental to the *intifada* and certainly did not extricate the army from the difficult pass in which it was caught in the territories.

Equally unhelpful, and perhaps the final indignity for the Israeli army, was a situation that it had never encountered in any previous war: finding itself at odds with a segment of the very population it was pledged to defend. As a true citizens' army and the cornerstone of a beleaguered country's survival, the IDF has always enjoyed the wholehearted support of the Israeli people. One could even say that for the better part of forty years it has been something of Israel's darling, the apple of the nation's eye—to the point where a mixture of admiration and protectiveness has sometimes got in the way of reasoned public criticism. In every past war, Israel has been united in the conviction that the IDF was doing its absolute best to protect and defend the country. But the *intifada* brought a striking change in this unfailingly supportive attitude, especially on the part of groups of Jewish settlers. Instead of pampering the troops, they showered the men with abuse, derided the army's conduct, and accused the high command of failing to end the rebellion for lack of trying. Never before in the century-long history of Jewish settlement had a group that defined itself as "pioneers," after wittingly choosing to settle in a trouble-prone area, so clamored for the government to provide it with "absolute security." The settlements on Israel's borders had always suffered from Arab terrorism, to say nothing of erratic artillery barrages from the surrounding Arab states; but their residents had never blamed the IDF for their vulnerability. Nor had Jewish pioneers ever maligned the army in the way that the militants in the territories did. Too often the soldiers had cause to complain that when Palestinian kids weren't making a mockery of the Israel Defense Forces, the Jewish settlers were.

The number of settlers injured during the course of the *intifada* was surprisingly low, considering the amount of stones and Molotov cocktails being thrown. Yet they tried to create the impression that their welfare was being deliberately neglected. Certainly the lives of the settlers had changed in some respects, though they had been attacked with stones and firebombs prior to the uprising as well. The most harrowing of these incidents was the tragedy that befell the Moses family in September 1987, when a firebomb set the family car ablaze near Kalkilya, resulting in the death of Ofra Moses and her five-year-old son and severe burns to the family's two other children. Yet despite the immediacy of such perils, life in the territories went on much as usual, just as it did throughout Israel even though terrorists could strike at any time there, too. Weeks, sometimes months, of relative quiet elapsed between one incident and the next, and Israeli cars regularly plied the roads of the West Bank and Gaza Strip as thousands of people drove to work and back, day in and day out.

The change engendered by the *intifada* was above all one of frequency. The stoning of Israeli vehicles became a daily occurrence, making the settlers' lives harder. Women no longer traveled alone; all drivers preferred to travel in convoys; and parents who sent their children to schools outside their settlements were understandably anxious about their safety. The army allocated its own vehicles to escort school buses and other means of transport, but the settlers remained unsatisfied. They seemed unwilling to accept the fact that they were living in an area rocked by violence, and rather than cope with the stress that inevitably attends such situations, they poured their ire out on the army, treating Israel's soldiers as though they were insurance agents who had broken faith with their clients. On a number of occasions, they even competed with the Palestinians in defying the army by blocking roads and holding demonstrations to express the depth of their grievance!

The ugliest expression of this anger was the suggestion, harped on like an *idée fixe*, that the uprising was being allowed to continue as a matter of army policy. *Nekudah*, a publication issued by the Jewish settlers in the West Bank and Gaza Strip, went furthest of all in its charges and practically accused the high command of treason. An editorial published under the heading "The Chief of Staff Does Not Believe in Victory" stated:

> Frequent statements by the chief of staff and other senior officers make it clear why they do not believe it is possible, or necessary, to achieve an absolute victory. Thus for the first time in the history of the state and the IDF, the chief of staff has declared that the IDF cannot emerge from this war . . . with the upper hand—and the soldiers and officers hear that. Tomorrow similar things may be said about an armored and air war on the Golan [Heights], for a chief of staff who says that the solution to an Arab uprising in Judea and Samaria* must be political, rather than military, is capable of saying that

* The biblical names for the mountainous areas of the West Bank.

the solution to Syria's threats is similarly political and that the army expects the government to make concessions to the Syrians.

Before the uprising the more militant of the settlers had challenged the IDF as part of their drive to achieve full parity in all decisions on security affairs. What they really wanted was to dictate the army's actions in the territories, but Rabin wouldn't hear of it. Moreover, he wasn't alone in his refusal to grant them such powers. Though supportive of the settlers on ideological grounds, Moshe Arens of the Likud (Rabin's predecessor in the post) had also tangled with them on similar issues. He was outraged, for example, when their representatives tried to stop him from inviting the then-head of Central Command, Maj. Gen. Ori Or—with whom they did not see eye to eye—to a meeting on security matters. The settlers wanted to establish local militias that would be permitted to operate beyond the bounds of their settlements. They almost got their way when the IDF agreed to form companies of settlers in a framework known as "area defense." This was the first time since the disbanding of the Palmach* in November 1948 that units with homogeneous political leanings were allowed to exist within the Israeli army. In another unprecedented step, the area-defense companies were assigned to operate on a domestic front, rather than along the border. This new arrangement prompted fears that having been armed and legitimized by the IDF, these militiamen would behave like vigilantes, "taking care" of their Palestinian neighbors as they saw fit. Central Command rectified the decision in a low-key manner: though never formally disbanding them, it simply stopped calling these companies up for reserve duty. Ultimately Gen. Mitzna reorganized them in a way that restricted their jurisdiction to the settlements proper, just as he blocked the establishment of a local Civil Guard to police the roads and otherwise operate outside the settlements alongside the IDF.

Some of the more militant settlers chose to take a positive view of the *intifada* as an opportunity to realize their political aims. Their thoughts ran toward deliberately aggravating the situation in the hope that the army would come down harder and harder on the Palestinians until they broke and left the country on their own—or, if not, were

* The shock troops of the pre-state Jewish underground. Five months after the establishment of the IDF, the Palmach's command was dissolved by order of Prime Minister David Ben-Gurion because of its strong identification with one of the country's political parties.

forcibly expelled. When the army failed to comply with this scenario, the militants could hardly bear their frustration and wanted to goad the Palestinians into greater violence so as to leave the army with no other choice. They also felt increasingly shut out of the corridors of power in Israel, for in addition to various brushes with Mitzna (and Ori Or before him) they had serious difficulties relating to Rabin. In fact, their chemistry with him was close to disastrous. They knew that he regarded many of their settlements as security burdens and found him to be distinctly cool in all their contacts with him. Rabin, for his part, could not help but sense the hostility of the settlers—who held him personally responsible for the *intifada* and branded him a "murderer" when one of their comrades was killed—so that whenever he needed their cooperation he prudently sent out his deputy, the Likud's Michael Dekel, to obtain it.

It must be said, however, that most of the Israelis living in the territories did not endorse the line prescribed by these militants. This "silent majority" comprised most of the people who had settled in the territories not out of ideological conviction or a pioneering impulse but in search of what the Ministry of Housing touted as "quality of life"—meaning anything from standard to luxury housing at prices unimaginable within the Green Line. How these neo-suburbanites thought they would improve the quality of their lives by settling amidst a hostile population remains unclear. However, they, at least, understood that without the support of the army their lives would become intolerable, and the last thing they wanted was to alienate its officers and men. Still, from time to time they too were caught up in the eddy of anger that swirled through the Jewish settlements whenever one of their inhabitants was killed or injured. At times like these, some of them were also tempted to join the militants in taking the law into their own hands.

To a certain extent many of the Israelis living in the territories were shocked by the realization that whether they liked it or not, the *intifada* spelled a radical change in their status and lifestyle. Despite the huge investment made in the infrastructure, thousands of people no longer streamed into the territories to buy up apartments and land at incredibly low prices. The dangers of travel kept even visitors away, forcing the local hotel in the Katif region to close its doors despite an advertising blitz promising sun, sea, and all the other amenities of a delightful family vacation. Perhaps the rudest awakening of all, though, had to do with the settlers' status. Despite the claims by some of their leaders that the settlements reduced the prospect of violence, most Israelis in the territories slowly began to see that instead of being a boon to their country's security, they were a burden on it—and that terrified them. Having acquired military experience from their own service in the army, they knew that the IDF could not be everywhere at all times and that it was impossible to provide them with complete protection. They also realized that the Palestinians had overcome their long-standing fear of Jews, in or out of uniform, and that led some settlers to opt for increasingly violent actions in a desperate effort to turn back the clock. Others responded forcefully out of a fear of things to come, for deep in their hearts they had all come round to seeing that the demographic situation affected them above all and that to deny or ignore it would be folly on their part. After all, not a single Jewish settlement had been established in the territories since Rabin's appointment as defense minister in 1984. Rather than bind the nation, the cherished vision of a Greater Land of Israel was more likely to divide it, and the settlers knew that without unqualified support their chances for holding out against the political and demographic odds were slim. The *intifada* made this problem so strikingly clear that some settlers spoke of accepting the fact that the Palestinians are a people represented by the PLO, and a few pragmatists even expressed a willingness to talk with the organization. Admittedly, these were isolated voices. Had it not been for the *intifada,* however, it is inconceivable that such "heresies" would have been voiced at all.

More than any previous challenge, the *intifada* has caused the IDF immense frustration, not least because the IDF has been unable to apply its power in this new form of warfare. There is no harm in generals discovering the limitations of military strength. It is a lesson that was learned by the Americans in Vietnam and the Russians in Afghanistan, and if the Great Powers know it from their own painful experience, it is all the more important for the army of a small nation to appreciate this reality. At any rate, frustration and all it implies are certainly preferable to the intoxication with power that swept over the IDF after the Six-Day War.

Unable to manifest its strength, the Israeli army has failed to achieve its objectives in the struggle against the uprising, objectives that were at any rate limited. As Gen. Mitzna explained in a letter distributed to the tens of thousands of IDF soldiers and members of the other security forces serving in the West Bank, "Our aim is to put a stop to the rioting, to restore order, and to bring life back to normal so as to provide Israel's government and citizens with the best conditions for making proper political decisions about the future of these territories." Two years after the start of the uprising, none of those aims have been met. The rioting has not been halted, and life has not returned to normal in the territories. Much to the contrary, the unruly Palestinians have been joined by fractious Israelis, and the *intifada* has begun to spread over the Green Line.

Another reason for the army's frustration is the undermining of its standing. Like it or not, the IDF has become the subject of a fierce political debate in which there can be no winners. Groups at both ends of the political spectrum are involved in this process. The Left is prepared to defend the General Staff against attacks from its opponents, but it is intent upon showing that the IDF has lost its moral stature in the territories. The Right has deplored the attacks by settlers on Israeli soldiers but continues to charge that the army's failure to quash the *intifada* is a deliberate one. It is but a short step from a claim of this sort to calls for a purge of the high command and demands that only officers wtih "ideological resolve"—meaning those who believe that the solution to the uprising lies in the exercise of greater force—should be appointed to "sensitive posts." At the same time, the army, perhaps more than any other sector of the Israeli public, has suffered from the collapse of the national consensus on the Israeli-Palestinian conflict. Clearly it feels that it has lost support from the nation it serves, and without question the decline in its standing is one of the leading achievements of the *intifada*.

For twenty years the conventional wisdom in the IDF, and the Israeli public in general, was that by adding a measure of strategic depth, the territories accorded Israel additional security. The *intifada* began to undermine that belief by showing that even if they could serve as a buffer in a war with Israel's neighbors, because of their indigenous population the West Bank and Gaza constitute a grave security problem on a daily basis. And even if the present outburst were to be brought under control, the best Israel can look forward to is a relentless war of attrition in the territories, forcing the IDF to revise its deployment in times of calm as well as war. Thus from a purely military standpoint, the comfortable situation that prevailed in the territories until December 8, 1987, will never be restored. The longer it takes Israel to accept that, the harder it will be to recover from the mistakes made while clinging to an illusion. In the meanwhile the IDF will remain caught in the middle—pleasing none, angering all, and losing its unique self-image in the process.

SIX | *THE ISRAELI PALESTINIANS*

"WE ARE PART of the *intifada*, but rather than employ violence we shall exercise our rights within Israel's democratic system." This seemingly paradoxical statement is almost the official line of the Arab community in Israel, and the ambivalence it betrays is in no way unexpected. For the complex identity of Israel's Arab citizens is itself a paradox and one of the more intriguing aspects of the Israeli-Palestinian conflict as a whole.

The uprising in the occupied territories has unsettled Israel's 790,000 Arabs more than any other crisis since the Six-Day War. Unable and unwilling to remain indifferent to the fate of their brethren across the Green Line, during the opening months they sat glued to their television sets, hungrily absorbing every scrap of information. Their feelings swayed between rage and sorrow over the mounting toll of lives and pride over the daring of the Palestinians in taking the IDF on. Yet at the back of their minds was a fear that fanatics would exploit the violence to massacre Palestinians, deport them en masse, and inevitably rock their own position as full citizens of a democratic state.

Despite such fears, however, the Arabs of Israel were in full sympathy with the Palestinian insurgents and boldly justified their actions. Many offered more than just moral support; in a flurry of activity, they sent food and drugs into the territories, held protest rallies, contributed to special emergency funds, and donated blood. Quickly formed "rescue committees" plunged into a round of public-relations work, focusing on the misery of life in the camps under curfew. Arab members of the Knesset visited Palestinian detainees and in some cases intervened on their behalf. Along with other prominent Israeli Arabs, they extolled the insurgents on their trips abroad, sometimes at rallies run by the PLO. A few Israeli Arabs were prepared to go even further in extending active aid to the uprising. When the Unified National Command had difficulty printing its handbills in the territories, it turned, through intermediaries, first to printing works in Nazareth and then to smaller print shops in the villages of the so-called Triangle,* where the reception was more cordial. Copies of Handbill Nos. 11 and 12 were in fact secretly printed in one of these villages, just as pamphlets and newsletters of the Islamic Resistance Movement were printed in the Israeli-Arab city of Um al-Fahm. When the Shin Bet decided to block the international-direct-dialing system in the territories, making it more difficult for the Palestinians to receive advice and orders from abroad, many Israeli Arabs helped them around this obstacle by offering them the use of their own phones. A few even made their bank accounts available to the PLO for transferring funds to its loyalists in the territories, and in a number of cases the sums involved were considerable.

Israel's security services were not unmindful of the danger that Israel's Arab citizens might slowly be drawn into active cooperation with the Palestinian insurgents. Their fears were in fact one of the reasons for the government's decision to stop the Palestinian "Ship of Return" from ever reaching Israel's shores. The PLO plan was to build around this ship a public-relations extravaganza in which deported Palestinians would attempt to return to their homeland. The point of the effort was to rouse not only international sympathy for the Palestinian cause but to set off a mass demonstration of solidarity by Israel's Arabs and thus import the *intifada* into Israel proper. The idea called for gathering tens of thousands of Israeli Arabs on the slopes of Mount Carmel as the "Ship of Return" tried to enter Haifa Bay. Issuing a demand that the boat be allowed to dock in Haifa, the Intifada Watch Committee, manned by leaders of the Israel-Arab community, called for demonstrators to mass by the thousands on the Carmel. By this point it was known that a number of leading Israeli Arabs were preparing to leave for Greece to join the deportees on their journey, and Knesset member Mohammed Miari of the Progres-

* Concentration of Arab villages just west of the Green Line between Wadi Ara in the north and Petah Tikvah in the south.

sive List for Peace had already reached Piraeus. At the same time, having obtained funds from a wealthy West Bank Palestinian, other Arabs were negotiating the purchase of an old ship that would set out to sea with a delegation of prominent members of the community to greet the "Ship of Return" on its way from Cyprus. Reports of these plans left the government decidedly uneasy, for other than complicating an already ticklish situation, there was a real risk that a mass assembly of Israeli Arabs awaiting the ship would end in bloodshed.

When the cabinet met to discuss the problem. it heard at least one surprising reaction. Ezer Weizman, who usually espoused a liberal approach to the Palestinians, said that everything possible must be done to stop the ship from even approaching Israel's territorial waters. He did not want Israel's Arabs to find themselves lured into collaborating with a PLO publicity stunt. With that kind of backing from a Laborite—and a dove, to boot—there was little question about how the government would act. A few days later a mysterious explosion created a gaping hole in the side of the "Ship of Return" while it was anchored in the Cypriot port of Larnaca. Its journey to Israel ended before it began. Unable to secure another ship quickly, the PLO was forced to scrap the operation, and the proposed passengers, along with hundreds of journalists who had flown in from all over the world to cover the event, departed in disappointment. In one of its few clear-cut victories during the *intifada*, Israel not only foiled the PLO's plot to cause it embarrassment but averted what could well have been a violent clash between its Arab citizens and the army or the police.

Defusing this one situation, however, still did not allay fears about how the Arab community in Israel would react to ongoing violence in the territories. Without question the Arabs of Israel were angry, and some were drawn into hostile actions. During the first months of the *intifada*, hundreds of attacks of one kind or another were aimed at targets inside Israel. Many were carried out by Palestinians from the territories, but some were definitely perpetrated by Israeli Arabs themselves. At their worst, these incidents ranged from throwing stones and Molotov cocktails at vehicles, on back roads and main highways, to a marked rise in the incidence of arson in forests and open fields. But there was also a steady stream of lesser offenses. Vandalism against agricultural facilities and the destruction of crops became a daily occurrence. Telephone lines were cut and roads were blocked regularly. Even Palestinian flags were flown in Israeli-Arab villages, and graffiti was scrawled on buildings in support of the PLO. These incidents reached their peak in March 1988, three months after the start of the *intifada,* and were denounced by the chairmen of local councils and other Arab figures. The leaders urging self-restraint still had the upper hand, but they could not discount the possibility of a violent outburst if the *intifada* continued to rage out of control.

Quite naturally, the PLO followed these developments with pronounced satisfaction, especially as it had become increasingly interested in the potential of the Israeli Arabs. Back in the 1960s Arafat and his colleagues had scorned them as a weak and listless minority incapable of contributing to the Palestinian cause; but now they expected that the Arabs of Israel would play a leading role in the struggle. Their change in outlook traced back to 1973, after the Yom Kippur War, when the PLO stopped thinking of the Arabs of Israel as a marginal group that was beset by traumas and beholden to the regime of the Jewish state. At about that time, the PLO adopted its "Ten-Point Plan" (1974), which spoke of striving for sovereignty over part of Palestine as an interim goal. The political weight of Israel's Arab minority and the growing self-confidence of its leadership may have had little to do with this change of strategy. But they were certainly not unwelcome, and the fact is that Arafat increasingly spoke of the Arabs of Israel as an integral part of the Palestinian people striving for self-determination. Dr. Asher Sasser, an Israeli orientalist who has followed developments in the PLO, has noted that "its political strategy and philosophy of [liberating Palestine in] stages . . . make it imperative to strengthen its links with the Arabs of Israel. If the philosophy of stages calls for the establishment of a state in part of Palestine as a step toward liberating the country as a whole, the Arabs of Israel become a prime political asset for pursuing the struggle beyond the 1967 borders."

Because the PLO could not operate among the Arabs of Israel as it did in the territories, rather than try to create clandestine frameworks, it built a dense network of contacts with legally recognized bodies. The PLO has a standing arrangement for holding frequent meetings with the Israeli Communist Party (Rakah), and on November 18, 1987, an agreement detailing the scope of cooperation between the two organizations was formally and "officially" concluded in Moscow. It effectively recognized Rakah as the chief representative of the Palestinian citizens of Israel. But Arafat has not accepted Rakah as the sole agent mediating between the PLO and the Israeli-Arab community. Instead, like any smart politician, he has actively cultivated the Progressive List for Peace—so actively, in fact, that a number of the party's younger members have been forbidden to leave the country to prevent these ties from growing any stronger. PLO activists have also been known to serve as mediators in disputes between Rakah and its rivals. As the 1988 elections approached, they tried to set up coordination meetings between the three Israeli-Arab parties (unsuccessfully, as it turned out) and pressured Rakah and the Progressive List (again unsuccessfully) to sign excess-votes agreements.* It must be said, however, that the flirtation between the PLO and these parties has been a two-way street. Sensing the mood among its constituents, on the eve of the 1988 elections both Rakah and the Progressive List, which are in fierce competition and freely air their rancor toward each other, openly courted the PLO for some expression of support. The same was essentially true of Abd al-Wahab Derauche's new list, the Democratic Arab Party, whose very establishment was cleared indirectly by representatives of the PLO.

It is likewise no secret to the Israeli security organs that particularly close cooperation has existed for years between parties and organizations in the territories and their counterparts in Israel. The Palestine Communist Party enjoys generous support and aid from Rakah; circles identified with the so-called Rejection Front† in the West Bank are in touch with radical groups like the Sons of the Village movement in Israel; and over the past few years a relationship of cooperation and dependence has developed between the factions of the Muslim Brotherhood in the Triangle and the movement's leaders in Gaza and Tulkarem—to the point where the fundamentalists in the territories advised their Israeli brethren on whether to vote for the Knesset and how to gear up for elections to the local authorities in February 1989.

Nevertheless, the PLO remains the leading outside influence on the Israeli-Arab community, and its means of enhancing that sway has been similar to its strategy in the territories: a steady flow of funds to support local organizations and institutions. This infusion of capital has been going on for over a decade now and increases from year to year, as does the number of people who benefit from it. It is the

---

* Understandings whereby two parties of a similar persuasion agree to turn over their excess votes (above the number required to obtain their last mandate) to the partner that would obtain an additional seat with the aid of these votes.
† The Democratic and Popular fronts.

PLO's way of reinforcing the infrastructure of the Israeli-Arab community, thus reducing its dependence on the government while winning supporters for its own endeavors. The potential recipients of these funds tend to regard them as offers they can't refuse. For while Palestinians abroad make generous sums available for the asking, the Israeli government has adopted a policy of benign neglect toward the Arab community and has been notably stingy with its appropriations. Far from rushing into this vacuum, the PLO has finessed its entry by means of purportedly independent endowments and funds. It has also been scrupulous about how its monies are used, ruling out all activities entailing violence or sabotage, which would give the government grounds for halting the transfer of capital. The availability of funds from Palestinian sources is an open secret among local councils and official bodies, and they take full advantage of it while applying to the government for their annual budgets, they regularly submit requests to foreign institutions controlled by PLO proxies.

One of these funds, the Geneva-based Welfare Association, which annually pumps millions of dollars into Israeli-Arab institutions, has Fatah activists on its executive committee and board of directors. It is headed by the managing director of the Arab Bank of Amman, Abd al-Majid Shouman, a former chairman of the Palestine National Fund. His deputy, Hassib Sabagh, is an active member of the Palestinian National Council and serves as an economic adviser to Yasser Arafat, while another member of the executive has served in the PLO's delegation to the United Nations. The Welfare Association is run in a highly professional manner and like any institution of its kind regularly sends out inspectors to report on how its donations are being used. In the months just prior to the *intifada* (September–November 1987), it transferred to Israel hundreds of thousands of dollars that found their way to a wide gamut of Arab groups, from societies that run kindergartens, women's organizations, and health services to an institute for Palestinian students in Acre and the Society for the Prisoner (which received a very impressive grant).

Israel's security organs have long had an interest in blocking these funds but have encountered an obstacle of their own in the State Attorney's Office, which argues that the state must first prove that the monies come directly from the PLO and are earmarked for illegal activities. There is of course ample precedent in Israel for applying for outside support. It is justly argued that since cities and institutions in the country's Jewish sector turn to the United Jewish Appeal and other outside sources for donations, the Arab sector is entitled to apply to Palestinian-run funds, especially as the government so blatantly discriminates against it in apportioning grants for development.

Statements of this sort bespeak a new-found assurance that distinguishes today's Arab leaders from their not-so-distant predecessors. Even a decade ago few would have been so outspoken on an issue that highlighted their ties to the Palestinian people. Long subject to a military government after the 1948 war, Israel's Arabs tended to remain insecure and wished to ingratiate themselves with the powers that be. Today, however, rather than cringe at whims of the state, they bask in the protection conferred by Israel's democracy. They have also come to appreciate the broad field of maneuver between their aspirations as Palestinians who take pride in their national heritage and the sensitivity of the Israeli law on matters of national security.

Much of this change traces to the younger, better educated, and more authentic leadership that has emerged among Israel's Arabs over the past few years. It is based mostly on an intelligentsia of at least 10,000 graduates of Israeli universities and others who have studied in the Soviet bloc on scholarships arranged by Rakah. This educated class, which grows from year to year and has lately enjoyed a much-improved standard of living, is marked by a strong political consciousness and a degree of self-confidence previously unknown among Israeli Arabs. Though confirming Israel's right to exist, its members feel a part of the Palestinian people and speak of themselves not as Israeli Arabs but as "Israeli Palestinians." Sympathizing as they do with the uprising in the territories, they directly and intensely experience the painful reality of "their people being at war with their country" and seek a formula to help realize the Palestinians' national dreams without turning against, and necessarily prejudicing their rights in, the State of Israel. One could go even further in saying that this first generation of Israeli Palestinians wants to help free its people from the yoke of Israeli occupation while enhancing its own status as citizens of Israel. If not quite a contradiction in terms, this is a tall order and rests on a delicate balance too easily rocked by fluctuations in the public mood. A committee appointed by Shimon Peres to recommend lines of policy toward the country's Arab minority wrote of the situation in 1984: "What we have here is a deep-seated, substantive conflict that can be resolved not in a radical, clear-cut manner but only by the mitigation of opposites, by mutual recognition and respect, and by the search for a common denominator." Under these circumstances, the committee's aim was to avert "a situation in which the national identity of the country's Arabs is expressed primarily by a display of hostility toward Israel."

The voting patterns of the Israeli-Arab community in successive national elections reflect the development of a new political consciousness. Whereas in past decades a good portion of this electorate voted for one or another of the Zionist parties (usually the ones in power), this is emphatically no longer the case. Gone are the days when Arab voters blindly followed the dictates of their clan heads. Today they think for themselves and have come to utilize the vote as a kind of protest action. In the 1981 elections to the 10th Knesset, two-thirds of Israel's Arabs were still giving their support to the mainstream Zionist parties or associated Arab lists; but by the following elections three years later, 51 percent of them were voting for radical, non-Zionist parties with a Palestinian-nationalist bent, such as Rakah or the Progressive List for Peace. This shift was especially noticeable among Muslim voters, who comprise the majority of Israel's Arabs, with 63 percent of them casting their ballots for non-Zionist parties. But the trend was also strong in the Christian villages, where over 60 percent of the Greek-Orthodox community and 40 percent of the members of the Western churches—mostly Catholics—voted for non-Zionist parties. Only the two small ethnic communities, the Druze and the Bedouin, continued to vote for the Zionist lists in great numbers: 92 percent of the Druze and 84 percent of the Bedouin electorate in 1984. In 1988 the trend away from the mainstream intensified, with some two-thirds of the Arab voters supporting non-Zionist parties, and it is believed that the *intifada* had an influence on channeling additional votes in this direction.

Since the start of the uprising, Israel's Arabs have effectively abandoned the old premise that it is possible to "influence policy from within"—meaning within the Zionist establishment. Perhaps the most salient expression of this change was the resignation, due to the *intifada*, of two Arab Knesset members from Zionist parties. Abd al-Wahab Derauche left the Labor Party to found an independent list (the Democratic Arab Party, which won one seat in the 12th Knesset), and Mohammed Watad left Mapam (in which he had been active since his youth) to join the Rakah-led Democratic Front for Peace. The status of the Progressive List for Peace—made up of two wings, the Arab majority and the smaller Jewish group called the Alternative—likewise attests to the new mood among the Israeli Palestinians. Despite appeals by the Jewish wing to unify both factions into a single party, the Arab majority spurned the notion of integration. The most it would agree to was the merger of the two wings' executives into a single political leadership. Observers have also noted discrepancies between the Arabic and the Hebrew versions of the party platform published in April 1988. The Arabic version presents the nationalist issue in more radical terms, and though not denying Israel's right to exist, it stipulates that the country's final borders should be determined in negotiations with the Palestinian state to be established alongside it. It also stresses the attachment of Israel's Arabs to this future Palestinian state, creating the impression that they will regard it as their homeland, too. Some Israelis read this clause as a sign of irredentist leanings, and its ambiguity has even been decried by a highly respected spokesman for Rakah, the writer and editor Emile Habibi.

These are but a few recent examples of the "Palestinization" of Israel's Arabs, a process that began slowly during the state's early years and has accelerated to new heights during the *intifada*. Until the founding of the PLO in 1964, it was mostly a latent process. But then the Six-Day War, by effectively erasing the Green Line, brought the Arabs of Israel into direct contact with the bubbling cauldron of Palestinian nationalism just as their domestic political status was undergoing a change. From 1948 to 1966 Israel's Arabs had been subject to a military government. Its final repeal a year before the Six-Day War freed energies for heightened political activity, and within a decade the expansion of this activism was reflected in two major political events. The first occurred on March 30, 1976, a date that has since been marked as a day of remembrance by Israeli Arabs—and Palestinians as a whole—as "Land Day." In the months preceding this protest, the Israeli government had expropriated some 6,000 acres of land in Galilee for development purposes. About 2,300 acres were owned by Jews and the rest by Arabs, yet the latter viewed the operation as a deliberate attempt to deprive them of their lands and as proof that the effort to dispossess the Palestinians, which had begun in 1948, was still going on in the democratic State of Israel. To make matters worse, the expropriations were carried out so callously that for the first time in the history of the state, the Arabs of Israel were moved to hold a community-wide demonstration and general strike. With feelings running high that day, the demonstrations culminated in a number of clashes with the army, in which five Arabs were killed. The community was shaken by the results of the protest action but emerged from it more determined than ever to stand on its rights.

The events of "Land Day" made a deep impact on the Arabs of Israel. It spawned a new resolve that has come out in the creation of the Lands Protection Committee to fight future expropriations plans. But on another level a more insidious reaction set in: many policies and actions that had once been interpreted as simply the government's insensitivity to the needs of its citizens were increasingly taken as deliberate discrimination against the country's Arabs. Community bodies and activities that had traditionally focused on social and municipal affairs began to take on nationalist overtones, the best example being the National Committee of Arab Mayors and Local Council Chairmen, founded in 1974. The movement known as the Sons of the Village, which began as an aid effort on the municipal level, has since become a radical force that essentially negates the existence of the State of Israel in its present format.

Israel's 1982 war in Lebanon was the other event that spurred the "Palestinization" of Israel's Arab citizens. Like their brethren in the territories and the diaspora, Israeli Arabs also regarded the war conceived and conducted by Ariel Sharon as an assault on the Palestinians. They saw it as a bid to arrest their development, expel them from yet another Arab state, and scatter them even further to destroy their national cohesion throughout the area that had once been Palestine. By the same token, the massacre perpetrated by the Lebanese Phalangists in the Sabra and Shatila refugee camps was perceived as part of a grand design to wipe the Palestinians out. The sense of danger created by the war infected Israel's Arabs as well, bringing the community closer together. Identification with the Palestinian struggle, and the PLO in particular, also rose appreciably.

The resulting quandary in which the Arabs of Israel find themselves is reflected in tortuous statements like: "We are part of the Palestinian people, which is represented by the PLO, but the PLO does not represent the Arabs of Israel." Such fancy footwork has been particularly and understandably vigorous since the passage of a law declaring the PLO to be a terrorist organization and making association or contact with it a criminal offense. Rakah has solved the representation issue in a more straightforward manner by stating: "We Israeli Arabs are represented by our government, but we may take issue with it." There are also more poignant expressions of the complex identity crisis weighing upon many Israeli Arabs, like that of a high school student from the village of Jaljulah. Asked by the prime minister's adviser on Arab affairs to define who he was, the youngster replied sadly: "I want to be an Arab Israeli, but you won't let me."

Added to their political predicament is a sense of deprivation, whether on the social or economic level, that has been expressed far more stridently. The Westernization (or as some observers prefer, "Israelization") of the community's intelligentsia has created greater expectations than ever before among Israeli Arabs as a whole. They gauge their collective standing and achievements not against the community's condition in the past but in contrast to the state of the country's dominant Jewish community, and such invidious comparisons have naturally sharpened their sense of resentment. The sociologist Dr. Majid al-Haj explains that the identity of Israeli Arabs is made up of two components: one is "the frank, strong desire for greater equality within Israeli society, while the other continues to be identification with the Palestinians in the territories." The problem is that the distinction between these two elements has begun to fade, and the stronger the feeling of inequality and deprivation grows, the more Israel's Arabs will stress the Palestinian aspect of their identity.

Certainly the deprivation cannot be denied. The living conditions of Israeli Arabs in certain neighborhoods of Jaffa, Lod, and Ramle, for example, are a mark of shame on Israeli society. A report written by Amos Gilboa, formerly the prime minister's adviser on Arab affairs, notes a huge discrepancy between the budgets of the Arab local authorities and their Jewish counterparts. The Arab cities lag far behind in their development, and the allocations they receive from the Ministry of Interior are strikingly low. While Jewish cities, towns, and settlements have long enjoyed support from both the central government and Jewish institution abroad (such as the United Jewish Appeal), it is only recently that the Arab settlements have had access to outside funding, and even then in nowhere near similar amounts.

Deprivation is all too obvious in the sphere of education, as well. It ranges from a chronic shortage of classrooms and low level of vocational and technological training to the obstacles placed in the path of those who attain academic degrees. About a thousand Arab students graduate from Israel's universities each year, but the decisive majority of them find that many jobs in the Israeli economy are closed to them. This is true not only of the military industries but of most government offices. Only a few graduates will find their way into teaching. Unless they can set themselves up in business or one of the free professions, the remainder must settle for unskilled jobs like the rest of the Arab workers in the Israeli economy, including thousands of high school graduates. Four-fifths of the Arab breadwinners are salaried employees who work at a considerable distance from their homes (earning them the sobriquet "workers on wheels"). In the commercial sphere, however, they usually remain segregated within the Arab sector, for they often find that Jewish Israelis feel uncomfortable with them and prefer to keep their distance.

Perhaps the most antagonizing indignity of all is that more than forty years after the establishment of the state, the Arab minority still has little impact on the decisions of any arm of the central government, even on matters that directly affect their own lives. The Arab members of the Knesset comprise one pressure group of many and have contributed little to advancing the interests of their constituents. As Amos Gilboa has reported, along with pride in the economic, social, and organizational progress they have made over the years, Israel's Arabs have experienced growing frustration and bitterness. The combination of the two has heightened their sense of national distinction within Israeli society, and Gilboa believes that they are going to start moving in the direction of communal autonomy.

If, despite the binds of inequality, the Arabs of Israel have nevertheless acquired a sense of power, it stems in large part from their success in creating a communal leadership in the National Committee of Arab Mayors and Local Council Chairmen. Today this body represents three Arab cities and sixty-two local councils, encompassing over 680,000 Arab residents. Thus for all intents and purposes, the National Committee is the Arab community's democratically elected leadership. Attached to it are a number of smaller bodies, such as the Arab Students' Committee, the High School Students' Committee, and watch committees monitoring a variety of issues. The committee's plenum—which is attended by representatives of all these smaller groups together with Arab members of the Knesset, representatives from the Histadrut (General Federation of Labor), the Teachers' Union, the Sons of the Village, and other leading Arab figures—is the equivalent of an unofficial parliament for the Israeli-Arab community. Rakah and its fellow-travelers hold about half the seats on these committees, but thanks to their organizational abilities and political experience, they usually carry the day in the plenum's votes.

Quietly and systematically, then, the Arabs of Israel have built their own elected leadership, a force that initially confined itself to local affairs but today addresses national issues. Traditionally the Israeli government has taken a jaundiced view of such centralized representation for the Arab community. During the 1970s this issue was the subject of heated debates, with the prime minister's adviser on Arab affairs, Shmuel Toledano, commending such a framework as a tool for influencing the Arab community and the Shin Bet countering that it could well develop into something far less benign. Earlier attempts to establish a body of this kind failed precisely because they were carried out in a clumsy, even menacing fashion. In 1980, for example, Rakah proposed holding a national convention of Israeli Arabs whose delegates would be drawn from all the country's Arab settlements on the basis of proportional representation. This convention was to become a standing body and function like a parliament exclusively for the Arabs of Israel. But when the idea became known to the country's security organs, a regulation was issued outlawing the convention's steering committee, and the notion of convening an Arab parliament in Israel—in this format, at least—was promptly shelved.

With the National Committee, however, the idea of a collective representative body for the Arabs of Israel has come to fruition through the back door. After the strike on "Peace Day" in December 1987, in solidarity with the *intifada*, it was suggested that the government should withdraw its tacit recognition of the body by ordering its ministries to sever all relations with it. But by then the committee was already too powerful for the government to boycott without severely straining relations with the Arab community as a whole. Besides, the built-in dissonance between the two main coalition partners, Labor and the Likud, extended to this subject as well. The Likud ministers naturally leaned toward boycotting the committee but Labor would not hear of it, so there was no point in even putting the matter to a vote.

Another source of the Arab community's self-assurance is its sense of ease with "the system" in Israel, especially with the ways of the country's democracy. This is particularly true of the younger generation. Their elders may have been traumatized by the tragedy that befell the Palestinians in 1948 and the years of military government that followed, but the generation born after the establishment of the state—which today comprises 80 percent of Israel's Arabs—feels quite at home in Israel. They have learned to take advantage of the country's democratic privileges and appreciate the prospects they offer. They have also learned to exercise their rights as full and equal citizens

and feel secure in the knowledge that large sections of the Jewish public will not allow these rights to be violated, as often happened during
the early years of Israel's existence. Yet they are also aware that they
will continue to enjoy this status only as long as they neither pose
nor are perceived to pose a threat to the nation's security.

As part of "learning the ropes," the Arab community has also
come to see that in the struggles for a share of the government's
strained resources, the meek finish last, every time. The rule of thumb
in Israel is that you can't get what you want without banging on the
table, demanding your due, and trumpeting the justice of your cause.
Internalizing this lesson, Israel's Arabs have begun to demonstrate with
greater frequency for full equality in practice as well as on paper. A
typical example of this strategy was the declaration of a general strike
on June 24, 1987, dubbed "Equality Day." Its success instilled confidence in the community that it could resort to this tactic whenever
necessary. And although no one could have foreseen it at the time,
"Equality Day" was also a dress rehearsal for the strike held in support
of the insurgents in the territories six months later.

Among Israel's Arabs are a number of radical groups that view
the *intifada* as an example that their own community should emulate.
The elected leadership usually takes pains to restrain these "reckless
elements." While supporting the Palestinian cause and accepting the
status of the PLO, it insists that all actions in Israel must fall within
the framework of the law. Yet there is no denying that the potential
for violence exists and will steadily grow unless the Israeli-Palestinian
conflict is resolved. Even the specter of civil war cannot be discounted,
for clearly the problems and tensions of Arab-Jewish relations are not
confined to the territories. In a future outburst, the unrest could well
spread to the Arabs of Israel proper.

Israel's Intelligence community is alert to this danger, just as it
is aware of the developing "Palestinian connection" among the country's Arab citizens and the inroads made by the PLO. Yet these same
experts believe that other factors are even greater cause for concern,
and they point first of all to the demographic trend. At the end of
1987 the total Arab population of Israel stood at about 790,000 (including the 110,000 or so residents of East Jerusalem), accounting for
17 percent of the state's population. In 1949, at the end of Israel's War
of Independence, the Arab minority numbered 156,000, or 13 percent
of the overall population. Since then Israel's Jewish population has
more than tripled, due primarily to the great tide of immigration in

the late 1940s and early 1950s, whereas the Arab population has quadrupled as a result of natural increase alone. Projections for the year
2000 show Israel's Arabs comprising some 20 percent of the population.
Although the rate of natural increase is now declining among this
community, especially among the Christians (falling from 2.71 percent
in 1955 to 1.2 percent in 1985), among the Muslims it was still as high
as 3.2 percent in 1985 (compared with 1.43 percent among the country's Jews).

Because of Israel's system of proportional representation, the political implications of this ratio go well beyond the community's
weight in purely demographic terms. In the 1984 elections, the Israeli-
Arab community had the potential to elect twelve deputies (out of
the 120 in the Knesset), and in 1988 its voting power rose to a potential of fourteen deputies. Yet the Arabs of Israel have not always used
this power to maximum advantage. A good proportion of them did
not vote at all, and many of those who did gave their support to the
Zionist parties. Over the years, however, a slow change has set in
regarding both voter turnout (73 percent in 1988) and a tendency
to vote for non-Zionist lists. In the 1984 elections, Israel's Arabs effectively voted in ten members of the Knesset—seven Arabs and three
Jews—but only four of them on Zionist lists. In 1988 the PLO openly
urged them to concentrate their votes on the non-Zionist parties to
create a "blocking force" that would prevent the establishment of a
right-wing government. In theory, this was indeed viable. But lack
of organization, competition between the Arab parties, and their refusal to sign excess-votes agreements prevented them from realizing
their potential. Moreover, the 1988 Knesset elections and 1989 elections
for the local authorities showed a rise in the fundamentalist factions
at the expense of Rakah, thus further fractionalizing the Arab electorate. With a more rational strategy, however, the Arabs of Israel—
like the block of religious parties in the 1988 elections—could become
the deciding factor in the forming of government coalitions.

Some Jewish Israelis find this prospect so unacceptable that they
would rend the fabric of Israel's democracy to avoid it. Ariel Sharon,
for one, has remarked that it is out of the question for the Arabs of
Israel effectively to decide which government will rule the country.
He pays lip service to the principle of equal rights but notes that they
go hand in hand with equal obligations and suggests that in return
for the franchise, Israel's Arabs should have to serve in the army
(though he knows quite well that both the IDF and the Shin Bet have

strong objections to the idea).* By some inscrutable logic, this condition would apply not to the Jewish yeshivah students, who are likewise exempt from military service, but only to the country's Arabs. Should it ever be passed, such legislation would bring the demise of equal rights in Israel. And once that goes, there's no telling where the erosion of democratic principles will end.

Another factor that threatens to undermine Israel's domestic stability if the Palestinian-Israeli conflict goes on much longer is the geographic concentration of the Israeli-Arab community. The Arabs already constitute a majority in two regions of the country: the Galilee, where they reached 50.3 percent of the population in 1985 (a majority that is constantly growing); and in the Triangle and Wadi Ara, where the Jewish population is quite sparse. In the Triangle, moreover, the Arab populace is entirely Muslim and has a strong attachment to the Palestinians living in the northern West Bank—relations that have grown considerably closer since the *intifada*. Intelligence experts fear that the existence of these two concentrations of Arab population may in itself encourage the rise of irredentism. In fact, sentiments in this direction have already been voiced by radical groups in suggesting that an autonomous Arab region be established in the Galilee. Such ideas are neither new nor especially linked to the uprising. Until 1959 the Arabs in the Communist Party espoused the right of self-determination "to the point of secession." In 1964 the al-Ard ("The Land") movement mooted the idea that the Galilee would eventually be annexed to one of the bordering Arab states. This notion caused such a stir that al-Ard was outlawed by the Supreme Court for sedition, and the attempt by some of its members to run for the Knesset on the Socialist List was similarly thwarted. A number of the movement's leaders subsequently found their way into the PLO leadership (outstanding among them being Sabri Jiryas) and alerted it to the benefits of reaching out to the Arabs of Israel.

In addition to being concentrated in these areas, Israel's Arabs live along the main arteries in the north and the Triangle. Even in the southern part of the country, where the Bedouin are definitely in the minority, their settlements tend to be located on the two main roads through the desert, one leading to Beersheba and the other to the Dead Sea. Natural increase and the style of building customary

---

* With the exception of the Druze, Israel's Arabs are exempt from military service on a combination of security and humanitarian grounds. Christians and Bedouin are accepted if they volunteer, but only the Druze are drafted.

among the Arabs—horizontal rather than vertical—has resulted in the spread of Arab towns and villages over broad areas. Thus while the Arab population of Israel has quadrupled since 1949, the area inhabited by it has multiplied tenfold during the same period, primarily by encroachment onto state lands. This spread has been abetted by the failure of the Israeli authorities to draw up master plans for the Arab settlements. The absence of plans has in turn led to the widespread violation of building laws and to the norm of infringing upon state lands. Thousands of destruction orders are issued by the courts against the houses built without permits, but the government has proved incapable of enforcing them.

As a result of this sprawl of existing towns and villages, a number of areas of contiguous Arab settlement have formed, particularly in the heart of the Lower Galilee and Wadi Ara. Neighboring villages have melded into urban clusters, each containing tens of thousands of residents, with the axes of transport passing through them like the main streets of newly formed cities. Clearly these conglomerates will continue to grow into blocs of homogeneous settlement within Israel. At the same time, the severe housing problems in these areas have spurred Israeli Arabs to move into the Jewish cities on the coast, though presently at a slow rate. The dependence on Jewish sources of employment is another factor that leads more and more Arabs to settle in these cities or at least purchase businesses there, despite the fact that most of them receive a chilly reception, at best, from their new Jewish neighbors.

It must be said to the credit of the Israeli-Arab community that for the forty-one years of the country's existence, it has rebuffed all calls and pressures from over the border to engage in hostile activity against the state. There have been few cases of espionage, and the number of acts of sabotage and murder have also been strikingly low and were usually perpetrated under the direction of Palestinians from the territories. For all that, numerous problems are seething beneath the surface. Yet every Israeli government to date has chosen to wink at them rather than work out a cogent policy toward the country's Arab minority. Every so often a committee is appointed to deal with one issue or another, but their reports are either rejected or simply ignored. Typical of this syndrome is the painful problem of the Arabs who were persuaded in 1948 to evacuate the villages of Biram and Ikrit—temporarily and for military reasons—but have not yet been allowed to return. Even when forwarded by a Likud minister with such impeccable political credentials as Moshe Arens, the proposal to allow them to resettle in the vicinity of their villages was soundly rejected by Prime Minister Shamir.

The present government's refusal to face up squarely to the problems suffered and posed by the Arab community will not make them disappear. Neither can it obscure the fact that if Israel's Arabs are drawn into the *intifada*, the country will face a genuine disaster. For once torn asunder, Israel's body politic as we know it today will surely be beyond repair. If only for that reason, the Arabs of Israel must be brought to understand that whether or not Israel will one day agree to the constitution of an independent Palestinian political entity in the West Bank and Gaza depends to a large degree on how they conduct themselves. If the radical forces flaunt the cause of irredentism and serve the PLO's aim of gradually bringing the *intifada* over the Green Line, the Jewish public will undoubtedly be convinced that the struggle between the two peoples is not just over the future of the occupied territories but over Tel Aviv and Haifa. And if the terms of the struggle are truly all or nothing, so that it cannot be resolved by compromise, then there is no point in relinquishing even a small section of the territories. Why give up Nablus or Rafah if the Palestinians intend to use them as a springboard for conquering Israel's heartland? This is the argument already being made by the Israeli Right. Whether or not it is embraced by the Jews of Israel as an unequivocal policy position may depend on the actions of their Arab compatriots in the months and years to come.

Finally, Israel's Arabs have been able to make their voices heard because of the strength of Israel's democracy. It is therefore in their own best interests to strengthen the state's democratic system, whereas trying to import the *intifada* into Israel would be like sawing the limb they stand on. In short, while asserting their identity and rights, the Arabs of Israel must beware of unintentionally abetting the forces that would gladly strip them of their franchise and reduce them to second-class citizens. The stakes are far too high to gamble with the future.

SEVEN | *THE UNIFIED NATIONAL COMMAND*

OUT OF THE *intifada* rose a new brand of leadership that tried to rein in the runaway violence and steer the Palestinians in the territories onto a more orderly course of struggle. The top echelon of this new force cloaked itself in mystery as a secret authority called the Unified National Command, while at the grass-roots level an array of "popular committees" sprang up in almost every city, village, and camp. In each case the impulse was a desire for coherence. The emergence of this new leadership was, as one of its more eminent members put it, "an attempt to install a conductor and pass out sheet music to an orchestra in which all the instruments were playing in the same meter but not at the same pace."

The birth of the Unified National Command brought to the Israeli-Palestinian conflict a breed of leaders that was quite unprecedented. Raised in the shadow of Israel's occupation, they had only vague memories of what life had been like before it. Diplomacy and intercession with the authorities, the hallmarks of their predecessors for the past two decades, were simply not their style. They went in for action and fresh ways of thinking, and their ideas caught on fast. Almost before anyone knew it, a unique way of doing things had taken hold in the territories along with a new vision of the population as a self-propelled body that was both leading and waging the struggle against Israel on its own.

From this perspective, the first months of 1988 marked a dramatic change in the political complexion of the conflict, for both Israel and the PLO were suddenly forced to accommodate a new partner in the long-standing strife between them. No longer were the lines of confrontation drawn solely by the policy of the Civil Administration or directives coming from the PLO abroad; now it was the Palestinians on the spot who decided what direction the struggle would take. Although it was composed of novices who had never extended their authority beyond networks of clandestine cells, the Unified National Command soon won unprecedented influence and prestige. In its heyday (through the summer of 1988) it challenged both Israel's control of the territories and the absolute authority of the PLO abroad, playing cat-and-mouse with the Israelis while deftly sidestepping the orders coming out of Tunis. Its members professed loyalty to the PLO but questioned the infallibility of its leaders. As Dr. Hisham Awartani explained it, they saw the organization as being not just the bureaucracy and military forces abroad but first and foremost the leaders and their following "on the inside." Thus the ground was shifting in two directions at once: while rubbing Israel's nose in the fact that the PLO, not the army or the Civil Administration, held exclusive sway over the local Palestinians, the Unified Command gave out equally emphatic signals that it would not kowtow to blasé bureaucrats ensconced far from the "theater of operations" in the West Bank and Gaza.

From the outset, then, the command labored under difficult constraints. While functioning underground to elude the Israelis, it had to contend with the PLO's intolerance for bold initiative and independent action. Ironically, the command's immediate success raised its members to a pinnacle of popularity that would prove to be their nemesis. In time, the pressure at home and bullying from abroad would dampen their ambitions and puncture their pluck. But for all its weaknesses, this new leadership soon became the helm of the *intifada*. It: florescence may have been short-lived, but it set down deep roots tha were never wholly destroyed. Who were these people? Where di they come from and where were they going?

To this day the names of the Unified Command's members d not ring a bell to most of the Palestinians involved in the uprising an certainly not to the Israelis who followed it in the press. Mohamme and Majid Labadi and their Gazan brother-in-law Jamal Zakut are fa from household words, just as very little is known of the role playe by academics like Samir Shehadeh and Taysir al-Arouri or by seasone activists like Yakoub Odeh, Adnan Dagher, Abd-al-Latif Ghaith, an

Mohammed Jaber. The same can be said of a long list of other figures. Not only did they all remain anonymous while serving on the command, their involvement was kept secret after they had been arrested and sometimes even after they had been deported by the Israelis! Throughout 1988 a strange conspiracy of silence was at work to shroud the true face of the new local leadership. Whoever uncovered their identity—whether Palestinian activists or Israeli security agents—was careful to keep it secret. Even the leaders themselves chose to remain silhouettes behind a screen of conjecture and rumor.

The obvious question is what benefit did they derive by clinging to their anonymity. Clearly it was not the demands of security that decided this course, for everyone knew that after groping around in the dark for a while, the Shin Bet solved the maze of compartmentalization surrounding the command and captured its successive memberships three times within a short interval. On the face of it, once arrested the members of the command had no reason to conceal their identity and every reason to want to bask in the admiration due people of their rank. Yet even the lawyers hired to defend them tried to protect their anonymity by deflecting the media's attention from the trials. Time and again, if Israel's military censors did not intervene first, their own self-censorship preserved the mystery surrounding these men, so that the Unified Command would remain a closed book.

This odd stroke of modesty can be traced to two basic sources. On one level the command's members feared the response of their own constituents if their masks were torn away and the rather conventional faces behind their pretentious collective title were suddenly revealed. After all, none of them could boast of being among the better-known Palestinian leaders. Few even came from one of the patrician Palestinian families that had traditionally dominated Palestinian politics. So the newcomers had good reason to fear that if their identities became known, the blind obedience to their handbills would quickly give way to questions about their judgment and perhaps even their motives. In short, they believed that self-concealment was in the best interests of the cause.

Then there were misgivings of the opposite sort: a fear that coming out into the open would be construed as a bid to supplant the PLO as an alternative leadership, or at least gnaw away at the outsiders' absolute hegemony. Early on, the command had learned how sensitive Arafat and his colleagues were to the least challenge, real or imagined, to their exclusivity. And there was no denying the command's potential to become a truly representative leadership for the people of the territories, thus posing a very real threat. The friction over this issue remained behind closed doors for many months but finally became public when some junior activists abroad complained that it was a grave mistake to rein in the men running the uprising. The loudest outcry came from Jamil Hilal, one of the most astute members of the Democratic Front, who wrote: "It is wrong to view the movement inside [the territories] as just an operational network that carries out the decisions of the leadership in exile. That will only stunt the growth of an organized mass base. Strengthening the role of the leadership inside means *removing obstacles* to the creation of a unified center of command . . . that will direct the day-to-day struggle while serving as the communications link with the leaders of the PLO."

But Arafat and the other veterans would not budge an inch to make room for a "sub-command" in the territories or anywhere else. They insisted that the "branch" of the PLO in the territories was there to follow orders and serve only as a local "display window" for the policies of the PLO Executive. To leave no doubt about who was in charge, Arafat demanded that the command's handbills bear the signature of the PLO alongside the cryptic title Unified National Command—especially as the first of these circulars had made only brief reference to the parent organization. He then dictated the definition of the Unified Command as merely an "arm" of the PLO, meaning an operational tool lacking powers of its own. When this term proved offensive to the command's most fervent partisans, a lecturer at Bir Zeit University proposed a compromise formula. It defined the Unified Command as "one of the organs" or "part of the body" of the PLO, implying that its members were partners and not merely minions. But Tunis rejected that too.

Inevitably, the local leadership made peace with the fact that it would not be allowed to assert its independence and that none of its members would ever be hailed as a hero of the *intifada*. Deportees grew accustomed to the stilted ceremonies held for them after being set down on Lebanese soil by an Israeli helicopter. First they were ordered to hold sit-down strikes in the local offices of the Red Cross. Then they gave interviews to the PLO's various publications (consisting mostly of charges against Israel). Finally they were relegated to middle-level positions in one of the PLO's branch offices. Arafat scotched every attempt to create a public standing for these men, as they were entitled to expect. At the end of 1988 a few of the people associated with the command considered striking back by allowing a young Palestinian journalist to write an unofficial version of their story, including the tensions in their relations with Tunis. Their condition for cooperating, however, was that the book must mention no names!

Thus even as they were being relentlessly pursued by the Shin Bet, the members of Unified Command had to efface themselves before the PLO. Under no circumstances were they able to wage a struggle on both fronts at once. Equally important was the fact that the command needed at least tacit endorsement from the PLO abroad to keep its credibility at home. Open to charges of harming the cause by dividing the movement or placing local interests above national aims, the command's members opted for prudence. They swallowed their resentment over the rigid guardianship of the PLO, and the more vulnerable they became at home, the lower they bowed before their prickly patrons abroad.

The annals of the Unified National Command began on one of the last days of December 1987 when Mohammed Labadi invited Nasser Ju'abah, a fellow Democratic Front activist, to his al-Bireh apartment. A twenty-seven-year-old bachelor who owned a small bookshop in Ramallah, Ju'abah was Labadi's personal driver and came to the job with sterling credentials, having chauffeured the front's leaders around the territories for years. Initially he had worked for Dr. Azmi Shueibi, head of the local front network until the mid-1980s. In February 1987, a few months after Shueibi had been deported to Jordan, Ju'abah visited him there and received instructions to report to "Abu Samer" (namely, Mohammed Labadi) and pick up where he had left off, ferrying activists to meetings in his Opel Ascona. As a rule Ju'abah brought his passengers to Labadi's apartment in the morning and then went off to run his store, returning for them only after dark. Occasionally he would also carry letters from Labadi to his brother, Majid, and in the summer of 1987 he was again sent to Amman to report to Shueibi and receive instructions from him orally. Reliable and clever, Ju'abah did these jobs with commendable dispatch.

Perhaps that is why Labadi had a more ambitious role in mind for him. "We're going to put out handbills to inflame the people to revolt," he told his driver at that late December meeting, "and you're going to be in charge of printing them." Dispensing with further preliminaries, Labadi produced the text of the first such document. It bore the signature of the "Unified National Command to Escalate the Uprising in the Occupied Territories," a body that was a fiction at that point but would soon become practically synonymous with the *intifada*. (Its name changed after Jamal Zakut of Gaza persuaded his comrades to drop the word "escalate.")

Labadi's handbill, written in the soapbox style so typical of the leftist organizations, called upon the "heroes of the stone and firebomb war" to "redouble the revolutionary content" of their protest, "shake the oppressive regime down to its foundations," and create "inviolable unity" around the PLO, "the sole legal representative of our Palestinian people." "The neo-fascists will be forced to accept the facts determined by your uprising, which paves the way to national independence," wrote Labadi. "Let us fly the flag of Palestine from the walls of Jerusalem the Holy!" After disposing of the obligatory rhetoric, the handbill got down to business, ticking off the means by which its aims were to be achieved:

> All roads must be closed to the occupation forces . . . Its cowardly soldiers must be prevented from entering refugee camps and large population centers by barricades and burning tires . . . Stones must land on the heads of the occupying soldiers and those who collaborate with them. Palestinian flags are to be flown from minarets, churches, rooftops, and electricity poles everywhere . . . We must set the ground burning under the feet of the occupiers. Let the whole world know that the volcanic uprising that has ignited the Palestinian people will not cease until the achievement of independence in a Palestinian state whose capital is Jerusalem!

Together with the ultimate goal, Labadi also enumerated a number of interim ones: the withdrawal of the army from the cities, towns, and refugee camps; the eviction of Ariel Sharon from his house in the Old City of Jerusalem; the repeal of the Emergency Regulations,* including all pending deportation orders; the release of detainees; a halt to the expropriation of land and the establishment of new settlements the abolition of Value-Added Tax; and above all the dispersal of all the municipal, village, and refugee-camp councils and the hold-

---

* The legal basis for measures such as administrative detention, deportation, the demolition of houses, and other collective punishments. Originally enacted by the High Commissioner during the British Mandate, these regulations have been repealed within Israel proper but continue to be applied in the occupied territories.

ing of "democratic elections" in the West Bank and Gaza Strip. This first handbill also established the format for all those to follow. It opened with a new slogan—"No sound will silence the voice of the *intifada*"—followed by an order to launch a general strike (in this case for three days, January 11–13) and to hold symbolic funerals as part of the mass demonstrations.

Accepting his mandate without question, Ju'abah took Labadi's draft to another comrade of the Democratic Front, thirty-two-year-old Abd-al-Rahim al-Baghdadi of Anata, who managed a printing press in East Jerusalem and was active in the Print Workers' Union established by the Labadi brothers. This was not the first time Baghdadi took part in producing underground leaflets. As the Shin Bet subsequently learned, a dry run of sorts had been held as far back as June 1987 with a document written to mark the twentieth anniversary of the Six-Day War. Labadi's printing and distribution system had passed the test back then, and what was now ready to go into operation was a well-oiled machine.

Baghdadi accompanied Ju'abah to the large printing plant in Isawiyeh, just under the terraced houses on the outskirts of French Hill, at the eastern edge of Jerusalem. Despite this proximity to a thriving Jewish neighborhood, a month was to pass before the Israelis discovered that the preparation of the handbills was going on practically on their doorstep in the flat-roofed building with orange-painted doors that were visible from afar. The two brothers who owned the press, thirty-two-year-old Moussa and twenty-six-year-old Ali Darwish, were also associated with the dormant network that was waiting to be called back into action. They had invested enormous sums in sophisticated equipment, which eventually prompted the suspicion that the funding had been obtained, in part, through Mohammed al-Kurd, a well-known East Jerusalem money changer and channel for bringing PLO funds into the territories. Incidentally, one of Kurd's outlets was later torched because of rumors that he had embezzled some of these funds. Neither were the Darwish brothers wholly above reproach: under interrogation they admitted, among other things, to charging the Democratic Front an exorbitant price for their services!

The chances are good, however, that the Darwish brothers will go down in Palestinian history for a very different reason. As Labadi's first handbill was being readied for printing and the two brothers were chatting up their client, they casually mentioned that two days earlier they had printed up 35,000 copies of another flier bearing the signature of the "Palestine Nationalist Forces." It was written in a style very different from Labadi's, but it too called for a general strike on the same days as the handbill currently in press. Ju'abah immediately grasped that two leaflets written in distinctly different styles over different signatures to achieve the identical aim of a three-day strike would make a mockery of the group that presumed to call itself the Unified National Command. Before the Darwish brothers had completed their work, he rushed back to Labadi's house to inform him of the duplication. Labadi deduced that the other handbill must have been written by Fatah people, and he was livid that they had outstripped him. Rather than scrap his own version, however, he told Ju'abah to have 40,000 copies printed up with one simple but crucial adjustment: the addition of the number "two" to its heading. To avoid having the truth of their disunity leak out, Labadi gave his post-factum approval to the Fatah leaflet bearing the date of January 8 and dated his own January 10.

Ironically, then, the Unified National Command was born in an atmosphere of strife and mutual suspicion, with at least two of its member organizations trading sharp accusations. Labadi chastised the Fatah men for their arrogance in failing to take their PLO partners into account (not, we might add, without a healthy measure of sanctimony, considering his own behavior). The Fatah people complained of the Marxist tenor of Labadi's creation, and the front's members rejoined that the Nationalist Forces' leaflet was "mealy-mouthed" and evasive about defining goals. The bickering ended within a few days, however, as the two sides reached an understanding on reconstituting the four-party coordinating committee that had existed in Jerusalem prior to the *intifada*. As before, it would be composed of representatives of the Fatah, the Popular and Democratic fronts, and the Communist Party, but its new name would be the Unified National Command. Word of the agreement was relayed to the PLO as a fait accompli.

Initially the command was but a direct continuation of the coordinating committee that had long existed in the Jerusalem area (representatives from other regions were not invited to join). Over the years such committees had emerged in a number of cities to facilitate the planning of demonstrations and assemblies and to ease the friction between the members of the rival organizations. In the middle of 1987 Feisal al-Husseini, the senior Fatah man in the territories, tried to revive the institution of a central leadership, but his efforts were cut short by his arrest and consignment to administrative detention. The Unified Command was formed to fill that vacuum.

Labadi wanted the new body to be a command in the fullest sense of the word, issuing orders that were binding on all the other bodies that had sprouted up in the territories. Predictably, the Fatah people saw things differently; the most they would concede was to empower the command "to state the population's demands." A compromise was reached by defining its role as "guiding" the inhabitants of the territories. It would not be just an instrument for articulating demands, but neither would it be able to issue definitive orders. The Democratic Front also wanted to hold secret elections to determine the command's membership—though exactly how to mount so ambitious a venture was never discussed, and the subject was quickly dropped. The format agreed upon instead was that each of the four participating organizations would appoint its own representative, according to its own considerations, and that all would enjoy equal status regardless of their size. Because of the desire to maintain unanimity, the smaller organizations had de facto veto power. In mid-April, for example, the threat of a Communist walk-out led to the defeat of a resolution tabled jointly by the Fatah and the Democratic Front. The Unified Command never had a chairman; most of the time an irregular system of rotation was in effect, with a different member seeing to the drafting and dissemination of the successive handbills. Each of the four constituent organizations continued to run its separate network. They did not share secrets, and they stubbornly reserved the right to act independently outside of their joint framework, so that essentially the command's decisions were implemented at the discretion of the people in the field.

The Democratic Front wasted no time in trying to create a similar command in the Gaza Strip, and once again it was Mohammed Labadi who set things in motion through his brother-in-law and close friend Jamal Zakut. A thirty-one-year-old laborer employed in Israel, Zakut had been active in the front since his student days in Bulgaria, where he also underwent military training. He raised the idea of a central command with an old prison mate, twenty-seven-year-old Tawfiq Abu Housah of the Fatah, who ran a press service in downtown Gaza. Over a cup of coffee, Zakut outlined his plan for a committee of representatives from all the organizations in the Strip, emphasizing that he also intended to draw in people from the Islamic movement and create a single roof for the *intifada*. When Abu Housah promised to pass the proposal on to his superiors, Zakut approached Marwan Kafarnah, a thirty-two-year-old teacher from Jebalya, who similarly asked for time to consult with his commander in the Popular Front. The only man who agreed to the idea on the spot was the Communist leader Tawfiq Mabhouh, who at forty-one was the eldest among them.

Once the Fatah and the Popular Front had come through with their approval, the first meeting of the Gaza command was convened in Zakut's crowded home in the Nasser quarter of Gaza. Five men turned up for the session, but Tawfiq Abu Housah of the Fatah bowed out immediately, leaving in his place a twenty-five-year-old student named Ihab al-Ashkar, one of the leading lights of the local Shabiba. (The change was made for reasons of security as well as prestige, lest it be said that the Democratic Front had effectively chosen who would speak for the Fatah.) The Gaza team was appreciably younger than the West Bank command, for other than the Communist representative all of its members were in their twenties or early thirties. Each reported to a superior for approval of their jointly planned measures, and following this system every handbill was vetted by the leaders of the constituent organizations in the Strip. The first of these handbills proclaimed that the Gaza command had been joined by representatives of the "national-religious force that holds with the PLO's programs," and a subsequent leaflet stated specifically that the Islamic Jihad was participating in the command's activities. The truth of the matter is that Zakut had done his best to bring the Islamic Congress into the Gaza command, but his entreaties fell on deaf ears, while the militants of the Islamic Jihad made their membership conditional upon having the Jihad's name appear separately on all handbills alongside the signature of the collective command. They also insisted that all communiqués open with the traditional salutation "In the name of Allah the merciful," but the leftists wouldn't hear of adding a religious note to what were essentially political manifestos.

The Gaza command never gained the stature of its West Bank counterpart. Its handbills, for example, were usually copies of those printed in the West Bank by the Unified Command. When the Gazans tried to purchase a mimeograph machine, they had to send to Ramallah for it, and the funds to buy it were transferred via money changers in Jerusalem. Some members of the Gaza command purchased food for the refugee camps under curfew and kept a correspondence going with Dr. Zuhdi Zuhami, Arafat's personal representative in Amman.

But because it was not joined or acknowledged by the fundamentalists, the young team in Gaza never achieved any serious influence over affairs.

In any case it was a short-lived phenomenon, falling to the Shin Bet in mid-February 1988. Zakut was the first to be interrogated but refused to cooperate with his captors. "Not a word of that is correct," he snapped when a list of charges was read out before him, just as he refused to sign the interrogation sheet or write out his own testimony in Arabic. Only after Abu Housah and the three remaining members of the command had made confessions did Zakut agree to give his version of events—and in the end he was the only member of the group to be deported. From Lebanon he spoke of the command as "the identity card of the *intifada*" and hinted that he expected others to pick up where he had left off. Zakut fully believed that his fledgling framework would be able to continue with a new lineup, but that was not to be. The arrest of its founding members spelled the end of the Gaza command.

Not that the West Bank group fared much better at the start. "Bureaucratic excrement"—no more and no less—is how Bashir Barghouti, the leader of the Palestine Communist Party, described that newly established framework. It was a surly expression of his pique over what he suspected was a Fatah bid to impose its will on the uprising by slapping together an assortment of local leaders. Barghouti decried the idea of a unified command as chicanery "imported from the outside," a "dismal example" of the PLO's style of dispensing orders from above. In one conversation he even mocked the new command as "a mid-summer cold," implying that it was both a minor annoyance and out of step with the times. One reason for the Communists' difficulty in accepting the command was that unlike the three other organizations involved, which were subject to executive councils abroad, the Palestine Communist Party was run by people living within the territories themselves. They did not have to wait for instructions by phone, telex, or fax—at best. On the contrary, it was the party's representatives in Tunis, including its member on the PLO Executive Committee, who took their orders from the West Bank. This structural difference set Barghouti and his comrades apart from all the others who were approached to join the command. They railed against the blind obedience to Arafat's every word, for as far as they could see the decision-makers in Tunis were ignorant of the real conditions in the territories and certainly could not be trusted to run the daily affairs of the *intifada*. The Communists insisted that the "interior" be granted full "freedom of initiative," as long as it toed the policy line set down by the PLO. They spoke of a division of labor whereby Arafat would set "limits" and primary goals but steer clear of the "damaging course of dictating orders and enforcing detailed plans that were inappropriate to the sensitive circumstances and incongruent with the mood of the masses or their ability to act."

In the end the Communists did not disrupt the consensus by refusing to join the command. It would have been out of character, particularly as they saw themselves as the catalyst in the process that had brought about a full reconciliation between the Fatah and the two fronts at the April 1987 session of the Palestine National Council.* But while not boycotting the command, they did readily show their displeasure with their associates' behavior and ideas. Not surprisingly, their influence in the command mounted as their warnings against making unreasonable demands on the population were consistently borne out. They poked fun at the handbills urging the Palestinians to climb up on their roofs en masse or remain closed in their homes for forty-eight hours at a stretch to "take stock of themselves," rightly predicting that such demands would largely be ignored. They also countered the Popular Front's pressure to escalate the violence, proposing that energies be invested in organizing the public instead. The Communists preferred a slow and measured canter over a reckless gallop.

Barghouti personally enjoyed considerable respect and prestige in the territories, and even his rivals acknowledged his rich experience in clandestine activities. He had spent years in a desert detention camp in Jordan during Hussein's rule over the West Bank (when the Communist Party was outlawed) and did not return to Ramallah until 1974. A chain-smoking, balding man in his fifties, he was known for an exceptionally keen mind and sharp pen and devoted most of his time to editing his newspaper, *a-Tali'ah* ("The Vanguard"), in East Jerusalem. It was Barghouti who oversaw the party's rehabilitation after the staggering blow it suffered in 1973 while trying to organize an armed underground. Many of its most prominent members were deported after that debacle. Others were sent to prison, and it took quite a while for

* This rapprochement ended the bitter rift caused by Arafat's attempts to reach an accommodation with Jordan's King Hussein. It was achieved through vigorous Soviet mediation, thereby ensuring that the Communist Party would preserve its status in any new framework.

the party to recover from this setback. But under Barghouti's guidance it returned to its traditional philosophy, dissociating itself from terrorism and accentuating the principle that had always distinguished the Communist Party from the other Palestinian organizations: recognition of the State of Israel within its 1967 borders. These two tenets were drummed into the comrades at cell meetings and through the clandestine organ *al-Watan* ("The Homeland"). The party's close-knit structure, the intelligence of its recruits, and their strict adherence to discipline and secrecy ensured it an effective presence during the *intifada*. More than any other organization in the territories, the Communist Party was deployed for swift action. Orders were conveyed efficiently. Activists were encouraged to demonstrate but not to draw attention to themselves or overstep the line between demonstrations and violence. Above all they were told to help establish local committees to guide the population through the turmoil.

Even though, strictly speaking, the Communists' secret network was an illegal body, for reasons of their own Israel's security services made no effort to destroy it. Their policy was to arrest Communist activists only on evidence that they had been directly involved in riots, and dozens of them were indeed hauled in during the *intifada*. But no steps were taken to dismantle the party's two-tiered organization—a token public presence and a large nonviolent underground—or to arrest its leadership. Instead, from time to time the Shin Bet signaled these leaders to revert to a more cautious and restrained line. One such signal was put out in September 1988 with the seizure of the secret press used for printing *al-Watan*. After a long search and patient stake-out, the Shin Bet discovered its hiding place in a rented apartment in the town of A-Ram, practically bordering on the fence of an army camp. Two offset presses were concealed within a sewing workshop. Their operator, a tailor employed in a Jewish-owned factory in the West Bank, was not known as a supporter of the Communist Party. He had run the presses for years, isolated from contact with any other party members, by collecting the manuscripts from one drop point and depositing the printed copies at another. The raid on the press put the Communists on notice that their clandestine network was not immune to danger if the party faltered again.

Despite what sometimes appeared to be a tacit understanding with the Shin Bet that even involvement in the Unified Command did not undo, other events showed that the Communists were vulnerable on their flanks. In the town of Salfit, widely known as the "Moscow of the West Bank" because of the party's prevailing influence there, the Communists began operating as a local government in the fullest sense of the term. They saw to it that the village maintained strict order and discipline even at the height of the uprising. The villagers were forbidden to appear masked at demonstrations, for example, lest members of other organizations infiltrate Salfit and incite the marchers to violence. But when the new "local government" flaunted its power by banishing the Palestinian police, the IDF intervened and treated Salfit to a dose of "dissuasion"—cutting off its electricity and arresting many of its residents. The irony is that on the Palestinian side, Salfit was held up as proof that the Communists wanted to repress the *intifada*.

The accusation was patently unfair, for what the Communists wanted was to have the *intifada* run intelligently, not as a reckless adventure. In a long leaflet explaining how they distinguished themselves from the other Palestinian groups, they stressed the importance of educating the population toward patience and reducing losses. It was no secret that the Communists wanted to shift away from violence toward building a solid social and political infrastructure. Worn down by the pace of events, they warned, whole sectors of the population might simply drop out of the uprising. So they pulled in the direction of forming popular committees and laying a firm organizational base. But in only one case, in April 1988—when they objected to mounting an all-out campaign of civil disobedience—did the Communists stand on their principles to the point of threatening to quit the command. Their resolve on that issue quickly had the desired effect and left them with the feeling that they could "train" their partners to stop dreaming and accept the facts of life.

But it cannot be said that the Communists' path was easy from then on. When they pressed the command to appeal directly to Israeli public opinion by issuing a handbill in Hebrew, they were slapped down by the Popular Front with the testy growl: "We're talking with stones now." Their attempts to end the frequent calls to break away from the Israeli economy and bring down the Civil Administration had only sporadic effect. And of course on the prime issue—the political question—the Communists stood entirely alone. The other members of the command not only avoided using the word "Israel" in their handbills, they stubbornly resisted any moderation of their political posture until the PLO "outside" changed its stand. At one point the Communist member of the command, Dr. Taysir al-Arouri, urged his associates to declare explicitly that the Green Line was to be the border of the future Palestinian state. He also pressed them to clarify that the *intifada* was a struggle against the occupation, not against the existence of Israel. But his efforts got him nowhere, and it was only after being arrested that Arouri returned to writing, from prison, of a solution that would include the signing of a peace treaty and cooperation between Israel and a sovereign Palestinian state.

The forty-two-year-old Arouri, an ex-security prisoner, was unquestionably the most seasoned political activist of all the members of the command in its successive incarnations. Added to the teaching post he held in the Physics Department of Bir Zeit University was his title as chairman of the Union of University Graduates from East European Countries. A close associate of Barghouti's, he supervised the party's underground in the Ramallah and Jerusalem districts, which were the Communists' main power base. Arouri was more of a pragmatist than most of his colleagues on the command, and he tried to discourage them from mouthing empty slogans as their way of dealing with problems. He wanted them to plan the work of the popular committees, make street demonstrations a lesser priority, and see to it that the uprising spread to the prisons and detention camps in the form of strikes. Though he harped endlessly on these themes, for the most part his sparring with his colleagues remained inside the family. But after his arrest, the tension came out into the open when the Popular Front launched a stinging attack on the Communists. From his seat in Tunis, George Habash's deputy, Abu Ali Mustafa, lashed the party for straying from the official PLO line by commending direct talks with Israel, mutual recognition, and the acceptance of the 1967 borders. Neighboring states need not recognize each other, he argued, pointing to the two Koreas and South Africa and Angola as examples. "Israel is not South Africa," the Communists rejoined sharply. "And besides," they added rhetorically, "will our refusal to recognize Israel make it go away?"

The Fatah teetered back and forth between the radical impulse of the Popular Front and the moderating effect of the Communists, one side flooring the accelerator while the other jammed on the brakes. If the Democratic Front could be said to control the gear shift of the *intifada*, the steering wheel remained firmly in the hands of the Fatah, Arafat's loyal foot soldiers. Though not quite a motley crew, the rank and file of this most developed and best funded of the Palestinian organizations was not committed to any rigid ideology; to join the Fatah—or so it was often said—one could believe in anything or nothing at all. The founding of the Unified Command required the Fatah leaders to engage in tough bargaining with their partners and concede some of the prerogatives of primacy. But they nevertheless continued to set the tone.

Despite the headaches it caused, the command's coalition arrangement ensured that a common front would be maintained—and that, presumably, was the benefit which drew all four organizations in. Yet it must be said that the Fatah agreed to join the shadowy Unified Command only after it had failed to provide the uprising with a highly visible leadership of its own. The up-front approach was consonant with its unique method of operating in the territories. Rather than invest in building an underground, since 1979 it had focused on weaving a colorful fabric of "popular organizations," with pride of place going to the Shabiba. What the others were trying to accomplish out of secret burrows, the Fatah was doing through public institutions—by the dozens. The credit for this ambitious operation goes to Abu Jihad, who kept the money flowing to fund the components of this system: charity societies, press services, trade unions, colleges, cultural institutions, and allowances to thousands of families. According to the estimate of one Defense Ministry expert, between 1977 and 1985 the PLO pumped about half a billion dollars into the territories—funds that were used to win the population over to the Fatah. People were no longer recruited by the PLO; they were "absorbed" into the seemingly innocent organizations it supported. Abu Jihad rightly believed that this was the one way to bring the masses, not just a smattering of volunteers, under his control. Even mayors known for their connections with Jordan were treated to generous sums of pocket money on their trips abroad. In a rare statement on this subject, Arafat noted that the PLO bore a burden that no similar movement in history had ever assumed. "I need the budget of a middle-sized state," he remarked in the summer of 1985, "and the burden grows from year to year. We are responsible for all higher education in the occupied territories. We fund the municipalities, we run the marketing of Gaza's oranges, and we handle the export of grapes and olive oil."

Though certainly aware of this steady arrival of funds, Israel chose to live by the motto (coined by Defense Minister Ezer Weizman in 1977) that "Money doesn't pick up bad odors." Asked for his opinion on the matter, Foreign Minister Moshe Dayan reasoned that "the important thing is not where the money comes from but where it goes. If this cuts into the PLO's budget, all the better." No attempt was made to stem the flow of these funds, and on one occasion Arafat even boasted that "there's no problem; everything's completely above board." The fact is that most of the money was brought in via the Jordan bridges and was declared at customs. In 1982 a regulation was issued barring the entry of PLO funds, but it was essentially ignored by the authorities—because it proved so difficult to enforce—and was rescinded three years later. In a sense, then, Israel acquiesced in the creation of a shadow administration that was hooked up directly to the PLO's coffers. Rarely were direct punitive measures taken against any of its institutions, whose activities were labeled "political subversion" to distinguish them from outright sabotage. Admittedly, there were juridical obstacles to clamping down on this system, whose arms ranged from newspapers to infirmaries. But the truth is that the notion was never seriously entertained. From time to time Shmuel Goren would come forward with a list of targets for closure, saying that he could not reconcile the policy of all-out war against the PLO with the freedom of action it enjoyed in the territories. But in light of the already tense relations in the National Unity Government, the cabinet decided not to decide. All subsequent deliberations ended in much the same limbo, and the regular warnings about the accumulative effect of these "subversive activities" fell on deaf ears. The money poured in; the PLO became more deeply entrenched; and when the *intifada* began, the figures who fell under the broad category of "subversives" were ready and waiting to go into action.

The senior and most identifiable of the Fatah activists came from the new Palestinian intelligentsia, a kind of lost generation wedged between the "notables" who had represented the inhabitants of the territories after 1967 and the young militants who were now manning the barricades. As men of the middle class and middle ground, their natural inclination was to set the *intifada* on a more familiar, "respectable" footing by calling a press conference in Jerusalem, inviting the international media, announcing a plan of action for the uprising, and establishing themselves as its leadership. The prime mover in this case was the editor of *al-Fajr*, Hanna Siniora, a Christian (which was always a sensitive point among the Muslim majority) and a pharmacist by training who had become a political functionary. Siniora enjoyed Arafat's full backing, and it was with this credential that he invited figures from all over the territories to his paper's East Jerusalem offices to work out a blueprint for action. There was nothing secret about these meetings. They went on under the vigilant eye of Israel's security services, and in their final stage a few of Siniora's colleagues even tried to ruin whatever surprise was left by leaking his plan to the press—and knocking it behind his back.

The first public meeting on the Siniora plan, held at the National Palace Hotel on January 4, 1988, included a dozen or so participants (only half of whom returned for the second session on the following day). Siniora proposed a campaign of civil disobedience to be carried out in stages. Then the author of the idea, Mubarak Awad, took the floor to explain the advantages of nonviolent protest on a mass scale. Objections were voiced almost immediately, and Siniora was even accused of trying to turn the *intifada* into a lark. Yet even had they agreed to the idea, all the participants at the meeting knew that the three leftist partners in the PLO would not stand for such thinking. In fact, the leftists already suspected that Siniora's efforts were "a ruse to snatch the uprising away from its true leaders."

The Popular Front was the most aggressive on this issue and lost no time starting a smear campaign against its centrist rival. "You can't play poker at night and call for a revolt the next morning in the same hotel," sneered Dr. Sufian al-Khatib—the target of his barb obviously being Siniora. Others complained that left to his own devices, the Fatah functionary would reduce the *intifada* to a sterile protest. Siniora, whose soft, round face often bore a warm smile, showed considerable courage in ignoring the anger of the Palestinian Left, together with the warnings he had begun to receive from the Israeli police. On January 7, after most of the figures invited to his consultations had dropped out of the venture, he appeared alone at a press conference in the American Colony Hotel and outlined the terms of a Palestinian boycott to be effected in four stages. It would begin with the symbolic step of giving up Israeli cigarettes; two weeks later the purchase of Israeli soft drinks would cease; then the Palestinians would withhold the payment of all taxes to the Israeli authorities; and finally Palestinian workers would stop going to work in Israel. By then he also had in mind, but did not spell out, the idea of having all the Palestinians burn their Israeli-issued identity cards.

Once the Siniora plan was officially out in the open, the Israeli security services weighed their options on how to respond to it. The most immediate, almost reflexive, recommendation was to arrest no fewer than seventeen of the men who had participated in Siniora's initial round of talks, all of them veteran Fatah figures. But the State Attorney's Office stubbornly resisted the idea, since there was no evidence directly connecting most of these men with violations of the law. With arrest ruled out, what remained was harassment. A force of policemen was stationed outside *al-Fajr*'s offices as a demonstrative threat. In private talks, Civil Administration officials cautioned the participants in the early consultations against pursuing the plan, while Siniora and his associates were publicly put on notice that any boycott measures would invite a forceful response. Defiance, they were warned—in whatever form—would hurt the Palestinians far more than it was worth.

Siniora soon ran into another, more daunting obstacle. Having made his initiative public, it took him just a day or two to see that it was not winning support. Incumbents like Elias Freij, the mayor of Bethlehem, and elder statesmen like Rashad a-Shawa, the ex-mayor of Gaza, fretted that "a boycott would mean starvation in the territories." Others were afraid to provoke the Civil Administration, while the young militants broadcast menacing hints to Siniora to simply drop the idea. He therefore called a second press conference on January 14 and confined himself to unveiling the "Fourteen Points" agreed upon in the preparatory sessions. Flanked this time by a group of respected Palestinians from different walks of life, Siniora read out the uprising's list of demands. Surprisingly, they were limited to immediate, local concerns. Among these demands were: rescinding the Emergency Regulations and abandoning the "iron-fist" policy; releasing all the detainees arrested during the *intifada* (especially the minors); canceling all deportation orders; lifting the siege on the refugee camps and stationing an international force in place of the IDF; halting the construction of new settlements and the expropriation of land; preserving the status of the holy places in Jerusalem; canceling all taxes imposed on the Palestinian population; permitting political organization and calling municipal elections under the supervision of a neutral party; rescinding all restrictions on construction, drilling for water, and industrialization in the territories; placing a ceiling on Israeli exports to the territories and ending discrimination against Palestinian products; permitting open contacts with the PLO and allowing representatives from the territories to participate in the Palestine National Council.

The outcome of this second press conference was far below Siniora's expectations. Though the PLO endorsed the Fourteen-Point Document, the Israelis reacted by arresting four of the participants in the event (for a few hours, as it turned out) and taking others in for questioning. And there the matter ended. The document itself was quickly relegated to the *intifada*'s archive, for the masses of Palestinians did not accept these demands as the true aims of their uprising. Siniora raised the matter with Secretary of State George Shultz in Washington a few months later. But his continued activity was so unpopular with the Palestinians themselves that he was forced to hire bodyguards and spend a good part of the year abroad on lecture tours. Lacking any real following, the people who had clustered around him quickly dispersed and tended to lie low or, to save face, wanly pretended that they still had access to the levers of power.

Some of them, however, had seen what was coming in time to withdraw from the Siniora effort and channel their energies in a direction more fitting with the popular mood. Sensing that Siniora's form of resistance was premature, the journalists Abdullah Awad and Salah Zahaika (editor of a-Sh'ab), Father Odeh Ghantisi, and Dr. Sari Nusseibeh, among others, authored the handbill signed by the "Nationalist Forces" (whose publication had so angered Mohammed Labadi). Siniora found that he had become a pariah—or at any rate that he was being excluded from the meetings to negotiate the establishment of the Unified National Command. Indeed, the whole affair of the Fourteen-Point Document was a fiasco for the veteran Fatah leaders in the territories. It showed that they not only lacked the mettle to stand up to the Israeli authorities but that a huge chasm yawned between these self-styled statesmen and the rioters in the streets. The thought of a genteel political struggle against the occupation struck the young demonstrators as ridiculous, a fatuous game played by people divorced from reality. Contempt for the veteran Fatah establishment was so widespread that its members even began to refer to themselves as the "whiskey drinkers," "creatures of the media," and the "Mickey Mouse leadership."

The Old Guard's swift retreat from its one attempt to assume the leadership of the intifada was also due to considerable Israeli pressure. Once the government decided that it would not stand for a local Palestinian leadership directing the uprising under the spotlight of the international media, it became impossible for people like Hanna Siniora to lead the population in a new kind of struggle. In retrospect it seems obvious that Israel's contribution to derailing the Siniora initiative is what opened the way for the appearance of another kind of leadership: the clandestine Unified National Command. The Fatah followed Labadi's lead only after it had been forced to conclude that it had no other choice. Should Israel have allowed Siniora to grasp the helm of the intifada and lead it openly? It is pointless to indulge in second-guessing now. Suffice it to say that by helping to bring down the familiar faces, it paved the way for the masked and nameless ones that were bound to take their place.

It was with a pronounced lack of enthusiasm that the Fatah leadership in Tunis gave its blessing to this changing of the guard. But chastened by his initial misjudgment of the situation, Arafat knew that a minimalist like Siniora was unfit to command during times of turmoil. Siniora's contacts with American diplomats and officials made him suspect in the eyes of the leftists, as well as the Palestinian man in the street, and his frequent appearances before Jewish audiences did little to improve his image. Another strike against him was his proposal, made in June 1987, to run an all-Arab slate in the Jerusalem municipal elections, become the deciding factor in coalition-making, and show the Israelis just how high the price of annexation could be. It was an ingenious notion, but the Palestinian response to it bordered on fury. Sharp graffiti appeared in East Jerusalem, Siniora's car was torched, and there were even rumors of plans to assassinate him. In the eyes of the younger generation, Siniora symbolized the ideological debasement of men who had risen to prominence by virtue of their connections, not their achievements.

As its first representative on the Unified National Command, the Fatah chose Dr. Samir Shehadeh, a lecturer in education at Bir Zeit University and leader of the Fatah supporters on the school's faculty and administration. Shehadeh made regular reports to his comrade Mohammed Matour, a lecturer in the Nursing School in al-Bireh, whose primary role was supervisor of the Shabiba movement in the Jerusalem-Ramallah district (making him something of a political commissar for the younger generation in the refugee camps). Men like Hanna Siniora paled in comparison with these younger, more militant leaders. They gave off an air of slackness and fatigue, just when the people were filled with fighting spirit. While others hoisted the banner of revolt, they busied themselves planning protests and boycotts like finicky old women. Their time had come to leave the stage, and the *intifada*'s numbered handbills—which began to appear soon after the abortive Siniora initiative—helped to ensure that they did so by denouncing them in conspicuously strong language.

Those handbills were the Unified Command's greatest achievement, the catalyst that made it into a recognized authority and gave the population the reassuring feeling that protest need not mean unending chaos.

Somewhere, these leaflets showed, a hidden hand was directing the *intifada*, setting realistic goals and establishing realistic means of struggle. Somewhere, perhaps deeply hidden in a cellar, cave, or bunker, a team of leaders with a flair for evading the authorities was giving the rebellion coherence. Their style echoed the mood of the people. They instilled a sense of pride, even euphoria, and defined new rules of behavior. They dictated strike days, and the public obeyed. They sneered at the enemy and heralded victory. They were also prolific: within a single month, the Unified Command produced six handbills in close succession, and the Israelis were helpless to stop it.

Three of these six documents were drafted by Mohammed Labadi and then sent to his partners for approval. Occasionally, the entire command met, each time in a different apartment in East Jerusalem, to discuss additions and revisions and agree upon the final text. It sometimes passed the draft on to Tunis, as well, but did not necessarily follow the dictates from on high. Thus like it or not, the Unified Command set the pace, while the "outsiders" were forced to live with its decisions. Frequent hitches in getting messages back and forth were another problem. Samir Shehadeh of the Fatah had been given a code book for deciphering instructions broadcast over the PLO Radio, but though he and Mohammed Matour listened to these broadcasts regularly, never once was this option used! Problems of this sort merely heightened the resolve of the local command to rely on its own judgment rather than march to the beat of a distant drummer.

The distribution system for these handbills was a particularly successful one. Once the final version had been settled upon, Labadi's driver, Nasser Ju'abah, would bring the manuscript to a twenty-two-year-old woman named Fa'izah Yusef of the Democratic Front, who typed it out on an electric machine. Then the typed version was photocopied in another apartment and taken to the print shop in Isawiyeh. After being printed the entire run (sometimes as many as 100,000 copies) was brought to Ju'abah's house, where it was divided up and tied into bundles for distribution. One of the people who helped transport the copies to their destination was Labadi's wife, Amal, who carted them about in her little Autobianci (as did a number of other women assigned this task). Every city sent out a small van or pickup truck with two people to fetch the handbills and transfer them to three or four smaller vehicles that would drop the bundles of 200 to 300 sheets on selected street corners. The drivers tried as much as possible to use vehicles with yellow Israeli license plates, making it easier to get past army roadblocks. In this way tens of thousands of leaflets were distributed throughout the West Bank, from Jenin in the north to Hebron in the south, in the course of a single night. It wasn't necessary to read them to know the most important thing; the very appearance of printed communiqués in such large quantities was proof in itself that a ramified and well-coordinated underground was now behind the *intifada*.

Israel's hunt for the source of the handbills did not bear fruit until the end of a month of frustrating surveillance. But on February 3, 1988, the Shin Bet finally picked up the thread that would lead it to the Unified Command. It came in the person of Nasser Ju'abah, who was stopped at a roadblock in a Peugeot pickup carrying 35,000 copies of Handbill No. 6. The remaining 30,000 copies of that issue were distributed that night, but through hard work the Israelis cracked the chain of distribution, link by link, from the press in Isawiyeh down to the individual drivers. Ju'abah immediately directed his interrogators to all the men involved in the operation, first and foremost Labadi himself. The Darwish brothers and Samir Shehadeh of the Fatah were arrested that same day, after which the presses were confiscated. Others involved in the distribution network were caught in the days to come, and the remaining pieces of the puzzle fell into place.

Except for one: Mohammed Labadi, who had utterly vanished. After lying in wait for him outside his home for four days, Israeli agents raided it on February 7 and found in his refrigerator door drafts of handbills and other documents confirming that they had identified the command's moving spirit. But Labadi himself had escaped. Two weeks earlier the order obliging him to sign in at the Ramallah police station had expired, and he dropped all pretense of not being involved in any clandestine activities. When the others were arrested he took refuge among comrades in Hebron and continued to serve on the Unified Command. It would take the Shin Bet another seventy days of feverish searching and patient surveillance before it would snare him in its trap.

The documents found on Labadi when he was caught on April 15 gave a clear indication of his plans. They included notes on expanding the role of the Unified Command beyond the publication of the handbills. In his mind's eye Labadi could see "revolutionary committees" taking command of the various districts. He intended to make sure that Palestinian businesses, factories, and members of the free professions stopped paying all taxes, as an example to the rest of the public. He also planned forcibly to remove the hucksters who set up stands on the sidewalks when the shopkeepers were observing the general strike. For quite a while Labadi refused to answer any of his interrogators' questions, telling them only that "when you start admitting to seemingly insignificant details, you end up confessing to important things, too." He was more forthcoming, however, when it came to his political outlook. "I intend to keep working until the rights of the Palestinian people are restored," he said, "and I am prepared to pay the price of resistance to the occupation." Asked about his political aim, Labadi clearly stated, "A Palestinian state *alongside* the State of Israel"— though he had never spelled this out in any of his handbills. In any event, before long his name was added to the list of candidates for deportation.

The authors of the command's first thirteen handbills (up until Labadi's arrest) never portrayed the *intifada* as a zero-sum game that only one side could come out winning. Even a scrupulous examination of their wording brought the experts to conclude that "an opening has been left for discussions, and there is tacit recognition of the State of Israel." Implied in these handbills—though no more than that—was a leaning toward political dialogue. The command rarely used the word "Israel," preferring terms such as "the artificial Zionist entity" or "the fascist neo-Nazi entity," and certainly was not about to recognize it. Yet Labadi and his associates were careful not to suggest that their goal was to dismantle the Jewish state. In part this pussyfooting was due to internal Palestinian politics. There was general agreement that the command must not try to usurp the PLO's role of establishing principles and setting down policy. Thus Labadi and the others obeyed the instructions they received from Tunis and announced early on that the *intifada* would continue until it had achieved the ultimate goal of establishing a Palestinian state. Akram Hanieh, one of Arafat's close aides, described this declaration as "raising the ante," for it officially replaced Siniora's demands to *change the workings* of the occupation with the aim of *ending* it altogether. This shift fit well with the image and approach of the Unified Command. Yet from time to time the handbills reiterated more modest, interim goals, signaling to Israel that the point of departure for winding down the revolt was not necessarily negotiations on a comprehensive solution; concessions on more mundane matters would be rewarded with a quid pro quo.

The Unified Command picked its way between the desire to make swift, visible progress and the need for a realistic view of the possible. Its members sincerely believed themselves to be revolutionaries and were moved by the conviction that the time had come for daring changes. Yet they were all aware not only of the lopsided ratio of forces with Israel but of the weaknesses of the people they were trying to lead. Often the command was torn between the dream of leading a fiery mass revolt and the lessons of their own experience, which were to lower their expectations. It was only gradually, and in the course of incessant debate, that the lines of a viable strategy began to take shape. If, at first, the command envisioned a full boycott of Israeli products and steps to bring production in Israel to a halt, it soon came to terms with reality. The result could be seen in the handbills, which lost much of their rhetorical zeal and muted their demands of the people.

Perhaps the most sobering factor in this process was a series of clumsy mistakes made early in the command's existence. The call to boycott Israeli products, for example, proved so outrageous that it forced the fledgling leadership to take a serious look at itself and forgo the ideal in favor of the attainable. On orders from the Fatah office in Amman, Dr. Shehadeh looked into the possibility of replacing Israeli-produced foodstuffs with Palestinian products and quickly concluded that it was a pipe dream. In their youth, many members of the command had committed to memory whole chunks of the writings of Mao Tse-tung and the history of the Vietcong. But now they found that leadership meant calculating the costs as well as the aims of their policies. Their conception of the uprising changed from one of fission that grows steadily more intense to a "long-range popular war" that must be carefully paced to avoid burn-out.

Most of the Palestinian public was prepared to be indulgent of the command's forays into the extreme. Its more outlandish orders may have been greeted with shrugs and snickers, but its basic authority remained intact. Occasionally there was outright resistance to its line of action—such as the circulars denouncing its threats against strike-breakers and certain well-known figures—but for the most part the Unified National Command preserved its stature as the one body deserving of a general hearing. Its flexibility in correcting mistakes and retreating from untenable positions was precisely the feature that established it as an authentic leadership that was responsive to the public and aware of its limitations.

It was also in close touch with the people. Naturally the command's members went into hiding, but despite their fear of exposure and arrest they did not drop out of political life. Most active of all was the Communist Dr. Taysir al-Arouri, who signed a manifesto advocating a political compromise, published jointly with Israeli writers, and even appeared at a public seminar on the *intifada*. Somehow activists in the field knew how to convey their recommendations to the proper address, so that the command received a steady stream of comments and suggestions from a wide variety of quarters. Most important of all, perhaps, was the backing it received from the academic world. A group of lecturers at Bir Zeit University put together a kind of think tank whose ideas found their way into the handbills. Faculty members took on urgent research projects to gauge the possibility of building a "closed economy" or to propose workable economic measures. Some of them pressed for the creation of an educational network completely divorced from the Israeli administration. Others devised ways of encouraging cottage industries, and one—Dr. Jadd Ishak, a lecturer at Bethlehem University—prepared an agricultural handbook that included tips on growing fruits and vegetables in yards and open lots. For much of 1988, in fact, debates on tactics led by faculty members from Bir Zeit (two of whom, Dr. Shehadeh and Dr. Arouri, were themselves members of the command) went on rather openly, practically within earshot of the Shin Bet and other Israeli authorities.

It is not surprising that the handbills reflected the ideological ferment at Bir Zeit. Originally a Christian college and practically a "family affair" built for the sons of the wealthy, the school had become a mecca for youngsters from the villages and refugee camps. It was a place where dedicated members of the Shabiba rubbed shoulders with the West Bank's academic elite; where faculty members schooled as classic Marxists mingled with teenagers fresh from street demonstrations—and the contact was often electrifying. All the major Palestinian organizations were represented in Bir Zeit through their campus extensions (known simply as the "blocs"). For years its cafeteria had been the most vibrant and important political club in the territories. The full array of activists collected there, from recruits to the Islamic Jihad to devout Trotskyites, all bound by a common drive to wage the struggle against Israel. Some observers believe that it was the breakdown of barriers between faculty and students that created the broad-based support for the Unified Command. For in Bir Zeit, more than in any other university, theorists (in the persons of the faculty) mixed with activists (in the persons of their students) to supply both the fuel and the feedback needed by the uprising's leaders.

The Unified Command was also nourished by another sector of growing importance in the territories: the released security prisoners. As veterans of a personal contest with Israel's security services, these men had been through the worst and were past their fear of the unknown. They had also been steeled by the tough discipline of the special committees that ran their lives behind bars. Most of these men had spent their years of internment in study, since they refused to engage in any form of labor (so as not to contribute, however obliquely, to the Israeli economy). Kept in overcrowded cells with only thin mattresses on the floor for beds, they turned these depressing conditions into the setting for political study groups and debating sessions. Far more important, however, they built an independent network within the prisons, and during the *intifada* the members of the Unified Command—most of whom were "academy graduates"—copied its format as the structure of the uprising. The committees in each of the cell blocks, which directed daily affairs, were the model for the popular committees. The central committee, which ran the Palestinian network in each prison on a coalition basis, was the prototype for the Unified Command itself. To obtain better conditions and privileges for the security prisoners, these central committees demonstrated their power by leading strikes and taking retaliatory measures against informers (sometimes to the point of murder)—and that is precisely how the Unified Command displayed its strength during the *intifada*.

This mixture of academic highbrows and hardened "ex-cons" as the mainstay of the Unified Command was less curious than it might at first seem, for all of the command's members came out of one of these backgrounds and frequently boasted them both. Moreover, it was only natural that the new leadership should enjoy the support of the two sectors of the Palestinian population that suffered the most from the heavy hand of the Israeli administration: the 100,000 or so politically conscious high school and college students and the close to 30,000 Palestinians (by the official Israeli estimate) who had served time for security offenses. It was they who composed the command's prime constituency, they who responded to its orders, and they who relayed back their own experiences and views. If anything could account for the extraordinary political unity attained during the uprising it was the tight weave of friendships formed between erstwhile rivals in Israel's prisons and the connections made through the "blocs" in the universities.

Upon returning to their villages, the students applied the doctrine of organization they had learned on campus, and in many places they were behind the activities of the popular committees. But always found working alongside them were released security prisoners, who were heroes in the eyes of the younger generation. This was especially true of the men freed in the 1985 prisoner exchange engineered by Ahmed Jebril. The deal was a coup for Jebril: six Israeli soldiers captured during the fighting in Lebanon were traded for some 1,000 security prisoners, practically emptying the jails of Palestinians and sending hundreds of trained and disciplined activists back into the field. The Israeli government debated long and hard before conceding to have some 650 of these prisoners remain in the territories. The Shin Bet fought fiercely against this clause, but its warning went unheeded. In time Jebril would boast that his deal had planted the seeds of the uprising—and with good reason. Authoritative estimates have it that within a year of their release, over a third of these freed prisoners had resumed some form of clandestine activity, and the rest went into action almost immediately upon the outbreak of the riots.

The capture of the Unified National Command (minus Labadi) upon the publication of its sixth handbill was far from a mortal blow. Within a few days the four organizations had put together a new team, this time with its center of operations in Ramallah. The fact that the command was made up of middle-level activists lent it a special durability, for it could easily be reconstituted after each wave of arrests. On the evening of March 19, 1988, the Israelis struck again, arresting the members of the new command in the Ramallah apartment of the Communist representative, Adnan Dagher. Caught in the act of writing Handbill No. 11, none of the five participants at that meeting resisted arrest. But after this second setback a system of rotation was adopted, so that there were times when one or more of the command's members was not present to approve the final wording of a text.

As fate would have it, the March 19 arrests followed a week of grave crisis within the Unified Command. After days of wrangling, its members had been unable to agree upon the wording of Handbill No. 10, so that no less than three different versions were printed and circulated in the territories. This was the first time that disagreements within the command had come out in the open. The dispute was essentially between the Fatah and the Popular Front over two issues: the call to the West Bank deputies to resign their seats in the Jordanian Parliament; and the demand that all Palestinians working for the Civil Administration's tax authorities resign their posts forthwith. The front was pushing for these moves while the Fatah resisted them. And when the command failed to produce any handbill at all, the Popular Front took action on its own, printing up circulars to present the demands—and issuing them over the familiar signature of the Unified National Command. Infuriated by this behavior, on the following day the Fatah responded with a handbill of its own—likewise signed by the Unified National Command—and five days later the Democratic Front joined the fray by distributing yet a third handbill over the same signature. Handbill No. 11 was therefore an unusually important document, for it was framed to clear up the confusion and lay to rest the understandable rumors of a split in the command. It was so important, in fact, that despite the March 19 arrests, the handbill was readied after only a short delay—thanks to the efforts of the new Fatah representative, Samir Sabihat, who was head of the Bir Zeit student council.

The capture of the command in the midst of a secret meeting showed the Palestinians that there was no way of guaranteeing its security. It also reinforced the fears, which were rampant by then, that the Israelis had penetrated to the very heart of the *intifada*. The suspicion that the Fatah was riddled with informers resulted in more stringent security measures to protect the command. But they did not prevent the capture of its third set of members as they drafted Handbill No. 13 at the beginning of April (after a wave of arrests throughout the territories had left some 700 activists in administrative detention). On April 10 deportation orders were issued against Adnan Dagher and the other members of the command: Ahmed Jaber Suleiman of the Democratic Front, Ghassan al-Masri of the Popular Front, and the Fatah's Ahmed a-Dik.

Time and again the Israelis closed in on the command, but it proved to be irrepressible. Each time one set of members was arrested, new ones appeared to take their place, so that the handbills continued to appear regularly within seven- to ten-day intervals. What the Israeli pressure did spawn, however, was a growing dependence on the PLO abroad. Since surveillance of the presses made it impossible to print up handbills in the vast numbers common at the start, they were also read out over the PLO Radio (at dictation pace so that members of the popular committees could copy them down.) Inevitably, however, this system of issuing handbills over the airwaves tightened the control over their content, so that the ultimate authority of the Unified Command was gradually lost to its handlers—and rivals—abroad. In time the handbills began to repeat themselves. Each week they set down the schedule of events and the hours of the general strike, but from the autumn of 1988 onward they contained no evidence of original thinking. Gone was the verve that had marked the command's early days. Its powers of invention were failing; its members had succumbed to routine. As each week passed the leaflets became more an instrument of the PLO establishment than the voice of the home-grown leaders. By 1989 even Hanna Siniora was coaching the writers of the handbills, and so the circle closed.

No one in Tunis, least of all Arafat, bemoaned the decline in the command's standing, for they had never wanted to yield power to the men in the field. From the start, Arafat had expected the command to be a rubber stamp for the plans he would devise himself. From his standpoint it was far more convenient to send orders directly to his loyalists than to work through a local command, and it must be said that the other partners in the PLO felt much the same. For months the "outsiders" had choked down measures they did not really approve, such as the resignation of the Palestinian policemen and local councils in the territories. But as the command grew weaker, the PLO's liaisons went over to the offensive and began to dictate what the handbills would say. The last time the command tried to block this trend toward subordination was on September 4, 1988, when the Fatah people sent two proposals to Tunis. The first was to formalize the command's link directly with Arafat's office, rather than have it work through each of its four component organizations. The second was to have all PLO funds sent to and distributed by the command, rather than apportioning them to each organization separately. In each case the aim was to enhance the command's effective control at the expense of its constituent bodies. The local Fatah people wanted to turn the command into the forward headquarters of the *intifada*, not just a relay station.

Needless to say, the establishment in Tunis was having none of these ideas, so the Unified Command continued to mark time in place. At one point a few of its members thought about revitalizing it by co-opting representatives of the organizations that were boycotting Arafat. Talks with Ahmed Jebril's Popular Front for the Liberation of Palestine–General Command, for example, reached an advanced stage in June 1988. But Arafat would not tolerate an alliance with his Syrian-backed rivals and easily foiled the move. Over the command's signature—though without first consulting its other partners—the Fatah put out a handbill denouncing the organizations of the so-called Salvation

Front and promptly sabotaged the ploy. In return, these Syrian-backed groups set out to poison the already frail relations between the territories and Tunis. Abu Moussa, head of the breakaway faction of the Fatah, secretly warned the command that it must protect itself against Arafat's "whims," intimidation, and efforts to preserve his standing by the tactic of divide and rule. "You must make sure that you are the organization in command and not the commander's organization," he quipped. "You must not agree that the control over funds turns into control over decisions." But harangues of this sort were nothing new in the fractious world of Palestinian politics and had little effect one way or the other.

The local leadership that arose in the territories never developed into a national command in the fullest sense because it could not withstand the pressure from Israel and the PLO combined. Before its path was blocked, however, the Unified National Command did manage to squeeze out the generation of urbane but ineffectual leaders who had held sway in the territories for the better part of a decade. The men who operated behind the title of the Unified Command were in their thirties and forties, often even younger. They came from a generation of militants who had spent months in prisons and detention camps before and during the uprising—time that was used for political consciousness-raising and ideological refresher courses. In a very real sense, then, Israel helped to cultivate the new Palestinian leadership by channeling some 20,000 young people through its prisons and then releasing them to participate in the changing of the guard. The mass identification with the Unified Command's handbills and the broad response to its appeals was due not to the charisma of the new leadership (which at any rate remained anonymous) but to the work of thousands of activists on the popular committees uniting the public behind it. When the latest lineup of the Unified Command was arrested at the beginning of 1989, it hardly mattered anymore, for the popular committees had become the real driving force, and Israel could not allow itself to place tens of thousands of activists behind bars as its way of paralyzing the uprising. The number of administrative detainees reached 3,000 as it was, and whenever an activist was hauled off to detention, new recruits came in to fill the gap.

Thus not even the command's decline could halt the effort to realize its program of civil disobedience and self-rule under the direction of the popular committees. The string of reverses in no way indicated the collapse of the new leadership; they merely meant that instead of supporting a strong central command, the *intifada* was being directed by many local ones. And it was here, at this lower level, that the struggle against Israel continued not only in the streets but behind countless doors where plans were being drawn for the government and "popular army" of a future independent state.

EIGHT | *THE ISLAMIC RESISTANCE MOVEMENT*

A RUTTED DIRT PATH that the rains reduce to mud was the only way to reach the humble home of Sheikh Ahmed Ismail Yassin in the Zaitoun quarter of Gaza. Passing by the large, domed mosque with a carved minaret that the sheikh built for the greater glory of Allah, a visitor on that road came to a low wall that barely concealed an unkempt yard and a rough single-storied structure bereft of even simple tile flooring. In the front room, on a battered mattress covered with a coarse woolen blanket, the sheikh would lie half crumpled in the gloom, and that is how he would receive his visitors. Occasionally he might ask one of the devout young disciples who guarded the building to carry him to a rickety chair, so that he would not have to gaze up at his guests from below. The thin, round-faced sheikh was almost totally paralyzed as the result of an illness, but his mind was razor sharp, and he was famed as an expert on Muslim law. His style of speech was terse, almost gruff, and was spiced with quotes from the Koran and other Muslim sources. Conversation seemed to be a chore for him as he sat propped up for company, his chin sunken into his chest. Only the glint of wit in his dark brown eyes suggested the contrary. He rarely left his house, and because of his handicap he found it difficult to lecture or even to write. Yet the *intifada* had made Sheikh Yassin one of the most powerful men in the Gaza Strip.

In 1984, despite his grim physical condition, Yassin was sentenced to a term of thirteen years in prison after sixty rifles were found cached away in his home. He was released in the following year as part of the

Jebril prisoner exchange but was not allowed to resume his position as chairman of the Islamic Congress. Instead, one of his close followers, the pharmacist Ibrahim al-Yazouri, assumed the title of chairman while Yassin continued to serve as the leader of the informal cultural and educational movement called the Muslim Brotherhood, for which the Islamic Congress was an official front. Since the Brotherhood's Gaza branch had long been independent of the mother organization in Egypt, Yassin was essentially the local movement's "supreme leader."

When the riots broke out in Gaza early in December 1987, some of the sheikh's followers urged him to abandon his policy of *tarbiyeh* (education) and *da'awah* (preaching) in favor of a more militant line. Although once involved in the concealment of weapons, Yassin had forbidden his disciples to indulge actively in terrorism. He knew just how easy it would be to slip into a bootless but costly confrontation with Israel, and he preferred to devote himself to constructive pursuits, like fostering a return to religion and establishing strong public institutions. Now his disciples argued that whether he wanted it or not, a revolt was underway, and he was obliged to try to guide it. Many Brotherhood activists were at any rate involved in the riots, and it would be difficult to stop them from continuing. The sheikh must not fall behind the times, these younger men warned him, for the moment of truth had come.

At first Yassin held his ground. But a few weeks later, when the violence persisted, he had more difficulty resisting their views and finally endorsed a handbill that joined in the incitement. It was signed not by the Islamic Congress, however, nor even by the Muslim Brotherhood but by an ostensibly new faction called the Islamic Resistance Movement. Only twice in the past had the cautious Yassin allowed his followers to use this cover: in a March 1987 handbill threatening pharmacists who did not cooperate in the war against drugs; and again in November in a handbill on resisting the tactics of the Shin Bet. In both cases the sheikh had been reluctant to involve the Congress directly and had therefore used a kind of code name, for most Gazans understood who was really behind these handbills.

As the rioting continued and the pressure on him mounted, Yassin relented more and more. For the past two years a slow process of "Palestinization" had been at work in the movement, shifting its accent from the broader scope of the "Islamic nation" and the "community of believers" onto the more narrow concerns of Palestinian nationalism. Some two months before the eruption of the riots, Yassin had allowed

his people to use the term "national products" at a fair of locally produced merchandise. This was a signal departure, for traditionally he
had ruled out any usage that detracted from the inclusiveness of Islam,
and he would only distinguish between "believers" and "infidels." The
new Palestinian cast became far more pronounced in the months to
come, but by mid-January 1988 Yassin knew that such concessions
were not enough; sooner or later he would have to permit his disciples
to direct their energies toward an active nationalist struggle. Just like
the Fatah, the Brotherhood found that it was being overtaken by the
militant mood in the streets.

It was in February 1988, after the establishment of the Unified
National Command (which he, too, perceived as a PLO bid to take
control of the uprising) that Yassin took the momentous step of creating a new fundamentalist underground. It took the name "Hamas," an
acronym for "Islamic Resistance Movement" whose literal meaning is
"enthusiasm," "courage," or "zeal." This sharp deviation from the
Brotherhood's policy of caution was not any easy decision for Yassin.
Moreover, to protect the institution of the Islamic Congress, which he
had built with such effort and care, he did his best to create the impression of a distinction between Hamas and the older public movement. The structure of the new organization was worked out at meetings in Yassin's home. Three Islamic Congress activists were appointed
to serve as a command: one to be responsible for political affairs, the
second for military matters, and the third for propaganda and especially
the printing and distribution of handbills (which required the sheikh's
personal approval). The Gaza Strip was divided into five districts,
each headed by an operations officer. A special liaison, Jamil a-Tamimi,
was assigned to maintain regular contact with Brotherhood activists in
the West Bank, most of them members of the religious establishment or
well-to-do businessmen who were quite uneasy about cooperating with
the new underground. Before long, however, young recruits were setting the pace for their elders there too, and gradually Hamas cells appeared in Nablus, Tulkarem, and other West Bank cities.

With its members joining Hamas almost automatically, the Islamic
Brotherhood in Gaza was swallowed up by the new framework and
turned into a quasi-underground. The first to be recruited from the
Brotherhood were its 'umal (full activists), whose cells were amal-
gamated into an 'usrah (family) or shu'abah (branch). Their activities
centered on certain mosques that were often used to conceal stores of
"cold weapons" (knives, clubs, and the like), secret correspondence,

and even people wanted by the authorities. Yassin became the bearer of the code name "100," and a special secret apparatus was created for him separate from Hamas's network of cells. It was a security and intelligence arm called "Majed" whose members collected evidence against Arabs collaborating with the Shin Bet and, once sentence was passed on a collaborator, saw to its execution. It also developed a new system for concealing firearms and other "hot weapons" (usually acquired from Israeli soldiers) and a method of "corresponding" about these caches by making tiny gashes on tree trunks and electricity poles. Gradually this super-secret arm was used to set fields and forests ablaze in Israel and torch the shops of strike-breakers in Gaza. Later it also went on to attack lone Israeli soldiers, even in Israel proper. But even before this special apparatus went into high gear, Hamas rose to prominence swiftly. By the second month of the *intifada* it was playing a leading role in the Gaza Strip, and by the summer of 1988 it had left its mark on the West Bank as well. In a matter of months, in fact, Hamas had become one of the most difficult challenges that Israel had to face.

In large part this scourge was self-inflicted, for the Civil Administration had contributed considerably to the development of the Muslim groups that came to the fore soon after the start of the *intifada*. Just as President Sadat had encouraged the growth of the Islamic Associations to offset the leftist elements in Egypt, many Israeli staff officers believed that the rise of fundamentalism in Gaza could be exploited to weaken the power of the PLO. Sadat's fate was to die at the hands of the same pious zealots he had allowed to flourish. The upshot in Gaza was similar: the Muslim movement turned on the very people who had believed themselves so clever in fostering it. Actually, the belief that it was possible to restrict the Islamic revival to conservative, apolitical lines was mistaken from the start, for the distinction between church and state does not exist in the mind or creed of the pious Muslim. Even novices who devoted themselves to the traditional pursuits of community welfare and saving wayward souls would eventually take a stand on affairs of the day. Indeed, as has been shown in so many Muslim lands, nothing can match religious institutions as tools of recruitment and control.

In Gaza this lesson was learned too late. For the better part of a decade, the Israelis had allowed fundamentalist Muslims to move into positions of power in the religious establishment. Once they had acquired that source of leverage, they began to flourish as a political force as well. The strange thing is that this quiet takeover was allowed to happen because of the superficial notion that the fundamentalists posed less of a threat to stability than the nationalists did. Any damage they might cause, the prevailing theory held, would be more than offset by the good they would do in finally neutralizing the PLO. It was not until about a year before the start of the *intifada* that senior officials in the Civil Administration showed the first signs of concern that their expectations were not being met and that in fact they might be on a collision course with a new wave of militant Islam. The fundamentalists had indeed sapped the strength of the PLO in Gaza. But they soon surpassed it in indoctrination toward fanatic zeal, which from Israel's standpoint was far more menacing than anything the nationalists could show for their efforts.

The potential of fundamentalism came as no surprise to the incumbent Muslim officials. As far back as 1978 Rafat Abu Sha'aban, the commissioner of the Muslim *waqf* (religious trust) in the Gaza Strip, had warned the Israelis against registering and thus officially recognizing the Islamic Congress. Abu Sha'aban had managed the *waqf* since the days when the Strip had been administered by Egypt. The position made him a man of some consequence, for in addition to its religious importance the *waqf* was a rich source of economic power. About 10 percent of all the real estate in the Strip—hundreds of shops, apartments, garages, public buildings, and about 2,000 acres of agricultural land—belonged to its trusts, and the *waqf* employed scores of people, from preachers and other clerics to gravediggers. Abu Sha'aban was unquestionably a moderate man and a seasoned public servant, yet his advice went unheeded. He feared that the fundamentalists would infiltrate the *waqf* and start controlling its assets, but the Israelis preferred to focus on the Brotherhood's abstention from terrorism, its stress on "winning hearts" (through charitable and educational activities), and its ideology of postponing a confrontation with Israel. Indeed, until the mid-1980s its leaders in the territories firmly declared that there was no point in rushing into a *jihad;* it was better to concentrate first on healing Muslim souls.

Delighted with that stand, the Israelis were quite willing to overlook the seamier side of the Brotherhood's doctrine calling for the destruction of Israel—once conditions were right. But above all, what made the movement so appealing to them was its rivalry with the PLO. Sheikh Yassin never concealed his distaste for Arafat. "Pork eaters and wine drinkers" is how he dismissed the PLO leadership, and he had special contempt for the leftists because they violated the precept (hallowed by every pious Muslim) that "a woman's voice is indecent." Being a prudent man, he was careful to explain that the PLO was not evil, merely misguided; the yardstick for judging Arafat, like every other Muslim, was not nationalist fervor but religious piety. Hearing these comments as signs of strong discord in the Palestinian camp, Israel was only too happy to let the "prayermongers" thrive.

And flourish they did, with a vengeance. In the space of a decade, Yassin built the Islamic Congress from a fledgling charitable association into an empire that ruled most of the religious life in the Strip. With funding mainly from sources in Saudi Arabia and Jordan, his loyalists conquered whole sectors of the religious establishment, enlisting the *waqf*'s institutions in the service of their cause. They built orphanages, infirmaries, libraries, and seminaries at an absolutely unprecedented rate. They won over the *waqf* employees and even gained a foothold in the local police! But without question Yassin's greatest achievement was his takeover of al-Azhar, the Islamic University in Gaza. Purging the school of PLO partisans, a group of academics headed by Drs. Abd-al-Aziz Ghantisi, Mahmoud Zahar, and Mahmoud Siam— all known to be the sheikh's disciples—turned the faculty and student body of 700 men into a reserve of disciplined "soldiers." The contest for al-Azhar was practically a mini-civil war between the Islamic Congress and its adversaries on the left (particularly the Popular Front and the Communists). The violence peaked in April 1986 in a series of stabbings and acid attacks, accompanied by a pamphlet war. But it was not until two months later, when the Fatah gave out signs that it, too, was about to enter the fray, that the Israelis called a truce. The lull lasted until the uprising, but after that round of violence in the spring of 1986 there was no doubt that the Congress was adept at fighting in the open—or that the Israelis were loath to take action against it.

Coincidentally or otherwise, these developments paralleled an extraordinary rise in prayer attendance and a return to the traditional Muslim way of life. In Gaza the number of worshipers doubled between 1967 and 1987. Gaza's 77 mosques at the end of the Six-Day War had multiplied to 160 in the following two decades, and in the West Bank new ones were being built at a rate of 40 per year! Many of these mosques were also used as community centers, especially as the religious revival had strong social overtones. Women took to covering their heads and wearing robes over their clothes. Young men grew beards, and wedding ceremonies returned to their traditional modest format. Even sports came into play as karate clubs sprang up in the mosques and soccer teams formed to join the Islamic League, whose players wore long pants and never let a curse slip past their lips.

In the West Bank the Muslim Brotherhood did not try to build a "front" organization along the lines of the Islamic Congress. But there, too, many of its members held key positions in the religious establishment (which was funded by Jordan), in the small Islamic College in Hebron, and in a score of charitable societies. In Nablus they also controlled the allocation of welfare to 10,000 needy families, granting loans and scholarships, hiring lawyers for detainees, paying compensation for property damaged by the army, and running orphanages, homes for the aged, and even an independent high school. The Brotherhood's branches on the West Bank kept in close touch with Yassin's people through mutual visits. They also made contact with Brotherhood members in Israel, albeit in a more circumspect manner. Though less effective in the West Bank than in Gaza, the Brotherhood nevertheless made itself felt there. In the Tulkarem district, for example, a Civil Administration survey completed just three months before the *intifada* cited a long list of warning signals linked to the Brotherhood's activity. Preachers were calling for a boycott of the Civil Administration and of the *mukhtars* cooperating with it. A religious injunction issued in the village of Ras Atiyah forbade Muslims to participate in the mourning rites for known collaborators. Bearded youths went on a rampage in Kalkilya, smashing display windows featuring photographs of women modeling dresses. (Such "manifestations of iniquity" were copied from Israel, so that the only proper response to them was a *jihad*.)

The truth is that incidents of this sort occurred throughout the territories, but for the most part people were afraid to complain about threats and harassment from members of the Brotherhood. Perhaps the most prominent example of such behavior was the crusade of the Salafiun groups in Khan Yunis. Pledged to return to the ways of the ancients, they attacked movie theaters, trashed shops and cafés selling alcoholic drinks, and tried to force the population to abstain from Western-style music, jewelry, and other non-traditional pursuits and tastes. They even made a habit of beating up people who ate with their left hand (which is considered contrary to the tradition of the

Prophet). Other thugs cast a veritable reign of terror over the Khan Yunis souk, but the Israelis made no attempt to intervene.

Besides signaling widespread disillusionment with the secular political movements, the popularity of the Muslim Brotherhood was something of a backlash against the permissiveness and materialism that had spread to the territories from Israel. It may also have been motivated by a desire to combat fear and loneliness by joining a sort of communion that would provide the strength to endure one's suffering. "When all doors are sealed, Allah opens a gate," Yassin soothed his flock. But beyond these possible attractions, the fundamentalist groups offered a special kind of activism that combined patriotism with moral purity and social action with the promise of divine grace. Sheikh Yassin offered the young Palestinian something far beyond Arafat's ken: not just the redemption of the homeland but the salvation of his own troubled soul.

Early in the uprising, a number of Israeli experts changed their thinking and came to the conclusion that the fundamentalists posed a far greater threat than the PLO. The conspicuous role of the Muslim Brotherhood and Islamic Jihad in fomenting the riots showed just how much the religious revival was fueling the revolt. The fundamentalists' self-sacrifice, pride in the simple life, blind obedience to orders, and adamant rejection of any dealings with Israel were all new and alarming signs of an emergent mood that could conceivably set the tone. One analysis of sermons preached in Gaza at that time showed that common to them all was the expression of deep animosity toward the Jews and the portrayal of Israel as the most pressing problem facing the Muslim world—and obviously these messages were getting through. One detainee arrested at an early stage of the riots earnestly and patiently explained to his interrogators that the resurrection of the dead at the end of days was conditional upon every last Jew being destroyed. More attuned to Western sensibilities, the PLO avoided any hint of anti-Semitism; but the fundamentalists gloried in it and made crude expressions of Jew-hatred a common feature of their publications.

Recommendations for constraining the Muslim Brotherhood had been framed by the Civil Administration prior to the outbreak of the riots, yet the steps that were taken failed to change the general drift of events. The proposals included keeping close tabs on the activities in the mosques; halting the illegal construction by the Islamic Congress and similar groups; prohibiting sports under the guise of religious activity; sending the army and the police out to halt acts of violence;

and firing members of the Brotherhood from jobs in the Civil Administration. All in all, though, these measures were a weak prescription,
considering that the Muslim Brotherhood and Islamic Jihad had already built a dense network of cells and dominated the political life
of Gaza and parts of the West Bank.

Then the Israelis turned tough, striking first at the Islamic Jihad.
The truth is that few of the groups going under this name were involved in leading demonstrations. Terrorism was their specialty, and
only one faction of the Jihad—the "revolutionary cadre" called the
Islamic Vanguard—cast itself into the whirlwind of the riots. One
reason for its low profile on the streets was that the Jihad suffered
from a sore lack of leadership. Dr. Fathi Shkaki and Sheikh Abd al-
Aziz Odeh were in prison; Dr. Ramdan Shalah and other leading activists
were abroad, so that essentially the movement took its orders from
its venerable ideologue, Bashir Moussa Naf'a, who was in contact with
the Fatah in Jordan and the authorities in Iran. But there were problems here too. Bassem Sultan ("Hamdi"), Marouin al-Kiali, and Mohammed Hassan Bahis, the Fatah officers in Amman assigned to plan
the Jihad's terror actions, were increasingly cramped by the surveillance of the Jordanian security services. King Hussein had repeatedly
promised the Israelis that he would not allow the three to expand their
operations. But Jerusalem was not satisfied with that assurance and
asked Washington to pressure the king into halting the flow of orders
altogether. This roundabout route did the trick: following a no-
nonsense demand from Washington, the three Fatah officers were
deported from Jordan on very short notice. A day after reaching
Limassol, they met their end in the explosion of a booby-trapped car,
and the PLO naturally accused Israel of engineering their fiery demise.

The Jihad suffered a second blow in May 1988 when the Shin Bet
rounded up a score of its members, including the two activists who
had published the movement's first ten handbills. A third central figure,
Ziad Nahal, was deported three months later, effectively depleting
the group's senior echelon. The result was that despite its enormous
prestige, the Islamic Jihad was unable to expand its operations or
move on to more sophisticated tactics. An appeal to Sheikh Yassin was
curtly rebuffed with the reply that the Islamic Congress had no need
of partners; and anyway, Yassin claimed, the Jihad had no more than
100 members, most of whom were under lock and key. Feelers put
out to the Unified Command were quickly withdrawn, for as Sheikh

Odeh explained (after being deported in April 1988), "We smelled a takeover by people looking out for their own interests and perverting the uprising for partisan aims."

In effect, then, the match that had kindled the uprising had begun to flicker out. There was no one left to lead the struggle, and for lack of choice, really, the Jihad's exiled leaders began to call for unity in the ranks. At one point they tried to introduce new rhythmic slogans into the uprising ("O Shamir, tell Rabin / that we are the sons of Saladin," or "O Rabin, tell Shamir / my great and mighty people to fear"), and when these chants caught on the exiles claimed that the Jihad enjoyed the support of the masses even without an organizational framework. But as each month passed, Yassin's Islamic Resistance Movement tightened its hold over the public, while the Islamic Jihad fell farther and farther behind. In a rare interview granted from his seat of exile in Lebanon, Sheikh Odeh was reduced to commenting sadly that "Allah does not forget to compensate those who have done well in his sight."

As might have been expected, the direction in which the battered Jihad turned at that point was back to terrorism. Odeh argued against taking up arms "because the Jews are waiting for that as an excuse to crush the uprising." But Dr. Shkaki (who was deported in August 1988) realized that many were "longing for an armed struggle." The summer of 1988 therefore saw a resumption of propaganda calling for suicide actions as an alternative to fighting with stones. One of the Jihad's publications reported that the PLO was unable to smuggle enough weapons into the territories and that in any case the Israeli troops were prepared to defend themselves against ambushes. Hence the only effective tactic was to drive cars packed with explosives into military installations, following the spectacular examples set in Lebanon. Such operations, the Jihad reasoned, would claim a large number of victims and boost the *intifada* onto a new plane.

The Ayatollah Khomeini, it seems, was equally interested in helping the Jihad embark upon a military struggle by creating a link between its remaining activists and the leaders of the Hizballah in Lebanon. After being deported Sheikh Odeh met with Sheikh Mohammed Hussein Fadlallah, the spiritual leader of the Hizballah in Lebanon, and was invited to dine with the Iranian ambassador in Beirut, but nothing tangible came of these talks. Meanwhile, the Jihad suffered another setback when its spiritual mentor, Sheikh Asa'ad Bayoud a-Tamimi, returned to Amman from Teheran with a suitcase filled with money and was promptly arrested. The result of these reverses was that the Jihad remained attractive as a symbol, but its drawing power as an organization never reached beyond a narrow sector of the Palestinian public—especially after the Islamic mainstream overcame its qualms and gave itself over to violence.

Because Hamas aimed to become a broad-based resistance movement, its immediate goal was to instruct its members in the rules of discipline and secrecy. Just as the PLO had to grapple with the problem of its permeation by Israeli agents, so Sheikh Yassin's aides looked for ways to prevent penetrations by double agents and to keep new recruits from falling under the Israelis' sway. Religion was itself a source of great strength in the contest with the Shin Bet, and the Hamas people were exceedingly tough nuts to crack. They maintained their silence or gave up only minor details even during long, debilitating sessions with practiced interrogators. Still, the movement wanted to arm its people with more than faith alone. A Hamas primer put out as early as February 1988 (in a miniature format for easy concealment) directed its members on how they were to behave from the moment they were summoned for a talk with the Shin Bet. An intelligence man, it explained, tries first of all to take the measure of his mark and then get him in his power so as to enlist him as a spy. To weaken the inexperienced candidate, he is kept waiting for hours and made increasingly nervous by vague talk of torture. During the interview itself, the Israeli officer often shouts at a youngster, threatening to prevent him from taking his matriculation exams or from traveling abroad and to see to it that his family suffers ruin unless he cooperates. The aim of all these threats, the booklet states, is to unnerve the youngster and lower his resistance.

As an antidote to these tactics, Hamas told its people that they must not allow their fear to get the better of them. They were not to answer even the interrogator's most polite and innocuous questions, for one thing leads to another, and in the next stage they would be given simple tasks that would grow more complex and demanding as time went on. The rules of behavior were listed in the booklet as follows:

- If you meet with an intelligence officer, answer him with "yes" and "no" and say nothing more.
- Act tough, not weak.

- Don't give him even the most elementary information and don't perform any service for him.
- Don't make any confession in his office or sign any documents.
- Don't agree to any further meetings.
- Don't drink any hot or cold beverage or taste any food. They may contain a tranquilizer or an aphrodisiac, and these can be your undoing.
- Tell your parents and friends about the meeting. Don't hold anything back and don't be afraid; someone will be able to advise you on how to behave.
- Let [the Israelis] know that you hate them and are not willing to cooperate.
- Don't be frightened by the threat that you will be placed under arrest. Detention is preferable to losing both this world and the one to come.

Another primer, published as a Hamas handbill, claimed that the Shin Bet was trying to trap agents with the aid of hashish and other drugs and that it caught young women in its net by having "stray dogs" (Palestinian collaborators) seduce them: "They keep pictures of the couple and the letters passed between them, threatening the girls with exposure unless they agree to serve the Intelligence [people]." More underhanded yet, the leaflet warned, the Shin Bet was known to photograph girls in their underwear while they were trying on dresses in shops and then blackmailing them into informing on their friends. Parents were therefore advised to make sure that their girls did not dally on the way home from school and that they did not frequent hairdressers, boutiques, or even shoe stores unchaperoned. Young men were warned off alcohol, pornographic magazines, and loose women who try to flirt with them in the street. Hamas elevated prudery from an embattled tradition to a weapon of the underground. Its handbills spoke of "a generation of informers" being succeeded by a people that refused to have any truck with the Jews, for by their very nature the "Children of Israel" were steeped in decadence, and they corrupted whoever came into contact with them. Anyone who recalls the Koran's prophecy that the Jews will come to a bitter end, one circular pronounced, cannot possibly serve them as a spy.

In April 1988 Hamas went a step further and brought out a sixteen-page handbook entitled *The Jihad Fighter Facing Interrogation and Torture* (printed in Cyprus, incidentally, with the aid of donations sent to a post office box in Tampa, Florida). It was an open secret that the detailed confessions extracted from PLO prisoners had brought disaster down on the armed struggle against Israel. Hamas feared that the Islamic endeavor would suffer a similar fate unless its disciples were taught to steel themselves against the worst physical and psychological pressure the Israelis could apply. The handbook therefore promised that those who proudly defied their interrogators would be rewarded as though they had died for the sanctification of Allah. But those who broke under interrogation would never know forgiveness, for more than just damaging the existing organization, confessions would deter new candidates from joining it. It could not be claimed that Islam was superior to secularism unless the Hamas people were known to "spit out their blood and teeth under the whip." An iron will, the handbook taught, was all one needed to withstand deprivation, whippings, electric shocks, and threats: "We must remember that the enemy's strength is naught compared with the Allah's grace."

In more practical terms, the authors of the pamphlet reminded their readers that the Israelis were sensitive about going too far and administering physical torture that would leave marks on the victims' bodies, for they claimed to be an enlightened nation that respected human rights. Faced with a detainee who clung to silence, they were doomed to lose in one of two ways: if the torture grew worse, their barbarism would be exposed; if it stopped, the prisoner would come out the winner. Prospective detainees were also warned not to believe an interrogator who told them that other prisoners had already made confessions, even if he trotted out a number of the detainee's friends or showed him statements bearing their signatures. A prisoner was best off telling his interrogators from the start that he was privy to secret information but would die under torture rather than reveal it. For the enemy had no interest in killing prisoners; he merely wanted to obtain information. The tactic of making partial statements in the hope of revealing a little and concealing twice as much was also ruled out, because such statements made it easier to send a detainee to trial. A prisoner who refused to confess had a better chance in court than one who made a statement but later repudiated it on the grounds that it had been wrung out of him by force. As a rule, the pamphlet explained, when no confession exists the enemy must bring his agents to court and is reluctant to do so, because even when testifying behind a screen, they run a much greater risk of exposure.

Cell mates were another potential hazard to beware of, for the Shin Bet was known to plant Arab agents disguised as hardened security prisoners. Even a great show of piety and prayer was no guarantee that fellow-prisoners were not "song birds," and since "even the walls have ears," the handbook stressed that silence was the best policy at all times. Particularly dangerous was the temptation to send messages to family and friends with visitors or with a prisoner slated to be released. As a final tip, the readers were encouraged to fabricate a logical but misleading story to explain their actions and to stick to it until their interrogators either fell for the alibi or just gave up. Whether due to all this detailed advice or simply to a greater dedication to their cause, the Hamas people exhibited far greater tenacity under interrogation than their PLO counterparts. They also displayed such strong qualities of leadership in the prisons and detention camps that many other prisoners were won over to their creed, adopting the practice of Islam and joining the new underground.

Hamas's strategy of offering itself as an alternative to the PLO but not stooping to violence against it held up throughout the first year of the *intifada*. Neither Sheikh Yassin in Gaza nor the Brotherhood's leaders in the West Bank had any illusions about where the loyalties of the Palestinian majority lay, and they admonished their people to exercise patience and restraint toward the nationalists, lest the Shabiba or other arms of the Fatah feel compelled to retaliate. Nevertheless, partisan feelings were known to be potent, and more than once scuffles broke out between the bearded followers of Hamas and their unrepentant rivals. In mid-June 1988 one of Hamas's demonstrations in Jebalya got so far out of hand that the crowd began to trample pictures of Arafat and burn Palestinian flags! The tension was almost as high in Nablus, and in one case it was only at the last moment that the Hamas people called off an ambush laid against Fatah loyalists who were about to emerge from a mosque on a protest march. So sensitive were the movement's leaders to the friction that in many villages they ordered their supporters to hold regular talks with their nationalist neighbors. The result was that each side continued to cover the walls with its own handbills and slogans but left the work of its rivals intact.

The Unified Command was prepared to live with competition, as long as it was contained and nonviolent. The Fatah, moreover, was particularly concerned that an outright clash with the new underground would destroy the *intifada* and play right into Israel's hands. It suspected the Israelis of a plot first to let Hamas gather strength and then to unleash it against the PLO, turning the uprising into a civil war. Evidence of such intentions seemed to pile up each day. The army never interfered with the Hamas strike stewards, who forced shopkeepers to close their businesses precisely during the hours when the Unified Command allowed them to be open. While blocking the PLO's sources of capital, the Civil Administration made no effort to stem the flow of funds from Jordan to Hamas and even permitted high-level emissaries of the Muslim Brotherhood to come from Amman for consultations.

The Israelis were not the only ones suspected of covertly helping Hamas along. By the summer of 1988 the Fatah had deduced that King Hussein was encouraging the fundamentalists for the same reasons the Israelis had: to weaken the PLO and shore up some measure of his own influence in the territories. There was ample evidence for this conclusion. Suddenly the editorial pages of Jordan's papers had opened up to the top men in the Muslim Brotherhood. Senior members of Hamas from Nablus and East Jerusalem were welcomed in Amman's ministries, and they even visited the offices of Jordan's General Intelligence Services! Sermons delivered in the West Bank made pointed reference to the role of the Hashemite family in the historical struggle and cautioned against detaching the area from Jordan. And of course Amman's regular payments to the *waqf* and its employees were seen as forthright aid in building Hamas's power at a time when the PLO suffered from steadily dwindling coffers.

To make matters worse, the fundamentalist challenge had begun to cause friction within the PLO itself. The Communists refused to engage in counter-propaganda on the grounds that it was Arafat's job. Together with the two fronts, moreover, they suspected that the ideologically supple Arafat would exchange his coalition with them for an alliance with Hamas. These fears were undoubtedly fed by Arafat's personal campaign to reach an understanding, however imperfect, with the fundamentalists. His route of approach was through the Muslim Brotherhood, and his plan was to place pressure on Yassin by courting his patrons in Kuwait, Egypt, and Jordan. He visited the Persian Gulf a number of times to meet with Brotherhood leaders there and work out the general lines of an agreement, but these efforts came to naught. In Jordan his emissaries approached Abd-al-Rahman Khalifa, the local leader of the Brotherhood, and parliamentary deputy Yusef al-Azzam, but likewise came away empty handed. In Egypt, however, his efforts finally paid off—far more than he ever expected. Beyond promising to ease the sheikh's hostility to Arafat, the Cairo branch of the Brotherhood—which is the strongest of all its arms—recognized the PLO as the uncontested leader of the Palestinian struggle, held fundraising campaigns on its behalf, and in the winter of 1988 even suggested that it would recruit volunteers for the organization! Only fools could miss the message of such effusive cordiality, and Yassin and his associates were anything but that.

In response, Hamas gradually wound down its campaign against the PLO without abandoning its basically hostile attitude. "Do you recognize the PLO as the leader [of the Palestinian struggle]?" Halil Koka, a founder of Hamas, was asked in Kuwait after being deported from Gaza. A bearded, heavy, forty-year-old father of nine, Koka had preached in the mosque of the Shati refugee camp, though he lived in a nearby quarter of Gaza. "We recognize the PLO as the leader of its constituent organizations" was the most he would concede, pointing to basic differences of ideology: "Allah brought the Jews together in Palestine not to benefit from a homeland but to dig their grave there and save the world from their pollution. Just as the Muslim pilgrim redeems his soul in Mecca by offering up a sacrifice, so the Jews will be slaughtered on the rocks of al-Aqsa." Since Arafat would not embrace this doctrine as the cornerstone of his policy, the most Koka would promise was that Hamas would not destroy the uprising in the course of trying to lead it.

In practice the PLO-Hamas rivalry centered on who had the authority to set the rules for the ongoing strike in the territories. That, at least, was the issue on which Yassin chose to challenge the Unified National Command through a series of numbered handbills that resembled the PLO circulars in form but were not at all like them in content. These handbills fairly crackled with pious zeal and were decorated with verses from the Koran for good measure. They hammered away at Hamas's credo, set forth its goals and slogans, and from June 1988 onward fixed the days of each week's general strike—often without any regard for the dates published by the Unified Command. Hamas proclaimed memorial days with roots in the Muslim tradition, from the anniversary of Mohammed's slaughter of the Jews of Haibar in the mid-seventh century to the 1969 fire in the al-Aqsa Mosque. In effect, it tried to create a calendar of events for the uprising as an alternative to the strike days observed by the PLO. Sometimes it even called the intifada by different names: sahwah ("awakening") or infijar ("explosion").

As its power grew, Hamas forced the population to strike on the days set down by both the Unified Command and its own leadership, thus doubling the burden on the already stressed population. Workers and businessmen were paying the price of the tough competition between the two camps, resulting in considerable disgruntlement, yet the new movement's success in enforcing its strike calls only bolstered its position. It was plain to see that the fundamentalists were even better at bringing life to a halt in the territories than the PLO. In the majority of towns and cities, the population took the path of least resistance and avoided the wrath of either of the rivals by going along with them both. Throughout 1988 even the Fatah was reluctant to break the Hamas strikes, though it was under heavy pressure from the labor unions and business community to assert its primacy and take the situation in hand.

Beyond this parallel system of strikes and handbills, Hamas's leaders set out to make their views known on other issues raised by the rebellion. They won considerable admiration for denouncing the ruffians who stoned Arab vehicles on non-strike days. They were the first to call for the reopening of the schools, echoing the desire of hundreds of thousands of pupils and their parents. And in the cause of community solidarity, they ran charity drives for the needy, chided drivers who played havoc with traffic laws (especially after the mass resignation of the Palestinian policemen), threatened the gangs of thieves who broke into homes and shops, and generally called for "sympathy" in human relations. On the other hand, they were enraged by the talk of civil disobedience coming out of the leftist organizations, decrying it as a crackpot notion that would drag the people down into despair while accomplishing nothing.

The symbols and images in the Hamas handbills were very different from those of the Unified Command. Instead of the promise of material rewards—alternative means of employment, lower rents, and protection against layoffs—Hamas spoke only of spiritual compensation: the building of a new identity for the people as an army of believers for whom the gates of Paradise were about to open. Israel was depicted as a satanic force that the faithful were to shun absolutely. For a while, in addition to the handbills, Hamas published a small underground weekly designed to break the "media boycott of the movement" in the Arab states. Expanding upon the content of the handbills, it added a survey of events in the territories, showered criticism on the Arab governments for their hypocrisy toward the Palestinians, and censured Arafat for his dealings with them.

On August 18, 1988, Hamas opened a new phase in its contest with the PLO by issuing its detailed manifesto, the "Covenant of the Islamic Resistance Movement–Palestine." Publishing this document was tantamount to waving a red rag in front of the nationalists, for it meant the renunciation of the long-standing Palestinian Covenant together with the formal institutionalization of the Islamic Resistance Movement as a separate political entity with a doctrine distinctly its own. Set down in forty pages of cramped type, the manifesto hailed a new era in the history of the Muslim Brotherhood and the changeover to an open, energetic struggle against Israel. Interestingly enough, it treated the nationalists with respect, promising that "on the day the PLO adopts Islam as its path, the Islamic Resistance Movement will become its army." In the meanwhile, it proclaimed, *jihad* was the "personal obligation" of every Muslim, for Palestine was the "soil of the Islamic trust till the end of days" and the Jews (in the spirit of the *Protocols of the Elders of Zion*) were an instrument of evil that turns the wheels of history. Reuven Paz, a leading Israeli expert on the development of the fundamentalist current in the territories, described this covenant as a sign that "the fight for the hearts of the Palestinian public [had] just begun." He believed that Hamas's prestige had led to an exaggerated assessment of its strength but that in any case only progress toward a political solution would be likely to drain off any of the following it had acquired during the *intifada*.

The debate over how to cope with Hamas wore on in the Israeli defense establishment until the summer of 1988, with certain quarters in the Civil Administration lobbying for forceful measures to check the practically unfettered activity of the fundamentalists. The main qualm about rounding up the Hamas activists had to do with Israel's vulnerability to charges of violating the Palestinians' freedom of worship by arresting clerical figures or curbing the institutions attached to the *waqf*. Yet cutting off the loudspeaker systems in the mosques and trying to restrain the preachers were obviously not enough, especially as many imams had gone beyond speaking in parables and were brazenly inciting their flocks to strike out at Israel. Still, the hallowed rule of keeping out of Muslim religious affairs was strictly observed, so that Hamas continued to gather strength and support within the religious establishment. But the indulgence shown toward middle-level activists no longer applied to the Hamas leadership.

What finally tipped the scales in favor of action was a buildup of reports that an armed underground was in the making. Halil Koka openly encouraged this course from his seat of exile in Kuwait, and in July 1988 the Hamas weekly showered praise on the young Gazan who had stabbed two guards while visiting a relative in prison, writing: "This is the most effective answer to all the laggards who claim that they can't rise up against the enemy without arms." Explosive devices were discovered by a main junction in the Strip, and the men who had planted them turned out to be members of Hamas. Yassin's people, it appeared, were close to embarking on outright terrorism. His young disciples were champing at the bit, and the crippled sheikh had difficulty controlling them. The Shin Bet found, for example, that they were preparing caches of arms and explosives. These activities (or so it came out in subsequent interrogations) were carried out by Hamas's military arm, whose volunteers received the title *"mujahedu Falastin"* ("holy fighters of Palestine"). They were under the command of Salah Shehadeh, whose code name was "101," and his two deputies, Yahya Sounar in the southern part of the Strip and Ribhi Moustafa in the north. All told, Hamas's military arm comprised over 200 men, many of whom had been borderline delinquents in their youth.

In light of these developments, the Israelis descended on Hamas in July–September 1988 and hauled in about 120 people, including Ibrahim al-Yazouri, one of Yassin's close aides, and Jamil a-Tamimi, the movement's liaison with the West Bank. The command established in February 1988 was completely liquidated, as was its clandestine press. In deference to his condition, Sheikh Yassin got off lightly with a sharp rebuke and stern warning against supporting any terrorist actions (banishing him from Gaza had been ruled out on the grounds that any form of direct punishment would only enhance his prestige). When the arrests were completed, an intelligence assessment pronounced the action as "the end of the Islamic camp's clandestine command." But in no way did it spell the end of Hamas. It took the movement's middle echelon several weeks to recover from the blow, and the next handbill—No. 30—had to be printed in the West Bank (for the first time). But thereafter Hamas's activity actually gathered momentum and increased in scope, spreading into many villages where sympathies for the fundamentalists had not yet been translated into a concrete organizational tie.

Meanwhile, within the Ketziot detention camp and Israel's prisons, the movement's arrested leaders continued to direct their organization, presiding over its swift recovery. They received reports in the form of notes that were passed on through kisses during family visits and immediately swallowed, to be read later in the privacy of their cells. The resumption of Hamas's activities despite the roundup of leading activists prompted a second blow by the Israeli security services in May 1989. This time Yassin himself was arrested, along with those of his aides who were still free and some 260 other Hamas activists, including Salah Shehadeh. Still, the Israelis had few illusions that they had broken the organization once and for all. They knew that the roots put down by Hamas would sprout new shoots, again and again, prompting more violence each time.

Fundamentalism remained a mass movement firm in its resolve not just to work toward the destruction of Israel but to change the face of Palestinian society by exorcising the demon of secularism. In a matter of months Hamas had become a factor to be reckoned with. It could not yet compete with the nationalists in numerical strength, but it had built an impressive infrastructure and held the power to ease or impede progress toward a political solution, as it chose. This, too, was one of the fruits of the Palestinian uprising whose bitter taste would linger for many days to come.

NINE | *THE PENDULUM OF CIVIL DISOBEDIENCE*

THE IDEA of civil disobedience existed long before anyone dreamed that the Palestinians in the occupied territories would actually rise up in revolt. For years it had been mocked by the PLO as the obsession of a naive misfit whose head was in the clouds and feet were planted anywhere but in the rocky soil of the Palestinian reality. For their part, the Israeli security services were aware of the doctrine being preached by Mubarak Awad and, unlike his detractors, even appreciated its potential. But because the response to it was practically negligible, they did not bother to close down his rather pathetic operation. Derided on one side and discounted on the other, the plan for a campaign of Palestinian civil disobedience slowly took shape as the initiative of one man who stubbornly promoted the strategy until it was absorbed into the pool of ideas that inspired the makers of the *intifada*.

"The greatest mistake Israel can make, where I am concerned, is to ignore me," Mubarak Awad had confidently announced upon returning to Jerusalem in 1983 after a fifteen-year stay in the United States. The Military Government's files contained entries on his brief stints in jail for helping to organize commercial strikes at the end of the 1960s. But considering what was known of him since then, his statement struck the Israelis as an odd and idle boast. During the long period spent in Ohio, Awad had completed a doctorate in psychology and engaged in youth work, yet as far as the Israelis could tell, he had not been associated with any arm of the PLO. He espoused methods that his compatriots had never considered before and that were diametrically opposed to the long tradition of armed opposition to the occupation. Nevertheless, Mubarak Awad persevered. Two years after returning to Jerusalem he opened the Center for the Study of Non-Violence (which, the Israelis suspected, was being funded by the PLO through donations from Palestinians in the United States). Working out of two small rooms, he ran a mobile library, led a number of quiet demonstrations (along the lines of planting olive trees), and began offering aid and guidance to villages whose land had been expropriated by the Civil Administration. Awad's work filled part of the vacuum created by the PLO's two-pronged policy of armed struggle from without and forbearance within, so that in time his center became an address for Palestinians with grievances of all kinds. Determined to make his philosophy work, he mounted a campaign (unsuccessful, as it turned out) to have Palestinians buy, on the first Monday of every month, only products manufactured in the territories. Undeterred by that failure, he tried (again to little avail) to boost the turnover at shops in Hebron being driven into ruin because they were located near buildings taken over by Jews; customers kept their distance from stores surrounded by barbed wire and military guards. One of his ideas was to organize a lottery to draw in a clientele but it never got off the ground.

Awad's ideological isolation and lack of organizational backing made it all the more difficult for him to put his ideas into practice, on even a modest scale. But they did not prevent him from trying to disseminate his doctrine in print. He personally translated Jean Sharp's classic on the benefits of nonviolent resistance into Arabic. On the eve of the *intifada*, he published *A Soldier of Nonviolence in Islam*, a biography of Padishah Khan, the "Gandhi of the Border"—an Indian Muslim who was allied with Gandhi and led the nonviolent movement in the northern part of his country—to prove that the doctrine of nonviolence was compatible with the Muslim tradition. These books, however, were barely noticed by the people he was trying to reach.

Greater interest was shown in Awad's call for civil disobedience, which was published in several versions beginning in November 1986. Setting out from the premise that the Palestinians could expect salvation from neither the PLO's armed forces nor the regular armies of the Arab states, he concluded that only the people themselves could halt the drift toward Israel's annexation of the territories. Without denying the justice of an armed struggle, Awad wrote, "I propose a better method at this stage." Nonviolent means, he explained, "would go a long way toward paralyzing Israel's destructive war machine" and allow broad classes of society to take an active part in the struggle, rather than just follow it over the radio. By winning over critical sectors of Israeli and Western public opinion, these methods would also lead to Israel's moral and political isolation.

Awad's plan was simple and straightforward: to change the accepted form of the demonstrations held in the territories from riots to prayer protests, silent processions, the wearing of yellow badges or prison suits, and clean-up campaigns. "These actions may sound strange, even amusing," he confessed to head off his critics, "but they get the message across." He proposed, for example, that when the Israelis set to building a new settlement, the Palestinians should throw themselves in front of the bulldozers, as well as cut electricity and phone lines, sabotage water mains, and block roads. "This is not madness," he assured his listeners. "It will work very well." If protesters were to aim for the same results by throwing stones, he explained, the Israeli response would be gunfire, and the construction of the settlement would only be accelerated. But if the Palestinians showed that they were prepared to die for their land, all would see that they had no interest in harming anyone. This was the ultimate form of guerrilla action, he argued—and for Palestinians the notion of unarmed *fedayeen* was a revolutionary one.

To reinforce these principles, Awad set down no less than 120 possible methods of action. They included refusing to work in Israeli settlements or factories, to cooperate with the military authorities, to produce one's identity card on demand, and to pay fines, so that the courts would be choked with cases and the prisons filled to overflowing. Other tactics were to refrain from applying to the authorities for licenses; to ignore summonses to the police or Civil Administration (and any other document written in Hebrew); to boycott all meetings and conventions in which Israeli officials or Palestinian collaborators took part; to withhold payment of all taxes, including Value-Added Tax (which is paid at point of purchase); to violate curfews and limitation-of-movement orders; and to ostracize anyone who collaborated or even cooperated with the Israeli administration.

Alongside these moves Awad called for the establishment of "alternative institutions" to replace the Israeli administration. He envisioned a "completely autonomous infrastructure" as the nucleus of future independence—a "shadow administration" that was in no way associated with or dependent upon any official body for funding or the running of day-to-day affairs. Instead of resorting to the courts, for instance, he proposed that the people revert to the ancient system of tribal law (*'ashiri*). Awad encouraged the organization of separate medical insurance for Palestinians. He wanted to set up committees to care for the needy, the families of prisoners, and settlements under blockade or curfew. He even spoke of drawing up an alternative curriculum together with a plan for moving classes into private homes in the event that the Civil Administration closed the schools (which it subsequently did). Above all, he advised stockpiling food and fuel, making arrangements to keep in contact with the foreign media, replacing the existent municipal councils with volunteer committees, and creating channels to generate local funding, rather than relying on aid from the outside.

This rich store of ideas was readily available to the Palestinian establishment in the territories, but for years it was sniffed at in disdain. Awad was snubbed by most of the Fatah spokesmen. They failed to invite him to their conferences and occasionally subjected him to subtle threats. In fact it was not until just a few weeks before the uprising that a positive reference in one of the PLO organs finally cleared him of suspicion of being connected with the CIA. His work in Jerusalem began inauspiciously. The first of his seminars to advocate nonviolence as the prime weapon of the Palestinian struggle antagonized most of its participants and sparked angry charges that after the PLO's retreat from Beirut, he was trying to discredit the doctrine of armed struggle. His American passport and American wife, Christian background, soft style of speech, and pursuit by the foreign journalists stationed in Israel set him far apart from the flinty field men like the Labadi brothers and their future associates on the Unified Command. But once the uprising broke out, it was the forty-five-year-old Awad who held the key to the problem that troubled all the rest: how to advance beyond violent demonstrations to a wholesale rout of the occupation.

Not that his climb up to acceptance was an easy one. During the early weeks of the rebellion, when the local PLO people still thought of his writings as an academic exercise, Awad began personally distributing his leaflets. With as much publicity as he could generate, he spent his days racing from one village and refugee camp to the next, reciting his philosophy to the youngsters of the Shabiba. Here and there he won a hearing, and in the Kalandia camp he organized a demonstration of residents holding olive branches and got the women to hold sit-down strikes. But in private conversations he admitted that convinced as he was that the demonstrators would make more of an impact by showering the soldiers with flowers than with stones, he had little hope of influencing the young to that extent. He was also disappointed by the widespread fear of boycotting the services supplied by the Civil Administration, for his goal was to cut all telephone connections and disrupt even the supply of water and electricity to the territories as expressions of their physical severance from Israel.

Mubarak Awad was finally let in from the cold in an almost abrupt process that began with the abortive Siniora initiative. Admittedly, when he addressed the first gathering of Fatah loyalists at the National Palace Hotel on January 4, he was practically hooted off the floor. But at least he had planted a seed. By the end of January, when the Unified Command was forced to consider the direction the revolt should take, it found that there were few suggestions other than to follow a course of civil disobedience. Men like Mohammed Labadi were good at spurring the masses on to the barricades, but they lacked a clear vision of where to go from there. It was then that Mubarak Awad stepped back into the picture and, unlike his experience in the past, found that his voice was being heard. Suddenly the Unified Command was pouncing on the pamphlets he had written over the years. From the end of January 1988 onward, it began to adopt whole parts of his program as the primary goals of the *intifada*. The fact that three months earlier Israel's Ministry of Interior had announced that it would not renew Awad's tourist visa, so that the threat of deportation hovered over him, only enhanced his image as a loyal patriot. And far from placing him under suspicion, the intercession on his behalf by American diplomats was now put to his credit as a sign of his influence in high places.

The next months were a heady time for Mubarak Awad. Early in February he met with senior members of the local Fatah and proposed that they declare a "Palestinian republic" forthwith. (The idea was a bit too daring for his listeners, but once again he had planted a seed—and it would bear fruit before the year was out.) His center's pamphlets, which for years had stood piled on shelves without any takers, suddenly became the hottest items in town. Leading lights who had refused to be seen with him were now lining up at his door. He was even called upon to mediate a dispute between the PLO's rival factions in Nablus! The press treated him as an outspoken leader of the *intifada*—and the only one with the courage to declare on camera that he was deliberately violating laws he believed to be unjust. In a matter of weeks, he had changed from being a curiosity on the fringe of the Palestinian rebellion to both a mentor on the doctrine of struggle and the leading propagandist of the uprising.

By the beginning of May the Israeli government had had enough. Under pressure from the security services, the "committee of prime ministers" (Shamir, Peres, and Rabin) weighed the matter carefully and decided to ignore the appeals from eminent American figures and to order Awad's deportation. As expected, he went out in a blaze of publicity. Appealing the order to the High Court of Justice, he let it be known that he would convert to Judaism, if it proved necessary, to obtain the right of return to his homeland. While waiting for the court to issue its ruling, he went on a hunger strike—and was joined outside the police station by a handful of Jewish supporters! When the order was upheld and he was led onto a plane bound for the United States, Mubarak Awad had the satisfaction of knowing that his ideas had finally taken root in the uprising. But like so many of the others who had had their hour upon the stage of the *intifada*, once in exile he was heard no more.

The appearance of the "Awad doctrine" in the Unified Command's handbills—stripped, of course, of its commitment to nonviolence—changed many of the rules of the contest going on between the Palestinian insurgents and the Israeli authorities. Though bloody clashes continued to erupt all over the territories, the real battle was now over the de facto self-rule that the population was trying to put into practice. In effect, the hundreds of violent incidents had become a smoke screen for the effort to build a "shadow administration" as the stamp of a state-in-the-making. The initial enthusiasm for driving the army out of the territories had been replaced by the more sophisticated aim of undermining Israel's rule as a whole. The more the insurgents had to concede the army's great advantage in street skirmishes, the more they invested in bringing down the Civil Administration and replacing it with an independent, grass-roots arrangement. By the early spring, what had begun as a wild lashing out at the troops had turned into a graduated assault on the machinery of occupation by a competing structure that answered to the Unified Command. And just as the IDF had been unable to quell the violence in the territories, so the Civil Administration found that it was losing ground to the institutions of self-rule that were meant to supplant it.

The administrative machinery of the *intifada* began to emerge haphazardly almost as soon as the riots had broken out. Its first manifestation was the "popular committees" that sprang up on their own in a number of places well before the establishment of the Unified Command. Envisioned by Mubarak Awad, these committees were formed, more often than not, by people who had never heard of him. They first emerged as a spontaneous effort by branches of the Shabiba, professionals, members of women's societies, and charitable organizations to aid the distressed population in the refugee camps under curfew. From Gaza supplies were sent to Jebalya and Shati; in Nablus residents administered to the refugees of Balata; in Ramallah the municipality was pressured into making up packages of food and drugs to be smuggled into the camps around Jerusalem; and in Jericho wealthy businessmen sent truckloads of fruits and vegetables to what was already being called (prematurely, it must be said) the "besieged areas." The scope of this aid was actually quite modest, for at the start of the *intifada* little was needed to ease the pressure on the camps, and there certainly was no shortage of food. But the symbolic value of these committees was enormous, for they opened the way to mass involvement in the revolt. Through them, even the most upright and law-abiding citizens could play a legitimate role in the *intifada*.

The idea of organizing caught on fast, and within a few weeks the aid committees boasted such offshoots as councils to run the villages that had declared themselves "liberated territory." From there the impulse to join forces spread to one of the mainstays of the uprising: the business community. During the forty-day general strike that began in December 1987, merchants in a number of cities and towns formed their own coordinating committees to deal first of all with pragmatic problems: the repair of locks smashed by Israeli soldiers and the stationing of guards to protect their shops against looting. They grappled with problems like price gouging, coordinated contacts with the tax authorities, and fought (unsuccessfully, as it turned out) against the peddlers who set up stands in front of the striking shops. Before long they were also dabbling in strategy and managed to persuade the Unified Command that if it wished to keep up the strike—which was the most prominent expression of popular defiance—it would have to relax its conditions. From February onward the merchants applied the redeeming formula of opening their businesses for three hours each morning—except, of course, on the dates declared full-strike days, or "Days of Rage," by the Unified Command. In accepting this compromise, the command averted the danger that countless businesses would fail and eased the tension between the shopkeepers and the members of the Shabiba, who watched their every move. Yet there was a deeper significance to the change. Looking back on this period, Ahmed Jaber of the Democratic Front, a one-time member of the Unified Command, observed that the shift in the terms of the strike was a mark of one of the *intifada*'s great innovations: its "democratic character." Rather than be issued from above, orders bubbled up from below—a pattern that would extend to other fields as well.

In the meantime, and for similar reasons, special committees cropped up in other spheres of Palestinian life. Health committees cared for the wounded who refused to turn to the hospitals for fear of being arrested. Groups of doctors and nurses gave lessons in first aid and were sometimes assigned to serve as paramedics at processions and demonstrations. Women's committees specialized in collecting donations for the needy, running blood banks for hospitals, passing out propaganda leaflets, educating housewives against waste, and looking after the families of the dead, wounded, and detained. Education committees tried to organize classes in youth clubs and private homes after the Civil Administration closed the schools in February 1988. (Until the Israelis put a stop to it, the "alternative-education program" in Ramallah, and to a lesser degree in Nablus, was quite a serious endeavor.) Judicial committees formed to settle disagreements, in place of the court system, and often based their rulings on the rural-popular legal tradition to stress their dissociation from both Jordanian and Israeli law. Occasionally special committees were organized to deal with problems particular to one place. The lands committee of Sur Baher, one of the Arab villages located within Jerusalem's municipal boundary, urged its residents to lay claim to every empty lot in the village, lest it be expropriated "for a Jewish settlement." As a result, the villagers began feverishly laying foundations for houses they never intended to build.

Perhaps the most conspicuous of these grass-roots efforts was the work of the agriculture committees, which encouraged the cultivation of abandoned plots. In Beit Sahur, to take just one example, a committee of this kind established a center to sell plants, seeds, and fertilizer at cost. Under the direction of a faculty member of Bethlehem University, its members taught the townsfolk how to raise vegetables in their yards and other available plots. At one stage they introduced the fad of raising rabbits and organized metal workers to turn out cheap iron cages that were snapped up in quantities, particularly by the classes that had always considered agriculture beneath their station. They also taught people how to turn old, unused refrigerators into incubators for chicks, and for a time makeshift chicken coops set up on roofs were a status symbol even in neighborhoods known for their posh villas.

Flashy campaigns called upon youngsters to plow "victory fields" in vacant lots, and "home economy" became one of the most popular slogans of the *intifada*. From vegetable patches and rabbits, these committees went on to promote the canning of preserves for marketing or home consumption. They even set up rudimentary sewing workshops in a number of homes and branched out into "home bakeries" along similar lines.

No one knows just how many popular committees existed in the territories, but there must have been hundreds of them. Like the Unified Command they were extraordinarily resilient; whenever their members were arrested, others rose to fill their place—lower-level activists who made up in enthusiasm for what they lacked in experience. The striking feature of the popular committees was their lack of uniformity, as befits a grass-roots operation. In some towns and villages a single committee reigned on a coalition basis. In others—mainly in the Gaza Strip—their activists came from only one organization, and occasionally these committees were made up of professionals with no organizational affiliations at all. There were committees that functioned completely independently and others that worked in concert or even joined into loose-knit regional frameworks. Regardless of these particulars, however, they all had enormous appeal. People who had always kept their distance from the PLO's institutions plunged into committee work with relish, despite the risk of being punished for their pains. The involvement of distinguished members of the community— doctors, lawyers, and educators—only added to the committees' prestige (though they were essentially controlled by released security prisoners). The fact is that by the spring of 1988, a sprawling network of popular committees was functioning in one form or another in every city, village, and camp, spreading the web of the uprising's machinery to the farthest corners of the territories.

The Unified Command quickly developed an ambitious outlook on the role of the popular committees. The Communists and Democratic Front appreciated their importance from the start. The Fatah lagged behind somewhat, preferring as much as possible to rely on its existing institutions—from labor unions and charity societies to the Shabiba. But once it realized that these committees were the wave of the future, it became the main supplier of their members. By February 1988 the establishment of popular committees had become a prime objective of all the nationalist organizations, and Hamas later followed a parallel course.

Beyond being the instrument for handling everyday problems, the committees were called upon to serve as the command's operational arm, enforcing the orders published in its handbills and compensating the people who had suffered for obeying them. This link between the popular committees and the Unified Command created the illusion of a hierarchy of command. Even when direct contact did not exist between the two levels, there was no doubt about who was directing the *intifada* and dictating its mode of action: the handbills served the popular committees as a canon on procedures. For the most part, however, the popular committees did have ways of communicating with the Unified Command. When arrested, for example, Mohammed Labadi was carrying lists of the committee members in the greater Jerusalem area and the tasks assigned to each, from gathering the names of people entitled to aid to instigating firebomb attacks on the offices of the municipality, tax authorities, and so forth. A detailed memo sent to Labadi in mid-March by a Democratic Front activist from the Tulkarem refugee camp (who identified himself only by the initials A.N.) illustrated the relationship between the Unified Command and a typical popular committee:

> In the last report I wrote about the work groups in the Tulkarem area, and I don't intend to return to the subject—though I must add that we have opted M.J., the commander of the shock forces operating in the villages of Sur and Aboush, onto the committee, so that it is today responsible for shock groups that have proven their determination in the course of the *intifada*. . . . In 'Anabta members of the Abu Moussa faction of the Fatah are also represented on the committee . . . Twenty-four members in Dir al-Ghousen have been cut off from us as a result of the latest arrests, and J.S. is in charge of checking out their situation . . . Unfortunately, no representative of the professionals comes to the meetings of the regional council, even though they have been allocated a seat. I would like you to deal with this matter . . .
>
> As to the tasks of the *intifada*, here is a report of what has been done: in [Tulkarem] we burned a minibus belonging to the collaborator Khaled al-Masrieh . . . We torched the offices of *a-Nahar* and threw three Molotov cocktails at army cars . . . A military bus was attacked and its windows smashed . . . The collaborator Jamal Ghazlan was stoned, and he shot back at the attackers. One of the members of the Sha'ar unit was arrested as a result. He was badly beaten in custody, so that his hand and foot were broken. There is a rumor, which I

cannot verify, that his eye was poked out . . . His arrest is
a great loss to us, since he was very active and carried out a
series of missions. But it has not created a security problem for
the rest of the activists . . .

The women led two processions in the city, to the offices
of the Red Crescent and to City Hall . . . The occupation
forces dispersed the march with tear gas . . . Each day we
also set up roadblocks and burned tires in two neighborhoods,
in the east and the west . . . In Danabah masked men hit one
of the soldiers in the head . . . In Dir al-Ghousen we had a
disagreement with the Popular Front during a demonstration
that began in the mosque. The march split in two with only
our people going on to the headquarters of the local council
and calling on its chairman to resign. . . . I have asked each
place for reports on their activities, in writing, but have not
received any to date; what I have written here is based solely
on conversations. I shall act to correct this problem and be
sure to send you a report from every settlement . . .

As for money: so far I have received 500 dinars in three
payments, in addition to 500 shekels. Out of this sum we have
paid comrade J.S. (who left his place of work) for gas to distribute handbills . . .

This particular report reflects the growing tendency to divert the
committees' energies into violent actions. But in principle all of the
PLO's factions wanted to turn them primarily into the seeds of self-
government, scattered pockets of independence. In May 1988 one of
the Popular Front's internal documents spoke of building the popular
committees into a "system of nerves that extend throughout our people" because they are "the machinery of popular rule" and express "an
advanced stage of our war of independence." A Democratic Front
document from the same period depicted the committees as "the long
arm of the Unified Command." Their role was not to make do with
the "mobilized forces" (the members of the Palestinian organizations)
but "to draw in a wider public" and create an "alternative popular
machinery" while destroying "the instruments of the occupation."
Soon afterward the Fatah wrote of "replacing the existing political
structure with national rule." As a result of these common approaches,
at the beginning of June 1988 the command's Handbill No. 19 called
for "constituting the machinery of rule in all cities, villages, and camps."
July was set as the last date for establishing new popular committees or
revitalizing flagging ones, and at the end of June Handbill No. 22 told
the committees to "consider themselves the government of the people."

The race to set up popular committees or gain control of existing ones placed the PLO in complete control of these bodies. Committee members were appointed by the constituent factions from above and were dependent on them for funds and other aid. Like the Unified Command, the popular committees eventually became local coalitions in which each representative acted according to instructions from his superiors while striving for consensus with his peers. As the committees gained experience, they began to issue special handbills that were often more influential than the country-wide circulars, because they dealt with problems specific to the residents of a particular area. Committee members also began to host foreign delegations and were usually eager to meet with journalists covering the uprising.

Nowhere was the tension between the disparate demands of violence and civil disobedience greater than at the level of the popular committees. As the mass demonstrations became less frequent, toward the summer of 1988, the popular committees felt obliged to instigate violent incidents, so as to prevent the uprising from dying out. Formed as classic civilian-support bodies, they were being transformed into local operational commands whose main interest was in fomenting unrest. At the same time, to ensure that the population would not slip out of their grasp, they began to subject it to increasingly brutal threats. In this new mode, the committees naturally drew attention to themselves and inevitably invited Israeli retaliation. In August 1988 Israel outlawed the popular committees and arrested hundreds of their members. Many of their successful community projects were also destroyed at that time. Israeli pressure on the teachers, for example, reduced the experiments in an alternate system of education to scattered token efforts. The campaign to encourage self-sufficiency by raising chickens, rabbits, and vegetables fell apart when the Civil Administration closed the stations run by the agriculture committees. Programs for providing aid to the needy were hard hit by the closure of many of the aid and charity societies. Even the clean-up campaigns were disrupted. In the end, the popular committees were forced to abandon their public activities and go underground. And because the public-spirited types who had initially flocked to join them were not cut out for the clandestine life, the committees invariably fell into the hands of the "hard-core cadres" of the Fatah, the Communists, and the two fronts.

Scattered among the popular committees, from the very start of the uprising, were "shock forces" dedicated to striking at both the Israelis and those Palestinians who broke ranks with the *intifada*. Evidently there is truth to the claim that these shock forces were first established on September 17, 1987, three months before the outbreak of the rebellion, to punish collaborators and presumably raise the morale of the dispirited Palestinian public. After the founding of the Unified Command, they were encouraged to "escalate all forms of resistance." Members were sworn to obey the command's orders, pay monthly dues, maintain absolute secrecy, and refrain from any action that might harm the forces' reputation. From February 1988 onward, it was these shock forces that led most of the riots, laid ambushes, built barricades, flew the Palestinian flag, and sprayed slogans on the facades of buildings. In the villages they organized the perimeter guard and posted lookouts to sound warning whistles if the army approached. In the cities they organized on a neighborhood basis, particularly in the local casbah and other rundown quarters of town. The young members of the shock forces in Nablus took to wearing ninja outfits and head masks made out of black cloth or plastic bags, completing the effect by wielding brass knuckles and iron chains. They were hailed for their forays against army foot patrols in the narrow alleys of the casbah. Sometimes they unnerved the soldiers at night by releasing cats with tin cans tied to their tails. At other times they set up wooden effigies in the pose of stone-throwers to draw Israeli fire.

More often than not, however, it was the Palestinians who felt the heavy hand of these shock forces, for out of their ranks came the local "fundraisers" and strike stewards who stopped laborers from going to work on the "Days of Rage." In many cases they backed up their threats with punitive actions that ranged from beatings and arson to cold-blooded murder. Handbill No. 22 described the shock forces as "the iron fist" of the uprising that "bears the burden of resistance to the occupation" and deters "those who would willingly turn away from us." In contrast to the popular committees, most of these forces were recruited by former security prisoners (who were naturally careful to keep a very low profile). As time went on, however, the distinction between the aid committees and the shock forces eroded, and many of the popular committees became all-purpose bodies whose "military" aspect steadily gained the upper hand.

The most far-reaching network of popular committees was created by the Fatah in the Gaza Strip. Abdullah Abu Samhadaneh, the son of Bedouin refugees from the Negev and an ex-security prisoner of some renown, took charge of building it and used a young journalist from one of the press services in Gaza to recruit its members. Beginning with the popular committees in the city of Gaza, Abu Samhadaneh systematically expanded the network into a new underground that was more ramified than the Shabiba movement, from which many of the recruits were drawn. It boasted a regular command structure and was rigorous in maintaining secrecy and internal compartmentalization. Recruits were usually brought in on the basis of personal acquaintance or family ties. Each new member joined an existing squad, but after proving himself in a few minor actions, he was ordered to break away and form a new squad of his own. From Gaza city the network spread throughout the Strip, with the formation of military, food-supply, and security committees (a kind of intelligence service that tracked down people suspected of strike-breaking and collaboration).

Money to fund the new underground evidently came in from Egypt by the incredibly simple method of tossing packages over the border fence in Rafah. In one instance $40,000 in cash was distributed among the committees, making its way not from hand to hand but via secret deposit points. Funds were earmarked for purchasing cans of spray paint and cloth to make flags, in addition to paying activists who had quit their jobs. But mostly they were distributed among the needy. Once a prospective recipient was approved, his name was written on an envelope and a $100 bill was placed inside it. The envelope and a short accompanying letter were then entrusted to a child, who slid them under the door of the addressee, making contact between the recipient and his benefactors unnecessary. In this way the underground played the classic role of an extended aid committee, but it was also responsible for a series of assaults on the recalcitrant. For example, it was known to be behind the torching of fourteen shops in the city of Gaza as punishment for keeping them open beyond the hours prescribed by the Unified Command's handbills. Its members forced the owners of garages to "contribute" tires for roadblocks, and in one case they laid siege to the house of a collaborator until the terrified man finally obtained help. Alerted by its more aggressive actions, the Shin Bet set to uncovering this new network and smashed it between June and August 1988, arresting dozens of people and adding its leading activists, including Abu Samhadeneh, to the list of candidates for deportation. Not that they yielded so easily. Abu Samhadaneh tried to rehabilitate his network from his prison cell, and his aging mother was placed in administrative detention for passing his orders on to its remaining activists.

In the early days of the Unified Command, when the issue was still how long the rebellion could possibly last, few dreamed that the organization of the population would ever get that far. Louai Abdo, probably the leading Fatah figure in Nablus, subsequently revealed that some of the Fatah's leaders did not believe that the population would bear up for very long under the strains of unemployment and disruptions in the economy. In their secret meetings they discussed the possibility of drawing out the initial riots for an unprecedented twenty to thirty days. But that was the best they had hoped for. All the organizations in the PLO were rife with pessimism and a deep sense of inferiority vis-à-vis the occupying regime. No member of the Unified Command ever really entertained the notion of an extended struggle, for experience had taught them that the population's staying power was invariably short-lived. Still, the thirty-three-year-old Abdo argued that events should be allowed to develop "naturally" and it would be wrong to assume any "closing date" for the *intifada*. In fact, the younger generation of the Fatah's local leadership agreed with Mohammed Labadi's approach that the higher the uprising set its sights, the more successful it would be, and that lofty slogans like "Freedom and Independence" should be spread around liberally. Rather than reconcile themselves to a brief flare-up, they wanted to keep the street battles going, reasoning that "when the people calm down, we will too." Some of these younger leaders knew very well that the residents of camps like Balata and Deheishe had been wrestling with the Israeli administration for years and had not given in, even though they had taken some pretty rough punishment. The kids in the streets had already gained control of "60 percent of the Palestinian public," they argued, and an achievement of that sort should not be relinquished easily. Instead, they spoke about mounting a "mass attack" (in the jargon of the Democratic Front) and a "war of attrition" (as the Fatah put it), though they stopped short of using these terms in their hand-bills.

By the beginning of February 1988, the members of the command had revised their assessment of the rebellion's longevity and were fore-casting that it might last "for about another six months." That was when the words "civil disobedience" began to appear in the handbills. Labadi's acceptance of this new strategy less than two weeks after his superiors in Tunis had lambasted Awad and Siniora for spreading untimely slogans showed the pace at which positions shifted under the impact of events. In a matter of weeks the taboo had become the commended; what had been treachery yesterday was patriotism today. Before long fierce competition broke out between Awad's erstwhile critics over which of them was better at manifesting his ideas. (Oddly enough, it was George Habash's Popular Front, the most shrill of the naysayers, that became the standard-bearer of the new philosophy.) Somewhere into its third month, the *intifada* adopted a long-range strategy that subordinated all its moves and considerations to the single goal of divorcing the territories from Israel's administration. Rather than step up the acts of violence to create an atmosphere of anarchy, the point was to lift the *intifada* onto a higher plane of achievement. Louai Abdo described the crux of this change as an attempt to "reduce the occupation from a weave of laws, maneuvers, and a controlling bureaucracy to squads of soldiers scattered through the streets." Israeli rule, in other words, would apply only where soldiers were present to enforce it. The uprising would "flex its muscles . . . at the full range of relations between Israel and the Palestinians."

Incredibly, most of the Israeli experts failed to see this change taking place. Steeped in scorn for the hyperbole of the handbills, they completely missed the real meaning of their words. The term "united front," for instance, was read as just another empty slogan to help unite the people around the Unified Command, whereas in fact it carried a specific operational message. During their stints in prison, men like Labadi, Abdo, and other men at their level had pored end-lessly over the writings of Mao Tse-tung and knew that "united front" was the special tactical approach of mobilizing as much of the popu-lation as possible by adopting a moderate policy line. Mao taught that a "united front, as a tactical principle, makes the revolutionary en-deavor more flexible by having the hardened cadres appear to mod-erate their zeal to achieve a broad consensus." In short, it made the revolution palatable to groups that were afraid to become involved in too perilous a struggle. Bearing this principle in mind, the command did its best to avoid wild leaps in one direction or another and tailored its demands to the circumstances of the hour. By defining the *intifada* as "a long-range popular war"—again following Mao—it was able to reduce the pressure to achieve a swift victory. This new approach also forced it to take into account the difficulties that the population faced in waging an all-out confrontation with Israel, so that it tried to make only demands that the people could reasonably fulfill.

Or so it believed. The reality of the situation was rather more complex. Due to their radical background and Marxist education, many members of the command tended to view their orders as the paragon of restraint, while in fact they far exceeded what most of the public was able to bear. The result was a pendulum of trial and error: presenting exaggerated demands and then withdrawing them; setting unachievable goals and then scaling them down in subsequent handbills. There were countless examples of this process of ebb and flow. In one of its first handbills on the subject of civil disobedience, the command pronounced that "to climb the rungs of [its] ladder" meant to cease all work in the Jewish settlements, deploy for slow-down strikes in Israeli factories, refuse to pay taxes, build a "home economy," and boycott Israeli products. Later on the call to boycott Israeli goods was modified to extend only to products for which Palestinian substitutes were available (such as chocolate, candies, and cigarettes). The demand to "paralyze the production lines" in Israel was reduced to a call to stay away from work only on strike days. The repeated appeals to stop paying taxes were converted into pressure on the employees of the tax authorities not to collect them—that is, to resign. Then there was the long list of orders that were simply ignored, such as the demands to cease all work in the Jewish settlements, destroy all the signs in the territories written in Hebrew, rebuild houses demolished by the IDF, and drastically cut prices and professional fees (down to 10 shekels, or just over $6, in the case of a visit to the doctor). Yet in the last analysis, these missteps were minor compared with the huge response to the command's leadership in two spheres: observing "memorial days" and the dates fixed for a general strike each week; and effectively crippling the Civil Administration in the territories.

By calling one to three full-strike days each week—in addition to the ongoing partial strike that enabled business to open for three hours each morning—the command created a special rhythm of reinforcement. Every few days the machinery of the uprising demonstrated its control of life in the territories all over again. By contrast, the weakness of the Civil Administration was glaring, especially after the command got the Palestinian policemen and employees of the tax, customs, and licensing authorities to resign and brought the various agencies and branches of local government to a standstill. These triumphs were joined by the darker side of "policing" the Palestinian public: the assaults on known collaborators. The perpetrators of mild offenses might be allowed back into the fold by taking an oath of contrition on the Koran or the Bible in special rituals held in mosques or churches. But the pressure on all the suspects was brutal, as was the intimidation campaign against the more prominent members of the pro-Jordan camp, especially the staff of a-Nahar.

Though concentrated on these targets, the destructive powers of the shock forces reached alarming proportions. Fearing a replay of the carnage in the Great Revolt of 1936, the command deliberately did not call for the assassination of collaborators. But about one-fifth of the 730 attacks recorded during the first four months of the uprising (including bombings, firebombs, arson, and stabbings) were nevertheless directed against Palestinians. In a number of places the popular committees explicitly ordered the shock forces to confine themselves to threats and the destruction of property, yet their message of restraint did not always get through. The command wanted to humiliate the Israelis by wooing away from them the members of the defunct Villages Leagues and wayward types who were serving the Shin Bet. But the shock forces had no patience for such subtleties, and they attacked the homes of thirty-five people described as "agents of Israel." The worst incident during the first year of the uprising was the march on the home of a collaborator in the town of Kabatya on February 24. In less publicized incidents, three people were murdered in Gaza on suspicion of passing information to the Shin Bet, and by July 1989 at least seventy suspected collaborators had been summarily assassinated. The statistics for December 1987–April 1988 on assaults against presumed collaborators include forty-five arson attempts, five cases of attacks with firearms or hand grenades, five assaults with non-explosive weapons, and fifty-eight attacks with firebombs. During these same five months there were thirty-four attacks against the Civil Administration, its Arab employees, and mayors or the heads of local councils; eighteen assaults on police stations or policemen (including one murder); seven attacks on the homes of mayors; and fourteen attacks on municipality buildings, tax and employment offices, and other symbols of the Israeli regime. All this added up to strong evidence that the writers of the handbills had sharp teeth, and fear of their wrath was justifiably strong, but that as often as not they failed to control their own forces.

At the end of April 1988, the leaders of the Popular Front in the West Bank met to draw up an interim report for Dr. George Habash that included recommendations for the future. Their first conclusion was that there were signs of a letup in the tension and drive of the uprising—not just a downturn in the enforcement measures taken on behalf of the popular committees but a decline in participation in demonstrations. Even the Palestinian policemen were trickling back to work. This slowdown was explained as the result of Israel's mass arrests, the imposition of blockades and intermittent curfews on "two-thirds of our people," and a relaxation in the army's guidelines on opening fire. On the other hand, the authors of the report credited the *intifada* for an increase in the number of Israelis who favored a political solution; the downfall of Israel's plan to annex the territories and grant the Palestinians limited autonomy; and the creation of new patterns of behavior for the Palestinian population. The problem, as they saw it, was that "you can't mark time in place: either you march forward or you fall back."

To halt the backsliding, these local Popular Front men prescribed a shift over to "all-out civil disobedience," albeit for a limited period. They understood that the Palestinian population was not yet ready to break with Israel indefinitely. But they believed it would cooperate in a more daring program if its duration was restricted from the start. Their main complaint was about the lack of funds available to help out the hundreds of thousands of strikers who would lose their wages. "The tragedy is that tens of millions of dollars are being wasted by the Right," they wrote in a typical swipe at the Fatah, "and no one knows where the money goes."

The date they proposed for embarking upon "all-out civil disobedience for a limited period" was during the Reagan-Gorbachev summit in May. But when the front's representative raised the idea before the Unified Command, he was astonished to find himself isolated on this issue. The Communists said they could see no logic to abandoning the limited approach to civil disobedience before the Palestinian breadwinners had some alternative to jobs in Israel and the Civil Administration. A similar feeling prevailed in the top level of the Fatah, whose spokesman in the command objected to rushing into a full-fledged revolt before some political gain could be assured. Conflicting views came out of the Democratic Front until Naif Hawatmeh decided in favor of accelerating the shift to the civil disobedience but not effecting it with undue haste.

Even Dr. Habash was not fully convinced by his eager disciples in the territories. The aging and ailing leader defined the path of civil disobedience as a "very difficult one" and cautioned his followers that although they had chosen "Freedom and Independence" as the slogan of the *intifada*, "we must not forget for a single moment the nature of the enemy who opposes us." Their struggle, he told them, would take a toll of hundreds, perhaps thousands, of dead, wounded, and imprisoned. As to its fiscal cost, Habash's comment was "You can't swim in a little puddle," meaning that to back up the plan to have 120,000

Palestinians stop working in Israel, the PLO would have to pump at least $12 million a month into the territories (calculated on the basis of $100 per family). "The worst mistake we can make," the front's organ, al-Hadaf ("The Aim"), warned its readers, "is to burden the uprising with tasks it cannot handle, for if it fails to fulfill them, it will be deemed a failure . . . The best aid to the intifada is to clarify that it cannot achieve strategic objectives, such as ending the occupation . . . We must strive to escalate the uprising as long as that is possible; but the command must be prepared to retreat, when conditions demand it, so as to advance again later on."

Despite these reservations, the people in the field stuck to their guns and circulated a position paper explaining that it was feasible to launch a series of disobedience campaigns, each for a maximum of a few weeks with periods of respite in between. They would not require major aid from outside, for the population could stockpile basic commodities and draw on aid from the Arabs of Israel. In reply to warnings about aggravating the hardship of the weaker classes, the authors of the paper pronounced, somewhat arbitrarily, that "there's no choice but to pass down difficult and increasingly stringent corridors of struggle."

The relentless pressure from the local Popular Front leaders eventually caused a breach within the Unified Command whose telltale sign was again the distribution of two variations of a handbill (No. 17). Repeating the ploy used in Handbill No. 10, the front published its own circulars over the command's signature, in this case portraying the situation as being on "the brink of civil disobedience," while the competing handbill published by the Fatah and the Communists made no mention of the subject at all. In the end, as a compromise, Handbill No. 18 (which was published on the eve of the Reagan-Gorbachev summit at the end of May) spoke of taking "preparatory steps" toward a transition to civil disobedience, withoupt citing a target date for the change.

In the months to come, those steps took the form of a lively propaganda campaign in which the various organizations disseminated explanatory pamphlets that spoke of civil disobedience as a springboard to independence. But each time the Popular Front's representative raised the matter for discussion in the command, the program was postponed again—mostly for fear of issuing an order that would not be obeyed, thus doing untold damage to the command's prestige and credibility. Meanwhile, the Democratic Front invested great effort in promoting an "open strike"—the complete cessation of Palestinian labor in Israel—to work up to a mass civil revolt in stages. The rationale behind this proposal was that it would be easier to cope with the distress of the 100,000 families that would lose their sources of livelihood than to tackle the difficulties of all the Palestinians at once when they were called upon to burn their identity cards and sever their ties with Israel. The "open strike," it was thought, would be able to draw upon special "compensation funds," to be set up for this purpose, as well as relatively modest sums smuggled in from the PLO. It would also place pressure on Palestinian employers to absorb additional manpower and encourage the creation of cooperative enterprises. To test the idea, the front ordered Palestinian field laborers to boycott the Israeli citrus harvest in the winter of 1988. The response, as it turned out, was negligible.

To restore the Civil Administration's grip on the Palestinian population and prevent any further advances into the realm of civil disobedience, the Israelis mounted a counterattack that hit at almost every class of the population—and hit them hard. Comprised of a mixture of punitive and deterrent measures, it aimed at damping the enthusiasm for a break with Israel by raising the price of involvement both in violent demonstrations and in the creation of an "alternative" or "shadow" administration. After the army had failed at forcing shops to close during the hours when the Unified Command permitted them to be open, the defense establishment resigned itself to defeat in the battle against the strikes. But on every other plane the IDF's punitive actions placed heavy pressure on the population, thwarting the popular committees and putting a drag on the uprising's momentum. The initiative had passed over to Israel in more ways than one, and with the Unified Command in a defensive position, the population began showing signs of fatigue.

Yitzhak Rabin and his aides knew by then that they could not turn the wheel of the rebellion back a full revolution. Yet they wanted at least to curb the gains being made by the *intifada* and to keep its ambitions in check. To accomplish this, legal procedures were revised to facilitate mass arrests, and the right to judicial review of sentences was rescinded, so that recourse to military appeal boards was all that remained. The establishment of new detention facilities—in Ketziot in the northern Negev and Daharieh near Hebron—made it possible to hold thousands of additional detainees for extended periods. About

50,000 Palestinians were arrested during the first eighteen months of the uprising, with over 12,000 of them held in administrative detention for periods of varying length. One out of every eighty Palestinian adults in the territories was imprisoned by administrative order, while one out of every forty spent over twenty-four hours in detention for his role in the *intifada*. There was hardly a household in the territories left untouched by the IDF's waves of arrests. Add to these figures the number of wounded, which was estimated to have reached more than 10,000 within the first year, and one gets a sense of what "iron fist" meant to all the strata of the Palestinian population—and this does not even take into account such blanket measures as imposing curfews and closing the schools.

Changes in the army's guidelines on opening fire, after plastic bullets* were introduced in August 1988, did not lessen the number of fatalities. Although most of the casualties were leaders of the riots, too many were people who had happened upon the scene by chance, including children. As the toll of random victims mounted, a debate broke out in Israel over the legality and efficacy of using plastic bullets. But it in no way detracted from their deterrent effect on many Palestinians, so that despite objections the new bullets remained in use. At about the same time, knowing that they were wanted men, hundreds of members of the shock forces and popular committees fled their villages or went underground, living in caves and wadis during the dry season or wandering from place to place in search of food and temporary shelter. Occasionally they banded together into groups— dubbed "roving ambassadors" by the PLO—and continued to punish collaborators while constantly on the move. Sensing the committees' weakness, the IDF began carrying out dawn raids on even remote villages that had held out as "liberated areas" (though after the soldiers withdrew, these areas reverted to the rule of their popular committees).

As its main method of punishment, the army chose extended curfews. Their application varied between the West Bank and Gaza Strip, with more localized curfews imposed in the former and broader ones used in the Strip. The statistics show that during the first year of the *intifada*, no less than 1,600 curfew orders were issued in the territories, 118 of them for five days or more. The Jebalya and Shati refugee

---

* These plastic-coated metal balls are designed to wound rather than kill, but at short ranges they can be as lethal as live ammunition, especially if they strike the head or a vital organ.

camps were held under curfew, intermittently, for over 120 days and Jelazoun for about 100. Even cities like Nablus, Tulkarem, and Kalkilya experienced curfews of a week or longer, and the entire Gaza Strip was shut down every single night. All in all, some 60 percent of the Palestinian population experienced life under curfew, including all the inhabitants of the Strip and the residents of at least 80 of the 450 Arab towns and villages in the West Bank.

Other punitive measures included the demolition or sealing of about 150 houses in the first year, the deportation of about 50 of the uprising's leaders, and the closure of the schools and the universities in the West Bank for most of the first eighteen months of the *intifada*. The branch offices of labor unions were closed down, and other institutions associated with defiance or self-rule—from the Society for the Cultivation of the Family in al-Bireh and the Friends of the Ailing Society in Tulkarem to the Environmental Protection Society in Kalkilya—were likewise forced to shut their doors.

These moves were reinforced by harsh economic measures, above all a series of dunning campaigns to break the tax strike. Carried out during curfews, with the army's full cooperation, these actions proved to be highly effective. In the Gaza Strip, for example, despite attempts to avoid paying taxes and a sharp decline in the amounts due to the government, because of a reduction in business activity, the income from taxes actually rose at the end of 1988 as a result of the forceful collection methods. In a variation on this theme, all export licenses were revoked in September 1988, to be reissued only to people who had cleared their tax debts. To prevent the infusion of aid from abroad, the sum that travelers were allowed to bring in from Jordan was cut from 2,000 to 200 Jordanian dinars. Blockades imposed on settlements were another form of economic pressure, since they prevented not only the free movement of the inhabitants but the shipment of their produce to market. Sometimes this measure extended to cutting off the supply of electricity and water, preventing the entry of fuel, and disconnecting all the phones. There were also individualized types of economic punishment. After the murder of the collaborator in Kabatya, the army halted the shipment of stone out of the nearby quarry. The villages in the Jordan Valley were forbidden to bring their harvest to market in Jericho except during the hours when the stores were already closed. The marketing of plums was halted in the village of Beit Omar; the sale of grapes was forbidden in Halhul; and Til was prevented from selling its figs and yogurt, the mainstays of its economy. In other problematic villages restrictions were placed on the production of olive oil, which is a major branch of the rural economy. (The Jordanians aggravated the stress by prohibiting the import of certain key products from the West Bank.)

Alongside the regular military patrols, the raids on villages, and harassment at army roadblocks, these potent economic measures were designed to prove that the Civil Administration could still pack a punch and that the Palestinians were best off not tangling with it by joining a campaign of civil disobedience. In a sense this policy finally changed the balance of forces in the territories. Where once there had been talk of an "*intifada* deluxe" in which the Palestinians would decide when to strike and when to work, wreaking havoc on sectors of the Israeli economy, from the spring of 1988 onward Israel showed them that two could play that game. In the course of that year, the Palestinian standard of living fell by as much as 30–40 percent. Economic hardship descended on whole classes of the population, be they villagers whose harvests were lost during curfews, laborers who had to live on the earnings from only 10–15 workdays per month, or merchants whose turnover kept plummeting. By the beginning of 1989 the number of Palestinian workers partially or wholly unemployed rose to the point where the industrialists in a position to offer jobs in the territories slashed the daily wage to a mere 10 shekels (just over $6). The number of people working in Israel—a critical source of income for the Palestinian economy—declined by over 25 percent, even during periods of relative calm.

Paradoxically, then, while the Palestinians disrupted life in the territories as an expression of defiance, Israel used the same tactic as a form of retaliation. In response to talk of building an independent economy, Israel saw to it that the Palestinian economic base was badly battered by exposure to both the Unified Command's policy and its own punitive measures. The tax strike was countered by collection campaigns and the confiscation of property. Hoarding, price gouging, and the exploitation of workers became increasingly common in the territories. In the shadow of such tribulations, the slogan of civil disobedience tended to lose much of its charm as the public's expectations were dashed. Rather than collapse under the weight of Palestinian resolve, the occupation became more oppressive. The more resistance to it mounted, the harder it was to bear.

Israel also paid heavily for its part in this war of attrition. As a consequence of the *intifada*, its commercial turnover fell 25 percent below the original forecast for 1988, which translated into a loss of almost a billion dollars. In the building and textile trades, the decline reached as much as 10–15 percent; the drop in tourism was by 14 percent; and the total export from Israel to the territories diminished by no less than 34 percent. Many experts concluded that the uprising was responsible for the country's state of severe economic stagnation, and Palestinian leaders saw this as a vindication of their old theory that Israel could be persuaded to forgo the occupation, since the days of easy profits made by controlling manpower and markets in the territories were gone forever.

By the summer of 1989 the score in this match of wills appeared to be a tenuous tie. The Civil Administration was still on its feet—if only as an instrument of punishment—and straitened circumstances had slowed the development of civil disobedience. But under no circumstances had the Palestinian determination to continue the struggle been destroyed. Instead, the two sides had settled into a routine of daily clashes that never reached the point of decision. There were ups and downs in the level of violence and the frequency of incidents, as well as in the number of casualties, but these fluctuations did not alter the basic patterns of the conflict. Having exhausted their capacity to bend the other side to their will, the Israelis and Palestinians had pretty much reached a standoff: Israel was unable to force total submission on the Palestinians; the Palestinians were unable to escalate the disturbances without limit.

In practical terms, what had evolved in the territories was a state of dual administration. Conditions varied from place to place and from one period to another, but the overall picture was of a limited degree of Palestinian self-rule, a state of crude autonomy. The *intifada* had produced cohabitation between two inimical systems of rule: the Civil Administration and the regime of the popular committees. Israel deployed its forces to curb the violence and prevent further erosion of its control, but it had no illusions about restoring the old order. On the contrary, it had effectively carried out an administrative retreat. Whatever hold it retained over the Palestinian population depended on its military presence, and bouts of "re-occupation" were necessary to exert it.

To many Palestinians, and not just the left-wing groups, this stasis had the feel of a setback. In the summer of 1988, Dr. Sari Nusseibeh, a Fatah loyalist and one of the most outspoken political thinkers in the territories, warned that a standstill in the *intifada* meant that the initiative had reverted to Israel. In an unusually candid article that appeared in the August 1 issue of *Al-Yom a-Sabe* ("The Seventh Day"), an Arabic-language weekly published in Paris by the PLO, he noted that most of the casualties in the territories were victims of the IDF's counteroffensive, not of clashes provoked by Palestinians. He spoke of the population fighting a defensive battle and pointed out the danger that the "mass resistance" of the uprising's early stages would shrink down to a modest-sized underground made up of members of the Palestinian organizations—effectively a return to the *status quo ante*. The Unified Command's reluctance to call for full-scale civil disobedience stemmed, he believed, from the lack of suitable financial backing. To make such a policy work, the PLO would first have to translate its declarations of support into "a loaf of bread that will reach the worker in the refugee camp and enable him to cope with the loss of his identity card." The conclusion of the piece astonished many readers, for Dr. Nusseibeh—who was obviously not writing solely on his own behalf—presented Yasser Arafat with a clear ultimatum: he must either come up with the necessary funds to set the territories on a course toward full-scale independence, or he should allow the Unified Command to pursue a course of retreat, halting the *intifada* in return for concessions on a few of its more modest demands. Predictably, the article prompted an outcry from indignant critics, some of whom accused Nusseibeh of having ulterior motives. Others pointedly reminded him that in the past he had urged the Palestinians to act with the resolve of "the [Arab conquerors] who landed on Spanish soil and burned their ships, in case they had a change of heart." But even these critics had to admit that the paucity of aid to the territories was the major obstacle to putting civil disobedience into effect.

Indeed, money came in at barely a drip, especially after Israel had blocked the existing channels of funding. In one case $4 million in cash was smuggled in (on behalf of Libya's Colonel Qaddafi), but part of it was later confiscated by the Military Government. On other occasions bank transfers of over $1 million were made to the accounts of Israeli Arabs. Cash was also carried in for the PLO by money changers, foreign delegations, and tourists entering the territories via the Jordan bridges. But the sums involved fell far below the amounts needed to solve the problem. Most of the money was quickly consumed by compensation payments to the families of the dead, wounded, and imprisoned; to people whose homes had been destroyed; and to the hundreds of people who had resigned their posts in the Civil Administration. Whatever was left over went toward the costs of legal aid and medical care or the overhead of the local Palestinian organizations. The Unified National Command never received anywhere near the tens of millions of dollars needed for the population to slam the door on Israel. The distribution of the supports, done secretly and with considerable confusion, stirred up bitterness on the part of people who believed themselves entitled to aid but never received it. As part of a campaign of psychological warfare, the Israelis circulated handbills noting the sums supposedly promised to various groups so as to play them off against each other.

When Sari Nusseibeh wrote his "ultimatum piece," he was driven by the fear that the *intifada* was turning out to be like the explosion of a star that generates incredible energy but ends up as nothingness. After eight months of unrelieved violence, it was incapable of moving up to the next stage of resistance by having the Palestinians divorce themselves from Israel. Instead, quite unexpectedly, a different sort of divorce took place. It was sheer coincidence, of course, but Nusseibeh's article appeared on the morning after the government of Jordan had officially renounced all responsibility for the West Bank. In a strange twist of fate, after the local leadership had held out for months against accepting the yoke of the "outsiders," it was King Hussein who decided this struggle by washing his hands of them both. For in bowing out of the arena, he set off a chain of events that would move the political center of gravity from the occupied territories to the PLO abroad.

TEN | *ON THE ROAD TO INDEPENDENCE*

"WE ARE CONVINCED that Israel is capable of putting a stop to the *intifada*," Marwan al-Kassem, the head of the Royal Cabinet, told American diplomats in Jordan.

"The Likud," said Crown Prince Hassan with equal confidence, "is deliberately squandering the opportunity raised by the uprising and is using the violence to justify its intransigence."

"Israel is allowing the PLO to assume the direction of affairs from outside," complained Marwan Dudin, the minister of occupied lands and himself a Palestinian from Mount Hebron. "It's even permitting the import of sophisticated presses to print up the handbills," he continued. "The Israelis must roll up their sleeves and take matters in hand. They must understand that their image is being tarnished because they're occupiers, not because they're beating people in the streets. It's so poor in any case, now, that they should at least put down the uprising quickly, without allowing press coverage."

As the *intifada* wore on through the winter of 1988, King Hussein and his advisers became convinced that the Israelis were deliberately not taking the steps necessary to quash it. They refused to believe that the government and army faced genuine difficulties in devising a strategy that would be effective but not too strong for the tastes of the Israeli public. So skeptical were the members of the Jordanian government and court that in meetings with delegations of Palestinian loyalists from the West Bank, they often wondered aloud whether Israel

267

wasn't carrying out a plot to heat the *intifada* to the boiling point so that it would justify a policy of mass deportations.

By the spring of 1988, the Jordanians' cynicism about Israel's apparent helplessness had turned to anxiety that the rebellious mood might spread to the million Palestinians living on the East Bank. They also continued to fret that Israel—following Ariel Sharon's claim that Jordan and Jordan alone was the Palestinian homeland—might begin to deport Palestinians over the river by the masses and severely destabilize the Hashemite regime. So nervous was Hussein that he turned to Iraq for assurances of military support in an hour of need, and the Iraqis—still mobilized to face Iran—offered to garrison units in Jordan. At the same time, whether to placate the genie that had escaped in the territories or to goad it as his way of staying in the political picture, Hussein chose to express support for the uprising. He had even made it possible for members of the Muslim Brotherhood to aid their comrades in Hamas. Not that the king was inviting the *intifada* into his own domain. Jordan's security services strictly prohibited demonstrations, confiscated all handbills brought in from the West Bank, and occasionally took Palestinians into custody as a precautionary measure. But Hussein would not defy the prevailing spirit in the territories or so much as lift a finger to help his loyalists there. They humbly lined up for audiences at the Basaman Palace and visited the head of the security services, Tarek Alla-al-Din, hoping for some sign of help and encouragement. But each of these meetings ended in disappointment. The best advice they received was to lay low and keep out of harm's way—and they took it quite seriously. Upon returning home some of them hired bodyguards, while others judged it more prudent to simply revamp their loyalties and swim with the current. In one of those palace audiences, a mayor from the northern West Bank related with satisfaction how hundreds of wrought-up demonstrators had passed under his office window shouting PLO slogans and waving Palestinian flags "without even glancing up in my direction."

"Don't kid yourself," one of the king's advisers said gruffly. "They only marched past your office to let you know that they haven't forgotten you and will be back to settle accounts when the time is right."

That was as sharp an assessment as any, considering that the pressure on the pro-Jordanian camp in the territories was growing more savage each day. Identification with the king was decried as "dual loyalty" and wholly out of place at a time of rising Palestinian nationalism. The drive to create a spirit of "unity in the ranks" meant not only smashing all forms of collaboration with the Israelis but undermining the "agents of Jordan" as well. In the absence of concrete support from the king, many of his loyalists chose to absent themselves from the West Bank for long periods. That left Jordan without "soldiers" to defend its "positions" in the territories and certainly without any champions of that old standby, the "unity of the two banks." Hussein had counted on Israel's government to act as he would have acted in similar circumstances. Instead he discovered that he had made an incredibly unsound bet and, politically speaking, had lost his shirt.

The ties by which Hussein had tried to bind the inhabitants of the territories to him unraveled with startling speed. Municipal leaders who had basked in the king's favor now shrank into paralysis under the eagle eyes of the popular committees. The much-touted Five-Year Development Plan came to an abrupt halt. Public expressions of loyalty to Hussein were considered sheer folly, and anyone foolish enough to commend the ties with Jordan was treated to a strong dose of intimidation or a Molotov cocktail—as happened to Dr. Moussa Abu Ghosh, a member of the Jordanian Parliament, for refusing to resign his position.

Despite the clear signs of alienation, some members of the Hashemite court still entertained the hope that the euphoria in the territories would dissipate before long. "People will start asking themselves what they have achieved," Marwan al-Kassem forecast, "and once they start sobering up, they'll take a more moderate approach." Hussein admitted in a talk with one West European leader that the PLO, which had long been the symbol of Palestinian nationalism, was in the best position to exploit the uprising for its own ends. Yet for a few months he nursed the hope that the *intifada* would give rise to a "sane and moderate" leadership that, while identifying with the PLO, would respect the West Bank's long-standing ties with Jordan. From their long experience with the mercurial Arafat, the Jordanians had good reason to doubt that he had the knack for getting the Palestinians what they wanted. "Arafat is not a leader," one top-ranking Jordanian official told some American guests, "he's a chairman of the board whose prime talent is avoiding decisions."

Hussein and his aides wanted to believe that the residents of the territories knew that too. They hoped, moreover, that the people behind the uprising were sane enough to see that no Palestinian state could get on its feet without Jordan's support as an economic prop and a gate to the Arab world. The strong family ties between Palestinians on both sides of the river and the common history of the two banks seemed enough to ensure that the bridges between them would not be burned. And from time to time the leaders of the Fatah shored up the the hope that all would be well by assuring Hussein that they had no interest in pursuing the campaign against his loyalists (fingering the leftists as the real culprits behind it). In a number of cases the Jordanians clutched desperately at the groundless notion that the uprising was actually hurting the PLO and would lead to an international conference in which Jordan would have star billing!

One by one, the king was disabused of these illusions. The expectation that Israel would quash the rebellion quickly turned out to be a pipe dream. Hussein's pleas to Washington to take some firm action toward convening an international conference went unheeded. As the summer rolled around, he admitted to himself that Jordan was fighting a losing battle in trying to defend positions that had already fallen to the PLO. The *intifada*, Hussein finally realized, was a "state of rage" that could not be controlled. He was told of stirrings of ferment in the refugee camps around Amman, of attempts to demonstrate, of the eager response to fundraising drives for the *intifada,* and of talk that the methods used against the IDF should be emulated in Jordan, a country with a Palestinian majority. For weeks he brooded in one of his periodic depressions and finally concluded that not only the fate of the West Bank was at stake but the future of Jordan itself. The king shared this assessment with only a few of his closest confidants. He sensed that after decades of trying to blur the difference between the Jordan's two banks, he must now reverse himself and draw a clear line between them. To the casual observer, the decision may have seemed abrupt at the time. But Hussein was essentially completing a slow withdrawal from the West Bank that had been in progress since 1972, when he reduced his claim to full sovereignty over the West Bank and agreed to a federation between Jordan and a Palestinian authority there. In talks with Arafat in 1985, that concept was further whittled down to a confederation between the two banks, and now he had decided to leave the West Bankers entirely to their own devices. Reading the collapse of support in the territories as a signal to deploy for defense, Hussein bit the bullet and decided "to save Jordan from the uprising," as one of his advisers told an Israeli acquaintance.

On July 31, wearing an especially somber expression, the king of Jordan went on television to announce his decision to "sever [Jordan's] administrative and judicial ties" with the West Bank. While not officially dissolving the union of the two banks that his grandfather King Abdullah had proclaimed in 1950, Hussein effectively renounced his claim to sovereignty over the West Bank, thus removing the last obstacle in the path of the PLO. Among the immediate corollaries of this move were the dispersal of Jordan's Parliament (half of whose members were appointed representatives from the West Bank); the abolition of the special Ministry for Occupied Lands and its replacement with a Department for Palestinian Affairs in the Jordanian Foreign Ministry; and the dismissal of the more prominent Palestinian members of the Jordanian Senate. Jordan also canceled the Five-Year Plan for developing the West Bank and Gaza Strip; discontinued the payment of supports to some 16,000 officials of the Civil Administration in the territories (which amounted to an average of one-fifth of their salaries); and pensioned off some 5,400 employees who received their wages directly from Amman. Then there were a series of purely symbolic steps, such as dropping the cities in the territories from Jordan's weather forecasts and, later on, publishing a new official atlas in which the Jordan River appeared as the kingdom's western border.

Though presumably designed as defensive measures, the king's moves also smacked of retaliation, and it was easy to read them as an outlet for his disappointment and anger. Hussein was careful to avoid the impression that he had washed his hands of the territories with the petulance of a sovereign scorned or with the cavalier attitude of "*Après moi le déluge!*" He wanted to convey the sense that his sole concern was for the needs and feelings of his erstwhile subjects; that he had bowed out of the contest, not stalked off in a huff. After all, the bridges remained open. So too did Jordanian banks in the territories and the institutions of the *waqf*, which were fully funded by the government in Amman. Yet behind closed doors even his greatest apologists in the territories moaned of being abandoned, wounded, on the battlefield and scored Hussein for letting his melancholy distort his judgment. Besides, it was obvious the king was feeling peeved. He chastised high-level American visitors for having paved the PLO's way to power by coddling Israel, rather than forcing it to make tangible concessions to Jordan. Arafat, said the king at one of these meetings, is the only leader of our time who has managed to do the impossible: to stumble from one setback to another until he finally made his way to victory!

From Israel's standpoint, the king's speech closed the door on the promise of salvation that the Labor Party had been dangling before the country's eyes for years: the so-called Jordanian option. "My brother," began Hussein's letter of condolence to Shimon Peres over the demise of their April 1987 London Agreement to convene an international conference on the Middle East conflict. But the message it bore was anything but comforting to Mr. Peres. Jordan was no longer prepared to deliberate the Palestinian problem with Israel; the only issue it would discuss was the matter of its own borders. The Israelis were stunned by the move and initially refused to believe that it was anything more than a ploy to force expressions of support (or at least remorse) out of the Palestinians. But when the king stopped his loyalists from circulating petitions that begged him to relent, the Israelis too were forced to accept that Jordan's move was an act of policy, not theatrics. Even the Likud was disturbed by the development because it realized that the forecasts of all the prophets of doom had come true: by refusing to reach an accommodation with Hussein, Israel now found itself completely alone in the arena with the PLO.

For their part, the senior members of the PLO were more suspicious than relieved, at first, and tended to regard the divorce as a trick to add Jordanian salt to Israeli-inflicted wounds. It took a week or two for them to accept that Hussein really meant what he had said about relinquishing all claim to the West Bank. After all, the Jordanian passports held by West Bankers were not invalidated, and a few other administrative arrangements remained in force. But these anomalies came under the category of "gratuitous gestures" on the king's part, not signs that he was going to reverse himself. Presumably, of course, there was still some room for maneuver. In the coming days, in fact, Hussein took pains to explain that he would not necessarily reject the idea of a Jordanian confederation with a future Palestinian state; nor would he demand agreement in advance on the precise construction of the framework. Yet few believed that he really meant business. Over a year earlier Hussein had told Shimon Peres why he was so leery of a partnership with Arafat. In their 1985 talks on a possible joint framework, Arafat had promised the king that any future Jordanian-Palestinian confederation would have a constitutional regime, ensuring that Hussein could retain his throne until the end of his life. "The moment he said that," the king remarked icily, "I knew that with him my days would be numbered."

After overcoming his skepticism, Arafat found that he had a much more irksome problem on his hands and, far from being delighted by the king's abrupt departure, he was furious at the Jordanians for not coordinating their move in advance. After all, without consulting him

in any way, Hussein had placed on his shoulders the enormous burden
of proving that the PLO could fill the vacuum effectively. All things
considered, he had no choice but to give his blessings to the fait accompli and announce that the PLO would assume all the responsibilities that the Jordanians had sloughed off. Thus the supports paid out
to the Arab employees of the Civil Administration would thereafter
be provided by the PLO—and they proved to be a heavy burden
indeed.

Ironically, then, though not on its agenda at all, the Jordanian disengagement was the first political gain of the *intifada*. The uprising
aimed at ridding the territories of the Israeli occupation; instead, it
had rid them of the Jordanian annexation. Even the greatest doubters
came round to seeing that Hussein's action was not just a ploy to place
more pressure on the Palestinians; it was a decision of historic import.
Having lost its appetite for tussling with the Palestinian state-in-the-
making, Jordan offered itself as a good neighbor instead, leaving the
PLO without rival for the Palestinians' loyalty. At one and the same
time the uprising had forced Jordan to forfeit the territories and
obliged the PLO to take on the role it coveted and feared in equal
measure: sole responsibility for the Palestinians. From the moment
Hussein had completed his address it was clear that Arafat would have
to take a decisive step of his own. The "Jordanian option" was history,
and he was now the only Arab party laying claim to the West Bank
and Gaza Strip. Yet at this juncture, as well, it was not Arafat but the
Palestinian leaders in the territories—the few associates of the Unified
Command still not in detention—who took the initiative. They had already drafted the document that would usher in the next stage of the
struggle.

Less than an hour after Hussein had completed his speech, an
Israeli police car pulled up in front of the East Jerusalem home of
Feisal al-Husseini, who was widely regarded as the senior Fatah per-
sonage in the West Bank. The tall, forty-eight-year-old Husseini had
taken no part in the first seven months of the *intifada*, for in the summer of 1987 he had been placed in long-term administrative detention.
Though released only a few weeks earlier, he did not seem to be rattled
by the arrival of the law. The policemen who entered his home found
him smiling in amusement at Israel's jitters over the PLO's newly
gained power. "I've been expecting you," he said calmly—and indeed,
a small suitcase packed with underwear and toiletries stood ready

against the living room wall. It was not until the squad car began moving through the streets of East Jerusalem that Husseini realized he was being taken to the offices of the Society for Arab Studies, the research institute he directed, and his cheer gave way to concern. "The Jews have gone mad," he muttered as they pulled up in front of the abandoned hotel that housed the institute, and he demanded that his escorts show him a search warrant. When the arresting officer began to chant the order, Husseini (who had used his time in prison to learn Hebrew) insisted on reading it himself, whereupon he blanched and retreated into silence.

In an unlocked drawer of his secretary's desk, the police found what they were looking for: a sheaf of typed pages headed "Plan for Making a Declaration of Independence." Husseini had difficulty hiding his consternation.

"How did you get involved in something like this?" the police officer asked snidely.

"I've already paid for my involvement," Husseini replied.

The bitter remark was an allusion to his earlier arrest at the height of secret talks with Moshe Amirav, a little-known member of the Likud Party, to reach an understanding between the Likud and the PLO. To this day, the truth about that strange affair remains buried under a clutter of contradictions and denials. Husseini had long been of the opinion that the Likud was the only fitting partner for talks on the Middle East imbroglio, and he made no secret of his hope that it would win the 1988 Knesset elections hands down. Labor, he believed, was in an irreversible state of decline, and he mocked Shimon Peres's courting of Hussein, whom the Palestinians regarded as a has-been. As the son of the most famous Palestinian hero of the 1948 war, a soldier who had himself attained high rank in the defunct Palestine Liberation Army,* and one of the few Jerusalemite leaders who commanded the respect of the Shabiba, Husseini was one of a kind in the territories. He justly regarded himself as a man of stature and a leader in his own right, not merely a pawn of masters abroad. And as such he assumed the authority to open new channels of political action. As far as he was concerned, a plan for achieving Palestinian independence was the logical next stage of the strategy he had embraced earlier when, together with Moshe Amirav, he had drafted a memorandum of understanding that was to serve as the basis of an agreement between Yitzhak Shamir and Yasser Arafat.

* The military arm of the pre-Arafat PLO made up of brigades attached to other Arab armies.

Those secret talks with Amirav extended over the course of a dozen or so meetings in the summer of 1987. Husseini and his partners, Dr. Sari Nusseibeh and Salah Zahaika, the editor of *a-Sh'ab*, acted with the knowledge and approval of the PLO leaders in Tunis. Amirav's credentials were somewhat less explicit. He was a veteran member of the Likud's Herut wing but, unlike Husseini, was far from a political personality or leader. It was assumed that he had the prime minister's approval for his venture, especially as he reported on his progress to certain Knesset members who were known to be Shamir protégés (specifically Dan Meridor and Ehud Olmert, both of whom were appointed as ministers in Shamir's next government). But the truth was probably that Shamir learned about these talks—much to his discomfort—only very late in the game. In any case, the existence of these contacts was kept a closely guarded secret from the Labor Party, as their purpose was to produce an alternative to the London Agreement that had pushed Shamir into a corner. It was envisioned as an interim agreement that would bridge the gap between the Likud's proposals for autonomy (as outlined in the Camp David accords) and the Palestinians' insistence on an independent state.

The transcripts of these talks give a clear sense of the outlook shared by Husseini and his comrades:

> NUSSEIBEH: Partition the country into two states or give all of its inhabitants full civil rights. We're prepared to accept either option.
>
> AMIRAV: The problem isn't Nablus or Ramallah, the problem is Jaffa. Have you really given up your dream of returning to Jaffa?
>
> NUSSEIBEH: Perhaps we will continue to dream about Jaffa, but we're practical people; we understand that we can only speak about a state in part of Palestine, and this will be the final settlement. What remains after that will be only dreams that obviously can never come true. And then perhaps even the dreams will evaporate, once there is peace.
>
> HUSSEINI: . . . As far as we're concerned, the State of Israel is a fact of life. For us Palestine is the whole country in your hands today, and in our dreams we want to have it all, just as you do. But I know these are dreams, and I don't want to force my dreams on you, just as I refuse to let you force yours on me. Both sides have the right to dream, but in reality we have obviously, if begrudgingly, given up on a state in all of Palestine. . . . When a Palestinian state comes into being, it will have open relations with Israel. There will be free

movement between them, and there won't be any need to put up a wall . . . I appreciate that Israel will not agree to any Arab military presence in the territories.

DAVID ISH-SHALOM [a left-leaning independent who was instrumental in setting up the meetings]: Will you agree to a national entity without an army? . . . Will you be satisfied, at most, with a police force equipped with light arms?

HUSSEINI: If I feel that I am protected against an Israeli attack, I will make do with that and forgo an army. An army is not an imperative if the state has defense [arrangements] in the form of reliable international guarantees . . .

AMIRAV: It's a pity that you didn't produce a great national leader like Ben-Gurion, who knew how to accept the partition and impose his leadership.

HUSSEINI: We were weak and could not afford to exhibit any readiness for concessions. But now we are strong and willing to compromise . . . As to demilitarization, I hereby state that we will be prepared to accept it. This idea is not new to us.

Sharing with the others his vision of a Palestinian state as a Hong Kong of the Middle East, Husseini explained in all seriousness that "we need international guarantees because you'll threaten us with armed intervention if we lower prices and compete with you!"

Husseini was prepared to be candid in these talks with the Israelis, but all along he was plagued by the suspicion that the Likud's intentions were less than sincere. He noted that Ehud Olmert had been reserved and cagey in a phone conversation with Sari Nusseibeh and that Dan Meridor had canceled a scheduled meeting with him at the last moment. He was also dogged by the feeling that "Amirav did not have Shamir's genuine backing"—although none of this kept him from continuing the talks.

On August 26, after weeks of exhausting debate, the two sides drafted, but did not sign, a joint memorandum. Its high point was the Likud's recognition of the PLO as the only partner for talks on the Palestinian question and its agreement to negotiate an interim agreement that would lead to the creation of a Palestinian "entity" in the territories, with its "administrative" capital in the Arab half of Jerusalem. This "entity" would maintain its status for a transition period of up to three years, during which a self-governing authority with the classic trappings of a sovereign state (its own currency, flag, national anthem, independent broadcasting service, identity cards, and travel documents) would operate in the territories. Discussions on the final settlement were to be postponed to a second stage that would begin after the three-year transition period. In effect, this arrangement was a kind of super-autonomy for the Palestinians, exceeding the terms outlined in the Camp David accords but still falling short of an independent Palestinian state.

Through their own networks in the territories, the Jordanians got wind of these talks and went into a panic. They had hitched their wagon to Shimon Peres's star, through the London Agreement, and now it appeared that the Likud was coming to an accommodation directly with the PLO! They didn't anguish for long, however, because meanwhile, back in Israel, someone pulled a double cross: on the very evening that the joint memorandum was completed, Feisal al-Husseini was arrested. "You're sabotaging a political initiative you don't even know about!" he railed at his interrogators. But the arrest was no bureaucratic blunder; the Shin Bet had consulted with Shamir before taking Husseini into custody and had received no instructions to the contrary. The truth appears to be that Amirav had gone far beyond what Shamir was prepared to swallow, and the prime minister had to wriggle out of the mess without losing face or causing an uproar in the Likud and the parties further to the right. To avert any misunderstanding, Shamir not only turned his back on the whole affair but saw to it that Amirav, who had already become the party's bête noir, was summarily expelled from it. Meanwhile, as part of the understanding, Sari Nusseibeh waited in vain for Amirav to arrive in Geneva, with Shamir's blessings, for a meeting with Arafat. Only Ish-Shalom, the "facilitator," showed up for that audience, and when he did so a translation of the memorandum prepared in Jerusalem was lying on Arafat's desk. But the PLO chairman seemed as qualmish about it as Shamir had been. "I am sending a message to the Israeli government," he stiffly told the emissary who actually represented no one. "I am prepared to enter into negotiations without prior conditions. When they begin, the sides will proclaim mutual recognition and the acts of violence will stop." But both men knew that this was just a perfunctory ritual, for there was nothing new about the offer and no reason to believe that the Shamir government would treat it any less scornfully than it had in the past.

The failure of this rather naive effort to leap the gap between the Likud and the PLO in a single bound held an important lesson for Feisal al-Husseini and his associates: the path to an understanding with

Israel—even a secret one—was paved with many pitfalls. Thus rather than aim for an agreement with the Israelis, they were better off making a unilateral move, since it was impossible to rely on Shamir and pointless to wait for Arafat.

The document confiscated in Husseini's office on the night of July 31, 1988, was just that move. It bore little resemblance to the memorandum worked out almost a year earlier with Amirav, for inherent to the new program was the partition of the country into two separate states. Husseini's plan was to have the local Palestinians proclaim, in Jerusalem, an independent Palestinian state within the borders laid down in the original 1947 partition plan. Its provisional government would be headed by Yasser Arafat, with the portfolios divided equally among other "outside" PLO leaders and figures appointed from the territories. Its administration would be formed out of the popular committees, and the Unified National Command would appoint the 150 members of the General Legislative Council, whose Executive would declare its readiness to negotiate a final settlement with Israel. The residents of the territories would be called upon to exchange their Israeli identity cards for Palestinian ones (to be issued with the help of the popular committees), while foreign correspondents, tourists, and other visitors would be required to obtain *laissez-passers* from the "provisional government." Husseini and his associates believed that an undertaking of this sort would knock the Israeli government off balance, because the country would be divided on the issue. It was his assessment that many of Israel's most respected citizens would be in favor of recognizing the new state, whose character would, in the document's words, "confirm that it is not aggressive and that the Palestinian people do not look forward to the destruction of Israel but wish, rather, to live as a neighbor in peace."

The uniqueness of this plan, which came to be known as the "Husseini document," lay not only in the determination to proclaim independence but primarily in the focal role earmarked for the activists in the territories. It was conceded immediately that Arafat and other leading PLO figures would receive high-ranking posts, but the privilege of proclaiming independence was reserved for the Unified National Command, with the Palestine National Council (PNC) merely ratifying the act. The General Legislative Council was to include only Palestinians living in the territories, just as the running of the administration was left to the new generation of leaders that had blossomed in the country. In short, what the "Husseini document" proposed was not only a fresh strategy but a new ratio of forces between Jerusalem and Tunis. The indigenous Palestinian leadership would be given the task of governing, while the "outsiders" would continue to represent and guide, with the country's delegation to the inevitable negotiations with Israel being composed of people from both categories. Beyond that, the document spoke explicitly of making peace with Israel.

Reaction to the "Husseini document," whose main points were disclosed after his arrest, was decidedly mixed. Arafat and his Fatah comrades, though not surprised by the drift of the proposals, chose reticence over praise. The leftists sniffed at it in familiar disdain, while many Israelis dismissed it as the vain posturing of bored intellectuals. This impression was reinforced by reports about the role played by Professor Jerome Segal of the University of Maryland, who three months earlier, during a visit to the territories, had touted the idea of proclaiming Palestinian independence. Segal's writings may have influenced some members of Husseini's circle, but for the most part they went their own way, denying his "paternity" and in any case rejecting most of the details of his plan.

Be that as it may, at the end of July 1988, for better or for worse, the "Husseini document" was the only program around. It addressed the problem that had been plaguing the Palestinians for months: how to "invest the gains of the *intifada*" (in Husseini's words) in tangible political achievements. Still, its backers hesitated. Proclaiming the independence of a state under occupation had already been tried by the Polisario in the Western Sahara, but there were fears in the territories that such a move was premature and, by enraging the Israelis, would quickly end in disaster.

That, of course, was not an unfounded assumption. Immediately after Husseini's rearrest, Israel made it known that it would do everything in its power to prevent the convention of an assembly on the Haram a-Sherif to proclaim Palestinian independence (the less impressive alternative being to call a press conference in Cyprus). At the same time Military Government officers began summoning Old Guard types who were known to be pro-PLO and warned them against joining in the initiative. The effect of these talks was immediate: all activity that appeared to be related to the declaration of a state was brought to a halt, and people singled out as probable candidates for the legislative council were quick to deny any connection with the affair. With Husseini back behind bars but his program on everyone's lips, the ball had been tossed into Arafat's court—and there was nothing Israel could do to stop *him* from adopting the principles of the plan. Arafat spent weeks agonizing over the question until he could no longer allow himself to waver. Independence was in the air, and the people on the "inside" were pressing him to decide.

The Unified Command's Handbill No. 24, written shortly after the disclosure of the "Husseini document," was quite blunt and insistent in its call on the PLO leadership to translate the fruits of the *intifada* into political gains. It demanded the framing of "a clear and complete plan that can enlist the widest possible international support." But while implying an acceptance of whatever the PLO decided, it definitely stressed that the people expected some genuine progress. Many Fatah activists in the territories were openly praising what Arafat's adviser Bassam Abu Sharif had written in May in the *Washington Post* commending mutual recognition between Israel and the PLO. In an editorial in *al-Fajr*, one of them even urged Arafat to put an end to his own "muddled rhetoric." Others began collecting signatures on a petition demanding a more moderate approach to solving the conflict. Emboldened by these signs of a mellowing mood, the leaders of the Communist Party came right out and said what they had been mumbling for years: that the PLO must state its willingness to recognize Israel in its 1967 borders. Opposition to these pressures came, as might be expected, from the Popular Front, which simply could not abide the thought of mutual recognition, and from certain quarters in the Democratic Front that wanted to save all concessions to Israel for the negotiating table. But the strongest propaganda against this approach was conducted outside the PLO by Ahmed Jebril's Popular Front for the Liberation of Palestine–General Command, which tried to build an alliance with Hamas and other radical groups to block any deviation from the traditional hard line.

In the end, the pressure to improve the prospects of negotiations won out—not least because they gave Arafat the opening he needed to maneuver back into the limelight. He used the letters and cables that reached him from the West Bank to persuade his colleagues that they must listen to the people who had wrought the *intifada* and understand their impatience. Yet he had no intention of sharing his powers with the Unified Command or allowing it to play an active role in shaping the PLO's policy. In fact he forbade any public discussion of the "Husseini document" and ordered his Fatah followers in the territories to cap their publicly tendered advice on the wording of the decisions that the PLO would ultimately have to make. Thereafter, all reference to the substance of the PNC's forthcoming deliberations were deleted from the command's handbills, for Arafat's message was unequivocal: let the PLO find its own way, without further chivying or chiding from afar.

As it turned out, Feisal al-Husseini and Sari Nusseibeh were not the only ones who had tried their hand at reaching a cautious understanding with the Israelis. Since the beginning of the *intifada*, Arafat himself had accumulated experience in what are probably best described as "contacts-once-removed." Through various intermediaries he had signaled Jerusalem of his desire for indirect communications, but they never elicited any meaningful response. Neither did his suggestion about placing a moratorium on hostilities as a prelude to talks. In the middle of February 1988, Arafat tried to reach the Israelis through the widow of Pierre Mendès-France. In three pages of Arabic text, accompanied by an English translation, the PLO chairman berated the Israeli leadership for not responding to his moves. "How many more Palestinians will have to die before Israel understands that the fate of the occupation is sealed?" he wrote angrily, adding near the end of the letter the veiled threat that "we must not be placed in a position that forces us to act in desperation." The main point of the communication, however, was to reiterate his proposal about holding an international conference based on "all the U.N. resolutions."

Observing to the letter the protocol for nonrecognition, Marie-Claire Mendès-France read the letter aloud to Labor's Ezer Weizman (whom she assumed would be the most open to its message) and Weizman did not address Arafat directly in dictating the reply: "I will meet with Arafat only on condition that he recognize Security Council Resolutions 242 and 338, which are also the basis for peace with Egypt; that he cease all acts of terror; and that he recognize the State of Israel and its right to exist." This was by no means a new formula, and Arafat was receiving similar messages from Americans like Dr. Landrum Bolling of Tantour College in the West Bank (who visited him with the full knowledge of the Reagan administration) and from European statesmen. Even the Soviets let him know that they expected him to move in this direction, and while visiting the Kremlin Dr. George Habash was told in no uncertain terms: Don't talk about returning to Jaffa now.

Throughout the summer, despite the upheavals of King Hussein's withdrawal and the energy generated by the "Husseini document,"

Arafat remained firm in his belief that the PLO must not make any concessions to Israel without being assured of a suitable quid pro quo. In all his contacts by proxy, his condition for halting the *intifada* was a no-nonsense countercommitment by Israel to recognize the PLO as a full partner to an international conference. In at least one case he also tossed out the idea (through an intermediary sent to Shimon Peres) that he would take the Gaza Strip off Israel's hands for a transition period to prove that the PLO was capable of controlling the population and maintaining order. But overtures of this kind were instantly dismissed by the Israeli government, and like Husseini before him, Arafat was forced to conclude that if Israel would not respond to his style of courtship, unilateral action was the only course left.

The setting for that action was the nineteenth session of the Palestine National Council convened in Algiers on November 12, 1988. It was the first PNC meeting since the start of the uprising, and the atmosphere was charged with expectation. Being the stronghold of the "outsiders," the PNC was also the perfect place to reassert their dominance. With that end in mind, perhaps, the first session began with a pathetic little drama that held an unmistakable message for the *intifada*'s leaders. When the hall was about half filled, some thirty exiled members of the Unified Command and popular committees were marched into it like a troop of boy scouts, singing the Palestinian national anthem with their fingers raised in a *V*, to be greeted by scattered applause. That humiliating entrance was the sum total of their role at the convention. None of these men, fresh from the battlefields of the *intifada*, was included in the press conferences or the closed sessions where decisions were hammered out. They had been invited to "decorate" the event, not contribute to it. One of these deportees, an early leader of the *intifada*, poured out his bitterness in a letter to friends:

> We're treated like dogs or thieves . . . I would be ready to have my hands and legs chopped off if only I could return . . . On the face of it everyone applauds us, but that's a lie . . . Things on the outside are not working out as we would like them to . . . They are difficult and complicated, and nothing can be decided without permission [from the PLO leadership] . . .

Needless to say, in the midst of a war and at the mercy of their "patrons," the deportees never made their grievances public.

With the problem of supremacy disposed of, the next drama took place behind the scenes, where a debate raged over the direction of the PLO's future policy. The intention to proclaim an independent state, following Husseini's lead, was by then a foregone conclusion. The struggle was over the wording of the declaration and the political program that would accompany it. The Fatah held that upon declaring the birth of the Palestinian state, it was necessary to make certain adjustments in the PLO's platform—though it continued to resist the Communists' coaxing to recognize the State of Israel and accept the June 1967 borders. It was also determined not to rush into the establishment of a government-in-exile or to tamper with the Palestinian Covenant. The leftists were less open to change, with George Habash arguing that since the uprising was still in full force, there was no need to make unilateral concessions, while Naif Hawatmeh was equally opposed to any retreat to conciliatory positions.

At the last closed session, the scales tipped in favor of the Fatah. As a sign of that victory the keynote speech was given, with great emotion, by Salah Halaf (Abu Iyyad), a veteran of the Fatah's founding generation and Arafat's deputy. "Is it logical to leave the liberation of the country and the mobilization of international support to women and children," he asked, "while we sit here and content ourselves with reports about their valor? If the sum of our role as leaders is to be hailed as hawks, then those who fight the Zionist enemy with stones are more deserving of that title." This was the gist of the new official line: the PLO must support the inhabitants of the territories, and they were demanding a policy that would move the *intifada* out of the impasse. To the leftists who advised waiting another few years until the ratio of forces against Israel would be even better, Abu Iyyad replied: "It is shameful not to fight with every weapon available. We have no choice but to use political means alongside the gun!" He later reluctantly admitted that the international pressure on the PLO to agree to Security Council Resolution 242 was unbearable: "Those who are interested in living like hawks have an easy life. But the wise hawk who knows his limitations is preferable to a high-flying hawk who is oblivious to what is happening under his feet." And of course there were also soothing themes: the willingness to accept an independent state in only part of Palestine was not necessarily the last word on the subject. "This is a state for the coming generations," Abu Iyyad reassured his audience. "It starts out small, but if Allah wills it, it will grow and expand."

To the ring of angry catcalls from the benches of the Popular Front, Abu Iyyad concluded on a confessional note: "Is [U.N.] Resolution 181 [on the Partition of Palestine] a good one? Who of my generation did not demonstrate against it? Even as a child I shouted against it in the streets. Until three months ago, I wasn't even prepared to consider it. I wanted all of Palestine all at once. But I was a fool. Yes, I am interested in the liberation of Palestine, but the question is how. And the answer is: step by step!"

Reactions to the new line were often ambivalent. "I am delighted by the declaration of Palestinian independence," Dr. Anis al-Sayegh, a senior PLO official later commented, "but I am also sad. For we're talking about the independence of one-fifth of Palestine for one-quarter of the Palestinian people. We must think of the rest!"

"I am not against the tactic of flexibility," said George Habash's deputy, Abu Ali Mustafa, "but I fear that we are going to lose our way."

In the end, though, by a majority of 253 to 46, with 10 abstentions and 29 delegates not voting, the PNC passed a resolution accepting Security Council Resolutions 242 and 338, together with the right of self-determination for the Palestinian people and all the other U.N. resolutions pertinent to the subject, as the basis for participating in an international conference for peace in the Middle East. George Habash, the most eminent opponent of the new policy, announced that he would act as a "loyal opposition" and give Arafat a chance to prove the value of achievements gained by political means. "If, in another two or three years, it turns out that this tactic was unwise," he said, "we will all have learned from the experience."

At close to 2 A.M. on the morning of November 15, 1988, when Yasser Arafat read out the Palestinian Declaration of Independence in Algiers, the West Bank and Gaza Strip were under tight curfew. The Israelis had cut off even the supply of electricity and had stationed reinforced units in the streets to prevent outbursts of joy or celebration at the declaration of statehood. No major incidents were reported that night. Here and there a flag was flown under cover of darkness and occasional whistles pierced the night, but for the most part the territories were wrapped in an eerie stillness. It may have been due to raw fear, or perhaps to defiance of a different kind: a determination to cheat the Israelis of yet another opportunity to humiliate the "citizens" of the new "state of Palestine" by treating even their happiness as a crime. In any case, as the hall in Algiers broke into wild applause, in the West Bank and Gaza, where there should have been joy, there was a void of sullen silence.

The Fatah and Communist activists in the territories saw eye to eye on providing a broad interpretation to the somewhat opaque wording of the Algiers declaration. They chose to focus on the moderate parts of the document as proof that, after much soul searching, the PLO had sincerely decided to recognize the State of Israel. But not everyone supported that view—or, for that matter, any of that changes that emerged from Algiers. The younger members of the Popular Front held a few demonstrations protesting the acceptance of Resolution 242, and at times it seemed that they might even rebel against their revered leader, Dr. George Habash, for not going to battle against Arafat. But the most vigorous campaign against the Algiers decisions came out of the ranks of Hamas. After covering the walls of dozens of villages with graffiti denouncing the "treachery" and "capitulation" of accepting partition as an equable solution, Hamas issued a series of petitions and handbills lashing the PLO for its implied recognition of the Jewish state. The ultimate test of strength, however, was postponed yet again.

The original proposals of the "Husseini document" on creating legislative and administrative institutions for the Palestinian state were ignored by the PLO. Instead, Arafat told the residents of the territories to keep the uprising going along familiar lines and steer clear of far-reaching innovations, for this was the hour of Palestinian diplomacy. In any case, the Israelis thwarted all the early attempts to create broad-based steering committees for the various sectors of Palestinian national life. Sometimes they had considerable difficulty coming up with legal grounds for preventing the conventions that were called in East Jerusalem, so that the police disrupted the meetings on such flimsy excuses as searching for bombs planted in the halls. The point was of course to prevent the founding of "shadow ministries" in the form of the Supreme Agricultural Council, the Higher Committee for Health Services, or the Council for Higher Education. All these local Palestinian institutions, like the unions of professionals, were prepared to take on increased responsibility for running life in the territories, from setting production quotas for farmers and planning school curricula to providing medical services in remote villages and coordinating between charity societies.

Nowhere was the desire to break with Israel and develop "islands of autonomy" stronger than in the sphere of health, precisely because the Palestinians had become so dependent upon Israel's medical services and because of the staggering number of people injured during the uprising. The moving spirit behind this effort, Dr. Mamdouh al-Ekr, spoke openly of developing a "national medical establishment," and dozens of health committees tried to extend their operations throughout the territories, sending medical teams to the villages, holding first-aid courses, developing neighborhood infirmaries, and even purchasing dozens of new ambulances.

But while a growing number of ailing and injured people availed themselves of these services, the high point of this new wave of Palestinian self-organization was the emergence of the so-called Popular Army. Working out of Tunis, with Arafat's permission, Mahmoud a-Natour (Abu Tayeb), the commander of the Fatah's Force 17,* set to creating this new "army" by reshaping the shock forces from small squads of ruffians into a quasi-military framework. This plan met with resistance from the territories, however. A number of public figures complained to Arafat that it was a superfluous and foolhardy adventure and pointed out that even if they were to condone it, they would deny his right to appoint an "outsider" as its commander. The Unified Command was instructed not to support the Popular Army, and in the end Abu Tayeb's attempt to force himself on the shock troops failed because the Fatah people refused to accept his authority.

In the territories themselves, however, the Declaration of Independence inspired new attempts to organize paramilitary formats. The popular committees in a number of villages began to recruit teenagers, divide them into "companies" and "battalions," and hold parades and exericses in which the "soldiers" brandished axes and clubs. In a few cases the Israelis discovered training grounds used for practice in throwing Molotov cocktails and in hand-to-hand combat with knives. Thousands of metal badges bearing the words "Popular Army" were smuggled in from Jordan to complete the force's "uniform," and mass swearing-in ceremonies were held in various spots around the territories. There were also some daring "shows of force." On one occasion hundreds of Popular Army members marched through the casbah of Nablus armed with "cold weapons," and on another hundreds more, all uniformly dressed, paraded down a side road in broad daylight.

Such attempts to establish the equivalent of a militia were naturally met by strong Israeli punitive measures. Blockades were imposed

* A unit of body guards for the PLO leadership that has been used for terrorist operations since the PLO's expulsion from Beirut in 1982.

on villages that joined the Popular Army, and many of its members were caught in ambushes or chases. The effect of these moves was to drive the Popular Army into hiding during the day, but it emerged again to rule the field at night. And the more the IDF scaled down the huge force sent in to secure the territories during the PNC meeting, the less often its patrols reached remote villages, giving the young members of the Popular Army free rein there. The countryside became the new bastion of the *intifada*. While the cities continued to set the political tone, it was in the West Bank's 420 or so villages that the drive to build local militias became a dominant theme.

By the spring of 1989 senior members of the Israeli defense establishment began to sound warnings that the Palestinians were likely to escalate the violence to armed attacks in the near future. The leaders of the PLO repeatedly stressed that under no circumstances had they abandoned their policy of "armed struggle" as a result of the uprising. Parallel with what they called the "stone war," they reserved the right to send armed squads over the border against Israel. As the *intifada* slowed, however, the Shabiba in the territories themselves began pressuring for the green light to mount armed attacks using explosives, rifles, and hand grenades. The lack of firearms in the West Bank and Gaza was only one of the factors that delayed developments in this direction. Arafat wanted to maintain the distinction between the rebellion of the Palestinians under occupation and attacks by armed squads sent from outside. He was determined to preserve the special character of the uprising as a popular movement, which was important for mobilizing international support. Still, in their closed sessions, senior IDF officers aired the view that neither Arafat's strategy nor the immediate absence of weapons could halt the trend toward armed violence. "Out of 100,000 youngsters in the territories will come hundreds who are prepared to risk their lives to take up arms," one officer warned darkly. The year 1988 had seen an alarming rise in the number of attacks with weapons (guns, grenades, and explosives), though they accounted for only 6 percent of the 2,100 acts of Palestinian violence recorded in the territories, and most of the shooting was directed against other Palestinians. In the first ten months of the *intifada*, the Shin Bet exposed no less than 300 cells organized for terrorist activity, three-fourths of them the result of local initiatives without any connection to commands over the border.

The IDF's assessment of the general drift of events was based on the assumption that without tangible progress toward a political settlement, and under continued pressure from the Military Government, further radicalization of the population in the territories was inevitable. "The time will come," read the minutes of one of these staff meetings, "when they'll be fed up with stones . . . and to keep from losing ground they'll have to move on to the use of rifles."

On the Israeli side, the chronology and pace of developments differed, but the general sway of the mood was dismayingly similar. It cannot be said that any palpable difference could be felt in Israel on November 15, 1988, the day that it awoke to the news of the Palestinian declaration of independence. Yet it was equally true that the country had been in the throes of a change since the start of the uprising over eleven months earlier. The *intifada* had sent a sharp jolt through Israeli society, forcing it to re-examine propositions that had long been taken for granted. Thoughts and feelings that most Israelis had repressed for years now came welling up to the surface. Fears that were associated with another time, often another place, suddenly had countless Israelis in their grip again. As the uprising stretched on from month to month, Israelis came increasingly to realize that their country was slipping back to the starting line in its conflict with the Palestinians, to the stage of visceral hatred and unbridled violence that predated even the 1948 War of Independence and centered on the most basic of issues. Does the country that Israelis call the Land of Israel and Arabs call Palestine belong to only one or to both the peoples that inhabit it? Can either of those peoples ignore the needs and aspirations of the other? These and similar questions were made all the more irksome by the realization that the threat to the Jewish state was not posed exclusively from the surrounding countries, as Israel's leaders had been claiming for two generations. It also existed within: on the average Israeli's doorstep, on the streets, on the buses, on the way to work and school. The war had come to the "home front" even though it wasn't raging on the borders.

After months of unremitting violence, it had become obvious that Israel was losing its composure along with much of its self-confidence, despite its military might. Israelis looked around them and saw that thousands of tanks and hundreds of planes were not enough to ensure their safety; that even nonconventional weapons could not solve a security problem that had seemed marginal for so long but now touched upon their lives every day. One Israeli psychologist ventured that Israel found itself in the paradoxical position of the victor feeling like the vanquished, an oppressor feeling itself oppressed. The *intifada* also raised a stream of questions about the kind of country the next generation of Israelis will inherit. Can Israel remain a democracy if it is caught in the vise of a civil war with the Palestinians in the territories and a struggle with its own Arab minority, which increasingly displays identification with the Palestinian people? In this condition, can it attract immigration from the Diaspora, even from communities in distress? Can it remain a Jewish state? And can the dreams of the Jewish national movement—of security, freedom, and creativity—come true under these circumstances, or will they necessarily collapse under the weight of an endlessly ugly reality?

If nothing else, the *intifada* has caused the Israelis great vexation and anxiety because it has defied the means used to suppress it, illustrating beyond question that this complex problem can only be solved by surgical means. For societies no less than individuals, the prospect of surgery is understandably frightening, and the tendency today is still to avoid reality by taking pain-killers or trying to discredit the diagnosis. Frustration also stems from the fact that many Israelis, of all political persuasions, have come to feel that where the conflict with the Palestinians is concerned, their country has been living a lie. They now believe that their leaders deceived them in pronouncing that the Palestinian people did not exist; that the Arabs in the territories did not want their leaders; that the PLO forced itself on the Palestinians by violence and intimidation; that the status quo of occupation could be maintained indefinitely; that Israel could control the inhabitants of the territories by punitive actions and never face revolt; and that only Israel wanted peace, while all the proposals coming out of the Palestinian camp were merely cynical ruses.

The resulting confusion and stress, together with the rage at the Palestinians for waking the country out of its delusion, have led to a wave of extremism in Israel. The most pronounced sociopolitical trend since the start of the uprising has been a sharp turn toward the right and the spread of fanatic behavior that at times is reminiscent of the frenzy of the Palestinians during the opening days of the revolt. Signs of this slide rightward had been evident long before the *intifada*, but the uprising accelerated the process considerably—so much so that it sometimes seems as if Prime Minister Shamir and his Likud Party occupy the center of the country's political spectrum! Contrasted with the line of the small but strident parties further to the right—Tehiyah, Tzomet, Moledet, and Meir Kahane's Kach Party, which has been

barred from running for parliament because of its racist platform—
Shamir's policies look like the epitome of sober pragmatism. Even the
Labor Party has been caught up in the drift, with certain of its leaders—including Defense Minister Yitzhak Rabin—arguing that the only
sane course open to the party is to bend with the new wind blowing
through the Israeli electorate, rather than try to lead the country toward a stance of compromise.

Considering this mixture of the Likud's satisfaction with the swing
rightward and Labor's lack of resolve, it was not surprising that extremism spilled beyond the bounds of the Israeli-Palestinian conflict to
color the view of Israeli life as a whole. Israelis were increasingly telling pollsters that their country was "more democratic than necessary."
Attacks on the media became more vicious as the press was accused of
being unpatriotic, of distorting reports, even of aiding the enemy. The
settlers and their champions published advertisements decrying the
"hostile media" and tried to persuade their countrymen that the press
enjoyed "too much freedom." Israeli reporters and cameramen were
beaten while covering the uprising—mostly by settlers but occasionally
by soldiers and policemen. In a variation on the ancient practice of killing the messenger who brings bad news, a secret group of right-wing
fanatics set fire to the home of one of the country's leading pollsters
because the results of her surveys angered them. Not even men in uniform were spared the violence and vitriol. Soldiers and officers who
tried to prevent inflamed settlers from rampaging through a West Bank
town and injuring innocent Arabs were beaten and subjected to hysteri-
cal abuse—curses like "Nazi" and "*Kapo*," the worst epithets one can
use in Israel. The abandonment of all restraint was becoming a norm
inside the Green Line, too. After the funeral of a soldier who had been
kidnapped and murdered in Israel by Palestinians from Gaza, a crowd
of angry young men tried to overturn the car of the chief of staff, who
had attended the burial service.

From overreaction it was but a short step to expressions of outright racism. Brought before a judge on charges of manslaughter, one
of the settlers' veteran leaders, Rabbi Moshe Levinger, told the court
of his regret that he had not been "privileged" to kill an Arab. Another rabbi, who headed a yeshivah on the outskirts of Nablus, proclaimed that there was a difference between Arab and Jewish blood,
implying that killing an Arab was a less serious offense than shedding
the blood of a Jew. Although a number of other rabbis sharply denounced this statement, it showed the degree to which rabid anti-Arab

feeling had penetrated the Jewish religious establishment, paralleling the radical-Muslim enmity toward the Jews. However, it cannot be said that such feelings were limited to religious circles. One Israeli mayor wanted to close the school in his city that was jointly attended by Jewish and Arab children. Another had a special enclosed area built for Arab laborers to prevent them from "loitering" in his city on their way to and from work. The attitude of many Israelis toward these workers is a study in ambivalence. On the one hand, there is a desire to punish the rebellious Palestinians by not allowing them to earn their living in Israel; on the other, Israelis are deeply afraid of being left stranded without cheap labor to work at the menial jobs that they have come to disdain.

Only the worst of the extremists have openly preached a racist line; the rest have been drawn into the new trend by a fear of war and the xenophobia so closely associated with it. Yet the *intifada* has also elicited reactions of the opposite sort, as the liberal and leftist camps have tried to make their voices heard. While consistently denouncing Arab terrorism, they have shown the Palestinians that the Israeli body politic is not all of a piece; that many Israelis support territorial compromise and even the establishment of an independent Palestinian state alongside Israel. They have also campaigned against the use of collective punishment in the territories and have made a point of visiting Arab cities and villages to express their identification with the people who have been made to suffer unjustly. A number of Knesset members have gone so far as to offer themselves as ombudsmen for the aggrieved Palestinians, becoming watchdogs over the sensitive problem of human-rights violations in the territories.

Nor are they alone in their work. A spate of new organizations and bodies have cropped up in Israel as a result of the *intifada*. One group calling itself The Twenty-First Year is dedicated to working against the occupation as an untenable moral condition, and a group of people with sons serving in the army have established a body called Parents Against Erosion to halt the deterioration in moral values that inevitably attends the suppression of a revolt by a civilian population. An information center has been set up to gather and publish details on Israel's conduct in quashing the uprising—especially the injury caused to innocent people—and the veteran movement Peace Now has concentrated many of its activities on reestablishing lines of communication between the two peoples, despite the daily clashes. These and many other groups, including the Association for Civil Rights in Israel, have worked tirelessly to prove that despite the confusion, skepticism, and slide toward extremism, Israeli society has not lost its sensitivity to injustice and human suffering; that the moral gauge on which Jews have prided themselves for centuries has not gone haywire in the State of Israel. But it was not at all clear that in this pitched battle for the soul of Israel, the forces of reason would prevail.

Many of the leaders of the *intifada* who had served on the Unified National Command heard about the successive political developments—the Jordanian retreat, the Husseini document, and the declaration of a Palestinian state—over the radio as they sat in the Ketziot detention camp in the Negev. By the autumn of 1988 there was no one left in the field capable of implementing what had been envisioned in the Husseini document, so as to give the declaration of statehood some tangible content. The Unified National Command was paralyzed. Immediately after the PNC meeting in Algiers, a new set of members was appointed to man it, but they were a different breed from their predecessors. Hassan Abd-al-Rabbo of the Fatah, Sam'an Khouri of the Democratic Front, Tahir Shaloudi of the Communists (fresh out of administrative detention), and Adnan Shalalda of the Popular Front were all middling journalists who had never been highly positioned in their respective organizations. Nevertheless, they tried to make an impact by proposing to Tunis that the territories be divided into ten sectors, each headed by a sub-command, and again asking that the distribution of funds be done through the Unified Command. Their most radical departure was in urging Tunis to let them appoint a fifteen-member team to enter into contacts with the Israelis—not negotiations (they realized that it was hopeless to try to wrest that prerogative from the PLO abroad), but at least discussions that could lay the groundwork for future bargaining between the sides.

The fact was that a unique opportunity had arisen to enter into a dialogue with the Israelis. Following the Knesset elections in November 1988, Yitzhak Rabin (who was reappointed defense minister in the new National Unity Government) ordered that attempts be made to engage local Palestinian leaders in talks. He even proposed that elections should be held in the territories to choose the people with whom Israel would negotiate a solution, and he went on record saying that he would not rule out even members of the Unified Command. But the command's request to react to these feelers, albeit gingerly, was ignored by Tunis until all of its members were finally arrested in one of the Shin Bet's periodic sweeps. By then no one in the territories would dare to respond to the Israelis without publicly granted permission from Arafat—and Arafat, needless to say, was not about to let anyone upstage him. Besides, he had something far better going by then: a series of political moves unfolding far from the scene of the conflict that promised to yield some very satisfying results.

ELEVEN | *THE TANGLED SKEIN*

"LET'S LEAVE THE MIDDLE EAST ALONE," Secretary of State George Shultz commented wearily to his aides at the end of October 1987. During that month Shultz had suffered yet another disappointment in his efforts to move the region closer to a viable settlement of the Israeli-Arab dispute. A plan worked out with Israel's foreign minister, Shimon Peres, to have King Hussein meet with Prime Minister Shamir in Washington during the upcoming Reagan-Gorbachev summit had run aground. The bad taste left by the Israeli involvement in the Irangate scandal still lingered in the State Department, and it suddenly seemed as though Shultz had tired of the players on the Middle Eastern stage, who always seemed to have a new card up their sleeves. The Reagan administration, he told his aides, had done what it could to solve the Israeli-Arab conflict; now it was best to leave this slippery subject to the president's successor.

At that point Shultz did not even know why King Hussein was so furious that he had vehemently rejected the invitation to talk with Shamir and the leaders of the two superpowers in Washington. He did of course know that Hussein had secretly met with Shamir a few months earlier but that their talk then had led nowhere. Worse yet, after the meeting Hussein had complained that Shamir was the most pigheaded man he had ever met. The king had gone to that meeting with the State Department's blessings and encouragement. He had also assured all involved that he would not let Shamir pry out of him any statement that could later be used as an excuse to avoid negotiations.

Though Shultz knew that the talk had been a dialogue of the deaf, he still believed that Shamir would be interested in any opportunity to push the PLO out of the arena—and that meant negotiating with the Jordanians. It was the format of those negotiations that had become a stumbling block. Hussein wanted them to be held as part of an international conference, and Peres had come through with his party's backing. Shamir would not hear of a parley of that sort but finally agreed to "an international opening" for peace talks—and the Americans considered that an achievement in itself.

It was with a heavy heart that Shamir had agreed to that much, especially as he took the subject of an international conference as something of a personal affront. For months, he knew, a three-way flirtation had been going on between the United States' ambassador in Tel Aviv, Thomas R. Pickering, Jordan's King Hussein, and his own foreign minister, Laborite Shimon Peres, to promote the endeavor. Since the previous April, when Peres and Hussein had come to their so-called London Agreement fixing an international conference as the vehicle for solving the Middle East dispute, Shamir had been feeling like the odd man out in his own government. The reports he received about the contacts between Peres and Hussein came not from his Foreign Ministry but from the American embassy in Tel Aviv—and of course only after the fact. Since he was not consulted on decisions in advance, it was only natural that he regarded the preparations for an international conference as going on behind his back, and his objections took on the tone of a personal feud with Peres. He also wanted to put the Americans in their place by proving that he was a man to be reckoned with and that the peace process wouldn't budge an inch if they tried to circumvent the prime minister of Israel. Almost without realizing it, Washington had been sucked into the chronic squabbling that went on between Shamir and Peres. The bickering even spread to the American embassy in Tel Aviv, where the staff was divided on whether such a complex endeavor as an international conference could succeed if the prime minister of the pivotal country opposed it.

Shamir was not the only intractable figure on the stage, however. What Shultz and his advisers did not know in October 1987 was that Jordan's envoys in Washington had become privy to details about the talks between American and Israeli representatives on how to get Hussein to a second meeting with Shamir, this time in Washington. As a result, Hussein was apprised of a number of points he would not otherwise have known, such as the fact that the Americans planned to publicize the king's meeting with Shamir—a step that would undoubtedly imperil Hussein. He had long suspected that Washington coordinated more closely with Israel than with Jordan on the peace talks, and after hearing of the latest consultations he was forced to accept his advisers' conclusion that the cunning Israelis and patronizing Americans were conspiring to manipulate him. The king's response was to turn down the American invitation with nary a word as to why.

That was not the note on which Shultz had wanted to conclude his record on the Arab-Israeli conflict. Well before the October setback, he had planned to make an "important speech" on the subject and told his speech writer, Dan Kurtzer, that he wanted it to focus on the human side of the conflict. Those who read the speech said that it would have been one of the best Shultz had ever made on the Middle East. As October drew near he postponed the address in anticipation of the Hussein-Shamir talks and to add elements of a plan for breaking the deadlock. Then came Hussein's dour rejection, throwing the secretary's plan out of kilter and leaving him exasperated with the entire subject.

While Shultz's aides were still puzzling over how to proceed after his decision to "leave the Middle East alone," the *intifada* broke out and forced the secretary to overcome his irritation and turn his attention back to the region. Washington could not remain indifferent to the explosion in the territories, especially as it was subject to pressure from all sides. One group in the State Department fretted that the continuation of the uprising, or too forceful an Israeli response to it, would damage beyond repair the relations between the United States' three friends in the Middle East: Israel, Egypt, and Jordan. Pleas to take action were even coming from American Jewish leaders, for the discomfort of many American Jews over the film clips of Israeli soldiers beating Palestinian youth grew deeper with each passing day. One of these Jewish leaders, Max Kampelman, who was the United States' chief negotiator in the talks on nuclear arms reduction, took advantage of one of his sessions with the president to urge Reagan to take action. So it was that less than five months after Shultz's decision to let the Middle East drift on its own course, without American coaxing or scolding, he found himself on a plane heading right into the thick of it. Shultz had not visited the area since May 1983, when he had proudly presented the doomed Israeli-Lebanese peace treaty to Syria's President Hafez al-Assad, and the subsequent Lebanese renunciation of that agreement still rankled. Yet upon returning to the region at the end of February 1988, he was at least convinced that unlike the circumstances surrounding previous American initiatives, his present mission would not meet with criticism at home. Positive signs were coming out of Israel, too. Shamir had even announced that he would be prepared to enter into negotiations without any preconditions, leaving Shultz and his staff feeling that the *intifada* might indeed be the long-awaited opportunity to score a breakthrough.

Hardly had they arrived in Jerusalem, however, when they discovered that this upbeat assessment was far off the mark. The Israelis were certainly stunned by the uprising, but they were still not prepared to make even minor changes in their approach to the conflict. Shultz left Washington with the intention of combining the Camp David accords and various elements of the autonomy plan with a new, accelerated timetable. The principle of autonomy for the Palestinians in the territories had been agreed upon by Israel and Egypt in 1978, though they differed on its translation into practice. The PLO had rejected the idea at the time of the Camp David accords, but given the pressure of the *intifada*, Shultz chose to hope that it might now have a change of heart. He planned to make autonomy more attractive to the Palestinians by stipulating that negotiations on the final settlement of the dispute would begin before it was clear whether the transitional stage— in which the self-governing authority would go into operation—had succeeded. To avoid characteristic foot-dragging, moreover, he laid down a rigid timetable for reaching the final settlement. But Shamir, who had never had much to say for the Camp David accords and had in fact been against ratifying them, resisted the idea of resuming the process at an even faster pace. He might have been reconciled to the notion of Palestinian autonomy if he could obtain assurances that the so-called Camp David process would never go beyond the transition stage of establishing the self-governing authority—in other words, that autonomy would be the final settlement. But all attempts to assure him that the United States remained firmly opposed to the establishment of an independent Palestinian state failed to make even a dent in his outlook.

The Palestinian response to the secretary's initiative was equally disappointing, for it added up to a chorus repeating the old refrain that the one and only address for any proposals was the PLO. The efforts to set up meetings with the organization's loyalists in the territories came to naught, as Tunis forbade the "insiders" to have any truck with Shultz. When a number of these local leaders called for a pragmatic approach, in the hope of establishing a direct connection with the American secretary of state, the most persistent in their pleas began to receive veiled threats. As a means of "reassuring" him of their backing, for example, Hanna Siniora was told that Arafat and Abu Jihad had foiled an assassination plot against him and Elias Freij, the mayor of Bethlehem, by one of the organizations of the Rejection Front. But the real message being conveyed to the territories was clear: the PLO's veteran leadership had no intention of letting these local parvenus steal their thunder by meeting with Shultz. If the secretary of state wanted contact with the PLO, its leaders would be happy to meet with him in Washington or any Arab or European capital; but the PLO Executive would decide who would attend such a meeting, not the "small fry" in Gaza, Nablus, or Jerusalem.

The Americans actually had few serious expectations of the PLO anyway; it was what they heard from the Israelis that dismayed them. Rather than promise to reflect on their proposals, Shamir merely groused that the Shultz initiative was a "retreat" from the Camp David agreements. He was particularly opposed to negotiating on the final settlement before the greater part of the five-year interim stage had passed. What shocked the Americans most, however, was Shamir's attitude toward Security Council Resolution 242. Suddenly Shultz realized that Shamir had his own special interpretation of the key U.N. resolution, for whereas 242 speaks of Israel's withdrawal from territories occupied in 1967 and is based upon the principle of "land for peace," Shamir categorically rejected that formula. He claimed to accept the resolution but did so on his own terms, stating that he was prepared to negotiate peace with King Hussein and any Palestinians he might bring along to the bargaining table, but he would not relinquish any territory for it.

"What is there to negotiate on when they state, from the outset, that they won't discuss territorial concessions?" Hussein asked Shultz when the secretary reached Amman on the second leg of his Middle Eastern journey. "Have you heard any other proposition from the Israelis?"

Shultz was forced to admit that at that stage, at least, he had not. Apprised of Hussein's reaction, Shamir's response was typically evasive: "And what about the king?" he asked, "Is he prepared to declare, publicly, that he is open to a territorial compromise?"

And so it went, with each side trying to keep one step ahead of the other while conceding nothing to Shultz. In one of the secretary's meetings with Shamir, the subject of the local Palestinian leadership came up, and Shultz raised the name of Feisal al-Husseini. Shamir, of course, knew quite well who Husseini was, after the close call of the previous summer's talks with Moshe Amirav. But he was loath to confess to the depth of his knowledge or admit the fact that Husseini was sitting in an Israeli prison, in administrative detention, even as they were speaking. All he would say was, "We have a file on him!"

"I don't know the man," Shultz admitted, "and I can imagine that there's some material on him. But it must be kept in mind that he can serve as a partner to negotiations in the future."

"It's a very heavy file," Shamir repeated to stress his point.

"Yes," said Shultz, equally determined to make his own point, "but the question is what one *does* with the file."

After exchanges like these, the members of Shultz's retinue were growing convinced that if the new American initiative had stalled, the main reason was Israel's prime minister. Such sentiments were never expressed openly, but some of the secretary's aides had the distinct feeling that American policy in the Middle East had fallen hostage to Israel's intransigence or inability to make decisions.

After the usual exchange of letters and expressions of disappointment—which were kept confidential by both sides—Shultz made another visit to the Middle East at the beginning of June. On the fifth of that month he held a closed session with members of the Knesset Foreign Affairs and Defense Committee. June 5 was a symbolic date, for twenty-one years earlier the members of the Knesset had huddled in the building's air-raid shelters while Jerusalem was being shelled by the Jordanians on the opening day of the Six-Day War, in which Israel was to capture the West Bank and Gaza Strip. Having been stonewalled by Shamir, Shultz hoped to get a step closer to the Israeli people by meeting with their legislators. But this meeting with the Knesset deputies confirmed to the secretary and his aides how deeply divided the Israelis were over a solution to the conflict with the Palestinians. The two main speakers at the session were the chairman of the committee, Abba Eban, and Eliyahu Ben-Elissar of the Likud. Eban was prepared to go even further than Shultz in commenting that Soviet involvement in the peace process was inevitable, while Ben-Elissar chose to scold the secretary by saying that his new initiative was opening the door to a Palestinian state.

"I must be something of a masochist to be coming back [to be] argued with by everybody," Shultz opened in reply. He sounded tired, as though he already understood that his efforts were doomed to fail.

Rather than chide the Israeli legislators, he tried to talk to them as a friend. Again and again he returned to the subject of the risks Israel would face if peace could not be attained. He spared no effort to reassure his audience that a secure Israel was a basic building block of peace, that only a strong Israel could rule out the Arab military option. But for peace, he told them, "you have to be ready to negotiate and recognize that there are other points of view, other interests, and compromise is necessary."

Neither did Shultz's soothing words hide the fact that his message had new overtones. In the past he had been skeptical about the good that would come out of an international conference; now Shultz was implying that the road to direct negotiations passed through a framework of that kind. It might not have the authority to make decisions or impose its will on the sides, but some sort of international conference would evidently have to take place. For the Likud members on the committee, that message alone was reason for dismay. But what really put their backs up that day was the new reading the Americans were applying to the "legitimate rights of the Palestinians"; for the first time, Shultz spoke of their "legitimate political rights."

"[That] sounds [like] some kind of modification to Camp David," Eliyahu Ben-Elissar objected. "I am afraid that you are heading towards a solution which will actually start movement towards the creation of an independent Palestinian state west [of] the Jordan River."

Uncharacteristically, Shultz cut him off. "I think that that would be a great tragedy," he countered, "would be unworkable . . . I am deeply convinced [from] my experience in talking with Arab leaders [that] whatever they may say at the Algiers summit* or elsewhere, they all recognize that an independent Palestinian state here in the West Bank and Gaza would be a disaster. They do not want that. Nobody in his right mind wants it. . . . [But the Palestinians] do have some kind of identity, and . . . that has to get recognized. The political aspect of it has to be recognized. . . . They want to have some control over their lives. That's what I think of as a political right."

That statement would return to haunt the members of the Knesset committee, and others who were informed of the session, months later when George Shultz instituted a dialogue with the PLO just weeks after the PNC's declaration of a Palestinian state. Whether he had planned

* The Arab Summit Conference in Algiers decided to demand the establishment of an independent Palestinian state.

that move long in advance, as the parting shot of his diplomatic career, or merely pounced on the opportunity presented by the changes in the PLO is something only Shultz can say. What cannot be denied, however, is that as a true friend of Israel who was close to the American Jewish community and concerned about the fate of Jews everywhere, no man was better suited to make the dramatic shift that placed America's policy toward the Israeli-Palestinian conflict on an entirely new footing.

Signs of an impending change had been in the air for weeks before the decision to recognize the PLO. Clearly the Reagan administration felt uncomfortable with the fact that it maintained ties with only one side to the conflict. It was a situation that cramped American foreign policy, leaving it strangely at the mercy of Israel's good will. It must be said, of course, that the PLO had done little to merit American recognition. Throughout the Reagan years it had stood fast behind a policy of reckless violence and barely hinted at a willingness to compromise with Israel. Yet neither can it be said that Israel had exploited these years to edge toward peace. All it had done for over a decade was maintain the status quo or add settlements in the West Bank and Gaza, making territorial compromise an ever more elusive prospect. For the most part, the United States related passively to this behavior. Occasionally the State Department issued mild admonitions to Israel about building new settlements, but they were hardly more than a slap on the wrist. During the Reagan years the United States launched two diplomatic initiatives in the Middle East, both in response to the outbreak of violence: the Reagan Plan during the war in Lebanon and the Shultz Plan at the height of the *intifada*. When each was rebuffed by the Israelis, however, the administration seemed to shrug philosophically and retreat into diplomatic lethargy. Given that discouraging history, by the autumn of 1988 Washington felt unable to do much more than pull its own wagon out of the mud.

After the failure of his February trip, Shultz knew that no suggestions for solving the conflict were likely to emerge from the Shamir government and that he would have to find a way to shake Israel out of its complacency. In September he chose the pro-Israeli Washington Institute for Near East Policy as the place to send the Israelis a signal. "Decision time is approaching in the Middle East . . . and these decisions must be based on a dispassionate and cold look at reality," Shultz told the select audience that filled the hall. "The status quo between the Arabs and the Israelis does not work. It is not viable. It is dangerous." Shultz balanced his reiteration of Israel's "right to exist in security" by stating that "Palestinian political rights must also be recognized and addressed." The solution to the problem was not an independent state, he qualified, but it was definitely based on the principle of land for peace and direct negotiations between the sides.

The secretary was careful not to upset the political apple cart on the eve of the American presidential election. It is doubtful whether he would have responded with the same alacrity to Arafat's almost forced declaration of recognition for Israel and renunciation of terrorism, made in Geneva on December 14, 1988, had it come weeks earlier— before the American electorate had chosen to install another Republican president in the White House. But one way or another, the dialogue between the United States and the PLO would surely have begun some time in the course of 1989 because as far as the administration was concerned, it was an idea whose time had come. Besides, the purpose of the dialogue was not to harm Israel but to help free it from the stalemate in which it seemed hopelessly ensnarled.

In retrospect it is clear that the American decision was arrived at through a series of twists and turns in national policy. The irony is that Shultz's firm decision to refuse Arafat a visa to the United States, so that he could address the United Nations General Assembly, was the catalyst that accelerated the process. From the moment that a visa request was made, the State Department knew that it had been maneuvered into a no-win situation: the administration would be the butt of criticism whether it granted the visa or not. Some officials argued for a line of reverse psychology, urging Shultz to approve the visa as a way of playing down Arafat's appearance at the U.N. "By refusing to grant Arafat a visa," a senior aide counseled, "we'll only focus world attention on his speech." And that, of course, was precisely what happened. When Arafat was denied entry to the United States, the U.N. retaliated by deciding to fly the General Assembly delegates to Geneva for a special session, making the Arafat speech into an extraordinary event and a media extravaganza. At a critical juncture Washington had incapacitated itself, and Arafat could not have chosen a better political backdrop for his appearance on the international stage.

Behind the scenes, meanwhile, various parties were involved in the moves leading up to the American decision to recognize the PLO. Support for the decision was unanimous in the National Security Council. The president's national security adviser, General Colin Powell, who was known to be well disposed toward Israel, wholeheartedly supported the idea and promised to persuade Reagan not to torpedo it. Feelers put out to the Pentagon showed that there was no opposition there either. The consensus seemed to be that recognition of the PLO would further strengthen the United States' standing in the Arab world without precipitating a major crisis with the heavily dependent Israelis or the American Jewish community.

The remaining problem was to bring the PLO around to taking the one step necessary to earn American acceptance—recognizing the State of Israel and renouncing terrorism—and here the American government received help from two unexpected quarters: Sweden's Foreign Minister Sten Andersson and a number of American Jews who were associated with Israel and active in the peace movement. Andersson, who assumed the role of orchestrator, paid special note to the fact that the *intifada* had created cracks in American Jewry's monolithic support for Israel; more than at any time in the past, Israel's policy vis-à-vis the Palestinians was being criticized publicly by Jewish circles in the United States. On the face of it, Andersson's initiative in helping Arafat see the light was an independent Swedish effort, but Secretary of State Shultz was in on it from the very start. Together with the Swedes, Rita Hauser, the president of the Center for Peace in the Middle East, had made a point of informing Shultz of her intention to meet with Arafat in Stockholm early in December and persuade him to fulfill the United States' conditions for recognizing the PLO. Shultz did not rush them, but he did react positively.

Andersson, who had been deeply affected by his visit to the territories a few months earlier, also had a personal interest in succeeding at the mediation effort. Long the object of attack at home for Sweden's arms sales to various countries at war, he looked to success in bringing the PLO in from the cold as a way of offsetting much of the damage he had suffered on the domestic front. It was equally plain to him, however, that if his undertaking failed, both he and his party would suffer quite a drubbing. In short, Andersson's prestige was at stake, and his acute sensitivity was felt not only in the exaggerated secrecy with which the preparations for the Stockholm session were made but also in his vigorous handling of the negotiations. At a certain stage, when the PLO delegation hesitated over the wording of the compromise statement that Arafat was to read out at a press conference, Andersson threatened that if the Palestinians rejected the proposed formulation, he would have no choice but to go public with the whole story—including exactly what had gone wrong.

But the little-known truth of the matter is that Arafat's declaration in Stockholm, and soon thereafter in Geneva, came in response not to Andersson's bluster but to an unmistakable signal he had received from the Reagan administration. On the occasion of Andersson's last visit to Washington, Secretary of State Shultz handed him, in the utmost confidence, a personally signed letter on the Palestinian question. It was addressed to Andersson but explicitly authorized him to show it to whomever he deemed proper, obviously meaning Yasser Arafat. The letter spoke in general terms of the United States' desire to see a settlement reached in the Middle East, but Shultz had been careful to delete from its draft any statement that could possibly be interpreted as a commitment to the PLO. When Arafat read the letter in Stockholm, he understood that the State Department was sending him a signal, for Shultz had included a subtle hint about a new American approach to self-determination for the Palestinians. The secretary had also taken the trouble to append the exact wording of what Arafat would have to say in order to gain the United States' recognition for the PLO. Finally, he added an assurance about the nature of the American response as soon as Arafat had publicly pronounced the magic words.

The Palestinian delegation was troubled mostly by two issues. First, they wanted to make sure that there would be a reciprocal tie between their recognition of the State of Israel and their right to establish a Palestinian state; they were not about to recognize Israel for its own sake. Second, they feared that recognition of a Palestinian state would be conditional upon a variation of the "Jordanian option"—a structural association of some kind between the Palestinian state and the Hashemite kingdom—and were determined to avoid that prospect at all costs. To gain time and perhaps an edge in the talks, Arafat never stopped complaining that the Americans had defaulted on earlier promises. Ambassador to the United Nations Vernon Walters, for one, had assured him that Washington would recognize the PLO in return for its help in getting the American hostages out of Lebanon. Arafat also had an unsettled account with the Americans over an incident in which—or so he claimed—the PLO had saved Henry Kissinger's life. After receiving word of a plan to shoot down the secretary of state's plane with a shoulder-launched surface-to-air missile as it came in for a landing at a particular airfield, the PLO quickly informed the United States, which had the plane diverted to another airport. "Even King Hussein doesn't trust the Americans anymore," Arafat explained. "He's replaced them with Margaret Thatcher, who has become his confidant."

"We'll find a queen for you, too," was Rita Hauser's impromptu reply, to the forced laughter of all present. Arafat extricated himself from a royal match by telling his listeners that he was distantly related to a king: Hassan II of Morocco.

Wary of acting in haste, Arafat refrained from articulating the American formula in Stockholm, pleading that he was having difficulty getting through to his comrades on the PLO Executive by phone. Instead he waited until arriving in Geneva for the U.N. General Assembly sessions—and then took two tries to get it right. Finally, at a December 14 press conference, he clearly renounced terrorism and accepted Resolution 242 as the basis for a settlement, as the Americans had demanded. In return, the United States fulfilled its promise by announcing that it would enter in a dialogue with the PLO.

At that point the Israelis had no idea that Shultz had been directly involved in prompting the PLO's acceptance of Resolution 242 and its renunciation of terror. (It was not until months after the fact that the details of what had transpired began to reach Jerusalem and the Israelis understood, for example, that Mrs. Hauser and her friends had only been the backdrop to the real drama that had unfolded in Stockholm.) Two days before the Geneva press conference, as the PLO Executive met to discuss the statement that Arafat would make to satisfy the American demands, Israel was informed that if the PLO accepted the wording proposed by the State Department, the United States would engage in a dialogue with it. Prime Minister Shamir shot off a letter to President Reagan expressing his concern and proposing that the two countries consult on the issue. But by that point events were moving too quickly for Israel to halt them; the Americans knew what they wanted and didn't need Israel's advice on the subject. While Arafat was performing his political balancing act in Stockholm and Geneva, the Israelis had become complacent about their relationship with the United States and were taken aback by the American gambit. During the years of the Reagan presidency, they had grown accustomed to dispatching any American political initiative just by turning their noses up at it. Committed as it was to dealing with only one side in the Israeli-Palestinian conflict, Washington appeared to have no leverage. But obviously all that had changed.

"This is the second time this administration has surprised us! The first was when you came out with the Reagan Plan in September 1982; now you've decided to recognize the PLO and enter into a dialogue with it. No one even hinted to us that you were holding talks with the

Swedes about bringing American Jews together with Arafat. Is this what you call a strategic partnership?"

The irate complainer was a ranking diplomat in the Israeli embassy in Washington speaking to a similarly high-placed official in the State Department. He may have had formal grounds for scolding the American, but the surprise he complained of was similar to Israel's being caught off guard by the outbreak of the *intifada:* only the perversely self-deluded could have believed that Washington would settle for the status quo indefinitely. When the Reagan Plan was being prepared, Israel really had no clue that such an initiative was in the offing. But in the case of the American dialogue with the PLO, the telltale signs were impossible to miss. Past experience, if nothing else, should have taught the Israelis that in response to violence the United States would propose a plan for negotiations. That had been the pattern at the close of the Yom Kippur War and again toward the end of the war in Lebanon. The crisis that grew out of the *intifada* was a fitting background for a new move, and if the Shultz Plan had come a cropper, Washington would probably try something else. For the Americans to have accepted the failure of the secretary's initiative and left it at that would have been tantamount to surrendering control over their own policy in the Middle East.

As surprises go, the real eye-opener was not the United States' recognition of the PLO but the muted reaction to it. While most of Shultz's aides expected the American Jewish community and Israel's friends in Congress to be up in arms about the dramatic reversal, the response turned out to be strikingly mild. Instead of assailing the outgoing secretary of state, they focused their criticism on the group of Jews who had met with Arafat in Stockholm and helped pave the way for the American dialogue with the PLO. One of the members of this group, Menachem Rosensaft, who is chairman of the Zionist Labor Movement in the United States and a member of the Conference of Presidents of Major American Jewish Organizations, was almost deposed for his involvement in the talks. Before long, however, even the anger of the American Jewish establishment died down, as did the broader American-Jewish opposition to the new policy.

The background to this unexpectedly subdued reaction was an Israeli blunder—and the rude awakening of many American Jews—that had occurred just a few weeks earlier. After the Knesset elections, Israel's two major parties had both agreed to cooperate with the country's Orthodox religious parties in voting for the "Who Is a Jew?" legislation. By invalidating (in Israel) religious conversions done by any but Orthodox rabbis, the proposed law implied that in the eyes of the Jewish state, anyone converted by a Conservative or Reform rabbi was not a Jew. The Orthodox parties had had this legislation on their agenda for over a decade, but 1988 was the first time they were promised the unqualified backing of both Labor and the Likud (as the price of their joining a postelection coalition). The prospect of such legislation naturally infuriated the majority of American Jews, not least because it smacked of an attempt to discredit the legitimacy of the Conservative and Reform movements, with which most practicing Jews in America are associated. It would also have disqualified as Jews (according to Israeli law) many Americans who regarded themselves and their offspring as members of the Jewish people in every way. Even those who would not be personally affected by the law were embittered by the cynicism that wafted their way from the Israeli political establishment. Although the law was ultimately tabled, the flap over it had soured many American Jews and left them feeling that the Israelis were ruining their vision of the Jewish state. It turned out, however, that the most critical element of the affair was its timing: the uproar over the "Who Is a Jew?" law was still reverberating when the American government decided to enter into a dialogue with the PLO.

Against this background it was difficult to expect that American Jews would stand up, as a man, and fight the secretary of state because he had taken a step defined as part of the peace process and benignly designed to help Israel help itself. Neither were Israel's friends in Congress willing to take up arms against Shultz, lest they appear to be sabotaging his efforts to coax the sides closer to peace. At most they hoped to ensure that the new dialogue would not culminate in outright American support for a Palestinian state. When members of Congress appealed to him, Shultz promised to try to coordinate with Jerusalem on the dialogue with the PLO—on condition that they would not come out against the new process. He needn't have been concerned; at any rate the criticism from Jews and pro-Israel elements in Congress was negligible. For the first time in decades there seemed to be a definite, relatively low limit to what Israel could expect of the American Jewish community. Under the circumstances even AIPAC, the purportedly all-powerful pro-Israel lobby, was reluctant to go to battle with Shultz, whose credentials as a friend of Israel were above reproach. Thus the Shamir government had suffered a double blow: not only had the administration broken out of the binds that effectively enabled Israel to exercise a veto on American foreign policy, the American Jewish community was raising penetrating questions about Israel's position on the Palestinian issue. The rift in the national consensus within Israel had spread to world Jewry, and nowhere was this more manifest than in the United States.

The American decision to recognize the PLO shocked and angered the Israeli government in equal measure, but the reactions to it varied. One response was Israel's stance of burying its official head in the sand. When American Ambassador Pickering tried to report to Yossi Ben-Aharon, the director-general of the Prime Minister's Office, on the first meeting between PLO representatives and the American ambassador in Tunis, Ben-Aharon snapped, "I don't want to hear it!" To which Pickering retorted, "I have been ordered to report. I can't force you to listen, but I am going to speak my piece!"

Ben-Aharon represented the school that believed even passive co-operation with the new process would ultimately bring Israel into indirect negotiations with the PLO. But there were other forms of response to the change. The people at AIPAC, for instance, were the first to recover from the blow and suggest that Israeli diplomats move quickly to achieve a new understanding with the United States and set limits on how far Washington would go in its negotiations with the PLO. They urged Israel to establish three cardinal points: that it would not return to its 1967 border; that the PLO must renounce a number of clauses of the Palestinian Covenant; and above all that the United States must not support the establishment of an independent Palestinian state. AIPAC believed that speed was of the essence, for it was crucial to reach an understanding with the outgoing Reagan administration that would be binding upon its successor. The problem was that neither the outgoing officials nor the representatives of the new administration were in the least amenable to the idea. Shultz's adviser and right-hand man Charlie Hill, who had done a tour of duty in Israel and had been instrumental in arranging a ceasefire between Israel and the PLO in 1981, let the lobbyists know that if Israel pressed the State Department to accept a new memorandum of understanding, it would have to commit itself to a number of things not at all to its liking. "You're too late," Hill explained. "The tide of history is no longer with you." Brent Scowcroft, earmarked to become President Bush's national security adviser, was likewise left cold by the notion of a new memorandum of understanding. He evidently feared that Washington would fall into the very trap from which Shultz had just extricated it, namely, having its diplomatic freedom of maneuver cramped by commitments to Israel—this time in its dialogue with the PLO.

The picture changed somewhat when the new administration began working out its approach to the peace process. Dogged by memories of his country's involvement in Lebanon and of the explosion that caused the death of 241 Marines stationed outside Beirut in 1983, the new secretary of state, James Baker, was easily persuaded that the chances of a peace initiative failing in the Middle East were far greater than the prospects of breaking out of the deadlock. To save Washington from falling into yet another pot of political molasses, rather than proceed with the method of major political initiatives he opted for a new approach: the United States would operate slowly, along a broader front, aiming to progress one step at a time. It would begin by trying to establish contact between Israel and the PLO via the residents of the territories. At the same time it would work to bring the Soviet Union into the picture, and while neutralizing the European Community for the present, it would hold the EEC in reserve to exert pressure on both sides, should that prove necessary. For the time being, the United States would exploit the *intifada* as an instrument to prod Israel along, but the time would come when all hostilities would have to be brought to a halt and the residents of the territories would have to enter into a dialogue with Israel. Washington accepted that the PLO was needed for that, and the price of its cooperation would be American assurances that it would be integrated into the peace process at a later date. From the start the PLO would have to be told that Washington's agreement to engage in a dialogue did not mean that the United States had changed its mind about the establishment of a Palestinian state. Then again, neither did it mean that the issue could not be raised in their talks. Israel would also have to undergo a process of "re-education" in which it would be forced to make peace first with what the PLO stands for and eventually with the organization itself.

Just before Israeli Foreign Minister Moshe Arens and Prime Minister Yitzhak Shamir visited Washington in the spring of 1989, the new administration was confident that it would not be difficult to integrate the eager PLO into the peace process. To get in on the action, American officials believed, the Soviet Union would also be prepared to accept certain conditions, such as dropping the demand for a full-fledged international conference. The problem really lay with America's own client, Israel, and the question was how to get the Shamir government to agree to a process in which representatives of the PLO—initially in the territories and ultimately from abroad—would take part. The Bush administration was not interested in a confrontation with Israel. And despite differences on a number of points, neither did Washington want to be seen twisting the arm of a friendly country regarded as a strategic ally. Ever since the Israeli elections in November, the State Department had known that the Labor Party was no longer the address for its ideas and proposals; Israeli foreign policy was being conducted exclusively by the Likud. The vital next step was therefore to find a fig leaf that would enable the Likud to get around the delicate subject of the Washington-PLO dialogue and enable the Americans to get that dialogue moving along fruitful lines.

Baker's and Arens's aides were prepared to create that fig leaf simply by having the two men avoid the subject during their meeting. Their talk was reminiscent of a conversation between a married couple when both partners know there's a lover in the background but neither wants to acknowledge it. The tacit agreement seemed to suit the Israelis; Arens, at any rate, emerged from the meeting feeling sanguine. Unfortunately, this cozy arrangement held up for only a day. What Baker refrained from saying to Arens behind closed doors he was forced to say to Congress publicly, namely, that at some point further down the road Israel would have to negotiate with the PLO. It was as if Baker had announced that the United States had a mistress in Tunis, and Israel was just going to have to live with it! Again the Israelis were caught off guard. Stung by the statement, Arens requested another meeting with Baker, but the secretary's schedule was full. Instead, the two held a telephone conversation in which the things they had deliberately not said to each other face to face now had to be discussed at a distance. None of Arens's arguments did any good; Baker was unwilling to retreat an inch from the gist of his statement that in the fullness of time Israel would have to make peace with the PLO, in both senses of the term.

The cards in the Israeli-Arab conflict were completely reshuffled by the Soviet Union, as well. While Washington was turning over a new leaf in its relations with the Palestinian national movement, Moscow was similarly reassessing its role in the Middle East—and both countries reached the conclusion that they would be unable to contribute to the solution of the conflict if they boycotted one of the sides. For years Washington would have nothing to do with the PLO, while

Moscow acted as though Israel simply did not exist. The Palestinian uprising, Israel's difficulties in quelling it, and the voices in the Palestinian camp finally calling for recognition of Israel were the main factors behind Washington's new attitude toward the PLO. But the change of heart in Moscow traced to different considerations entirely. On one level, the profound changes in Soviet domestic policy inevitably affected the country's foreign relations as well. Regional conflicts were a subject that greatly troubled the Gorbachev regime. In light of the Soviet Union's grave economic condition, the very last thing Moscow wanted was for one of its client states to become embroiled in a runaway war that could draw the Kremlin into a confrontation with the West and force it to squander its resources. As a result, Moscow traded in its old aggressive demeanor for a policy aimed at averting international crises. Rather than stir the cauldron of superpower rivalry, the Russians were out to seek solutions to local disputes.

Suddenly the kind of thinking that Moscow had taken for granted for decades was being openly challenged from inside the system. Had the huge Soviet investment in arms supplies to the Third World, and particularly the Arab states, justified itself? Certain quarters within the KGB were suggesting that the astronomical sums laid out for these arms be made public, while other voices were insisting that the provision of weapons for free must be halted immediately and that economics should be the sole factor governing the sale of arms. Friends who pleaded indigence would simply receive less—and certainly not the most advanced and expensive weapons systems—unless they could find some way to cover the costs of their acquisitions.

Syria's President Assad was introduced to this new approach rather bluntly at a dinner that Gorbachev hosted in his honor in Moscow. What was the point of pouring huge sums into more and more weapons systems, the Soviet leader asked rather bluntly before all the invited guests. Wouldn't it be more logical to invest these funds in Syria's economy? The message to Assad was more than clear: Syria might be the Soviet Union's most important client in the Middle East, but that did not mean that Moscow would automatically support its plans for war. The Kremlin would continue to help Damascus build its defenses, but Gorbachev made it quite plain that he was not about to bankroll any Syrian military escapades.

This shift in emphasis was not as abrupt as it might have seemed to Assad that night. For quite a while Moscow had suspected that when the Syrians spoke of achieving "strategic parity" with Israel, they really meant the ability to mount an offensive against Israel without the aid of other Arab states. Moscow was prepared to accept the need for "strategic parity," but only in defensive terms. It was willing to supply Syria with sophisticated weapons systems that would deter Israel from taking any military initiative, but sanctioning Syria's efforts to build its own, nonconventional weapon systems was another matter altogether. Soviet Intelligence knew that Damascus was relying on more than just Russian weapons in its effort to reach this coveted "parity" with Israel. Assad was reported to be courting the Chinese in order to obtain medium-range ballistic missiles, which the Russians were not prepared to sell him, and he had recruited European experts to develop chemical and biological weapons. After secretly accumulating information on the weapons systems already in Syrian hands, the Russians had also come to the disconcerting conclusion that their client had secretly built a plant for the production of chemical weapons. Moreover, with the help of experts from Western Europe, it was trying to place chemical warheads on the missiles purchased from the Soviet Union. Naturally the Russians feared that this information—which they assumed was known to Jerusalem as well—might drive the Israelis to mount a preemptive attack on Syria. One way or another, it seemed increasingly likely that future hostilities in the Middle East would not be limited to conventional weapons.

When Moscow sent the commander of its anti-chemical-warfare unit, General Pikolov, to Syria in 1987, the visit was mistakenly interpreted in Israel and the West as evidence of collusion between the two countries. In point of fact, Pikolov's mission was to admonish Damascus against becoming involved in a war with Israel, and especially against drawing on its arsenal of nonconventional weapons. The Soviet general wanted to clarify Syria's intentions in this respect, but the Syrians kept from him as much information as possible and managed to keep him well away from their highly sensitive facilities for producing chemical weapons. To make their message unmistakable, at the International Conference on Halting the Dissemination of Chemical Weapons, held in Paris at the end of 1988, the Russians pointedly kept their distance from the Arab camp. Iraq (which had been accused of employing chemical weapons in its war with Iran) and its sister states in the Arab world, tried to shift the spotlight off their activities by pointing an accusatory finger at Israel. Rather than deny their involvement with chemical-warfare programs, they argued that since Israel was developing a nuclear arsenal, it was pointless to prohibit the Arab countries from producing chemical weapons in self-defense. In the past Moscow would have jumped at an opportunity of this sort to embarrass Israel and the United States. But this time the Russians felt that the danger arising from the spread of chemical weapons was the most pressing issue, and they insisted upon facing up to it immediately.

It cannot be said, however, that the Arabs were the only side in the Middle Eastern imbroglio that worried the Soviets. Long before these developments, the Russians had ordered their intelligence experts to find out just what the Israelis were up to in the sphere of nonconventional weapons. Reports that they were testing a new ground-to-ground missile capable of reaching the southern marches of the Soviet Union troubled Moscow greatly. When a group of American generals and experts visiting the Soviet Union at the beginning of 1989 raised the question of how to prevent the transfer of missile technology to the Third World, one of the Americans remarked offhandedly that the Russians had more reason to be concerned about the matter than the United States, because the range of Middle Eastern missiles would ultimately cover part of the Soviet Union. Yet even before that barb slipped out, Moscow had begun to send out signals of its displeasure over the Israeli missiles. When reports on Israel's launching tests leaked out of Washington, the Kremlin's reaction was instructive. The Russians said that they could not remain indifferent to what was happening near their southern border, but they did not threaten Israel. And the main channel for their expressions of concern was not the Soviet Foreign Ministry but the Hebrew-language broadcasts of Radio Moscow. Clearly, on this sensitive issue the Kremlin had chosen to conduct a dialogue with Israel, rather than resort to its old style of bullying, in the hope that the Israelis would appreciate the change in attitude and content themselves with shorter-range missiles.

In broader political terms, Moscow's conclusion from all these developments was that the time had come to join in cultivating and accelerating the peace process in the Middle East. The Russians were obviously feeling edgy about the region. On a variety of occasions the Soviets reiterated that the superpowers must act quickly, because various countries in the Middle East were developing capabilities of mass destruction, and the region had a history of spinning out of control as the result of a sudden deterioration in the political situation. When the Iraqis tried to supply FROG short-range ground-to-ground missiles to the Christian forces in Beirut, the Kremlin moved, in concert with the United States, to prevent them from being stationed on Lebanese soil. The last thing it wanted was the spread of a conflict that might draw in both Syria and Israel, as had happened in 1982. Given this new outlook, it should not be surprising that, like Washington, the Soviets regarded the Palestinian uprising as a prime opportunity to prod both sides closer to a compromise.

Since their only real leverage was with the Palestinians, the Soviets spared no effort to coax the PLO into adopting a new line at its Algiers Conference. They realized, of course, that what the Palestinians wanted above all was recognition from the United States, which would be forthcoming only if they recognized Israel and renounced terrorism. But rather than try to prevent their chief rival from gaining direct influence over one of their traditional clients, the Soviets encouraged the PLO to fulfill the American prerequisites for recognition. All they asked in return was not to be left out of the subsequent peace process—as they had been from the Camp David accords, which were exclusively a "Pax Americana."

The Russians were also prepared to be flexible. They believed that the best instrument for negotiations was an international conference in which the Soviet Union would participate alongside the United States. But when it transpired that Yitzhak Shamir was vehemently against the idea and that Washington was not about to force it on him—at least not at that stage—the Kremlin exhibited its readiness to retreat. Russian envoys told the Israelis on any number of occasions that if Israel could come up with a better proposal than an international conference, Moscow would be prepared to embrace it. And to prove their eagerness, the Soviets appointed a senior Foreign Ministry official to deal with the Middle Eastern peace process, while making various conciliatory gestures toward Israel and agreeing that other countries in the eastern bloc do the same. These gestures still fell short of renewing the diplomatic relations that the Soviet Union had severed with Israel during the Six-Day War, but they communicated a new-found consideration for Israel's sensitivities. When a Palestinian from Gaza sent a bus hurtling off a mountainside, causing the death of sixteen of its passengers and injuries to all the others, a representative of the Soviet Foreign Ministry was quick to define the incident as an act of terrorism—far outstripping the State Department, which took two whole days to arrive at the same conclusion.

The flurry of diplomatic activity brought on by the *intifada* has also forced Israel to reassess its stand on the role that the Russians can play in the peace process. Israel's attitude toward the Soviet Union has long been marked by sharp suspicion—and with good reason, considering the fact that successive Soviet regimes have displayed an openly hostile attitude toward Israel and that diplomatic relations between the two countries have been severed for longer than they were active. Moscow's support for all of Israel's enemies, its direct military involvement against Israel after the Six-Day War, and its massive supply of arms to Arab confrontation states were all taken as decisive proof that no good would come of the Soviet Union's involvement in the Middle East. Added to Moscow's aggressive bias was the fact that it had worked against the first peace treaty between Israel and an Arab state and for decades had subjected its own Jewish population to abuse.

Then came Gorbachev's turnabout, forcing Israelis to consider whether a profound change had not indeed taken place in the Kremlin. Before long members of the Israeli political and diplomatic establishment had begun to argue that despite the unhappy history between the two countries, it was best not to freeze the Soviet Union out of the peace process. If Moscow took an active part in engineering an agreement, they reasoned, there was a better chance that it would restrain Syria and the other radical Arab regimes that were opposed to peace. On the other hand, if Moscow were kept out of the political process, the peace it might yield could not possibly be a stable one.

What Israel lacked at the early stage of the *intifada* was a policy that would counter its image of intransigence. The government slowly realized that instead of being dragged, kicking, to the conference table behind the PLO (which was now dictating the moves both in the territories and on the diplomatic plane), it must break free of its old way of thinking and stop seeking negotiating partners that had long departed the scene or had never been more than a mirage. For a number of reasons, however, that was no simple task.

More than any other event in Israel's history, the *intifada* has exposed in all its grimness the snarled state of the country's political system, which has grown brittle in its approach to the Israeli-Palestinian conflict and has a way of crippling itself the moment the issue comes up. Whenever this system appears to be making some progress, its wheels immediately jam. Each time it takes a step forward, it is promptly fettered by self-restraints that send it staggering two steps back. The result is that in terms of the Palestinian problem, at least, the decision-making process of the Israeli government is effectively para-

lyzed. The cabinet is not even able to discuss vital questions surrounding this issue. It addresses itself exclusively to the most immediate
tactical and operational concerns—and then only when forces outside
the cabinet raise them for discussion. Any deliberation in long-range
policy is repeatedly postponed; the ministers simply dodge the subject.
It has been argued, for example, that the deportation of most of the
intifada's leaders will soon deplete the local Palestinian leadership capable of negotiating with Israel. Is this policy really in Israel's national
interest? By refusing to grapple with the question, the cabinet inevitably opts for the position that "whatever is, is right." It has never even
managed to hold a thoroughgoing discussion of Israel's policy toward
its own Arab minority.

The flight from the Palestinian question has been going on for
years now, and while the *intifada* has forced the political system to
take the matter more seriously, it has done little to change the old
habits of procrastination and avoidance as ways of gaining time. The
government's behavior has been based upon the dubious assumption
that time is on Israel's side, as well as on the more empirically solid
premise that, given time, people tend to adjust to a persistent reality.
As the *intifada* survived all of Israel's attempts to quash it, the country's
political leaders and the public at large grew accustomed to the fact
that the IDF was being forced to kill and maim Palestinians almost
every day. As the months passed, Israelis became thoughtlessly accepting of a shocking level of violence and bloodshed, particularly as the
casualties were almost always Palestinian, rather than their own. The
consensus in Israel was a kind of dug-in-heels attitude that the status
quo must be maintained—and certainly that it must not be altered as
a result of anything done by the Palestinians. The alternative premise—
that in the absence of a solution to the conflict, the extremist forces
in the Arab world would only gather strength—was either dismissed
out of hand or welcomed as proof that no one was willing to discuss peace with Israel. And the prospect that Israel would one day be
seated at the bargaining table facing the most radical of the Palestinians,
while its own social, economic, and military strength had been sapped
by the relentless violence, was not considered at all.

On the face of it, Yitzhak Shamir's second National Unity Government was eminently suited to grapple with fateful decisions, both
because it incorporated Israel's largest parties and because many of
its ministers were highly experienced in matters of national security.
With three men who served as prime ministers (Shamir, Peres, and

Rabin), five ex-defense ministers (Rabin, Peres, Arens, Weizman, and Sharon), and three former chiefs of staff (Rabin, Chaim Barlev, and Mordechai Gur), it boasted an impressive lineup of men with a long history of making difficult national decisions. Yet despite these sterling credentials, the cabinet has proved incapable of holding a trenchant discussion of the Palestinian issue and arriving at decisions on anything beyond the most immediate needs. The main reason for this grave lapse in good government is as much structural as it is ideological. The cabinet is composed primarily of members of the country's two equally weighted major parties. Each of them is further divided into competing camps that are able to balance and cancel each other out whenever it appears that an impending decision will be to their rival's advantage. And in the unlikely case that a decision of import is made, it is quickly trussed up with crippling qualifications and limitations.

Seeing how this equilibrium operates, the various experts who serve the cabinet, such as intelligence people, are reluctant to lay their heads between the two grindstones of Labor and the Likud. Most of them assume that if they honestly speak their minds, they will only be rebuked and branded as partisans of a particular political view. On the most sensitive of issues, they tend to say no more than is absolutely necessary for an understanding of current affairs. They speak only when invited to and volunteer no information that might spark off a ministerial squabble or leave them open to demeaning criticism as a cat's-paw of narrow political interests. This minimalist trend in sharing experience and expertise was evident even before the *intifada*, but the incessant sparring and backbiting in the cabinet has now made it the rule.

For all the effort invested in evasion, it must be said that the Palestinian uprising did send a tremor, however short-lived, through the sclerotic Israeli political system. The shock was felt mainly when the events in the territories caused a sharp turn in international public opinion, and particularly the erosion of support for Israel in the United States and the American Jewish community. Coaxed by a number of concerned ministers, Shamir finally began to see that it was vital to take some action to stop the slip in support from getting out of hand. The Likud people held that a public-relations effort would suffice. There was no need to go as far as a genuine peace initiative, they argued, for the turn in public opinion traced primarily to Israel's failure to explain itself effectively on the Palestinian issue. Thus the problem of sagging support—to say nothing of expressions of outrage and dismay—was conveniently laid at the door of the professional diplomats. The new Likud regime in the Foreign Ministry, headed by Moshe Arens and his deputy Benjamin Netanyahu, charged that a few of Israel's diplomats were unable to convey the government's position because they themselves doubted the justice of Israel's cause. The fault lay not with the policy but with its exponents—people who are "of two minds when they explain the Israeli position."

Working against this trend, a few of Shamir's advisers—particularly Justice Minister Dan Meridor and Government Secretary Eliakim Rubinstein—ultimately persuaded him that Israel could not afford to restrict its efforts to a public-relations campaign. What was needed was a new political tactic: an Israeli peace initiative. In devising it Shamir would have to coordinate closely with Minister of Defense Rabin, who commanded a strong following in the Labor Party and would force Shimon Peres to either back the plan or split the party in the course of opposing it. Schooled in the byzantine ways of the Israeli political system, Shamir also knew that to avoid attempts at sabotaging his effort before it got off the ground, he would have to keep the details of the plan secret from other ministers, above all from his own colleagues in the Likud. To present the program for the cabinet's approval would mean having it watered down to pure bombast before he had had a chance to run it past the Bush administration. Not that any new idea could be kept a secret for very long; Shamir's explanations of his intentions and what lay behind each of the plan's clauses were immediately leaked. Nevertheless, fearing that he would be hamstrung by the system, the prime minister refused to discuss his new policy in the cabinet prior to his departure for Washington. And despite requests by senior Likud ministers David Levi and Ariel Sharon to participate in the working sessions on the initiative, Shamir consistently failed to invite them.

That Shamir and Rabin agreed on the substance of the initiative was due less to the fact that they concurred on all the issues than to a readiness to bypass the points that would have derailed it. Consequently their peace proposal made no reference whatever to Resolution 242 or the principle of exchanging territory for peace. Neither did it state whether the Arab inhabitants of East Jerusalem—which Israel annexed in 1967 and regards as its sovereign territory—would be allowed to run and vote in the elections to be held in the territories. In this way the two men were able to reach a temporary, tactical understanding that made the initiative possible but left the impression that it was more an attempt to call a truce between Labor and the Likud than to make peace between Israel and the Palestinians.

While the new proposal opened the way to negotiations with the Palestinians in the territories, Shamir clearly meant to shut the PLO leadership out of the political process. The main Israeli concession achieved by the *intifada* was one of timing. Whereas in the past Shamir had been prepared to hold elections in the territories only after the five-year transition period stipulated in the Camp David agreement, he was now amenable to starting the process with elections and then going on to negotiate the final status of the territories.

The notion of holding elections as a prelude to talks was not original to the Shamir-Rabin initiative. As a matter of fact, it was first suggested by the Palestinians, about a month after the start of the *intifada*, as a step toward negotiations between Israel and the PLO. Israel did not even bother to respond to the idea then. But it evidently left its mark, for a few months later security experts approached Rabin with the suggestion of launching a political initiative built around the conduct of elections in the territories. It took a while for the Labor Party to embrace the idea, and Shamir—who was initially put off by the suggestion—began to warm up to it only when he realized how strongly American feeling was running against Israel. Ultimately he was won over by the argument that a plan offering the Palestinians a genuinely democratic process would be well received by the new American president. It was also the least perilous course for Israel— assuming, of course, that Shamir could persuade Bush to keep the PLO out of the game.

Were Shamir's intentions sincere when he presented his initiative to the Bush administration in April 1989? The Americans certainly had reason to wonder, if only because just days after returning from Washington the prime minister publicly characterized his own peace initiative as just "an idle fancy." No mere slip of the tongue, this statement was ostensibly made to mollify the members of the Likud who had not been let in on the plan in advance. There were other signs that the powers that be in the Likud were eager to lay the fledgling plan to rest as soon as possible. After the May Arab summit in Morocco spoke critically of the initiative, Moshe Arens, who was Shamir's leading ally in the party, was quick to announce that the Arab states had rebuffed it. After that hair-trigger reaction, it was all too plain that a number of the plan's authors were actually hoping the Arabs would reject it.

Be that as it may, the body that really did reject the Shamir-Rabin initiative, by trying to drain it of all content, was the Likud's own Central Committee when it met to debate the plan in June. After weeks of psychological warfare Shamir knuckled under to his arch-rivals in the party, Sharon and Levi, by telling the committee, and thereby the world, that his conditions for holding elections in the territories were such that no Palestinian could possibly accept the Israeli initiative. For Shamir, the prospect of an open clash in the Likud was so daunting— more than the risk of an American crisis of confidence in Israel or the consequences of having daily confrontations in the territories go on indefinitely—that it brought him to repudiate the initiative bearing his name.

After publicly humbling himself before his rivals at the Central Committee session, Shamir tried to backpedal by claiming that what *really* counted was not what he said to the party but what he told the cabinet—and he then proceeded to tell the cabinet that his original plan had not changed in any way. But he only managed to create confusion and more than a modicum of skepticism. Like Arafat and the other Arab leaders he assailed for saying one thing in Arabic and quite another in translation, Shamir resorted to the frail explanation that sometimes a politician must say things to please his constituency, but no one else need take them seriously. Had he gone for a floor fight, Shamir could probably have defeated his challengers at the Central Committee meeting. That, at least, was the strategy he had agreed upon with Meridor, Ehud Olmert, and the other young ministers he had appointed to the cabinet. But a last-minute talk with an old friend, who warned him that he would have great difficulty winning an open confrontation, caused him to back down.

The Likud Central Committee obliged its representatives in the cabinet to lay down preconditions for any negotiations with the Palestinians or any other Arabs. It cannot be said that Shamir was fundamentally opposed to this approach. His problem was that for the first time he was duty-bound to translate it into official policy, turning the tables on Palestinians just when they had finally come to terms with Resolution 242. For decades Israel had been calling on the Arab states to enter into talks in the spirit that everything would be open to negotiation. Now it was weighing down its own offer with so many provisos that for all intents and purposes it had adopted the traditional Arab stance. In effect Shamir was giving the Palestinians advance notice that in no case would Israel negotiate over the establishment of a Palestinian state; that they would not be entitled to choose their own representatives (because Israel would not sit down with anyone appointed by the PLO); that the residents of East Jerusalem would not be permitted to run and vote in elections for the institutions of the autonomous administration; and that in any case the negotiations would not begin until the *intifada* had come to a halt. On the face of it Shamir was speaking from a position of strength; in practical terms, however, the constraints stripped Israel of its political maneuverability and effectively handed the most extreme of the Palestinians veto power over its plan. As for talks with Jordan, officially speaking King Hussein was still invited to enter into them without prior conditions, but Shamir made it known that he would not abide by the formula of land for peace. Thus by a neat sleight of hand, the master magician Yitzhak Shamir managed in rapid succession to launch and shoot down his own peace plan, making it look suspiciously like a clay pigeon devised for nothing more than a bit of harmless sport.

The political knot into which the Labor Party has tied itself is no less a study in contradictions, with squandered opportunities, an addiction to half-truths, and a sheer lack of political courage added for good measure. During the course of the *intifada*, King Hussein pulled the rug out from under the Labor Party and the policy it had brandished for two decades. While the Labor people toyed endlessly with the idea of a "Jordanian option" as the trap door through which Israel could always escape from the odious problems of the occupation, Hussein stunned them by doing his own disappearing act in severing Jordan's administrative ties with the West Bank. For weeks after that move, Labor's leaders clung to the belief that it had just been a maneuver to revitalize the ties between the West Bank and Jordan by giving the Palestinians a taste of what life would be like without them. As it turned out, the king's bill of divorcement was no mere ploy, and it exposed the cornerstone of Labor's policy for what it really was: a finely crafted political illusion.

It is doubtful whether Hussein had ever been capable of delivering what Labor expected of him. But even if he had, the Labor Party was itself working so assiduously against the realization of a "Jordanian option" that it doomed the very policy it advocated. After all, it was Labor that had governed Israel for the decade between the Six-Day War and the Likud's electoral victory in 1977—critical years for the turn of events in the territories and relations between Israel, Jordan, and the Palestinians. Throughout that decade one opportunity after another was blithely disregarded; one feeler after the next was scornfully repulsed until arrogance and disdain became almost reflex actions. Moshe Dayan, the party's "strong man" until the Yom Kippur War, deported hundreds of Palestinian leaders from the territories, the most influential of them from the pro-Jordanian camp. It was also Dayan who coined the smug phrase about waiting for a phone call from King Hussein, though he never did anything to encourage it while there was still a chance of restoring Jordanian control over all or part of the West Bank.

Hussein's 1972 proposal to establish a federation between Jordan and the West Bank was rebuffed by Prime Minister Golda Meir before any Palestinian had had a chance to react to it. Mrs. Meir made equally short shrift of Hussein's vision of a territorial compromise—which the Labor Party would jump at today. The last chance for direct Jordanian involvement in the West Bank came after the Yom Kippur War, when Israel withdrew from captured territory and signed interim agreements with Egypt and Syria. Dr. Henry Kissinger suggested that a similar agreement be contracted with Jordan, giving Hussein control over Jericho and its environs. But the Labor Party rejected the idea, prompting Hussein to snap: "Do I have to attack Israel to get what Syria and Egypt got?" A few months later the Rabat summit conference passed the resolution recognizing the PLO as the sole legitimate representative of the Palestinian people, thereby stripping Hussein of the right to negotiate on its behalf.

As if to complete the undoing of the "Jordanian option," after the Yom Kippur War Prime Minister Rabin and Defense Minister Peres allowed Gush Emunim, the newly formed Jewish settlers' movement, to create facts on the ground that contradicted Labor's political and strategic doctrine. Thus by the time Shimon Peres, as foreign minister in Yitzhak Shamir's first National Unity Government, reached an understanding with Hussein on negotiating within the framework of an international conference (the 1987 London Agreement), the Jordanian option had long been a dead letter. The king might just as well have sold Peres the Brooklyn Bridge.

The *intifada* left the Labor Party in a state of ideological and political disarray. Its chairman, Shimon Peres, understood that there was no hope of reaching an understanding with the Palestinians without the involvement of the PLO, but he feared that admitting such "heresy" would only earn him, and his party, the wrath of the many Israelis who preferred to dwell in the comfort of delusion. Instead he took cover behind a screen of double talk and obfuscation, which cost him the support of many loyalists. A reluctance to swim against the current that was sweeping Israel further and further to the right was shared by Peres's colleague and chief rival in the party, Yitzhak Rabin. The defense minister justified his stand by arguing that he would not be able to get any peace initiative going without Shamir's approval and had no chance of getting Shamir's cooperation if he did not bend with the wind. He consequently sought the lowest common denominator with the Likud, and the result was predictable. Instead of exhibiting leadership, the Labor Party tailored its positions to fit the public mood, while Israel backed itself further and further into a corner.

Piqued by the results of the Likud's Central Committee meeting, Rabin shared with Labor's leadership his own thinking on the political initiative and whether or not the party should leave the government over the damage done to its credibility. The most obvious substantive difference between Rabin and Shamir was that Rabin backed the principle of exchanging land—though not all the land occupied by Israel—for peace. Yet there were subtle, tactical differences between them as well. For example, the terms of the Israeli plan clearly ruled out the PLO's involvement in negotiations, but Rabin told his party that he was willing to have Egypt (as a partner to the original Camp David accords) draw up a list of Palestinians to be included in talks on the ground rules for the elections. He realized, of course, that in writing that list the Egyptians would consult the PLO; but he chose to play the matter down by saying that the Egyptians had the right to consult with whomever they wished. He was even prepared to have Palestinians from outside the territories participate in future negotiations on a permanent solution, provided that their names were cleared in advance with Israel, Egypt, and the local Palestinians. In effect, Rabin was leaving a back window open to the PLO. It would not be able to stroll into the negotiations through the front door, but neither would it be categorically barred from the peace process.

Like Shultz before him, Israel's defense minister was essentially speaking about granting the Palestinians political rights (once the transition period had begun) and at the same time placing a moratorium on the creation of new Israeli settlements. In the course of the *intifada*, Rabin had changed his thinking on three critical issues. He realized that Hussein would not bring the Palestinians to the negotiating table but rather the opposite, that the king would follow in their wake. He came to see that Israel must negotiate directly with the local Palestinians, not just treat them as "mailmen" bearing messages to Jordan and the PLO.

Finally, he appreciated the benefit of holding elections in the territories—a prospect he had earlier refused to consider. In addressing his party comrades, Rabin emphasized the points that distinguished him from Shamir. But he nevertheless recommended that the National Unity Government be kept intact—if only to hold Shamir to his word that the peace initiative had not changed—and Labor's Central Committee accepted his reasoning.

Though it has not been allowed to create political chaos in Israel, the *intifada* has sharpened the polarization of Israeli society and radicalized thinking on the Palestinian issue. The longer it drags on and the more casualties it claims, the more it will generate deep distrust between the two peoples. On the Israeli side, the government's self-induced paralysis has contributed to the spread of a national malaise and the pernicious conviction that the conflict is inherently insoluble. At the same time there seems to be a growing realization that the Palestinians and their leadership cannot be ignored forever and that Israel's government is not telling the whole truth about contacts with the PLO. None of the political camps in Israel has been left untouched by the *intifada,* and some have even reversed the positions they held sacred for years.

Perhaps the most salient change has taken place among the settlers in the occupied territories, who have been torn in opposing directions. On the one hand, isolated voices have been prepared to admit that the PLO represents the Palestinians, which is a radical departure in itself. But the far more significant trend among the settler population is its despair of solving the conflict by peaceful means. Until the *intifada* most of the Israelis living in the territories made known their belief, at every opportunity, that Jews and Arabs can live together in peace. Along came the uprising and shattered that claim, so that now the settlers dwell on the need to part ways with the Palestinians, since the two peoples are incapable of sharing the same patch of land. Equally sobering for the settlers was the realization that the uprising is fueled by serious grievances and that even if it is put down for the present, it will only break out again, perhaps with even greater force, in the future. It was for this reason, as much as their political tenet that the whole of the Land of Israel belongs exclusively to the Jews, that the more radical settlers were shocked by the Shamir-Rabin initiative. They perceived it as the first crack in Shamir's hitherto impenetrable wall. It signaled to them that even if the prime minister did not intend to pursue a political solution, he might capitulate to pressures or circumstances and bring his proposal to fruition. And it forced them to see that even were the current initiative to fail, sooner or later another one would arise or, worse yet, a more vicious wave of violence would spawn more drastic and far-reaching solutions.

The new approach engendered by these fears was an urgent drive to "encourage the emigration" of the Palestinians. The settler's spokesmen refrained from advocating the outright expulsion ("transfer") of the Palestinians but pointed to economic pressures as a way of prodding them to leave their native land of their own volition. They harped on the line that the *intifada*, even in its mildest form, is intolerable to the Israelis—even worse than the actions of terrorists along the country's borders. The irony is that by portraying the situation in such dramatic terms and insisting that the only solution is to separate the two peoples, without intending it the settlers have played right into the hands of their worst enemies. Arafat could not have phrased his own ambitions better.

After almost two years of fruitless combat with the Palestinians, the thinking in Israel seems to be stalled at a strange juncture. While frustration and enmity have taken hold of much of the Israeli public, they have not yet led it to any clear-cut political conclusions. The same citizens who want to bar Palestinians from working in Israel or are frightened by the knowledge that tens of thousands of them walk freely on Israel's streets each day have yet to deduce that the way to relieve these threatening circumstances is by political disengagement, rather than by continuing to bend the Palestinians to Israel's will. Despite the evidence of the past years, the majority of Israelis still believe that they can have their cake and eat it too: hold on to all of the territories and control the Palestinians without being the object of rebellion and hatred. At the same time, the mainstream in Israel is steadily losing ground to the groups at the extremes commending radical solutions, from the wholesale deportation of the Palestinians, on the one hand, to an unconditional withdrawal from the territories, on the other.

The trend toward extremism in the army is expressed in a different but no less ominous way. The inability to suppress the uprising, despite the major commitment of human resources, has left the army carrying a huge burden of frustration. Unfortunately, the consequent anger of many of its officers is being directed against what they see as the "unlimited" freedom of expression in Israel that is being "negatively exploited" by the press and electronic media. Such feelings have seeped up from below into the middle ranks of the officer corps, and while the army's top brass is committed to combating anti-democratic feeling in the ranks, its relentless spread continues to be one of the most alarming consequences of the uprising for Israel's future. At the very least, then, the *intifada* is forcing Israelis to take a fresh look in the mirror, and what they see is the emergence of dark spots on their democracy, blemishes that threaten to mar the face of their society for years to come.

EPILOGUE

THE *intifada* NEED NOT necessarily go down in the annals of Middle Eastern history as just another tragic chapter of the Israeli-Arab conflict. Despite the losses in life to both sides and the mounting hatred and bitterness that have resulted from the uprising, it has also opened up opportunities for negotiating an end to the dispute. As a painful shock and sobering experience, it has forced Israelis and Palestinians to take a harder look at themselves and their adversaries, to weigh the risks and prospects they face, and to arrive at a reasoned assessment of what is possible and what must necessarily remain a dream. Certainly this clash in the occupied territories has highlighted both the power and the resolve of the two sides, but it has also exposed their limitations and the sharp internal divisions within each of the camps.

The latest flareup of this long struggle has further eroded the faith in outworn slogans by exposing a number of basic truths from which there is no escape. Rather than repress the reality of their situation, Israelis and Palestinians must begin to accept it as a condition that precludes an absolute victory for either cause. Not only has the view of the present reality changed radically, the hopes for the future and dreams of unqualified redemption must be subjected to renewed scrutiny. Israelis must ask themselves how it will be possible to redeem the whole of the Land of Israel in a situation of protracted indecision and what life will be like in a country that is preoccupied with suppressing a large part of the population living within its bounds. Palestinians must take a fresh look at their own assumptions and ask themselves whether

327

the determination to destroy the State of Israel will not in fact prolong the occupation and the suppression of Palestinian national aspirations.

The *intifada* will surely be remembered as one of the milestones in the contest for this country of two peoples. It has pushed the arena of struggle back from the borders, against regular armies, to the interior, where it is a people-to-people affair. It has set the Israelis and the Palestinians at a fateful junction where they must choose between striving toward compromise or continuing to batter each other in successive rounds of mutual attrition. Many already see that in the absence of a settlement, extremism will thrive on both sides. A standoff can only sharpen the discord and heighten the feelings of alienation and hostility, as well as the thirst for revenge. There is a real danger that those who call for a *jihad*—a holy war to the death—against Israel will win out among the Palestinians, while the advocates of "transferring" the Palestinians over the border will gather strength among the Jews.

There is no longer any question that by their uprising the Palestinians have smashed the status quo beyond repair. Though unable to impose a new order in the territories, they have opened up a third front against Israel, forcing it to be on the ready to fight against regular armies and terrorist actions along its borders while contending with a mass civil uprising that shuns standard weapons but uses other forms of violence quite effectively. Thus not only has the Palestinian uprising gravely affected Israel's internal security, it has changed the country's very perception of what security means. The territories, long viewed by Israelis as a defensive belt providing their country with strategic depth, have now become a woe to be reckoned with. The cost of administering areas teeming with a hostile population has been made painfully clear to Israel, as has the need to reexamine the advantages of holding onto them. Without doubt the territories are important to Israel's security, but they pose a threat as well. For the first time since 1967, the uprising has seriously forced Israel to consider the effect that the occupation has had on the occupiers: their ethos, their image, and their democratic way of life.

Israel has not managed to "wipe out the *intifada*," as the slogan shouters have been demanding, because a democratic society, by its very nature, has trouble coping with a rebellion of this kind. What may seem vital to people in charge of security is unthinkable to citizens concerned with the health of their nation's democracy—a paradox that has come to the fore countless times in the past two years. It was not by chance that Justice Minister Dan Meridor—a Likud man who was raised on the doctrine that the whole Land of Israel, stretching over both banks of the Jordan, is the patrimony of every Jew—has seen fit to reject prescriptions for more punitive action. Israelis can have no illusions about the cost to themselves of trying to restore the status quo ante. Occupation and democracy cannot dwell together for long; the uprising has been a pointed reminder of that.

By their rebellion, the Palestinians have taken the initiative into their hands and made partial gains in their struggle against foreign domination. Jordan's renunciation of its claim over the territories and the United States' recognition of the PLO have been their prime strategic victories. On another plane, however, the new Palestinian leadership has managed to snatch the population of the territories out of Israel's control. The Palestinian population has adopted the stance of a "mobilized society" prepared to make great sacrifices. It has even dictated policy changes to the PLO, though in the final analysis the new local leadership has not posed a critical challenge to the authority of the PLO abroad, and the organization's superiority over such homegrown rivals as Hamas has clearly been demonstrated. In short, the *intifada* has shown that there is no way to bypass the PLO on the road to a settlement.

At the same time, the uprising has sparked a deep crisis of confidence in many existing conventions. The Israeli public is far from convinced that its government knows how to reach the goals it has set for itself, and similar doubts have arisen among many Palestinians regarding their own established leadership. Members of both peoples have been shocked and alarmed by the expressions of brutality and indifference on both sides of the barricades, leading diehards to insist that "there's no one to talk to." Far more compelling, however, is the conclusion that it is imperative to strive toward disengagement by means of negotiation. The Israelis negotiated agreements even with the Germans just a few years after Nazi Germany had sought the life of every last Jew within its sphere of control. The fact that atrocities have been committed by Palestinians does not justify denying the rights of the Palestinian people, just as complaints about callousness and cruelty on the part of Israelis is no excuse for refusing to engage in negotiations.

The failure to exploit the opportunities that opened up after the Six-Day War has caused inestimable damage. For over twenty years, history smiled on Israel and expected that it would choose a definitive course of action. Instead it has wobbled and waffled in an attempt to avoid decision. Its control over the West Bank and Gaza Strip has not inspired a flood of Jewish immigration or even resettlement on a scale that has changed the demographic map of the territories. On the other hand, the opportunity to lay the foundations of a solid peace with the Arab world has been squandered. This tragedy is reflected in the figure of Yitzhak Rabin, who as chief of staff in 1967 brought the territories under Israel's sway and as minister of defense since 1984 has seen it lose control over them. Throughout these wasted years Israel also contributed to the revival of Palestinian nationalism, which has been nurtured not only by aspirations for political independence but by social and economic privation.

Today Israel finds itself trapped by the binds of its own occupation regime. In the end it will have to do what other nations have done in similar circumstances: invest its efforts in working toward a compromise. The demand to halt all acts of violence before negotiations can begin, the illusion that the Palestinian "silent majority" is not interested in a rebellion, and a fear of the risks inherent in a settlement—of which there are no few—will all have to defer to the understanding that it is better to seek an accommodation with the Palestinians than to dig deeper and deeper into an untenable situation. This realization, which is slowly dawning on parts of the Israeli public, will undoubtedly grow with the changing of the guard that is already in effect. A new Palestinian leadership has emerged out of the *intifada*, and there have been signs of faltering support for the veteran leadership in Israel, with the infighting in both major parties essentially centering on the issue of succession. Proposals that have been turned down in the past by Israel will be accepted in the future—just as the idea of holding elections in the territories has—but they will carry a far higher price tag. Men who are being cast into prison today will be the preferred negotiating partners in the future (as were Archbishop Makarios, Habib Bourguiba, Jomo Kenyatta, and Kwame Nkrumah in their day). The important thing is that Israel not exhaust its energies in a fruitless bid to avoid the inevitable and thus arrive at the negotiating table in a considerably weakened state.

The reigning outlook in Israel for the past two decades has proven itself bankrupt. Claims by the Right that annexation of the territories—de facto if not de jure—is viable as well as desirable have been rudely disproved by the *intifada*. Labor's belief that the solution could be reached via Jordan was also demolished by the truth about the tilt in the balance of forces toward the PLO. As to the Israeli Left, its naive sermonizing about making room for a PLO-led Palestinian state without links to Jordan clashes with Israel's most basic security needs. It is the frustration created by these unrealistic approaches that accounts for the scurry after simplistic and wholly pointless solutions such as "transfer" or, at the other extreme, an unconditional withdrawal from the territories.

The path of a workable solution leads to only one meaningful alternative: the tripartite option that brings Jordan, a Palestinian entity in the territories, and the State of Israel together in a single settlement package. Only in this broad context is it possible to solve the problems raised by every other formula. Since the Camp David accords, various diplomatic initiatives based on this general concept—the Reagan initiative (1982), the London Agreement (1987), and the Shultz initiative (1988)—have foundered one after the next. The reason for their failure, however, was less their substance than their methodology. All efforts to ensure progress by the step-by-step approach have become bogged down after the initial move. That is why it is necessary to make the opening step a major leap forward that will advance the sides well into a transition stage and provide the momentum for reaching a full-fledged settlement.

In our view, the two components of this move should be:

• An Israeli "administrative withdrawal" from the West Bank and Gaza Strip, which essentially means turning the machinery of the Civil Administration over to Palestinian institutions. This move, to be taken prior to elections or any negotiations on autonomy, must be accompanied by an agreement on working in tandem with the Israelis and be independent of progress on political issues. It is envisioned as a kind of disengagement-of-forces agreement between Israel and the leadership of the *intifada* and as a test of their ability to cooperate with one another, preferably after the reduction of the Israeli military presence in the population centers. An administrative withdrawal of this kind will require the creation of channels for active negotiation and coordination until the official establishment of Palestinian self-rule.

• Alternatively, or at the same time, the transfer of the Gaza Strip over to the PLO and a locally elected leadership to test the Palestinians' ability to hold to an agreement and provent acts of terrorism. Gaza is more suitable than the West Bank for such a trial since its residents are more dependent upon Israel for water and their livelihoods. The area is at any rate surrounded on three sides by Israel, and since it is well isolated from Israel's eastern front, the risks are considerably less than they would be if the same conditions were granted initially to the West Bank. Under this arrangement the Palestinians will have to make a commitment not to declare an independent state in the area evacuated by Israel, while Israel will have to allow the residents of the Strip to continue working in its territory. During the trial period development programs such as the rehabilitation of the refugees and the construction of a harbor will be carried out in the Gaza Strip with the aid of Arab and international funding. The success of this experiment will go a long way toward persuading the Israelis that it is possible to trust and cooperate with the Palestinians in the West Bank as well.

These two steps are calculated to overcome the main difficulty that has prevented negotiations from getting under way, namely, disagreement over the nature of the final settlement. By transferring the whole of the Gaza Strip to the Palestinians and effectively placing them in charge of administering the West Bank, it will be possible to move on to negotiations without agreeing on their outcome in advance—although there will have to be a general understanding about what the broad contours of the final settlement will be.

To prepare for negotiations, sooner or later Israel will have to ask itself what its minimal terms are for a settlement with the Palestinians. What is the point beyond which it cannot retreat without compromising its security, if not its very existence, and tempting the other side to violate the peace? Why set down minimal conditions? Because neither side can realize all of its aspirations in a peace treaty, and the insistence on maximum claims is what has dragged the conflict out for so long. Yet any agreement that makes one side feel that its vital interests have been prejudiced is a sure formula for the renewal of hostilities at the first opportunity. Thus the aim in sketching out minimal terms is to ensure that peace, once achieved, will be protected. At the same time, even these basic conditions cannot be presented as dictates by one side to the other, for that will only encourage the next generation to renounce them. They must be spelled out clearly and make it possible for the two peoples to engage in fruitful cooperation, so that it will not be in the interest of either side to violate them. In short, the minimum demands must be modeled on the conditions of cooperation that have developed in Europe since World War Two, not on the humiliating dictates that emerged from Versailles.

The agreement to be negotiated between Israel and the Palestinians will necessarily have two main elements: a military and a political one. The events of the past two years, since the start of the *intifada*, bring us to the conclusion that it will be impossible to end the conflict without reaching an accommodation with the PLO. Any other settlement will be only a partial one and thus liable to collapse. The military aspect of the agreement requires that not only the West Bank and Gaza Strip but Jordan, too, be included in the settlement. Current developments in military technology and those envisioned for the future, as well as the growth of the armies in this region, make it imperative that Jordan be part of both a political and military settlement with the Palestinians—regardless of who rules it. Jordan's participation in the peace treaty will directly affect the size and deployment of the force that Israel will have to keep in the West Bank. If it does not take part in the settlement, Israel will not be able to reduce its forces on the West Bank at all, for there is little point in demilitarizing the Palestinian entity if a large military force can deploy against Israel immediately to the east of it.

In these circumstances, Israel must insist that the solution to the conflict be a confederative arrangement that will include Israel, Jordan, and the Palestinian entity to be constituted in the West Bank and Gaza. Such a confederation must have a binding constitution that cannot be abrogated without the unanimous agreement of its members. It must also require the Palestinian entity to remain demilitarized and abstain from signing any military pacts. A confederation is also the one solution from a legal standpoint; according to international law it is the only way to oblige a sovereign entity to honor agreements that limit its independence. The Palestinian entity will not be entitled to pull out of the confederative framework, alter its political status, annex areas to its territory, or be annexed by another political entity. Thus besides protecting the Palestinians' sovereignty, a confederation will rule out the possibility of a future Palestinian takeover of Jordan to establish "Greater Palestine" from Jordan's border with Iraq to its 1967 border with Israel. As part of a peace treaty, Jordan will have to pledge not to enter into military alliances against Israel. Similarly, the stationing of troops from countries at war with Israel will be forbidden on Jordanian soil. In this way Jordan will be detached from the countries of the "eastern front" that Israel regards as a military threat.

Whether and when the military presence imposed on the Palestinian entity is lifted will depend to a large degree upon the surrounding Arab states. Their conduct will also affect developments during the transition stage in which the final status of the Palestinian entity will be established. Put simply, the duration of the transition stage will necessarily be determined not by a rigid timetable set down in advance but by whether or not the Arab states bordering on Israel remain in a state of war with it. For as long as this state of war continues and Israel faces the risk of attack, the IDF will have to station its forces in the West Bank and Gaza Strip. However, if Jordan joins in a peace treaty and agrees to certain necessary military arrangements, the IDF will be able to lower its profile on the West Bank and concentrate its forces mainly on the northeastern sector facing Syria. And if Syria joins in the treaty and military arrangements, the IDF will be able to change its deployment on the West Bank substantially.

The transition stage regarding internal security can be shorter and need not be linked to the conduct of the bordering Arab states. Instead, it will depend upon Palestinian willingness to cooperate with Israel in the war on terrorism. This stage should be composed of two phases; the greater the cooperation in the war on terrorism and the maintenance of public order, the sooner it will be possible to transfer responsibility for various aspects of internal security to the Palestinian entity. Only close cooperation between Israel, the Palestinian entity, and Jordan can yield positive results in the struggle against terrorism and the extremist groups that are capable of disrupting the peace process. During the transition period, the command of the war on terrorism, to be established on the territory of the Palestinian entity, will be a joint Palestinian-Israeli one. The Jordanians may be invited to join in this effort, but United Nations police forces and observers should not. Since experience shows that only strong Arab governments succeed in preventing terrorism, the governing authority of the Palestinian entity will have to be deeply committed to maintaining the peace.

In the last analysis, Israel cannot settle solely for the demilitarization of the West Bank; it must be prepared for the possibility that the peace will be broken. Thus during the transition period its military presence must be designed for defensive purposes, to deter the forces that would exploit the reduction in its troop presence in the territories. For this purpose it is sufficient for two or three concentrations of armored forces to be stationed on the eastern slopes of the West Bank and in the Jordan Valley. Access to these deployment areas will be from two directions—the north (Beit Shean) and the west (Jerusalem via Ma'aleh Adumim and then on to the Jordan Valley)—so that the friction between the IDF and the local population can be kept to a minimum. In the Gaza Strip the IDF will deploy in the Katif area, which separates the main body of the Strip from Sinai, and will man observation posts on the shore. Israel will also reinforce its early-warning stations and anti-aircraft batteries in these designated areas of deployment. At the end of the transition period, it will be entitled to demand the establishment of a joint early-warning station in the West Bank to be operated by Israelis, Palestinians, and Jordanians and commanded by Americans (or manned by Americans alone, as in Sinai).

In making passing reference to the key American role in the peace process, we must also mention the possible involvement of the Soviet Union. There can be no hope of reaching a comprehensive peace in the Middle East without Russian cooperation. Even on a modest scale, it is preferable to receive Soviet help in resolving the conflict than to forgo it—not least because Damascus will think twice about disrupting a peace process in which the Soviet Union is involved. However, Moscow can be integrated into the peace process only if it accepts certain conditions, namely, that it will not sign any military pacts with the Palestinian entity or with Jordan, will not send them military forces or advisers, and will not supply the kind of offensive arms that would be in violation of the demilitarization agreement.

The terms of demilitarization must state that the Palestinian entity may not have military forces or weapons systems such as tanks, combat planes, and field guns. This prohibition must also extend to military fortifications and electronic weapons systems, reducing the chances that Israel will be surprised by an attack from the east. Neither will the Palestinians be permitted to transfer, station, or train foreign military forces, policemen, or advisers on their territory. They must not be allowed to produce chemical, biological, or nuclear weapons and should be entitled to manufacture only the light weapons necessary for their police forces. In this sense, the demilitarization of the Palestinian entity will be only partial, as the Palestinians will be allowed to have their police. On the other hand, it will be for an unlimited period. During the first phase of the transition period, the police will be a local and village force; afterward two regional police forces can be established, one for the West Bank and the other for Gaza, and finally a single force will cover both areas.

In negotiating the final status and borders of the Palestinian entity, Israel will have to insist upon adjustments along its eastern frontier. These changes are necessary not only because Israel's "narrow waist" is located along this border but primarily because uncontrolled drilling on the western slopes of the Samarian Mountains can cause severe damage to Israel's most important subterranean water reserve. Smaller border adjustments will undoubtedly be demanded for security reasons in the area of Lod (to widen the air space by Israel's international airport), the Jerusalem corridor, the Hebron Mountains, Greater Jerusalem, and the road connecting Jerusalem to Ma'aleh Adumim.

The residents of the Jewish settlements not included in these ceded areas will have to choose between remaining in place and being subject to the laws of the Palestinian entity—just as Israeli Arabs obey the laws of the State of Israel—or evacuating their settlements. The Jewish settlers who remain within the Palestinian entity will not be entitled to have a military force of their own, just as Israel's Arabs have no such force. In this way mutuality will obtain between Israel and the Palestinian entity in this sensitive area of communal security.

The most basic condition of a final settlement is that it must put an end to the conflict between the two peoples. Signing a peace treaty will signify that the two sides renounce all further claims against one another. This condition must be spelled out clearly in the agreement, for it will comprise one of the guarantees that the Palestinians will indeed abandon what they call their "plan [to dismantle Israel] in stages." Another equally important condition is that the Palestinians must forfeit what they call the "right of return," which is essentially a means of destroying the State of Israel from within. This issue cannot be open to negotiation. Israel should of course agree to the reunification of families; but it cannot assent to the return of the 1948 refugees, whose resettlement has deliberately been prevented by the Arab states for over forty years and who will have to find a permanent place in the Palestinian entity, in Jordan, or in one of the other Arab countries. Israel must also insist that the Palestinian entity, in cooperation with the Arab countries and with aid from international sources, will act to solve the refugee problem. Naturally, Israel will contribute its share to this effort, for it appreciates that the peace cannot be stable if refugee camps containing hundreds of thousands of people living in substandard conditions continue to exist along its borders.

The last important condition is that the Palestinian entity will not claim to represent the Arab citizens of Israel or the Palestinians living in Jordan. The PLO must make a firm commitment not to take any action that would amount to inciting the Israeli-Arab community to irredentism, promoting the secession of parts of the State of Israel, or commending the establishment of another Palestinian entity.

There remains the question of what will happen if the peace treaty is violated. To cover this possibility, the agreement should state that in the event of a major violation of the demilitarization agreement—for example, by permitting a foreign army to enter the Palestinian entity, or acquiring prohibited weapons systems, or allowing extensive terrorist operations to originate from Palestinian territory—Israel will be entitled to exercise the right of ex-territorial defense.

Unless the *intifada* leads to an agreement along these general lines, the Israeli effort to quell it will at best have the effect of sprinkling sand on burning embers: the violence will go on smoldering until the next wind comes along to fire it up again. Keeping the *intifada* at a low simmer may convince many Israelis that it is possible to live with the difficulties of controlling the population in the territories, so that Israel need not consider making concessions. But if Israelis reconcile themselves to this grim prospect, the younger generation of Palestinians will surely deduce that a civil uprising is not an effective vehicle of political expression and that they must return to the path of an armed struggle. There seems no avoiding the conclusion that unless sincere negotiations get under way, both sides will suffer considerably for the foreseeable future and the ultimate outcome of the *intifada* will be much to Israel's detriment.

It is only natural to ask whether the risks to Israel will disappear if the minimal conditions outlined here are achieved. The answer is of course negative. No solution is risk-free, and every step forward brings with it new fears and uncertainties. Nevertheless, the risks of peace are accompanied by the prospect of better times to come, whereas the existing risks offer nothing beyond the promise of a further deterioration, greater repression and extremism, and ultimately, perhaps, a war. What, then, are the incentives that will move the sides to take risks, reach an agreement, and guarantee that it will not be violated? The Palestinians will receive political independence, albeit limited in certain respects so that their right to self-determination will not infringe on the same right of others. If they violate the treaty, however, they stand to lose their sovereign status, perhaps forever. By joining in a peace agreement as part of a confederation, Jordan will ensure its own independence for the future. And Israel will finally be able to put the Palestinian conflict behind it and concentrate its energies on advancing the welfare of its own people and of the region as a whole.

INDEX